www.wadsworth.com

wadsworth.com is the World Wide Web site for Wadsworth and is your direct source to dozens of online resources.

At *wadsworth.com* you can find out about supplements, demonstration software, and student resources. You can also send email to many of our authors and preview new publications and exciting new technologies.

wadsworth.com
Changing the way the world learns®

THE WADSWORTH CONTEMPORARY ISSUES IN CRIME AND JUSTICE SERIES
Todd Clear, Series Editor

1995   **Close/Meier:** *Morality in Criminal Justice: An Introduction to Ethics*
Klofas/Stojkovic: *Crime and Justice in the Year 2010*
Silberman: *A World of Violence: Corrections in America*
Wooden: *Renegade Kids, Suburban Outlaws: From Youth Culture to Delinquency*

1996   **Belknap:** *The Invisible Woman: Gender, Crime, and Justice*
Friedrichs: *Trusted Criminals: White Collar Crime in Contemporary Society*
Johnson: *Hard Time: Understanding and Reforming the Prison*, Second Edition
Karmen: *Crime Victims: An Introduction to Victimology*, Third Edition
Walker/Spohn/DeLone: *The Color of Justice: Race, Ethnicity, and Crime in America*

1997   **Golden:** *Disposable Youth: America's Child Welfare System*
Hickey: *Serial Murderers and Their Victims*, Second Edition
Irwin/Austin: *It's About Time: America's Imprisonment Binge*, Second Edition
Messner/Rosenfeld: *Crime and the American Dream*, Second Edition
Shelden/Tracy/Brown: *Youth Gangs in American Society*

1998   **Bailey/Hale:** *Popular Culture, Crime, and Justice*
Chesney-Lind/Shelden: *Girls, Delinquency, and Juvenile Justice*, Second Edition
Johnson: *Death Work: A Study of the Modern Execution Process*, Second Edition
Pollock: *Ethics, Crime, and Justice: Dilemmas and Decisions*, Third Edition
Rosenbaum/Lurigio/Davis: *The Prevention of Crime: Social and Situational Strategies*
Surette: *Media, Crime, and Criminal Justice: Images and Realities*, Second Edition
Walker: *Sense and Nonsense About Crime and Drugs: A Policy Guide*, Fourth Edition
White: *Terrorism: An Introduction*, Second Edition

1999   **Arrigo:** *Social Justice/Criminal Justice: The Maturation of Critical Theory in Law, Crime, and Deviance*

2000   **Walker/Spohn/DeLone:** *The Color of Justice: Race, Ethnicity, and Crime in America*, Second Edition

2001   **Austin/Irwin:** *It's About Time: America's Imprisonment Binge*, Third Edition
Karmen: *Crime Victims: An Introduction to Victimology*, Fourth Edition
Shelden/Tracy/Brown: *Youth Gangs in American Society*, Second Edition
Pope/Lovell/Brandl: *Voices from the Field: Readings in Criminal Justice Research*
Walker: *Sense and Nonsense About Crime and Drugs: A Policy Guide*, Fifth Edition
Wooden/Blazak: *Renegade Kids, Suburban Outlaws: From Youth Culture to Delinquency*, Second Edition

✦

Youth Gangs in American Society

Second Edition

RANDALL G. SHELDEN
University of Nevada-Las Vegas

SHARON K. TRACY
Georgia Southern University

WILLIAM B. BROWN
University of Michigan-Flint

WADSWORTH
✦
™
THOMSON LEARNING

Australia • Canada • Mexico • Singapore • Spain • United Kingdom • United States

Executive Editor, Criminal Justice: Sabra Horne
Development Editor: Teri Edwards
Assistant Editor: Ann Tsai
Editorial Assistant: Cortney Bruggink
Marketing Manager: Jennifer Somerville
Project Editor: Susan Walters
Print Buyer: April Reynolds

Permissions Editor: Bob Kauser
Production Service: Shepherd Incorporated
Copy Editor: Bruce Owens
Cover Designer: Joan Greenfield
Cover Image: Tony Stone Images
Compositor: Shepherd Incorporated
Text and Cover Printer: Webcom Limited

pp. 89-90, and 92-94, examples of graffiti from the National Law Enforcement Institute, *Gang Manual,* 1992. Reprinted by permission of N.L.E.I. pp. 1, 34, 61, 97, 128, 159, [?, ?, ?], photos by William B. Brown.

Printed in Canada.
1 2 3 4 5 6 7 04 03 02 01 00

Wadsworth/Thomson Learning
10 Davis Drive
Belmont, CA 94002-3098
USA

For more information about our products, contact us:
Thomson Learning Academic Resource Center
1-800-423-0563
http://www.wadsworth.com

International Headquarters
Thomson Learning
International Division
290 Harbor Drive, 2nd Floor
Stamford, CT 06902-7477
USA

UK/Europe/Middle East/South Africa
Thomson Learning
Berkshire House
168-173 High Holborn
London WC1V 7AA
United Kingdom

Asia
Thomson Learning
60 Albert Street, #15-01
Albert Complex
Singapore 189969

Canada
Nelson Thomson Learning
1120 Birchmount Road
Toronto, Ontario M1K 5G4
Canada

Library of Congress Cataloging-in-Publication Data
Shelden, Randall G., 1943-
    Youth gangs in American society / Randall G. Shelden, Sharon K. Tracy, William B. Brown.—2nd ed.
        p. cm.
    Includes bibliographical references and index.
    ISBN 0–534–52745–0
    1. Gangs—United States. I. Tracy, Sharon K.
    II. Brown, William B. III. Title.

HV6439.U5 S527 2000
364.1'06'60973—dc21

00–040426

Contents

Foreword

As editor of the *Wadsworth Contemporary Issues in Crime and Justice Series,* I am delighted to announce the second edition of *Youth Gangs in American Society,* by Randall G. Shelden, Sharon Tracy, and William B. Brown. The *Contemporary Issues* series is devoted to furthering our understanding of important issues in crime and justice by providing an in-depth treatment of topics that are neglected or insufficiently discussed in today's textbooks. *Youth Gangs in American Society* is an excellent example of the kind of work the series was designed to promote.

Can there be a more important topic in contemporary studies of crime and justice than gangs? The very existence of gangs is a tremendous concern to all Americans. In part, we are concerned about gangs because of our fear of violence. It seems to be daily newspaper fare that some young person has been shot by another, stemming from gang conflict. Few images are more searingly painful than that of the drive by shooting—after all, we expect to be safe in the warmth of our homes. But even more troubling than the violence we associate with gangs is the thought that generations of youth are turning away from pro-social activity to embrace anti-social affiliations associated with crime and savage-like behavior. We fear the tangible harms of gangs, but we bemoan the loss of order among our nation's young.

The irony is that so much of what we think about gangs is deeply embedded in popular myth and inconsistent with factual knowledge about the reality of gangs. Popular thinking has it that all gangs are violent, but studies show this is untrue—and that even violent gangs are not typically engaged in violent activity. The popular media portray gangs as minority youth from impover-ished neighborhoods, but social science tells us there are gangs in middle-class America, too. We like to think of gangs as a modern reaction to the difficulties of contemporary society, but the existence of gangs in urban settings goes back centuries. Indeed, many of our beliefs about gangs are only partly accurate, and getting a more accurate understanding of the gang is an essential first step in developing a policy to deal with gangs effectively.

The need for accurate, dispassionate analysis of the realities of various as-pects of gangs in America is why the second edition of this book is such a contribution to the field. No other book provides such a thoughtful, detailed investigation of gangs as does this popular text. Professors Shelden, Tracy, and Brown have brought together a wide body of evidence about gangs that takes the reader through each of the important aspects of the study of gangs. The book begins with a critical history of gangs in society, and shows how ubiqui-tous gangs have been to urban life. The authors then describe the various kinds of gangs and how they "work": what it takes to be a gang, join a gang, lead a gang and, for some, even leave a gang; how girls gangs come to mirror and dif-fer from their boys' counterparts, how gangs are a part of criminality. From this analysis, we begin to get a more vivid picture of the complexities and varieties of gang life: social class, criminality, and ethnic identity.

After giving us this foundation of understanding, Shelden, Tracy, and Brown then help us to place gang life in social context. We read about gang members and their families, and learn how closely linked some gang members are to their closest kin, and how troubled some of these relationships can become. We begin to understand the phenomenon of gangs as a reflection of contem-porary society: theories of social disorganization in inner cities and growing economic inequality between the well-born and the poor help us to under-stand why gangs develop and why they operate as they do. By the time they have taken us through this careful and detailed analysis, we begin to develop a richer view of the gang and a more critical understanding of its importance as an aspect of contemporary society.

The final question is: What shall we do about gangs? Here, we learn that many strategies—from unremittingly tough to seductively soft—have been tried with gangs, and the best have met with only partial success. It is not that the situation is hopeless, but that gangs are such an integral part of the sub-societies within which they operate that to effectively change gangs requires changing much within those sub-societies. But we must develop the broad-based strategies we can to respond to gangs; otherwise, we are left with the re-volving door of the criminal justice system and lives of despair and suffering.

There is so much about this book that is good that I commend it to you with enthusiasm. Read it, and you will understand gangs. Learn from it, and you will be not just more knowledgeable, but a more effective citizen, when it comes to helping shape national policy about gangs.

Todd R. Clear
Series Editor

Preface

This book is in reality a contradiction, for it is about a subject that no one can precisely define. It is a book about "youth gangs," yet, as we note in the first chapter, there is hardly a consensus on what a "gang" really is. Perhaps what we are dealing with is a process that Richard Quinney several years ago defined as the construction of the "social reality of crime" (Quinney, 1970). In this case, we are specifically dealing with the "social reality of gangs." In the preface to his book *The Social Reality of Crime*, Quinney wrote that "a thing exists only when it is given a name; any phenomenon is real to us only when we can imagine it. . . . So it is with crime. In our relationships with others we construct a *social reality of crime*" (Quinney, 1970:v). Later he wrote that "crime" is socially constructed through "the formulation and application of criminal definitions, the development of behavior patterns related to criminal definitions, and the construction of criminal conceptions" (ibid:23).

So it is with "gangs." We think we know what a "gang" is because we read about it in the papers with headlines about "gang-related homicides" or "gang drive-bys," or we see specials on television about the "Bloods and the Crips," or we see pictures of members of gangs like the "Latin Kings" or the "Hoover Street Crips" or "White Fence" or the "West Coast Bloods." But what does it mean, exactly, when we label these groups "gangs"? And once they are so labeled, how do the individuals respond to the labeling process? Are these "gangs" real, or are they, in part, artifacts of our modern media, an institution that can "create reality" better than any magician? Are "gangs" creations of politicians or law-enforcement officials, who often use them to describe an event or series of events when no other explanation fits the facts (as in the phrase "It was probably 'gang-related.' ")? And as Stryker (1980:32) has pointed out, "Children cannot create their own definitions independently of society, or behave in those terms without social interference." Thus, the problem of defining a "gang" may have fallen into the hands of many who have long since stopped listening to these "children."

It is indeed a difficult task to write a book, a "survey of the literature" so to speak, about a subject matter no one seems to agree how to define. This we have tried to do here. In this preface, we want to give the reader the following warning: If you are looking for an easy answer to a serious social problem and a quick, step-by-step guide on how to control or even eliminate "gangs," then you had better not read any further, for you will be disappointed. The phenomenon of "gangs," like the phenomenon of "crime," is something that is seemingly easy for one to know what it is being talked about (as in "I know a crime when I see one" or "I know a gang member when I see one"), yet when pressed further, it can be as difficult to comprehend as the meaning of life itself.

In this book we are not denying the reality of "gangs," nor are we saying that "gangs" are "merely" the creation of the news media and law-enforcement officials. We know that there are individuals who are called and call themselves "gangs," and some of them engage in behavior we fear and abhor. But like other aspects of our "social reality," the phenomenon of "gangs" cannot be understood without an examination of the social conditions within which it exists—something that policymakers have chosen to ignore and that social control agents are unable to respond to, given their "official" mandate. One of the major themes of this book is that the "problem of gangs," like the "problem of crime" (or any other "social problem"), is a product of the existing social order at a particular point in history. And in order to understand this "problem" we must place it in a much larger context, a context of modern society at the end of the twentieth century. Quinney (1980:45) argues,

> Social reality is more than that which we consciously attend to in our everyday lives. Once created, it gives structure to life, whether or not we consciously grasp the existence and meaning of that structure. There is a structure of reality (including elements that are social, economic, and political) that is there for our understanding, a structure that is constantly changing as we understand and act upon it. Social reality is thus within the structure of our historical condition.

Pertaining to youth gangs, response to our "historical condition" has been less than a willingness to grasp the meaning of the obvious: poverty, frustration, segregation, isolation, and despair. In part, this book attempts to raise our consciousness about these issues.

In writing this book our goal was to look at what others had to say about youth gangs and to formulate from the plethora of information an explanation for, or at least an understanding of, this cultural phenomenon. The book was written by three individuals with vastly differing backgrounds, attitudes and philosophies, opinions, and approaches to research. Shelden, a sociologist and academician, has focused his research on the theoretical nature and subculture of youth gangs and has tried to place gangs in a much larger context of the society of which they are a part. Tracy, a female and public administrator, views the impact on the public at large and the organizational response to gangs. Brown, a sociologist and Vietnam veteran, has used direct ethnographic field research in Detroit and finds parallels with the concept of "war zone" and a "combat" mentality.

When the first edition of this book was "put into production" (as they say in the book publishing world), we had no idea of how successful it would be. We knew at the time that there were few books on gangs that took the approach we were taking, namely, a sort of textbook treatment of the subject. We believed at the time (and obviously so did the editors of Wadsworth) that such a book was needed. We are pleased to be able to present the second edition, which always signifies that the first edition was a success. For that we are grateful to all of those who have used this book in their college and university classes and to those who have purchased it for their own personal use.

Since the time the first edition was "in production," several additional books about gangs have been written, plus numerous journal articles and government publications (e.g., from the National Institute of Justice and the Office of Juvenile Justice and Delinquency Prevention). We have made every effort to update the information that was contained in the first edition, which has not been an easy task, given the incredible accumulation of published works during the past five years. In this edition, the works of two noted gang researchers (Klein, 1995; Spergel, 1995) have been included. This edition has benefited greatly from the work of these two experienced researchers and they are cited on numerous occasions. We took the advice of several reviewers and made several changes (most notably in the chapter on gang typologies and girls).

We have entered into the much-hyped "new millennium," a term that has, in our opinion, been overused and even abused by the media. As far as the subject of gangs is concerned, it is merely a new year, but with some of the same problems confronting us at the end of the old year and the last century. The problems we see that relate directly to gangs center around the issue of what is known as *social justice*. Despite the "boom times" of the American economy, the conditions of the majority of Americans have not improved that much, especially those who are found at the very bottom of the social order. While many in more privileged sectors have benefited from the recent economic boom, as usual certain segments have been left behind. All one has to do is to drive or walk around neighborhoods in places like downtown Detroit, the west side of Las Vegas, south-central Los Angeles, the barrios of East Los Angeles, on the south side of Chicago, Hunters Point in the southern part of San Francisco, or the Matapan area of Boston, among many others, to see evidence of this. For the majority of these inhabitants, they receive neither *legal* justice nor *social* justice: In the case of the former, they are most likely to be arrested, convicted, and imprisoned than any other segment (African-Americans have an incarceration rate fully eight times that of whites), and the jobs and wealth created by the booming economy have not yet "trickled down" to them.

As we note in Chapter 1, the definition of "gang" and "gang member" remains illusive and open for varying interpretations, although given the fact that in every jurisdiction (where estimates have been provided) the percentages of gang members who happen to be either African-American or Hispanic continues to hover between 80 and 90 percent, one cannot help but conclude that something quite conscious and intentional is being done by those in authority. After all, politicians (including those running for local criminal justice positions, like police chief or district attorney) wishing to be elected or reelected, rely on a very small group of mostly upper- and upper-middle-class white suburbanites for their source of campaign financing. It is these groups that tend to fear crime the most (at least according to public opinion polls), and the kind of "crime" they fear the most is that which is committed by the previously mentioned racial groups (for a more detailed examination of this issue, see Dyer, 2000).

Since the first edition, the number of gangs and the number of gang members have continued to increase. However, we strongly question (and urge the reader to question) the bases of these estimates. We strongly suspect that the one fact that correlates most strongly with these rising numbers is the increase in the amount of funding being provided by the federal government in the "war on gangs" (and also the "war on drugs"). The metaphor of "war" does not escape us here since declaring a "war" by definition creates an "enemy"—in this case, the enemy consists of the urban poor and racial minorities. In other words, we have declared a war on racial minorities and the poor and using the word "gang" serves to mask what is really going on, in our opinion.

Our desire is that this book can provide a lens through which to view and begin to answer the many questions pertaining to gangs. Chapter 1 provides an introduction to the historical context of gangs and explores the difficulty in defining what is meant by the term "gang." In this chapter we have added a new section on the topic of gang migration and have expanded on the discussion of "moral panics." We then explore the illusive topic of what gangs "look like" in Chapter 2 (which has been extensively rewritten), followed in Chapter 3 with a discussion of the uniqueness of the gang subculture and the question of how and why youths join gangs. The variety of crimes committed by gangs and their members is discussed in Chapter 4. A new chapter has been added for this edition.

The chapter on girls and gangs (Chapter 5) has been expanded with much new material (provided by the meticulous research of coauthor Tracy). Here we explore the question of gender and the phenomenon of girl's participation in gang activity. The chapter on theories of gangs has been moved further ahead in the book and is now covered in Chapter 6. At the suggestion of several reviewers, we added a discussion of rational choice theory and expanded on our discussion of anomie theory. Chapter 7 is a new chapter, which is actually an expanded version of the last portion of chapter 2 in the first edition. Here we expand on the problems of capitalism within American society and the growing inequality that has occurred during the past 20 years or so and how this impacts gangs and gang behavior.

Finally, in Chapters 8 and 9 we have expanded on the discussion and assessment of the multitude of responses to the problem not only of gangs but also of crime and delinquency in general, beginning with a look at community and societal responses (Chapter 8) and ending with an examination of the response of the criminal justice system (police, courts, legislatures) (Chapter 9). Finally, our concluding chapter (Chapter 10) is designed to expand and/or change the way in which research is conducted and, more important, to challenge the way we think and respond to gangs. The concluding chapter in this edition includes an update on the story of "Jimmy," which, sad to say, is not a happy ending.

These are just some of the issues we discuss in the second edition of this book. We certainly do not make the claim that this book will be the final word on this subject. We hope that the book can serve as a useful reference for probing this subject in more detail and for asking more questions about this problem.

We all want to extend our appreciation to the several reviewers who made excellent suggestions for an improvement of the first edition of this book. We could not include every suggestion that was made but took to heart most of them. Thanks go to the following reviewers: Peter Kratcoski, Kent State University; James J. Nolan III, West Virginia University; Kevin Thompson, North Dakota State University; Charles Tittle, Washington State University; Douglas S. Wallace, Kansas State University; and Lawrence Salinger, Arkansas State University.

Once again, our thanks to the people at Wadsworth for their generous support throughout this entire project. Special thanks are extended to editors Sabra Horne and Dan Alpert. Both have been wonderful to work with and were always there with support.

Shelden extends his thanks and love to his wife, Virginia, for once again putting up with the subject of gangs. Tracy would like to extend special thanks to Kathy Ruebel, her birth sister, and to Florence Ferguson, her soul sister, for giving support. She also extends her love and thanks to her parents for giving love and guidance. Finally, she gives thanks to her husband, Rusty, for giving her faith, fortitude, loyalty, and love. Brown once again extends his thanks and love to his wife, Judy.

1

✦

Introduction

A BRIEF HISTORY OF YOUTH GANGS

I
t should be noted at the outset that youths have formed groups (usually with their own age cohorts) from the beginning of time. Some of these groups have committed various kinds of activities that have been considered harmful and even crimes. Some of these groups have been called gangs, while many have been labeled rowdies, bad kids, troublemakers, and other negative terms.

Youth groups known as gangs are certainly not inventions of twentieth-century American society, for such groups have existed since at least the early fourteenth and fifteenth centuries in Europe. For example, descriptions of life in England during this period note that gangs committed various forms of theft and robbery, along with extortion and rape (Hay et al., 1975; Pearson, 1983). One report noted that in London during the fourteenth and fifteenth centuries citizens were "terrorized by a series of organized gangs calling themselves the Mims, Hectors, Bugles, Dead Boys . . . who found amusement in breaking windows, demolishing taverns, assaulting the watch. . . . The gangs also fought pitched battles among themselves dressed with colored ribbons to distinguish the different factions" (Pearson, 1983:188). In France during the Middle Ages, there were groups of youths who fought with rival groups from other areas and schools and who also committed a variety of crimes. Youth gangs or groups reportedly existed in Germany during the seventeenth and eighteenth centuries (Covey, Menard, and Franzese, 1992:90–91).

Deviant youth groups (and no one knows for certain the extent to which these groups were referred to as gangs) did not exist in any large number in the United States until the nineteenth century, although one report notes that they were found in some areas during colonial times (Sanders, 1970). During the latter part of the nineteenth century, with the rapid expansion of the capitalist system following the Civil War, some citizens in cities such as Philadelphia and New York expressed a concern about the problem of delinquency in general and gangs in particular. Herbert Asbury wrote about various youth gangs in and around the five-points area of New York City in the late 1800s. Among the most famous gangs were the Plug-Uglies, Dusters, Bowery Boys, Roach Guards, Shirt Tails, and Kerryonians (Asbury, 1927). An early study by the Illinois State Police noted that a gang called the Forty Thieves was founded in New York around 1820; this is believed to be the first youth gang in the United States (Goldstein, 1991:8).

A study of a Philadelphia newspaper covering the years 1836 to 1878 found 52 different gangs identified. The report noted that in the pre–Civil War era Philadelphia was "plagued" by gangs. A report by the *New York Tribune* stated that the northern suburbs of Philadelphia during the years 1849 and 1850 was crawling with "loafers who brave only gangs, herd together in squads," and mark their names on the walls. In New York City in 1855 there were an estimated "30,000 men who owed allegiance to gang leaders and through them to the political leaders of Tammany Hall and the Know Nothings or Native American Party" according to one contemporary account (Spergel, 1995:7).

Over the past few decades public attention to gangs has oscillated. For example, during Prohibition and its immediate aftermath (the Depression years), the public seemed enthralled with gangland activities and many of gangland's colorful characters (e.g., the Mob, Al Capone, Bonnie and Clyde, the Ma Barker Gang, and others). Several decades later mass media glamorized those flamboyant actors. Throughout much of the 1940s Americans were distracted by World War II events in Europe and the Pacific and the healing process associated with the closure of a world war. Fascination with the gang was revitalized during the 1950s and early 1960s (the West Side Story era) by academics who marched behind a theoretical banner that questioned lower-class allegiance to middle-class values (e.g., Cloward and Ohlin, 1960; Cohen, 1955; Miller, 1958; Short and Strodtbeck, 1965). By the end of the 1960s Americans were tuned into nightly exhibitions of civil disorder (related to the civil rights movement and the Vietnam War), the Vietnam War, and a new type of gang—the hippies. Strangely, with high levels of crime and violence occurring throughout most of the 1970s, very little attention was paid to gang activities. America's loss in Vietnam, inflation, fuel shortages, existentialism, and disco captivated the public's attention.

Public concern about gangs was reinvented during the 1980s and continues today. The rediscovery of gangs has been augmented by an escalation of media presentations about youth gang activities—particularly those gangs located within America's inner cities. The media have experienced great success in raising the public's level of fear about youth gangs. Gangs are a hot topic in the media with the amount of coverage increasing tremendously during the past two decades. Two gang researchers have noted that during the 1980s "newspapers, television, and films were suddenly awash with images of gun-toting, drug-dealing, hat-to-the-back gangstas. With the hue-and-cry came a massive mobilization of resources. Federal, state, and local funds were allocated to create anti-gang units in law enforcement and prosecution agencies." Then came the rapid deployment of technology, databases and the proliferation of gang "experts" (typically police officers or former gang members), and all across the country they went spreading the word that gangs were everywhere. "In public schools across the country, gang awareness and resistance techniques were incorporated into the curriculum, gang-related clothing banned from campuses, and teachers instructed on how to identify gang members and spot concealed weapons" (McCorkle and Miethe, 2001:3).

One indication of the growth in such coverage comes from a search of the Reed Nexis Database, which accesses the files of major newspapers and magazines. This database revealed the number of articles on the subject of gangs between 1983 and 1994 increased from a mere 36 references in 1983 to more than 1,300 in 1994, as shown in Table 1.1. Yet, there has been a downward trend in media coverage in recent years, especially the noteworthy drop in 1999. Still, surveys of law enforcement agencies indicate steady growth in the number of gangs and the number of gang members. This demonstrates that media reporting of events does not always conform to reality.

A detailed study of the role of the media in Nevada (specifically in the two largest cities, Las Vegas and Reno) show a similar pattern (McCorkle and Miethe, 1998:2001). While media coverage has obviously declined since a peak in the mid-1990s, the number of gangs, gang members, and gang-related crimes, according to every estimate from official sources, has actually increased (see below). In actual fact, media coverage of most major topics rarely conforms to reality but rather conforms to the need for profits. There is abundant research showing how the media portray a reality according to the perceptions of groups in power who control the media.[1] The famous phrase, "If it bleeds, it leads," is an appropriate way of expressing this point.

More often than not, the true causes and the surrounding social context of social problems, like gangs, is totally ignored. This is not surprising when you consider that one of the major roles of the corporate-dominated media is to divert the public's attention away from real problems and keep them entertained. Many, if not most, "news" stories are presented in an entertainment

**Table 1.1 Gang-Related Articles in Major
Newspapers and Magazines, 1983–1999**

Year	No.	Year	No.	Year	No.
1983	36	1989	403	1995	1208
1984	33	1990	533	1996	1317
1985	159	1991	522	1997	1008
1986	142	1992	686	1998	1018
1987	148	1993	1,098	1999	877
1988	249	1994	1,313		

SOURCE: Reed Nexis Database (GANG W/5 YOUTH AND VIOLEN! AND DATE = [year]). Search conducted on January 9, 1995.

format (witness the coverage by CNN of the Gulf War and the conflict in Bosnia, the death of Princess Diana, the O.J. Simpson trial, and so on, where each one of these events had their own theme music). Debra Seagal's research about a prime-time television "real crime" show, which was based on video-tapes of real police arrests, illustrates this problem. In her article Seagal discusses how focusing on individual criminals diverts our attention away from the social context of crime and, indeed, communicates the idea that these offenders exist in a social vacuum. Seagal writes as follows (Seagal, 1993, quoted in Reiman, 1998:157):

> By the time our 9 million viewers flip on their tubes, we've reduced fifty or sixty hours of mundane and compromising video into short, action-packed segments of tantalizing, crack-filled, dope-dealing, junkie-busting, cop culture. How easily we downplay the pathos of the suspect; how cleverly we breeze past the complexities that cast doubt on the very system that has produced the criminal activity in the first place.

In a similar vein, one writer has noted that the big hoopla about "family values" by Dan Quayle over both the riots in Los Angeles following the Rodney King verdict and an episode in the television series *Murphy Brown* (where the main character is a single woman who decides to have her baby out of wedlock and raise it herself) completely ignored the "social context" of the lives of most women and most inner-city African-Americans. She noted that

> the erasure of the L.A. uprising in the *Murphy Brown* incident moved the debate away from issues of race, from the condition of inner cities, and from the deteriorating economic base in the United States, to a much safer, symbolic ground. By shifting the debate from the material conditions of inner cities to the discursive field of "family values," both parties occupied a much more comfortable terrain for debate (Stabile, 1995:289).

This is an example of what is known as "symbolic politics" (Gordon, 1994:4). Similarly, TV crime shows constantly inform the public about the dangerous criminals in our midst without any attempt to try to explain why. The viewer is left with the impression that these criminals come out of nowhere! Reiman concludes by saying that (1998:157, italics in the original):

> to look only at individual criminality is to close one's eyes to social injustice and to close one's ears to the question of whether our social institutions have exploited or violated the individual. *Justice is a two-way street—but criminal justice is a one-way street.* Individuals owe obligations to their fellow citizens because their fellow citizens owe obligations to them. Criminal justice focuses on the first and looks away from the second. *Thus, by focusing on individual responsibility for crime, the criminal justice system literally acquits the existing social order of any charge of injustice.*

Throughout the 1980s and well into the 1990s, the media, with the generous help of law enforcement, created many myths about gangs and gang crime, which understandably created much fear among the public. Similarly, the "war on drugs" has been largely a media-driven event. For example, shortly after the 1988 election, public opinion polls revealed that only about 10 percent of the public believed drugs to be a major problem facing the country. Following an intensive media blitz, this percentage soared to almost 40 percent within one year (Miller, 1996:157).

It did not take long for citizens to become alarmed about the threat of gangs. In Salt Lake City, for example, a 1993 poll found that the "majority of Salt Lake County residents are increasingly anxious about expanding gang violence and would accept a tax increase to combat that problem" (Shellety, 1993). *U.S. News and World Report* (July 16, 1984, 108–109) noted that the city of Miami is faced with the problems of Cuban immigrants forming gangs, while Seattle has Asian immigrants in competition with both African-American and Hispanic gangs.[2] Many reports on gangs are highly exaggerated and based more on anecdotal rather than scientific evidence. An example of such media exaggeration comes from a 1987 *Time magazine* article on the subject of gangs, which stated in grossly exaggerated form that

> despite the fratricide among gangs, most of their victims are innocent bystanders. Gangs are prospering because crime pays in the ghetto. Many gangs have made the deadly transition from switchblade bravado to organized crime, serving as highly efficient distributors for Colombian cocaine dealers. Stiff competition has prompted bloody firefights in broad daylight over market share, while the influx of drug money provides topflight weapons, fancy cars and high tech surveillance equipment. Gang membership is now a full-time job, lasting well into the 20s and 30s (22).

Not surprisingly, the media usually rely on various "official" sources for good "sound bytes." Here is a rather typical description of a "gang" by the California State Task Force on Gangs and Drugs:

> Today's gangs are urban terrorists. Heavily armed and more violent than ever before, they are quick to use terror and intimidation to seize and protect their share of the lucrative drug market. Gang members are

turning our streets and neighborhoods into war zones, where it takes an act of courage simply to walk to the corner store (Klein, 1995:7).

The fear of crime in general (including gang crime) has been linked to political phenomena that are related to ethnic heterogeneity and social change rather than to crime itself (Heinz et al., 1983). Similar circumstances, with corresponding relationships, may paint our current beliefs and fears about youth gangs. Ethnicity, race, and subcultural differences have been found to play major roles in the promotion of the public's fear of crime (Covington and Taylor, 1991). Youth gangs are intrinsic to American society. Since the mid-1980s youth gangs have been found to exist in many small and mid-sized cities throughout the country. Gangs have become somewhat permanent institutions of large urban areas with a heavy concentration of the poor and racial minorities. Youth gangs exist, in some form, in all 50 states (Spergel, 1990). As the famous French sociologist Emile Durkheim once proposed, there is a certain inevitability of crime, and so perhaps there will probably always be some groups within society that are going to be, at the very least, labeled gangs (Durkheim, 1950). Gang members come from an array of economic backgrounds (e.g., poor, middle-class, and wealthy socioeconomic statuses) and ethnic backgrounds (e.g., African-American, Asian, Latino, and a multiplicity of European ethnic groups). Each of these ethnic groups, at various junctures in history, has been viewed as representing a threat to the existing order. Their behavior has habitually been portrayed as destructive and/or violent.

For at least 20 years our society has experienced significant pivotal economic and structural changes (e.g., accelerated deterioration of the inner cities, increased levels of poverty, high unemployment among ethnic minority youth, displacement of workers, and a shrinking middle class). Amidst these dramatic social transformations we seem to have acquired an uncanny interest in, and concern for, two interesting diversionary topics: (1) crime and (2) youth gangs. Overall, crime rates have been relatively stable over the past two decades. In fact, while the overall crime rate has dropped significantly in the 1990s, going back 20 years one finds that there has been little overall change (Maguire and Pastore, 1998).[3] It is rather curious that during the recent drop in official crime rates, the number of gangs and number of gang members has increased, or so we are told by the National Gang Survey (U.S. Department of Justice, 1999). One could logically make the argument that as gangs and gang members increase, the crime rate drops! Arguments have been raised that youth gangs today are a new breed (Stover, 1986). The most significant behavioral differences between contemporary youth gangs and their early 1900s counterparts, however, seem to center around variations in their methods of activity.

Concerning gangs in the early part of the twentieth century, several researchers noted episodes of violence and theft by youth gangs in Chicago (Shaw and McKay, 1942; Thrasher, 1927). Thus violence and crime are not the innovations of contemporary youth gangs. However, during the past decade youth gangs have become more involved in illegal drug marketing, drive-by shootings, and the acquisition of more sophisticated weaponry. These changes in gang activities parallel economic, social, and technological transformations that shape social change in the greater society (e.g., declining employment op-portunities, widespread acceptance of violence promoted by the mass media, social fascination with draconian modes of punishment, and the development and sanitized/impersonal use of high-tech war machinery). One gang mem-ber in Detroit stated, "Fuck, man, we don't make no 9 millimeters. Business makes 'em and we make business with 'em. That's capitalism, ain't it?"[4] Sub-stantive attributes of youth gangs may not have changed significantly since the days of Thrasher; rather, gangs may have simply taken advantage of modern technological advancements (the abundance of automatic weapons), become more willing to expand their business-venture options (drug dealing), and up-scaled their level of violence to keep up with social trends and interests (drive-by shootings).

Much of our concern about youth gangs is precipitated by an interest in issues germane to decaying urban areas. Our preoccupation with youth gangs almost exclusively targets African-American and Hispanic gangs; both are re-flections of ethnic minority groups that the dominant class has perceived to be the most threatening to social stability. Historically, the dominant class has sponsored legislation that portrays concern for the general public. However, this legislation often results in the adoption of social control policies over the lower classes, particularly ethnic minorities, while the real beneficiary is the privileged class.[5] Musto describes how support for the Marijuana Tax Act (1937) was obtained by painting Mexican-Americans—believed to be the principal consumers of the drug—as potentially violent while under the influ-ence of marijuana (Musto, 1973). Two studies have offered evidence that infor-mation linking African-Americans with cocaine use was employed (for political purposes) to solicit support from Southern legislators to make co-caine illegal (Cloyd, 1982; Helmer, 1975). It was argued that African-American males under the influence of cocaine presented a potential threat to white women. One of the most recent examples of legislation targeting ethnic mi-norities can be found in the overwhelming approval of California's Proposi-tion 187, which, among other things, forbids certain illegal aliens living in California from obtaining various benefits, such as welfare, and even prevent-ing some children from attending school.[6]

African-Americans and Hispanics are ethnic groups that many people strongly associate with the inner city. The inner city is frequently envisioned as an area constituted predominantly of these two minority groups. Policymakers communicate their concern about the plight of the inner city. However, one question continues to surface from the center of this political "concern": Are policymakers actually concerned about the social conditions of citizens resid-ing in our inner cities, or are they simply worried about their ability (or in-ability) to contain this lower-strata population? Perhaps this "concern" is little more than a superficial reflective response—catering to dominant-class demands driven by the fear that their domain is threatened by inner-city inhabitants who want to flee the gang-occupied territories.[7] How else might one explain, in a humanistic context, their reluctance to institute structural changes that offer real hope and opportunities to inner-city residents? Instead, they pass scores of legislative rubbish that foster the social control of an underclass, particularly those elements of the underclass who find themselves trapped within the inner cities of America—ethnic minority groups. For decades, American society has been successful in its geographic isolation of these disenfranchised groups (Harrington, 1962; Massey and Denton, 1993; Piven and Cloward, 1971; Shaw and McKay, 1942; Wilson, 1987).

One of the important implications of these recent developments is the fact that today's gangs are becoming much different from the gangs of years ago, especially those studied by the "Chicago School" (see Chapter 7). For those groups, the gang was a transitory experience of recent immigrant groups. Most members eventually matured out of the gangs and settled down to jobs and families. Recent studies indicate that this is no longer the case. More and more gang members remain within the gang well into their adult years, as there are fewer opportunities available to them in terms of well-paying jobs. In short, gangs have become part of an emerging underclass of marginalized minority youth. Virtually all the research within the past 10 to 15 years has documented this (e.g., Duster, 1987; Hagedorn, 1998; Huff, 1989, 1996; Klein, 1995; Moore, 1978, 1991; Quicker, 1983; Short, 1990a; Spergel, 1990, 1995; Zatz, 1985, 1987). During a follow-up study of the original 47 gang founders in Milwaukee, Hagedorn found that over 80 percent of them were still involved in the gang although they were in their mid-20s, a time when most have typically matured out of the gang (Hagedorn, 1998).

The next section of this chapter explores the recent growth of gangs and how such growth is linked to changing social conditions. Brief case studies of three cities—Los Angeles, Milwaukee, and Chicago—provide some insights into this phenomenon.

THE RECENT GROWTH OF GANGS: A FOCUS ON LOS ANGELES, MILWAUKEE, AND CHICAGO

There is little doubt that the number of gangs, as well as the number of gang members, has grown in recent years. What is not well understood, however, is how and why this has occurred. There has been an increasing amount of research during the past decade on this subject. This research is important, as it provides us with some insight into the gang phenomenon that will be helpful in the years to come. It places the recent growth of gangs in a much larger social and economic context.

Los Angeles Gangs

Prior to World War II, gangs, as we understand them today, did not exist in Southern California, although some important changes beginning in the 1920s began to set the stage for their emergence. The economic boom of the 1920s helped bring thousands of Mexican immigrants to the area. These Mexicans were primarily rural and poor and brought with them a tradition known as *palomilla* (in Spanish this means a covey of doves), in which a number of young men in a village would group together in a coming-of-age cohort (Vigil, 1990:118). In the Los Angeles area these young men began to identify with a particular neighborhood or parish during the 1920s and 1930s. These groups, called boy gangs by an early researcher on gangs, were to be the forerunners of the modern Chicano gangs of East Los Angeles (Bogardus, 1943). It is important to note the tradition of such youths identifying closely with a specific geographic area, such as a village, parish, or neighborhood. These areas are now referred to as *barrios*.

Vigil notes a process of *choloization* (or *marginalization*) within the *cholo subculture*.[8] This is a process whereby various cultural changes and conflicts have made some Chicano youth especially vulnerable to becoming gang members. In the Southern California area during the Depression, thousands of Mexican immigrants were repatriated and deported. This process had a very negative effect on the Mexican-American population, with many feeling that they were unwanted. Racist policies and widespread discrimination set in, culminating with the famous *Zoot Suit* riots of 1943. About the same time a death at a party in East Los Angeles resulted in sensational press coverage (which included stereotypic descriptions of Chicano gangs). The police arrested 22 gang members for conspiracy to commit murder, resulting in 12 convictions (this was called the "Sleepy Lagoon" case). Also, police began to engage in periodic sweeps within gang areas.

These two events, perhaps more than any others, helped bring youths closer together and transformed informal youth groupings or boy gangs into gangs (Moore, 1988, 1991:1–2). In regard to the Zoot Suit riots, those "that fought the marauding sailors in East Los Angeles were seen by their younger brothers as heroes of a race war" (Moore, 1978:62). In fact, one particular boy gang known as *Purisima* (the name comes from a local parish) began to call itself *White Fence* (named after the surrounding barrio). Currently, this gang is one of the oldest, most well established gangs in Los Angeles, having offshoots in other cities, such as Las Vegas (Moore, 1988, 1991).

All of these events took place during a time when many positive male role models left the barrios because of repatriation. Thousands of other such role models were removed from the area because of World War II. Upon returning from the war, many took advantage of GI benefits and purchased homes in the growing suburbs of Southern California. Unfortunately, the males who remained in the barrios for the youths to look up to were those rejected from the service, those with criminal records, and typically those among the poorest of the poor (Vigil, 1990:119). These gangs continue to flourish throughout

Southern California and indeed throughout the West (including Northern California, Nevada, and Arizona).

The origins of African-American gangs in Southern California are similar to those of the Chicano gangs, even though they emerged a generation later. The most popular of these gangs are the Bloods and the Crips and their various offshoots (called "sets"). Like their Mexican counterparts, African-Americans came from rural areas (mostly the rural South) to Southern California, a sprawling urban and industrial society. Their traditional way of life in the South was mostly church based with close family ties. However, the second-generation children (again like the cholo youths) faced many pressures in the new culture in Los Angeles. By the late 1960s these African-American youths (concentrated in a few areas near downtown Los Angeles and in the San Fernando Valley) "found themselves alienated from the old rural values that had sustained their parents. They were racially locked out of the dominant Anglo culture and, in most cases, economically locked out of the African-American middle class. Their futures were as bleak as any cholo's, maybe bleaker" (Reiner, 1992:5). They had come in search of the "American Dream" of good-paying jobs in the booming aerospace, automobile, and construction industry, only to find the jobs filled by mostly whites. From the late 1950s to the time of the Watts riots, unemployment among African-Americans in south-central Los Angeles went from around 12 percent to 30 percent, while median incomes dropped by about 10 percent. In 1964 one of the major causes of growing discontent (leading to the Watts riots) occurred, the repeal of the Rumford Fair Housing Act (Davis, 1992:296).

One of the earliest references to a "gang problem" appeared in African-American newspapers during the late 1940s, and this was in reference, ironically, to *white* youths ("gangs"?) who attacked black people. There were reported "racial wars" on several Los Angeles area high schools during the late 1940s and early 1950s. Much like the response by Hispanic youths to the Zoot Suit riots, African-American "gangs" emerged as a *defensive* response. These African-American gangs defined themselves mostly in terms of school-based turfs. Some of the earliest of these gangs went by such names as the Slausons, Gladiators, Watts, Flips, Rebel Rousers, Businessmen, and the like. Some of these "gangs" modeled themselves after the white "car clubs" so common throughout Southern California (e.g., the Slausons and the Flips). Some of these groups divided themselves into two factions, one group on the "West Side" (usually with more money and more sophistication) and the other on the "East Side" (less money and less sophistication). Some of these "gangs" were merely the extension of intermural athletic rivalries, common in those days (Davis, 1992:293–294).[9]

The Watts riots of 1965 did for African-American gangs roughly what the Zoot Suit riots did for Chicano gangs. One result of the Watts riots was that young African-Americans were seen in a more negative light by the media and by the rest of society. Also, African-American youths began to see themselves differently. It is important to note that although African-American youths did not have the palomilla tradition of their Mexican counterparts, they did have already-developed Chicano gangs to imitate. As Reiner notes, "Given the emasculating circumstances of ghetto life a quarter-century ago, it is small wonder that the cocky, dangerous style of the Latino gangs had a strong appeal for African-American youths. It responded perfectly to the need for repackaging defeat as defiance, redefining exclusion as exclusivity" (Reiner, 1992:5).

During the late 1950s some African-American youths (and a few whites) began to imitate some of the cholo style of the Mexican-American youths. They formed car clubs and other organizations and had such names as the Businessmen, the Slausons (named after a street in Los Angeles), the Black Cobras, the Gladiators, the Boozies, and others. These groups consisted of "guys who banded together for camaraderie and, to a certain extent, for protection" (Bing, 1991:148–149). These gangs were different from today's gangs in many other ways. While they had certain neighborhoods where they lived, they usually did not consider such areas as their territory or turf. They did not usually fight other gangs, they had no colors, and they did not paint graffiti (Los Angeles County, 1992:20).

During the mid-to late 1960s a transformation began with the emergence of groups that called themselves Crips. There is some debate as to the exact origin of this term; some say it came from a movie staring Vincent Price, *Tales from the Crypt,* while others say it comes from the word cripple because the original gangs crippled their enemies or suffered a similar fate. Another story was that it referred to a style of walking (i.e., walking like one was crippled in some way). The most popular story was that the Crips were founded by a group of youths from Fremont High School (a youth named Raymond Washington is generally credited as the founder) that had one member who walked with the aid of a stick and who was referred to as a "crip," short for cripple. Some have suggested that the original gang used walking sticks as a sort of symbol and that the police and the media began to apply the name and so eventually the gang did, too (Davis, 1992:299; Los Angeles County, 1992:5; Reiner, 1992:6). Several imitators came from the city of Compton. One group called themselves the Westside Crips, founded by a student from Washington High School known as Tookie. They borrowed one of the cholo traditions of wearing railroad bandannas and added to this the color of blue. Other Crip sets soon began to imitate them by wearing blue bandannas and other blue clothing, a color that set them apart from others. (Some of these sets currently wear the colors brown, purple, and black; Reiner, 1992:6–7.)

Still another version is that the Crips emerged in the wake of the demise of the Black Panther Party; in fact there is some evidence that both the Crips and the Bloods more or less took the place of the Black Panther Party, at least at first. It is well known how the FBI and other police organizations engaged in a systematic elimination of the Black Panther Party in the 1960s, largely under the infamous COINTELPRO program. This was an elaborate counter-intelligence program established by the FBI to "disrupt, harass, and discredit groups that the FBI decided were in some way 'un-American,' " which even included the American Civil Liberties Union (Chambliss, 1993:308; Davis,

1992:298). This effort was largely responsible for infiltrating just about every African-American political organization in the country whose views were in any way militant, including committing murder. Many believe that "the decimation of the Panthers led directly to a recrudescence of gangs in the early 1970s" (Davis, 1992:298). In fact, as *Los Angeles Times* journalist Bob Baker suggests, Raymond Washington (see above) himself was influenced by some of the beliefs of the Panthers (Baker, 1988c). This version of the story indicates that the first "set" of Crips was in part the result of the destruction of housing and of neighborhood ties with the building of the Century Freeway. Within this area was the original "107 Hoover Street Crips," who split off from a gang called the "Avenues." The area around 107th Street was where Raymond Washington lived. In fact, one of the "O.G.s" of this gang told journalist Bob Baker that Crip originally stood for "Continuous Revolution in Progress" (Davis, 1992:299).

The next important development was a reaction to the emergence of the Crip gang sets, both on the "East Side" and the "West Side" of Figueroa Street. Such independent gangs as the Brims, Bounty Hunters, and Denver Lanes, among others, came together wearing red handkerchiefs, calling themselves "Blood," and arose in defense of the Crips (Davis, 1992:299). One group of African-American youths who lived on a street called Piru in Compton began to get together for protection from attacks by Crip sets. They called themselves the Compton Pirus and are believed to be the first gang to borrow the term *blood brothers* and apply it to their gang name. The term suggested, of course, the color red, which they selected as their gang's color. Soon Blood sets wore red bandannas, shoes, and jackets to set them apart from the Crips. Within just a few years Blood and Crip offshoots or sets spread throughout the Los Angeles area. These gangs began to borrow other traditions of Hispanic gangs—flying colors, defending their turf, using graffiti, hanging with homeboys, and jumping in new members. By the 1970s gang culture was firmly established in the Los Angeles area (Reiner, 1992:6–7).

One interpretation of the Crips was that they were a "radical permutation of Black gang culture" and "however perversely, inherited the Panther aura of fearlessness and transmitted the ideology of armed vanguardism (shorn of its program)." Even some Crips insignia "continued to denote Black Power," but "Crippin' " eventually "came to represent an escalation of intraghetto violence to *Clockwork Orange* levels (murder as a status symbol, and so on) that was unknown in the days of the Slausons and anathema to everything the Panthers had stood for" (Davis, 1992:299).

A turning point in the history of African-American gangs in Los Angeles came with an incident that took place outside a movie theater in Westwood, about two blocks from UCLA and near the wealthy neighborhood of Beverly Hills. Two members of rival gangs faced off, and a young woman who was standing in line was shot in the head and killed. Bing reports as follows (Bing, 1991:xiv):

> Her death snapped people into a new and horrified awareness: The beast had slithered out of its cage to prowl streets where insularity is the rule

and privilege the norm. Suddenly the specter of South Central LA—a nightmare landscape where shadowy figures of young men stalk the streets and cars burn unattended in alleyways, where there is a nightly roar of wind from the rotors of the police helicopters that hover overhead at tightly spaced intervals, where everything is illuminated by the surreal beams of their searchlights . . . descended like nuclear ash over a city that had not been more than marginally aware of its existence. . . . Suddenly the lead stories on local newscasts were about the latest gang-related shootings.

Milwaukee Gangs

In Milwaukee, gangs emerged within the context of major economic and social changes in the midwestern and northern parts of the country. As factories began to close, more and more young males became marginalized as unemployment rates in Milwaukee increased. Most gangs emerged through conflict either with the criminal justice system or with other groups of youths. Some of Milwaukee's gangs evolved from ordinary street-corner groups, while others began as break-dancing and drill teams, which became fads within the African-American community. Very often fights broke out at these events. Negative police-minority relations, protests, sensational press coverage, and other conflicts helped solidify these gangs. A few gangs were offshoots of some famous Chicago gangs, but these were mostly formed when ex–gang members or their families just happened to move to Milwaukee rather than through active recruiting by Chicago gang members. Further, school desegregation ironically contributed to the problem by placing rival gang members in the same schools and in the process destroying some of the turf connections of these gangs (Hagedorn, 1998).

In Milwaukee, a study by Hagedorn identified 19 major gangs, only four of which originated in Chicago. In the latter case former Chicago gang members moved their families to Milwaukee (which is about one hour's drive away from Chicago), where in time their own children formed gangs and named them after such Chicago gangs as the Kings, Cobras, and others (Hagedorn, 1998: 58–59). Hagedorn could find no evidence of any sort of "franchising" by these gangs—that is, Chicago gangs did not move to Milwaukee to "set up shop." (Later in this chapter the problem of "gang migration" will be discussed.)

In most cases gangs develop in a way described years ago by Thrasher (see Chapter 7), that is, through normal youthful group processes (Thrasher, 1927). In the majority of cases, gangs are formed only after some sort of conflict, either with other groups or, more often, as a result of the response by the criminal justice system. In Milwaukee, four of the 19 gangs studied by Hagedorn developed out of break-dancing groups, while 10 emerged gradually out of ordinary street-corner groups that selected their names based on either the street they lived on (e.g., the 2–7 gang was named after 27th Street) or their housing project (e.g., Hillside Boys was named after the Hillside Housing Project). Two other gangs were female auxiliaries (Hagedorn, 1998:58–59).

Some gangs were originally both a dance group and a corner group. All 19 of the gangs Hagedorn studied started while most of the members were attending middle schools between 1981 and 1983. Each gang's roots were in a group of friends in a particular neighborhood, and each gang developed the same way. Break dancing and drilling were the main social activities of African-American and Hispanic youths in the early 1980s, and the dance groups formed very spontaneously. They practiced frequently, had dance contests, and were highly competitive. Often during these contests fights would break out, and the groups would act as units (not unlike fighting during other sporting events, especially hockey). These groups formed all over Milwaukee (and other cities, too), each group assuming its own name and identity. Most simply disappeared.

Corner groups formed the same way: A few youths who were not in school (or were cutting classes) had nothing to do except hang out. Many adopted a name and eventually became strongly integrated through conflicts with other corner groups and gangs.

The Chicago gangs did not merely migrate as a gang. They left Chicago (or, rather, their parents moved) in order to escape the gangs and other problems in their neighborhoods. However, ironically, some of the youths found that they had to band together in Milwaukee for protection (a common scenario throughout the country).

Hagedorn reports that many gang members blamed the police both for the creation of gangs and for giving them their name. They reported that they used to play games in playgrounds but were often chased away by the police. Having nothing else to do, they resorted to stealing instead of playing (stealing, it should be noted, is often a form of play for youngsters). Also, the police often identified these groups according to the addresses, blocks, or street corners where they hung out.

The gangs studied by Huff in Cleveland and Columbus, Ohio, had similar origins. Many originated from break-dancing or rappin' groups (rather informal groupings of young men and women who evolved into gangs because of conflict with other groups). Others evolved from regular street-corner groups as a result of conflict with other street-corner groups. Some had moved to Ohio from either Chicago or Los Angeles and brought with them leadership skills learned in gangs in these cities. With these skills they founded their own gangs (Huff, 1989).

Chicago Gangs

The gang problem in Chicago dates back at least to the early 1900s (originally appearing as athletic clubs) before Thrasher did his classic study. Some significant changes came after World War II, when membership in Chicago gangs became generally younger and more nonwhite. Sometime during the 1960s the so-called supergangs (People and Folks) first appeared (Bensinger, 1984). The largest gang in Chicago currently is the Black Gangster Disciples. Other popular gangs include the Cobra Stones, El Rukns (previously the Black P. Stone Nation), Blackstone Rangers, Vice Lords, Latin Kings, and Latin Disciples.

Each gang has its own identity. The Black Gangster Disciples use a six-pointed Star of David to symbolize the gang's founder, David Barksdale. They wear one earring in their right ear and tilt their caps to the right. The El Rukns use the five-pointed star and a pyramid with a half-crescent moon within it (symbolizing their affiliation with the Nation of Islam). The Cobra Stones, affiliates of the El Rukns, feature two half-crescent moons along with the five-pointed star. They wear an earring in their left ear. The Latin Kings use a crown with three crests, while the Latin Disciples use a devil's head or crossed pitchforks, and the Vice Lords use a complete circle surrounded by fire, tilting their hats to the left (Bensinger, 1984).

A recent survey sponsored by the National Institute of Justice found that in Chicago there are more than 40 active street gangs, with the four largest being the Black Gangster Disciples, Latin Disciples, Latin Kings, and Vice Lords. The combined total membership of these four gangs is around 19,000, about half the total gang population in Chicago (Block and Block, 1993). (There is some dispute about these numbers. According to an ABC investigative news report airing September 28–29, 1994, the Gangster Disciple Nation of Chicago claims 35,000 members).

According to the report by Block and Block, the Black Gangster Disciples are descendants of the Woodlawn Disciples and are the strongest on Chicago's South Side. They are most commonly known for their turf wars with the Blackstone Rangers in the late 1960s and early 1970s and, more recently, with the Black Gangster Disciples.

The Latin Disciples are a racially and ethnically mixed gang allied with the Black Gangster Disciples (in the Folks nation). They are found in a mixed-race neighborhood in the northwest part of the city in and around Humboldt Park and Logan Square. The Latin Kings are the oldest and largest of the Hispanic gangs, having been in existence for about 25 years. They are found in several different (usually racially and ethnically mixed) neighborhoods. They are especially active in the growing Hispanic neighborhoods on the southwest side. The Vice Lords are the oldest of the four gangs, dating from the 1950s. Although they operate throughout the city, they are found mainly in poor West Side neighborhoods. The Latin Kings and Vice Lords formed an alliance known as the People nation, mostly in response to the formation of the Folks nation (Block and Block, 1993:2–3).

Short gives an interesting historical portrait and comparison of two different Chicago gangs, the Vice Lords and the Nobles. In his study we can see the importance of local social conditions. The former gang is still quite active, while the latter no longer exists. Short notes that this is because they came from two completely different kinds of communities—Lawndale and Douglas, respectively (Short, 1990b).

Between 1934 and 1961 Lawndale showed the greatest increase in delinquency out of all Chicago communities, while during the same period Douglas had the greatest decrease. The Nobles were a neighborhood play group that was solidified through conflict with other gangs and as a result became a gang itself. As the members aged, they left the gang and assumed normal adult lives.

The Vice Lords, in contrast, began around 1958, when several incarcerated gang members agreed to pool their gang affiliations so as to become one of Chicago's toughest gangs. There were 66 original Vice Lords when the gang formed. In about two years, membership grew to over 300 in five branches. In the 1960s they incorporated as a nonprofit organization with around 8,000 members in 26 divisions.

Short accounts for the difference between the two gangs by citing important differences in the characteristics of the two communities in which the gangs lived. The Vice Lords emerged in an area of rapid population growth, especially racial changes. This community has lacked a stable population base and social institutions. Short notes that such communities as Lawndale are in direct contrast to what he terms functional communities. Functional communities (and Douglas resembled this type of community) are more apt to have a consistent pattern of norms and sanctions. Such communities offer more educational and job opportunities to their youth. Communities like Lawndale are populated largely by what Wilson has called the "truly disadvantaged," with a large segment of the households headed by young women (Wilson, 1987).

Some Concluding Thoughts on the Recent Growth of Gangs

As indicated at the beginning of this chapter, the first known youth gangs in recorded history began to appear in London during the fourteenth and fifteenth centuries as England was shifting from an agrarian to an industrial society. As many scholars have noted, this revolutionary change displaced thousands of people, and they, in turn, flocked to the growing urban areas, such as London (Ignatieff, 1978; Marx, 1964; Marx and Engels, 1976; Rusche and Kirchheimer, 1968; Shelden, 2001). Similarly, in several segments of American society a very similar process has been occurring. Displaced by the shift from an industrial to a service/information society with the corresponding need for better education and training, literally millions of minority youths have been displaced and become marginalized (or choloized) during the past 20 to 30 years. The formation of gangs can be seen as a method of adapting to such changes. The comparison between seventeenth-century London and late twentieth-century Los Angeles has not escaped notice. "Both cities were among the preeminent urban magnets of their time for huge rural populations displaced from the land (as was nineteenth-century New York). That status brings a city enormous benefits—growth, wealth, diversity. It also brings tremendous social dislocations—including gangs" (Reiner, 1992:9).

Along with the recent growth of gangs has come a flurry of research activity from both academic and nonacademic settings. Unfortunately, our knowledge base is still limited, and there is much disagreement about the nature and extent of youth gangs. In fact, there is little agreement about what a gang actually is.

WHAT IS A GANG?

We must initially consider the problem of defining what exactly constitutes a gang and a gang member. If four youths are standing on a street corner or are simply walking down the street, is this a gang? If this same group of youths hang out together frequently and occasionally engage in some form of deviant activity, does this mean they are a gang? Suppose this same group invents a name for itself and even purchases special shirts or jackets and invents slogans or hand-signs—does this mean it is a gang? If a young person is seen giving special hand signals or heard uttering gang phrases because he thinks it is cool or hip to do so, whether he may fully understand the implications, is he then to be considered a gang member? Or, if a youth lives in a neighborhood inhabited by a gang (but no one in the gang considers him a member), just happens to be passing the time on a street corner with a gang member he has known for several years, and is coincidentally questioned by a police officer, who subsequently fills out a field investigation card on him, is he therefore to be counted as a gang member? And how does race enter into the picture in the definition of gangs? If three or four white youths spend a considerable amount of time together, occasionally commit crimes together, and are often seen wearing the kinds of clothes typical of adolescents in general and some gangs in particular, are they considered a gang? We suspect that the average white citizen (and many police officers) would respond to this group differently than if they saw a group of three or four African-American teenagers hanging out together (e.g., at a shopping mall). Perhaps this is one reason why most official estimates of gangs and gang members tell us that less than 10 percent are white and the majority are African-American or some other minority group (usually Hispanic). In other words, could it not be argued that the very definition of *gang* is racially biased? Even these few examples illustrate the difficulty in defining gangs and gang members.

The term *gang* can have many different definitions. Gil Geis has provided one of the most interesting comments about the etymology of the term, noting that the early English usage of *gang* was "a going, a walking, or a journey" (quoted in Klein, 1995:22). The definition given by the Random House College Dictionary (1975:543) provides similar meanings of a positive or neutral nature, such as "a group or band"; "a group of persons who gather together for social reasons"; "a group of persons working together; squad; shift; *a gang of laborers*"; along with the more negative meanings. The thesaurus of the word processing program used to type these words gives such synonyms as "pack," "group," "company," and "team."

Not surprisingly, there has existed little consensus among social scientists and law-enforcement personnel as to what these terms mean. One writer defined gangs as "groups whose members meet together with some regularity, over time, on the basis of group-defined criteria of membership and group-defined organization" (Short, 1990:3). In many studies researchers have often used whatever definition was used by the police. Many researchers have apparently confused the term *group* with the term *gang* and have proceeded to expand the definition in such a way as to include every group of youths who commit offenses together. One of the most accepted definitions comes from the work of Klein:

> [A gang is] any denotable . . . group [of adolescents and young adults] who (a) are generally perceived as a distinct aggregation by others in their neighborhood, (b) recognize themselves as a denotable group (almost invariably with a group name), and (c) have been involved in a sufficient number of [illegal] incidents to call forth a consistent negative response from neighborhood residents and/or enforcement agencies (Klein and Maxson, 1989:205).

The dominant law-enforcement perspective is that gangs are essentially criminal conspiracies with a few hard-core members (often described as sociopaths) and believe that arrest and imprisonment of these individuals are required as a viable social policy. An example is provided by the California Penal Code (Section 186.22), which gives a definition of a "criminal street gang" as "any organization, association, or group of three or more persons whether formal or informal . . . which has a common name or common identifying sign or symbol, where members individually or collectively engage in or have engaged in a pattern of criminal activity" (Spergel, 1990:18–19). A report from the Los Angeles County Sheriff's Department defines a gang as "any group gathered together on a continuing basis to commit anti-social behavior" (Los Angeles County, 1992:1).

Adding to the ambiguity of the term *gang* is the most recent National Youth Gang Survey (1996) sponsored by the Office of Juvenile Justice and Delinquency Prevention (OJJDP). In this survey of about 5,000 agencies, a *youth gang* was defined as follows: "a group of youths or young adults in your jurisdiction that you or other responsible persons in your agency or community are willing to identify or classify as a 'gang.' " Omitted from this definition were such groups as motorcycle gangs, hate/ideology groups, prison gangs, or "other exclusively adult gangs" (U.S. Department of Justice, 1999:57). In other words, a "gang" is whatever an agency says it is!

Modern researchers have argued that gangs and delinquent groups are significantly different, but most now generally agree that gang offenders are usually older; are more homogeneous with regard to age, sex, race, and residence; and tend to commit more violent crimes than ordinary delinquent groups. Curry and Spergel distinguish among the terms *gang, street gang, traditional youth gang,* and *posse/crew.* They define *gang* as

> a group or collectivity of persons with a common identity who interact in cliques or sometimes as a whole group on a fairly regular basis and whose activities the community may view in varying degrees as legitimate, illegitimate, criminal, or some combination thereof. What distinguishes the gang from other groups is its communal or "fraternal," different, or special interstitial character (Curry and Spergel, 1990:388).

They define *street gang* as "a group or collectivity of persons engaged in significant illegitimate or criminal activities, mainly threatening and violent." The emphasis is placed on the location of the gang and their gang-related activities (ibid.).

The *traditional youth gang*

> refers to a youth or adolescent gang and often to the youth sector of a street gang. Such a group is concerned primarily with issues of status, prestige, and turf protection. The youth gang may have a name and a location, be relatively well organized, and persist over time. [They] often have leadership structure (implicit or explicit), codes of conduct, colors, special dress, signs, symbols, and the like. [They] may vary across time in characteristics of age, gender, community, race/ethnicity, or generation, as well as in scope and nature of delinquent or criminal activities (ibid:389).

Still another variation is the *posse* or *crew*, which, while often used in conjunction with the terms *street* or *youth gang*, is more commonly "characterized by a commitment to criminal activity for economic gain, particularly drug trafficking" (ibid.: 389).

Spergel and Curry also note that there are various kinds of deviant groups, such as "Stoners, punk rockers, neo-Nazi Skinheads, Satanic groups, motorcycle gangs, prison gangs." These may resemble traditional youth gangs or street gangs. They also caution that these gangs should be distinguished from what have often been called *youth groups* and *street groups*, common in an earlier era (e.g., as when Thrasher wrote in the 1920s). These groups are often called *street clubs, youth organizations,* or *athletic clubs.*

Spergel and Curry also note that there are *delinquent groups* and *criminal organizations.* The former are far less organized and criminal than the gangs defined previously and do not have distinctive dress, colors, signs, and so on. The latter refers more to a relatively well-organized and sophisticated group of either youths or adults (often a combination of both) organized mainly around the illegal pursuit of economic gain. Finally, there are gang *cliques* or *sets* that are often smaller versions (or subgroups) of larger gangs, usually based on age (ibid.: 390).

Huff alerts us to another distinction, which has gained more significance in recent years, namely, that existing between gangs and organized crime. As he notes, *youth gangs* historically were largely groups of adolescents (mostly male) who engaged in a variety of deviant activities, especially turf battles and gang fights. Now they are increasingly involved in major crimes, especially those that are violent or drug related. *Organized crime* has meant *adult* criminal enterprises operating businesses. Today such organized activities characterize many youth gangs. Huff defines a *youth gang* as a

> collectivity consisting primarily of adolescents and young adults who (a) interact frequently with one another; (b) are frequently and deliberately involved in illegal activities; (c) share a common collective identity that is usually, but not always, expressed through a gang name; and (d) typically express that identity by adopting certain symbols and/or claiming control over certain "turf" (persons, places, things, and/or economic markets) (Huff, 1993:4).

In contrast, Huff defines an *organized crime group* as a

> collectivity consisting primarily of adults who (a) interact frequently with one another; (b) are frequently and deliberately involved in illegal activities directed toward economic gain, primarily through the provision of illegal goods and services; and (c) generally have better defined leadership and organizational structure than does the youth gang (ibid.).

There are several key differences between these two groups. First, they differ significantly in terms of age, youth gangs being much younger than organized crime groups. Second, whereas the organized crime group exists almost exclusively for the purpose of economic criminal activity, youth gangs engage in a variety of both legal and illegal activities, with their illegal activities usually committed by individuals or small groups of individuals rather than by the entire group.

It is obvious that the majority of these definitions focus almost exclusively on delinquent or criminal behavior as the distinguishing feature that differentiates gangs from other groups. This is consistent with a strictly law-enforcement perspective. Several other researchers disagree and argue that gangs should not be defined as purely criminal or delinquent organizations (i.e., the reason they began in the first place and the reason they continue to exist is the pursuit of delinquent or criminal activity). In this context, it is important to consider one of Huff's most pertinent comments. He notes that

> in analyzing youth gangs, it is important to acknowledge that it is normal and healthy for adolescents to want to be with their peers. In fact, adolescents who are loners often tend to be maladjusted. Because adolescents go to dances together, party together, shop together (and, in many cases, shop *lift* together), it should not be surprising that some of them join together in one type of social group known as a gang. Group experience, then, is a familiar and normative phenomenon in adolescent subculture, and gangs represent an extreme manifestation of that age-typical emphasis on being together and belonging to something (Huff, 1993:5–6, emphasis in the original).

Hagedorn believes that gangs are not merely criminal enterprises or bureaucratic entities with formal organizational structures. Rather, as other researchers have noted (e.g., Moore, 1978; Suttles, 1968), gangs are age-graded groups or cliques "with considerable variation within each age group of friends" (Hagedorn, 1998:86).

It is difficult to conceive of gangs as purely criminal organizations. Most gang members spend the bulk of their time simply hanging out or engaging in other nondelinquent activities. Jackson notes that many researchers, accepting the popular imagery of gangs, have spent a considerable amount of time (perhaps months) "waiting for something to happen" (Jackson, 1989:314).

It should be noted that a new category has been invented recently. According to the most recent National Youth Gang Survey, respondents were asked to identify how many "troublesome youth groups" they had in their jurisdiction. This term apparently is a combination of the term "unsupervised peer groups" and "troublesome youth groups." Citing several sociologists (Sampson and Groves, 1989; Short, 1996; Warr, 1996), the report notes that these adolescent groups typically have three or four members and are not well organized and rather transitory (what adolescent groups are *not?*). Also, they occasionally get involved in delinquent activities (again, what adolescent groups do *not?*) but are not committed to a life of crime (once again, what adolescent groups are any different?). Despite any connection to full-fledged youth gangs, survey respondents were asked to estimate the number of these kinds of adolescent groups (how they were to identify them and what criteria were to be used is not spelled out in this report). Not surprisingly (given that those doing the data collection were all adults), the vast majority of jurisdictions reported the existence of such groups (U.S. Department of Justice, 1999).

An equally difficult task is trying to determine what constitutes a *gang-related offense*. If a gang member kills another gang member in retaliation for the killing of a fellow gang member, few would argue over whether this would be gang related. However, what if a gang member is killed as a result of some sort of love triangle, or if a gang member is killed by someone not in a gang, or if a gang member kills someone while committing a robbery on his own? Decisions about these kinds of incidents must be made, and police officials have procedures for such reporting. However, as Klein and Maxson observe, such procedures are conducted "not always according to reliable criteria, not always with adequate information regarding the motive or circumstances of the crime, not always with extensive gang-membership information on file, and—most clearly—not by the same criteria from city to city" (Klein and Maxson, 1989:206).

Klein and Maxson reviewed this process in five cities around the country and found that each city had somewhat different methods for defining gang-related incidents; for example, in two cities, only violent incidents were counted. In one city the policy was to include only gang-on-gang crimes, but the authors found that robberies where the offenders (but not the victims) were gang members constituted gang-related crimes. In another city any offense committed by a gang member was counted as gang related (Klein and Maxson, 1989:208).

In short, there appears to be little consensus on what a gang-related crime is. Given the complexity of the problem, it is highly unlikely that such a consensus will ever be achieved. Quite often we will find that a gang member is engaging in offending behavior by himself, without any assistance from his fellow gang members. Also, rarely will one find an entire gang (if, for example, there are 100 members) involved in a single incident. A method used by the Chicago Police Department seems as good a solution as any that has been offered or presented.

CHICAGO'S USE OF DESCRIPTORS
TO DEFINE GANG-RELATED CRIME

Based on the definition of gang-related crime provided by Bobrowski, the Chicago Police Department uses the term *descriptors* to aid in their recording of data on gang crimes. These descriptors Bobrowski defines as "certain features which serve to distinguish street gang related cases from those which are not." Based on the research by this police department, there "emerges a finite set of descriptors which can be thought of as trademarks of the street gang crime" (Bobrowski, 1988:15).

The term *descriptors* implies more than just motives, as it suggests a certain "commonality of circumstances" of street-gang crime. The Gang Crimes Section of the Chicago Police Department chose seven specific descriptors "which serve to categorize the event data found in case narratives." The seven are representing, retaliation, street fighting, vice related, recruitment, turf violations, and other. The first four descriptors together constituted about 94 percent of all street gang-related crimes during the period under study (January 1, 1987, through July 31, 1988). The seven descriptors are summarized as follows (Bobrowski, 1988:17–29):

1. *Representing.* This term is used to denote any incident in which, in the process of committing a crime, the offender represents himself as being a member of a particular gang. This can be a verbal statement, a hand-sign, a display of colors, or any other similar symbolic gesture. In a recent period of time (January 1, 1987, through July 31, 1988) Chicago police noted that this descriptor was found in 32 percent of all street-gang-related cases.

2. *Retaliation.* This term denotes when one gang resorts to some form of violence to solve certain conflicts with one or more other gangs. Examples include attempts to protect its own interests, uphold its interests, and seek revenge (for example, for a harm done to one of its own members). Such behavior arises out of insults, chance altercations, and infringements on one's criminal activities. This descriptor was found in about 8 percent of gang-related activities in Chicago.

3. *Street Fighting.* This is similar to the classic rumble, whether it be spontaneous or planned, an execution or hit, or simply a fair fight. The most common are "spontaneous assaultive engagements among small groups (three to five persons), random encounters among antagonistic rivals, and small bands of two or three persons assaulting non-gang victims" (Bobrowski, 1988:22). These actions constituted 24 percent of gang-related crimes in Chicago.

4. *Vice-Related.* This category accounted for 30 percent of all the street-gang-related offenses. About 92 percent of these were narcotics, liquor-law violations, gambling, and prostitution offenses. It should be noted that less than 1 percent of all nonvice offenses involved drug activities (for

example, evidence of vice activity was found in only 2 out of 82 homicides during the period under study).

5. *Recruitment.* This refers to activities in which a gang member in some way attempts to force a nonmember to join the gang. Usually it is a type of "join or continue to pay" situation. Recruitment is probably grossly underrepresented in these statistics. Victims are often fearful of further actions against them by the gang and simply distrust the police; therefore, reporting does not occur. Also, if the youth joins the gang, the likelihood of the incident's being reported to the police is almost nil. Statistically, recruitment efforts constitute only 3 percent of the reported gang crimes.

6. *Turf Violations.* These include the defacing of gang graffiti and passing through a designated gang territory, frequently a favorite hangout of a particular gang (for example, a restaurant, street corner, or bar). These events are also woefully underreported for basically the same reasons as noted in recruitment. Officially, these violations accounted for only 1.5 percent of all street-gang crimes in Chicago.

7. *Other Descriptors.* These include such crimes as extortion (mostly forcing people to pay turf tax to cross into and through gang territory), personal conflicts among gang members, and prestige-related crimes, which may be greater than reported. These offenses "may include acts committed to satisfy membership initiation; to establish a special reputation, a position of responsibility, or a leadership role; to respond to challenges or avoid reproach; or to prevail in internal power struggles" (Bobrowski, 1988:27). Together all of these constituted only 4 percent of the officially reported gang crimes in Chicago.

Reiner notes that there are two different ways of defining gang crimes. On the one hand there are *gang-related crimes,* and on the other hand there are *gang-motivated crimes.* The former is the broader definition that states if either the criminal or the victim is a gang member, then the crime is gang related. This is known as the *member-based* definition. This makes it a lot easier for law-enforcement authorities to count gang crime. However, some believe that it will tend to overstate the amount of crime attributed to gangs because many, if not most, of the individuals involved would probably commit crimes and/or be a victim whether or not they were in a gang (Klein, 1995:15).

Some believe that focusing on motivation is using a more narrow view. From this perspective, gang-related crime is caused by *gang activity.* Supporters of this view claim that one of the main virtues of using the *motive-based* definition is that it eliminates unrelated kinds of crime and focuses on crimes that are "clearly due to the presence of gangs" (e.g., drive-by shootings), although it may understate the gang problem (Reiner, 1992:95–96).

Using the *motive-based* definition may in effect obscure the extent of the gang problem in an area, perhaps hoping that the problem will "just go away" (Knox, 1991:343). Indeed, there are significant differences in the amount of "gang-related" crime, depending on which definition one uses.

Klein compared homicide rates in Los Angeles and Chicago. In Los Angeles, with a member-based definition there were about twice as many gang-related homicides as in Chicago, which uses a motive-based definition (Klein, 1995).

STEREOTYPES OF GANGS

Part of the problem in arriving at a consensus definition of *gang* and *gang-related crime* is that we are dealing with widely accepted stereotypes of gangs, most of which are derived from the biased information of law enforcement and the media. From many years of research, Joan Moore has compiled the following list of the most common stereotypes: (Moore, 1993:28–29):

> (1) They are composed of males (no females) who are violent, addicted to drugs and alcohol, sexually hyperactive, unpredictable, and confrontational; (2) They are either all African-American or all Hispanic; (3) They thrive in inner-city neighborhoods where they dominate, intimidate, and prey upon innocent citizens; (4) They all deal heavily in drugs, especially crack cocaine; (5) "A gang is a gang is a gang"—in other words, they are all alike or "you see one and you see them all"; (6) There is no good in gangs, it is all bad (a corollary to this is that anyone who would want to join a gang must be stupid or crazy); (7) Gangs are basically criminal enterprises and that youths start gangs in order to collectively commit crimes; in other words, there is a tendency to confuse individual and group criminality; (8) The "West Side Story" image of aggressive, rebellious, but nice kids has been replaced in recent years by the "gangster" image of a very disciplined criminal organization complete with "soldiers."

According to Moore, stereotypes shape the definitions of gangs and therefore determine policies structured to deal with gangs. Especially important is the stereotype of gangs as criminal enterprises, which confuses individual and collective criminal activity. Quite often the police, as well as the media and the public, will label as gang related criminal behavior that is individually motivated. It should also be noted that stereotypical thinking is a common phenomenon in the world. To stereotype is to think in terms of rigid and inflexible categories. Most of the time such thinking is normal and harmless, but when it is associated with anxiety or fear, it is very different. "Stereotypes in such circumstances are commonly infused with attitudes of hostility or hatred towards the group in question" (Giddens, 1990:303). As was stated earlier, it is not uncommon for white citizens, for example, to have a completely different response when they see a group of three or four young African-American males together in a shopping mall as opposed to a group of three or four young white males, even when each group is wearing clothing and/or colors that are stereotypically associated with gang attire.

Stereotypes have a great deal to do with what researchers have called *moral panics*. This term was originally popularized by British criminologist Stanley Cohen when describing the reaction to various youth disturbances (by youths called "mods and rockers") in Britain during the 1960s (Cohen, 1980; see also Goode and Ben-Yehuda, 1994). Cohen defined a moral panic as a "condition, episode, person or group of persons" that "emerges to become defined as a threat to societal values and interests." The nature of this problem "is presented in stylized and stereotypical fashion by the mass media," while the "moral barricades are manned by editors, bishops, politicians and other right thinking people" (Cohen, 1980:9). These kinds of threats are "far more likely to be perceived during times of widespread anxiety, moral malaise, and uncertainty about the future" (McCorkle and Miethe, 2001:19).

These panics build on already-existing divisions in society, usually based on race, class, and age. (Typically the most visible crime is the focus of attention, which just happens to be the outrageous and, it should be noted in the case of gangs, the rare "drive-by" shootings.) The moral panics typically focus on youth because they always represent the most serious challenge to conventional values held by adults. The recent growth of the underclass—consisting disproportionately of minorities and the young—in an isolated and deteriorating inner city is where the greatest concentration and growth of gangs have been.

Moral panics have three distinguishing characteristics (Mc Corkle and Miethe, 2001:19–20). First, there is a focused attention on the behavior (either real or imagined) of certain groups, who are in turn transformed into sort of "folk devils" with the corresponding emphasis on negative characteristics over any positive one. There is an "evil" in our midst, and it must be eliminated. Second, there is quite a gap between the concern over a condition or problem and the objective threat that it poses. Typically, as in the case of gangs, the objective threat is far less than popularly perceived. Third, there is a great deal of fluctuation over time in the level of concern over a problem. The threat is "discovered," then concern reaches a peak, and subsequently subsides—but perhaps reemerging once again.

Besides gangs, there have been many examples of such moral panics during the 1980s, when gangs emerged as a "problem." One was the panic over "satanic cults" in the 1980s, and another was the problem of "missing" or "stolen" children around the same time. Also, there was the "crack epidemic" around the same time, which corresponded with the antigang hysteria. Still another panic was that over "serial killers." All of these panics were eventually proven, through careful research, to far exceed the objective nature of the threats alleged by the media and law-enforcement officials (McCorkle and Miethe, 2001:22–32).

HOW MANY GANGS AND GANG MEMBERS ARE THERE?

Gangs can be found in all cities with populations of 100,000 or more. Gangs are also found within both the federal and the state prison systems and in most juvenile correctional systems. Gangs are found within practically every major urban high school in the country (Camp and Camp, 1985; Curry and Decker, 1998:125–132; Howell, 1998: 4; Klein, 1995:168–170; Shelden, 1991; Spergel, 1995:116–127).

Exactly how many gangs and how many gang members there are in the country is presently not known with any degree of certainty. In fact, there are as many estimates as there are estimators![10] In the 1920s, Thrasher estimated that there were 1,313 gangs in Chicago alone (Thrasher, 1927). Miller's nationwide survey in the 1970s estimated anywhere from 700 to almost 3,000 gangs in the largest cities in the country (Miller, 1975, 1982). The most recent estimate is that there are more than 30,000 gangs and over 800,000 gang members (Howell, 1998; U.S. Department of Justice, 1999). What is especially interesting about estimates is that over the past 20 years during which such surveys have been conducted, the number of gangs and gang members increases every year. What is also interesting is that in almost every case the estimates come almost exclusively from law-enforcement sources (especially the most recent surveys, such as the latest National Youth Gang Survey). Moreover, during all these years the amount of money going to police departments keeps increasing as well, in addition to the number of "gang units" and police officers assigned to these units (see Chapter 10). As noted earlier, in virtually every survey in recent years the definition of *gang* and *gang member* has been left entirely up to the reporting law-enforcement agencies.

Estimates from individual cities and states have been provided throughout the years and may be used for comparative purposes. Spergel (1990:26–27, 31–33) provided some estimates from the 1980s in several major urban areas. These estimates show how the gang problem increased during this decade, according to law-enforcement sources. For example, in Dade County, Florida, the number of gangs in 1980 was estimated to be only 4, but by 1988 there were 80; in Los Angeles County in 1988 there were about 800 gangs, up from 239 in 1985, whereas estimates of the number of gang members range from 50,000 to 70,000 (one estimate said there were about 25,000 Crips and Bloods gang members alone); in 1975, in San Diego County, there were only three gangs with about 300 members total, but by 1987 there were between 19 and 35 gangs with a total membership of about 2,000. In some cities, the numbers have been fluctuating: Phoenix in 1974 reported about 34 gangs but 31 in 1986 (however, these numbers have recently increased again); in New York City, the number of gangs declined from 315 (with about 20,000 members) in 1974 to 66 in 1987 (with only about 2,500 members); Louisville reported about 15 gangs in 1985 but only one gang in 1988; and in Fort Wayne, Indiana, six gangs existed in 1986 (with more than 2,000 members), but only three gangs and about 50 members were noted in 1988.

The 1995 national survey noted that California reported the largest number of gangs at 4,927, with Texas having 3,276, followed by Illinois with 1,363 and Colorado with 1,304. Not surprisingly, California topped the list for the number of gang members, with an estimated 254,618, with Illinois a distant second with 75,226 and Texas third with 57,060. It should be no surprise to find that Los Angeles had the largest number of gang members at 60,000 (county estimate; the city estimate was 58,197), followed by Chicago with 33,000 (U.S. Department of Justice, 1997).

A reporting system known as GREAT (Gang Reporting Evaluation and Tracking) was established in the early 1990s by the Los Angeles Police Department. Reportedly this has become one of the most sophisticated gang-reporting systems in the country. As of October 1991 this system listed a total of 936 gangs in Los Angeles County. Of this number, there were 298 African-American gangs (213 Crips, 85 Bloods), 467 Chicano gangs, 63 Asian gangs (plus 16 Samoan gangs), 61 Stoner gangs, and 18 Anglo gangs. In the early 1990s it was estimated that there were in excess of 100,000 gang members in Los Angeles County. Of this number, 94 percent are male, and just 6 percent are female. About 57 percent are Chicano, while 37 percent are African-American, and about 4 percent are Asian (Reiner, 1992:109–110). The more recent estimate of 60,000 gang members suggests one of two conclusions: There has been an actual decline in the number of gang members in Los Angeles County, or improved reporting techniques account for the "decline." We are not certain which of these reasons is correct, but we are inclined to support the second interpretation.

These differing estimates may reflect many factors, including how local criminal justice officials define *gang* and *gang member*. Some agencies provide conservative estimates (sometimes to preserve a safe image of their city or to promote tourism), while others highly exaggerate the numbers (often in hopes of obtaining more funding). The changing numbers noted above may reflect changing perspectives and definitions.

Some comments about the sources of the above statistics are in order at this juncture. The fact that those providing most of these estimates are law-enforcement bureaucracies and that the amount of federal dollars flowing into these bureaucracies should arouse the curiosity of any critical reader. And naturally so, given the vested interest in producing high numbers. It is also curious that every year a national survey is done, there seem to be more gangs and more gang members identified. Moreover, it is certainly no surprise to find gangs and gang members in just about every suburb and rural hamlet in every part of the country since federal dollars will certainly flow to these small departments (according to the 1996 survey, 25 percent of all rural counties and 57 percent of all suburban counties reported having gangs). As noted earlier, a new category was invented for this most recent survey, called "troublesome youth groups." Almost three-fourths of large cities reported having these groups, while just over half of all rural counties have them (U.S. Department of Justice, 1999:15). Given the vagueness of the definition of "troublesome youth groups," is this not surprising? It should not come as any surprise to the reader that the authors are very skeptical of the above numbers. What really bothers us is the existence of this new category of "troublesome youth groups." Why? Simply because almost any youth (especially a minority youth) can be identified as belonging to such a group! (How many groups of three or four adolescents will not be perceived as "troublesome" to some adults?) Once so identified, it may be easy to eventually classify them as a gang and thus more easily controlled. The civil libertarian in each of us raises some alarms, as it should for all of us.

As this is being written (April, 2000) one of the biggest police scandals in the history of Los Angeles has emerged (*Los Angeles Times,* 2000; *Washington Post,* 2000). It is important to note that the scandal involves a group of officers affiliated with an anti-gang unit known as Community Resources Against Street Hoodlums (CRASH), who has been accused of making false arrests, extorting money from drug dealers, unjustified shootings, and, most importantly for the subject at hand, falsely accusing many individuals of being "gang members." One report noted that these accusations (corroborated by several police officers) cast doubt about the authenticity of the gang data based in Los Angeles. The report claims there are 112,000 gang members in Los Angeles County—62,000 of whom have been identified by the CRASH unit that was disbanded (see Chapter 9). Police officials and police gang "experts" claim that the data are accurate, but we wonder. So far, at least 100 convictions of "gang" members have been overturned and 20 officers have been fired or have quit (Jablon, 2000; O'Connor, 2000).

According to self-report studies (most often a random sample of youths in high school or junior high asked about their delinquent behavior), the percentage of youths who report being in a gang or engaging in gang-related behavior has not changed significantly during the past two decades. Typically, no more than 10 to 15 percent of all youths report being in a gang (and this estimate includes areas with a high rate of crime and gang membership) (Johnstone, 1981; Sampson, 1986; Savitz, Rosen, and Lalli, 1980). However, in certain areas the numbers are still quite large, especially for minorities. For example, the previously cited estimate for Los Angeles County Crip and Blood members means that over 25 percent of the total African-American male population between 15 and 24 in Los Angeles County are members of these two gangs. In Chicago, there are estimates ranging from 12,000 to 120,000 gang members. Spergel (1990) provided the following percentages of those within a particular school population in the Chicago area who reportedly are in gangs: 5 percent of the elementary school youths, 10 percent of all high school youths, 20 percent of those in special school programs, and, more alarmingly perhaps, 35 percent of those between 16 and 19 years of age who have dropped out of school!

Even higher numbers are found when we consider those who are on probation or elsewhere in the criminal justice system. A 1990 survey of juvenile correctional institutions found that more than three-fourths had a gang problem inside these institutions. Another survey found that two-thirds of the inmates reported belonging to a gang, likewise in detention centers (Howell, 1998).

Regardless of the numbers, there is some evidence that gang members commit a disproportionate amount of crime, especially violent crime. Yet this aspect of the problem may be exaggerated because the violence captures the public imagination and makes the headlines. Also, the violence is heavily concentrated within certain neighborhoods or within certain schools in large cities. If we consider an entire city or county we find that gang members do not contribute that much to the overall crime problem. In Chicago, for example, it has been estimated that gang crime constituted less than 1 percent of all

Part I crimes between 1986 and 1988.[11] More recent estimates suggests the same, although in certain neighborhoods gangs contribute a lot to the overall crime problem (Howell, 1998). Most of the offenses committed by gang members continue to be property crimes (often these are committed by gang members independently rather than as part of an organized gang activity).

Many believe that gang members commit a disproportionate number of homicides, but this may be distorted. Some recent estimates indicate that gang homicide accounts for a disproportionate share of the violence committed in some areas (Howell, 1998). In many cities, such as Los Angeles, the problem of gang homicide has grown worse. For example, Klein reports that the number of gang homicides in Los Angeles County increased dramatically during the late 1980s, going from 271 in 1985 to 803 in 1992 (Klein 1995:120). Since 1992, however, there has been a significant decrease in gang homicides, with about 400 in 1997. In 1992 gang-related homicides constituted about 45 percent of all homicides but just 25 percent in 1997.[12] We will have more to say about homicides and other crimes committed by gangs in the next chapter.

GANG MIGRATION

Quite a bit of controversy revolves around the issue of "gang migration" with suggestions that gangs have engaged in a nationwide "franchising" operation. The term *migration* often gets confused with a similar term known as *proliferation*. The latter term signifies the increase in the number of communities in the nation reporting that they have gang problems. While it is true that more communities report having gang problems in recent years, this is usually the result of social conditions within the communities themselves that have caused gangs to grow. On the other hand, we would also suggest that such an increase may stem from changing definitions of *gang* and *gang member* and the tendency for law-enforcement agencies to exaggerate the problem in order to obtain more funding. We are not the only researchers who have raised this issue, for Cheryl Maxson argues that some of the increase in gang proliferation may stem from a "heightened awareness of gang issues, redirection of law enforcement attention, widespread training, and national education campaigns" (Maxson, 1998:2).

On the other hand, the term *gang migration* suggests something entirely different. This term suggests "the movement of gang members from one city to another." Maxson's study of gang migration defined migration rather broadly to include (1) "temporary relocations" (e.g., visits to relatives); (2) "short trips to sell drugs or develop other criminal enterprises"; (3) "longer stays while escaping crackdowns on gangs or gang activity"; (4) "residential moves (either individually or with family members)"; and (5) "court placements" (Maxson, 1998:2).

Much research has documented the "proliferation" of gangs in many communities and even noted some "connection" to gangs in other cities, but for the most part the exact nature of this "connection" has not been explored often, until Maxson and her colleagues began to study the issue in depth (Maxson, 1998; Maxson, Woods, and Klein, 1996; See also Curry, Ball, and Decker, 1996; NDIC, 1996).

What emerges from more recent studies is a very complex picture of gang migration. First, according Maxson's survey, out of 1,000 cities, 710 had experienced gang migration by 1992. Second, gang migration has been concentrated in just a few large cities, especially in the San Francisco Bay Area, Southern California, Chicago, and southern Florida. In fact, almost half (44 percent) of the migration was in the western part of the country. Third, almost all of the cities that have experienced gang migration also have gangs that have been "homegrown" (only 45 of the 710 cities had no homegrown gangs). Fourth, most cities already had a gang problem before new gang migration began, which clearly contradicts the notion that gang problems are the result of "franchising." (Maxson notes that the majority of those interviewed, 81 percent, disagreed with the statement "Without migration, this city wouldn't have a gang problem." Most reported that migration was not the major cause of the gang problem, contradicting reports by the media and by politicians.) Fifth, "emergent" gang problem cities (gang problems have emerged during the past 20 years or so) and "chronic" gang problem cities (those with gangs dating back several decades) are about equally as likely to report gang migration.

What is most important from Maxson's study was what she found when she asked law-enforcement officials what they thought were the major reasons why gang members move to their cities from another area. The most common reason (stated by 39 percent) was that the gang member simply moved with their families. Another major reason was to stay with relatives and friends. Combined, these "social" causes of migration constituted more than half (57 percent) of the cases. Drug market expansion was cited in 20 percent of the cases, with another 12 percent citing other criminal opportunities (for a total of 32 percent), what Maxson calls "pulls." Finally, in about 11 percent of the cases, the reason given was that the gang member was forced out in some way—either by police crackdowns, court order relocation, or simply a desire to escape gangs. It was also discovered that these gang members are about equally as likely to join already existing gangs in their new city as remain with their original gang (Maxson, 1998:7–9).

This complex picture suggests that gang members move mostly for the same reasons that others move—moving with their families or to be closer to friends or relatives. What is also clear is that most of these moves are by individual gang members rather than large segments of one particular gang. Clearly, there is little evidence to suggest that gangs migrating from one city to another are the major source of the gang problem. Nor is there any evidence of "franchising" or the "outside agitator" hypothesis. Maxson (and many other researchers) suggests that the popular perception of gang "franchising" stems mostly from "the diffusion of gang culture in the media." The nation's youth "are hardly dependent on direct contact with gang members for exposure to the more dramatic manifestations of gang culture, which is readily accessible in youth-oriented television programming, popular movies, and the recent spate of 'tell-all' books from reputed urban gang leaders" (Maxson, 1998:9). What is perhaps most interesting from Maxson's study is the fact that the only sources are those in law enforcement. Perhaps a more complex picture will emerge when others are interviewed about such moves, especially the gang members themselves, their families, school officials, and so on.

SUMMARY

Gangs are not something new to the social arena. They existed in fourteenth- and fifteenth-century Europe and colonial America. Throughout the twentieth century social researchers have devoted extensive time and resources to the understanding of youth gangs in America. First, many studies point out that discriminatory policies and practices by the government have contributed to the emergence of gangs in various parts of America. These policies and practices include the promotion of social disorganization in Chicago, the deportation of immigrants in Southern California during the Great Depression, and police brutality in Watts during the 1960s, among others.

Second, we have pointed out that public perception (and fear), crucial to policy development, is shaped largely by the mass media. It is clear that the media have done little to differentiate fact from fiction in their portrayal of youth gangs. Moreover, the media, over the past few years, have capitalized on the incidents of gang activities by significantly increasing their coverage of youth gangs between 1983 and 1994. The media have contributed to the stereotypical images of how we think about gangs and gang members.

Third, the only agreement about what constitutes a gang, its members, and its activities is disagreement. Often, this discord is linked to location (e.g., type of neighborhood), age (e.g., adolescent versus young adult), and purpose (e.g., play group, organized crime, drugs). We have found that one of the major problems associated with the study of gangs is the identification of gang-related crime. Each jurisdiction seems to create its own criteria to determine whether a crime is gang related.

Fourth, this chapter addressed the issue of *how many*. How many gangs are currently active in America? How many individuals are in these groups? There are a significant number of projections and estimates related to these questions. Frequently, the argument is raised that because gangs come and go, it is difficult to determine accurately the number of gangs and gang members. It is our contention, however, that in order to determine how many gangs or gang members are active in America, we must first determine what exactly a gang or gang member is.

Finally, the subject of "gang migration" was explored, especially the suggestion that there is a sort of "franchising" method working here. Contrary to popular belief, gang members who move do so for the same general reasons that young people in general move—with their families.

NOTES

1. See the following studies of the media that support our contention: Herman and Chomsky (1988), Bagdikian (1987), and Chomsky (1989).

2. Several different terms are commonly used to describe persons of Hispanic or Mexican descent. Some prefer to use the more generic term *Hispanic,* while others prefer terms such as *Chicano, Latino,* or *Mexican-American*. Different sources cited in this book use different words to describe these gangs. We will be using all of these terms throughout the book, depending on the sources we are citing.

3. Contrary to popular belief, the most significant increases in crime in recent years has been for the adult age-groups, especially those over 25 (Males, 1999).

4. Interview by Brown of a gang member in Detroit, Michigan.

5. Enactment of the Chinese Exclusionary Act (1882) was encouraged by the American Federation of Labor and by the belief that opium use by Chinese immigrants facilitated production advantages for this minority group over white workers (Abadinsky, 1993; Latimer and Goldberg, 1981). Helmer (1975) points out that the 1875 economic depression in California was yet another motivating factor for this legislation.

6. Attempts to control ethnic minorities with legal "rationalism" in America is not a new phenomenon. A Supreme Court case illustrates this, as it dealt with an African-American woman named Mildred Jeter, who was married to a white man named Richard Loving. The couple moved to Virginia and established residency. Both were arrested for violation of Virginia's miscegenation law (prohibiting interracial sex and marriage). Both parties were found guilty and sentenced to one year in jail. The sentence was suspended for 25 years on the condition that they would leave the state. In his opinion, the trial judge stated, "Almighty God created the races white, black, yellow, Maylay and red, and He placed them on separate continents. And but for the interference with His arrangement there would be no cause for such marriages. The fact that he separated the races shows that He did not intend for the races to mix" (388 U.S. 1, 1967).

7. This is similar to the "concern" about the so-called dangerous classes during the last half of the nineteenth century (see, e.g., Brace, 1872). For a complete history on the control of the "dangerous classes," see Shelden (2001).

8. The term *cholo* is used to describe a Chicano gang member or the Chicano subculture itself. It is derived from a term used to describe a marginal position between two cultures—the older Mexican culture and the newer Mexican-American culture—thus the term *marginalization*. To better understand "marginalization," think of the margins of the typical notebook pages, and you will note that this part of the page is literally off to one side and not part of the main body of the page. We can also speak of the marginalization of dissent, whereby alternative perspectives are not allowed within the mainstream press or political discourse. Chapter 4 elaborates on the cholo subculture in more detail.

9. Davis provides a more complete history of African-American gangs, including an insightful analysis of the role of the Los Angeles Police Department in helping to perpetuate gangs, partly by trying to eliminate them, starting with Chief Parker in the 1950s and ending with Chief Gates in the 1980s and early 1990s. One example cited by Davis was the efforts by Chief Parker to engage in an "all-out war on narcotics" in both the south-central and East Los Angeles areas, which translated into a "war on gangs." This included an attack on the Group Guidance Unit of the Los Angeles Probation Department, which had been set up after the Zoot Suit riots to help young offenders. To Parker, these were mere unreformable criminals who needed stiff prison sentences (Davis, 1992:294–296).

10. This apparent obsession over how many gangs and gang members there are is typical of he positivistic orientation in the

social sciences, and in the larger society in general, which too often gets reduced to a mere numbers game. Part of this obsession is the need to "control" or "manage" gangs. For this to be done it is apparently important to know the exact size of the "problem." What is lost in this procedure are people, both the victims and the victimizers, of social disadvantage and oppression. What is also lost are the various social conditions that create gangs (see Chapters 7 and 8 for more detail about these social conditions).

11. Spergel (1990:34). *Part I* crimes include homicide, rape, robbery, aggravated assault, burglary, larceny, motor vehicle theft, and arson.

12. Personal communication with Cheryl Maxson.

2

$\blacklozenge$

What Do Gangs
and Gang Members
Look Like?

A WORD OF CAUTION

It is uncertain whether an accurate profile of the typical gang and typical gang member can be presented. As was noted in the first chapter, there is little consensus among professionals of what a gang is and how a gang member is identified. Therefore, the present chapter should be read with this caveat in mind. Also, this chapter should *not* be interpreted as a tool to identify who is or who is not a gang member or what group is or is not a gang. Unfortunately, any such typology presented is going to be used by some (e.g., law enforcement) merely to control or even eliminate the groups and individuals so categorized. We do not want to contribute to this kind of control.

AN OVERVIEW OF GANG STRUCTURES

It is important to emphasize that there is not only a variety of *gangs* but also a variety of gang *members.* Gangs and gang members come in many forms and can be differentiated by several criteria, including age, race or ethnicity (all Hispanic or all African-American, Asian, or mixed), gender composition (e.g., all male, all female, or mixed), setting (e.g., street, prison, or motorcycle), type of activity (e.g., social, delinquent/criminal, or violent), purpose of the gang activity (e.g., defensive versus aggressive, turf defense), degree of criminality (e.g., minor or serious), level of organization (e.g., simple or corporate, vertical or horizontal), and group function (e.g., instrumental or cultural) (Spergel, 1990:60).

Most common gangs are rather loosely structured groups who "come together for periods of weeks, months, or as long as a year, but then disintegrate" (Klein and Maxson, 1989:209–210). One of the most common types is the traditional, vertical, or area gang. Characterized by a common territory, these gangs are age graded, typically all male, often with female auxiliary groups, and mostly ethnic minorities (usually African-American and Hispanic but often Asian). Another variation is the horizontally organized groups. These usually include divisions that cut across different neighborhoods and include youths in different age brackets. Many have spread across cities, states, and even countries. Often they are referred to as supergangs and nations. Examples of these horizontal alliances include the Crips and Bloods (who started in Los Angeles) and the People and Folk (starting in Illinois). It should be emphasized that these large groupings often consist of gangs with very little in common with one another other than their name. To a gang member what is most important is the particular set or neighborhood of origin. As a gang member told Bing, "See, 'Crip' doesn't mean nothin' to a membership. Like 'I'm a Crip, you're a Crip—so what? What set are you from? What neighborhood are you from? What street do you live on? I may live on Sixty-ninth, he may live on Seventieth' " (Bing, 1991:244).

An example of the vertical type of gang organization could be found in New York City in the early 1960s. The age groupings there included Tots (11 to 13 years of age), Juniors (13 to 15 years of age), Tims (15 to 17 years of age), and Seniors (17 and older). But these age groupings are not consistently the same from one point in time to another, as evidenced in New York City. For example, by the 1970s the most common groupings included the Baby Spades (9 to 12 years of age), the Young Spades (12 to 15 years of age), and the Black Spades (16 to 30 years of age). In Philadelphia the following age groupings were recently identified: Bottom-Level Midgets (12 to 14 years), Middle-Level Young Boys (14 to 17 years), and Upper-Level Old Heads (18 to 23 years). Members of these gangs usually can be divided into such categories as hard core, fringe, cliques, and wannabes, with the latter grouping reserved for the very young, usually 12 or younger (Spergel, 1990:55–56).

Regarding gang leadership, gangs "present a shifting, elusive target, permeable and elastic, and thus inherently resistant to outside intervention. It presents not a cohesive force but, rather, a sponge-like resilience" (Klein and Maxson, 1989:211). Gang leadership tends to shift over time "with changes in age, gang activity levels, and availability of members (owing to marriage, work, or incarceration, for example)" (Klein, 1995:62). The stereotype of the gang leader is someone who is tough, with a long criminal history, and who has strong influence over the members. To the contrary, the typical leader does not maintain influence over a long period of time. Leadership tends to be very situational, and contrary to the belief that to eliminate the gang all you need to do is "cut off the head" and the rest will die off, someone else will generally take his place. This is because gang leadership is, as with most groups, a function of the group rather than individuals (Klein, 1995:63). In other words, gang leadership fluctuates. It is normally undertaken by youths who are the most stable members, who possess good verbal skills, who are cool under pressure, and who are generally looked up to by other members. But, like life in general, it constantly changes.

One of the most important distinguishing features of gangs continues to be that of territory, or *turf*. However, this must be interpreted with caution, for there have been many changes in recent years (even since the first edition of this book). Klein's most recent research notes that most cities that he surveyed reported the existence of "single or autonomous gangs." These are gangs that occupy smaller territories than was once the pattern, such as single blocks, a school, a "project," and so on. They tend to have shorter histories and fewer ties to traditional neighborhoods, or "barrios," than the more traditional gangs. Many of the more recent gangs are what Klein describes as "geographically connected gangs." These are more like "branches" of the same gang but located in a neighboring territory or totally separate areas and sharing an affiliation but not the residence (Klein, 1995:102). No doubt part of the declining importance of turf is because of the growing sophistication of some gangs and their greater involvement in criminal activities (which means that the actual physical location becomes less important) and the increasing use of the automobile.

Among the more traditional gangs (those who have been in existence for the longest time) the notion of turf or neighborhood remains of critical importance. In many areas, especially in Los Angeles, the term *gang* is often synonymous with *barrio* (sometimes spelled *varrio*) or *neighborhood* (Moore, 1978, 1991). The notion of turf centers around two important ideas—identification and control—with control being the most important. At least three types of turf rights can be noted. The first is that of basic ownership rights, in which a gang "owns" a particular area and attempts to control practically everything that occurs there. The second is occupancy rights, which means merely that different gangs share an area or tolerate one another's use. The third is enterprise monopoly, in which a certain gang is said to have control of certain criminal activities occurring within a specified area (Spergel, 1990:71–72).

Age seems to be one of the most important characteristics of gangs because the clique is one of the basic building blocks of gangs. "Gangs are loosely organized into small age/friendship cohorts or cliques. These groupings are called 'klikas' in cholo gangs and 'sets' in African-American gangs, where they are somewhat less rigidly age-bound" (Reiner, 1992:38–39).

ILLUSTRATIONS OF GANG TYPOLOGIES

When it comes to categorizing gangs, two methods are generally used: types of *gangs* and types of gang *members*. The distinction is important because not only are there a variety of *gangs* in existence (more than a dozen specific "gang types" have been identified) but there are about an equal variety of gang *members*. This idea is consistent with a point made in the first chapter, namely, that there are a variety of adolescent groups existing at any one time. In fact, the adolescent subculture itself is famous for the infinite variety of groupings.[1] In the next two sections we will review some of the more common typologies, starting with *gang* typologies and ending with gang *member* typologies.

It should be noted at the outset that the following typologies should be considered as *ideal types,* to use Max Weber's famous concept.[2] Ideal types are used frequently by researchers in all fields of study to help make sense and organize a vast array of research findings. Ideal types do not necessarily reflect reality in that there are no "pure" types of anything (e.g., no person is a pure "authoritarian personality" type, and there is no such thing as pure "capitalism" or "democracy") since human life and nature itself can fit perfectly into any types. These ideal types merely serve as ways to clarify one's investigation. What normally happens is that the researcher suggests that a phenomenon *tends to fit into one or another type* more often than not. For example, using "democracy" as an ideal type a researcher can compare different political systems in terms of the extent to which they are "democratic," realizing that there will be no perfect "democracy." Or, to use gangs as an example, there may not be a pure "hard-core" gang member or a pure "predatory" gang, but a particular individual may come close to the pure type of "hard core" but also have certain characteristics that could place him into the category of "peripheral" member; likewise with a "predatory" gang in that a specific gang may have some characteristics of this type of gang but yet have some characteristics of a "territorial" gang as well, but it is more "predatory" than "territorial."

Types of Gangs[3]

Types of *gangs* can be based on many different criteria. The most commonly used criteria seem to be certain behavioral characteristics, especially deviant and/or criminal behavior but also certain nondeviant or traditional groups behaviors. Research in six different cities by three different researchers uncovered the following major types of gangs.

1. *Hedonistic/social* gangs—With only moderate drug use and offending, these gangs are involved mainly in using drugs (getting high) and having a good time, with little involvement in crime, especially violent crime.

2. *Party* gangs—A group with relatively high use and sales of drugs, but with only one major form of delinquency (vandalism).

3. *Instrumental* gangs—Those whose main criminal activity is that of committing property crimes (most members use drugs and alcohol but seldom engage in the selling of drugs).

4. *Predatory* gangs—Those heavily involved in serious crimes (e.g., robberies and muggings) and seriously involved in the abuse of addictive drugs such as crack cocaine; some with much lower involvement in drug use and drug sales than the party gang; some may engage in the selling of drugs, although not in any organized fashion.

5. *Scavenger* gangs—Loosely organized groups of youths who are described as "urban survivors," preying on the weak in the inner cities, engaging in rather petty crimes but sometimes violence, often just for fun. The members have no greater bond than their impulsiveness and the need to belong. They have no goals and are low achievers, often illiterate, with poor school performance.

6. *Serious delinquent* gangs—With heavy involvement in both serious and minor crimes, but with much lower involvement in drug use and drug sales than the party gang.

7. *Territorial* gangs—Those gangs associated with a specific area or *turf* and who, as a result, get involved in conflicts with other gangs over their respective turfs.

8. *Organized/corporate* gangs—Heavy involvement in all kinds of crime and heavy use and sales of drugs; they may resemble major corporations, with separate divisions handling sales, marketing, discipline, and so on. Discipline is strict, and promotion is based on merit.

9. *Drug* gangs—These gangs are smaller than other gangs, much more cohesive, focused on the drug business, and have strong centralized leadership, with market-defined roles.[4]

Many prefer to describe most of the above gangs (except for drug gangs) by using the term *street gang* (Klein, 1995:132). This is a rather all-inclusive term that refers to most of the above typologies.

Types of Gang Members

The most common method of distinguishing among different gang *members* is to base on the *degree of attachment to, and involvement in, the gang.* It might be useful to think of a *continuum* from complete involvement and attachment to very little attachment and involvement. To use an analogy, think of attachment to, and involvement in, a local church. At one extreme are those who rarely attend church services or any church-related activity, except perhaps for weddings, Easter Sunday, or Christmas Eve services. Otherwise you may never see them at church (perhaps one or two other times during the year). Next on the continuum are those who attend Sunday services perhaps once a month on the average and on occasion will participate in a church-related activity (a picnic, a lecture, or a play sponsored by the church). Then there may be another type who attends church services almost every Sunday but rarely participates in church-related activities. Closer to the other end of the continuum are those who attend church every Sunday and get involved in many church-related activities during the course of the year and who have several friends that are also similarly involved in the church (but they have many friends not involved in the church). At the other extreme are those who not only attend every Sunday but also may serve as an elected officials of the church (may even teach Sunday school) and participate in church-related activities almost on a daily basis or whenever these activities occur. However, in addition to the above, this person literally has no friends who are not connected with the church in some way. In short, the church is, for all practical purposes, *their life.* They have no identity apart from their roles within the church.

Gang members may be similarly classified. The following gang *member* types have been discovered by researchers:[5]

1. *Regulars/hard core*—Those who are strongly attached to the gang, participate regularly, and have few interests outside of the gang (in other words, the gang is practically their whole life). Vigil describes these individuals as having "had a more problematic early life. They became street oriented earlier. They became gang members sooner, and they participated in the destructive patterns over a longer period of time." These individuals also lacked a consistent male adult in their lives, which made the streets even more attractive as they began to emulate other gang members. For these persons, getting into the gang was seen as a rite of passage. They also began experimenting with drugs and engaging in street fighting at a much earlier age than other kinds of members (Vigil, 1988:66, 81–85). The *hard core,* or simply *core,* members of the gang tend to be a smaller number of members who are the most influential and active members of a particular gang. This is the inner clique who "interact frequently and relate easily to each other." They may be "those few who need and thrive on the totality of the gang's activity." These individuals "may make key decisions, set standards, and provide support and sanction for the action of the leaders. They are the key recruiters" (Spergel, 1990:64–65). The hard core are "the most gang-bound in terms of lifestyle. For these young men, life outside pretty much ceases to exist. They have few friends outside the gang and recognize no authority beyond its existence" (Reiner, 1992:42).

2. *Peripheral* members (also known as *associates*)—These individuals have a strong attachment to the gang but participate less often than the regulars because they have other interests outside the gang. This person is "just as intense as the regulars once he is a member of a gang, but his level of commitment is mediated less by a problematic early life and more by a life-turning event (for example, incarceration), which causes him to contemplate pursuing another lifestyle" (Vigil, 1988:66). The *associates* are sometimes called *fringe* members. They may belong to the gang but are not considered part of the hard-core group. Using the fraternity analogy again, these may be like those students who only recently completed "hell week" and were formally initiated into the fraternity.

3. *Temporary* members—These are only marginally committed, join the gang at a later age than the regulars and peripherals, and remain in the gang

only a short period of time. This individual "is neither as intense nor as committed as the others and primarily associates with the gang during a certain phase of his development" (Vigil, 1988:66).

4. *Situational* members—These are very marginally attached and join the gang only for certain activities (avoiding the more violent activities whenever possible).

5. *At risk*—These are not really gang members but are *pre-gang* youths who do not as yet belong to a gang but have shown some interest. They live in neighborhoods where gangs exist. They often fantasize about being members and also might have friends or relatives who belong to the gang and whom they admire. Often they begin experimenting with certain gang attire and/or language. This may begin as early as the second grade (Reiner, 1992:40–44).

6. *Wannabe*—This is a term gangs themselves often use to describe "recruits," who are usually in their pre-teen years and know and admire gang members. They are perhaps one notch above the "at risk" youths in terms of commitment and involvement. They have already begun to emulate gang members in terms of dress, gang values, and so on. Such young people are mentally ready to join a gang and perhaps just need an invitation or opportunity to prove themselves in some way. They may be called *Pee Wees* or *Baby Homies*. An analogy may be made to freshmen college students aspiring to join fraternities. One researcher called this type an *emulator* (Taylor, 1990).

7. *Veteranos/O.G.s*—This group usually consists of men in their 20s or 30s (or even much older) who still participate in gang activities (sometimes referred to as *gang banging*). There are two major subtypes within this category. *Veteranos* have traditionally been regarded as a type of elder statesmen who are somewhat retired but still command respect. The title is more honorable within Chicano gangs than African-American gangs. *O.G.s* are *original gangsters* and are those referred to in African-American gangs as men who have earned respect through a combination of longevity and achievement. Often they are expected to teach younger members the ways of the gang and/or to straighten out younger members causing trouble within the gang. Sometimes they are literally the founding member or members of the gang.

8. *Auxiliary*—These are members who hold limited responsibility within a gang. This is a very common role for female members. These individuals do not participate in all gang activities. A related type is the *adjunct* member, who is a permanent part-time member by choice, often because of holding down a regular job (Taylor, 1990).

Some gangs have formed unions in order to achieve certain uniform objectives (especially self-protection) and have thus formed so-called supergangs. Still others have simply been described as "gang nations" or "gang sets." Examples of the latter often include the famous (or infamous) "Bloods and Crips" that began in the Los Angeles area. However, the most popular grouping of gangs into "gang nations" or "supergangs" are known as *People and Folks,* originating in Chicago in the 1970s.

THE SUPERGANGS OF CHICAGO: PEOPLE AND FOLKS

There are currently a least 132 active street gangs in Chicago, with from 30,000 to 50,000 "hard-core" members. Four of the most active and largest gangs account for about 19,000 members, and they are alleged to be responsible for about two-thirds of all "gang-motivated crimes" and for about half of Chicago's "gang-motivated homicides" (Howell, 1998:4; see also Block et al., 1996; Block and Block, 1993; Chicago Crime Commission, 1995). These gangs "show varying degrees of internal structure ranging from loosely knit groups cohered by one or two focal personalities to well developed, highly structured hierarchies of authority with a leader who oversees several layers of subordinates in a definite chain of command" (Bobrowski, 1988:30). Until the late 1970s there were several alliances, mostly informal, and many rivalries among the gangs of Chicago. However, a turning point came when informal alliances and rivalries came together to form two major supergangs (or nations), known as *People* and *Folks,* at the end of the decade (Bobrowski, 1988:30; Hagedorn, 1998:67).

This formation began within the Illinois prison system when the mostly white Simon City Royals agreed to provide drugs to inmates who belonged to the Black Disciples in exchange for protection; this group came to be called Folks (and is represented in graffiti by a six-pointed star). Shortly thereafter, and in response to this alliance, the Latin Kings aligned themselves with the Vice Lords and the El Rukns and became known as the People (represented by a five-pointed star).

Presently there are more than 30 Chicago gangs that identify themselves as *Folks,* including Spanish Cobras, Latin Disciples, Imperial Gangsters, Latin Lovers, Braziers, Insane Popes, and Simon City Royals. There are at least as many gangs identified as *People,* including Latin Kings,[6] Vice Lords, Future Stones, Gay Lords, Latin Lords, Bishops, and War Lords. Also, there are numerous factions within each major supergang (the Latin Kings have more than 13 different factions, and the Black Disciples and Vice Lords reportedly have about 20), while an estimated 19 gangs are independent (Bobrowski, 1988:34). In terms of the actual number of gang members, these numbers are almost equally divided between People and Folks. In terms of racial distinctions, about 70 percent of Folks are Hispanics, while about 19 percent are African-American, and 10 percent are white. Among the People gangs, around 56 percent are Hispanic, 22 percent are African-American, and 19 percent are white.[7]

These two nations have apparently spread into different parts of the country. One report noted that the Folks nation has a chapter in the city of Atlanta.

They are apparently well organized, as they even provide a somewhat formal application for membership that asks potential members about their qualifications, asking them, among other questions, "What can you do for our organization that we can't do for ourselves?" According to the Atlanta police, out of a total of approximately 1,500 gang members, 1,000 are members of the Folks. The police also report that numerous gangs are in the Atlanta area vying for territory. A police official is quoted as saying that "the South is wide open. It's brand new virgin territory. It's like taking Coca Cola to Russia, like a great new market. There's more accessibility and it's easier to recruit" (Speir, 1994:7–9).

ETHNIC AND RACIAL TYPOLOGIES OF GANGS

Another common method of characterizing gangs is by ethnicity or race. The most utilized is the distinction between African-American, Chicano/Hispanic, and Asian gangs. This section explores some of the differences among these types of gangs. It should be noted at the outset that there may be much more ethnic heterogeneity today than in the past, although for the most part ethnic homogeneity is still the norm (Klein, 1995:106). In some cities there are a few gangs that are ethnically mixed; usually this is white plus Hispanic.

Chicano Gangs

Chicano gangs in Southern California have perhaps the longest history of any gang in America; they have been in existence for over 50 years. Family and community ties are most apparent among these gangs, which may often be traced back several generations. The individual gang member is expected to assist other gang members in times of need and to uphold the neighborhood gang name. Those who join these gangs are among the most marginal youths within this area. There are economic, social, cultural, psychological, and ecological stressors in the barrios. Most barrio residents suffer from at least one of these, but those who suffer from more than one of these stressors constitute those who are victims of *multiple marginality,* and these are the most likely to become Chicano gang members (Vigil, 1988).

Most of these gangs do not identify with specific colors the way Bloods and Crips do. However, some colors favored include black, white, browns, and tans (Dickie pants are favored). Pendleton shirts are also favorite attire (Atlanta Gang Conference, 1992). Some use red bandannas, which stand for Northern California Hispanic gang allegiance, signified by the notation *Norte 14* (from the California prison subculture); others wear a blue bandanna, which stands for Southern California Hispanic gang allegiance, signified by the notation *Sur 13* (from the California prison subculture).

Several other differences have been noted. Unlike the gangs Thrasher studied in the 1920s, Chicano gangs (particularly in Los Angeles) are not a transitory phenomenon because they are based in neighborhoods where Chicanos have lived for several generations. These gangs are Mexican–Americans, meaning that they have not assimilated into mainstream American society as did the Europeans. Also, some Chicano gang members remain affiliated with their gang well into middle age (Moore, Vigil, and Garcia, 1983:183).

Chicano gangs can be divided into two distinctive categories: institutionalized and noninstitutionalized. Two of the more important institutionalized extensions of membership are intertwined with the very nature of the Chicano traditions of kinship and alliance. The first is self-explanatory; the second occurs when others come to the rescue or exhibit loyalty and an interest in friendship with gang members. Other categories include an expansion of boundaries (absorbing small nearby barrios) and the formation of branches (occurring when gang members move into new neighborhoods). Noninstitutionalized categories include family motives for moving out of the barrio, ecological displacement (making way for public improvements), and factional struggles within a particular group or klika/clique (Moore, Vigil, and Garcia, 1983:193).

Moore's study, which concentrated on three major Chicano gangs in the Los Angeles area, reaffirms some of these findings and reinforces some traditional sociological theories, especially those of Thrasher. She observes that "the age-graded gang is one among many barrio structures in which boys play a role; it may be the only structure in which they play a reasonably autonomous role" (Moore, 1978:52). She also notes that the Chicano subculture is more than just machismo, as there is a sense of belongingness, a feeling of family. "The isolated individual is a rarity in the barrios. . . . It is no accident that gang members refer to each other as homeboys. Even in adulthood, when two strangers discover that they are homies they open up to each other as if they were, in fact, members of the same family" (Moore, 1978:53).

Two of the oldest gangs in East Los Angeles are White Fence and El Hoyo Maravilla. As described by Moore, the White Fence gang began during the 1930s as a sports group for young men and was associated with a local church. The younger brothers and cousins of these boys started the gang after most of the original group got drafted into World War II. By the time they began (1944), there were already several established gangs in the area. White Fence was considered more violent than other gangs, probably because they challenged older boys from other gangs (such as the Veteranos from El Hoyo) (Moore, 1993:25–34; see also Moore, 1991).

In the Maravilla neighborhood there were several gangs, mostly named after streets (Arizona Maravilla, Kern Maravilla, Ford Maravilla, and others). The first clique of El Hoyo was actively involved in sports and often competed with White Fence neighborhood kids. The early El Hoyo gang was more like a modern gang than the original White Fence group. These were the zoot-suiters, or pachucos, and their neighborhood was one that was invaded by white servicemen during the Zoot Suit riots in 1943. As in the original White

Fence group, the war separated them and left many younger kids to carry on the tradition (Moore, 1991:27).

By the late 1940s the gangs became permanent fixtures, more or less institutionalized agents of socialization in the form of peer groups. An age-graded structure developed as the older members matured and broke with the gang and younger kids formed their own cliques. For example, the White Fence Monsters, who were formed in 1946, were followed by a gang called the Cherries in 1947, who in turn were followed by the Tinies in 1949. Later cliques went by such names as the Santos (1960–1963), Locos (and the girls' branch of Las Locas) (1964–1968), Jokers (1970–present), and Cyclones (1973–present). The Veteranos in El Hoyo Maravilla (formed in 1933) were followed by the Cherries in 1939, Jive Hounds in 1943, Li'l Cherries in 1945, Cutdowns in 1946, Midgets in 1950, and Li'l Spiders (1974–1980) and Winitos (1974–1976) (Moore, 1991:31). These cliques are reproduced in Figure 2.1.

Asian Gangs

In the United States there are several varieties of gangs of Asian descent. Among the most common Asian gangs are Chinese, Japanese, Korean, Vietnamese, Cambodians (including Mien, Hmong, and Eurasian), Pacific Islanders (most notably the Filipinos but also Samoan, Tongan, Fijian, Guamanian, and Hawaiian), Haitian, Cuban, Jamaican, Guatelalan, Salvadoran, and Honduran. There are probably some other examples, but these are those cited most often (Klein, 1995:106–109). (Space does not permit a complete discussion of each and every one of these varieties. We will concentrate on the most common: Chinese, Vietnamese, and Filipino.) Asians immigrating into the United States enter gang life and often pursue the same kind of activities that they pursued in their native countries. In general, the crimes they commit are much more often property offenses than other types of gangs. What little violence they commit is mostly of the instrumental variety (e.g., threats, retaliation, warnings, and "paybacks") (Klein, 1995:110). Police find that Asian gangs are difficult to penetrate, as they are extremely secretive. Also, most members are clean-cut and polite and act with respect toward law enforcement. They are highly entrepreneurial in nature (Reiner, 1992:46). Asian gangs generally victimize people from their own culture; therefore, the victims usually fail to report the crimes to the police.

Vietnamese Gangs

In recent years these gangs have been widely publicized in the press, especially in Southern California towns like Garden Grove and Westiminister. They are also found in such cities as Atlanta, Houston, New Orleans, St. Petersburg, Washington, D.C., Boston, New York, Denver, St. Louis, Chicago, and Vancouver, British Columbia (Klein, 1995:109–110). Obviously they have become quite mobile!

Hoyo Maravilla	Dates	White Fence	Dates
"Originals"	1935–1945	*"Originals"	1944–1952
"Cherries	1939–1950	*Honeydrippers (girls)	
Vamps[a] (girls)	?	*Monsters	1946–1954
Jive Hounds	1943–1953	*Lil White Fence (girls)	
Lil Cherries	1945–1954	Cherries	1947–1960
*Cutdowns	1946–1956	WF Cherries (girls)	
*Jr. Vamps (girls)		Tinies	1949–1961
*[Big] Midgets	1950–1955	Spiders	1953–1960
Lil Cutdowns	1951–1969	Chonas (girls)	
Las Cutdowns (girls)		Midgets	1957–1966
Penguins	1954–1960	Peewees	1960–?
Lil Midgets	1958–1965	Los Termites	1964–1970
*Las Monas (girls)[b]		Lil Cherries	1964–?
Dukes	1958–1966	*Monstros	1968–?
Tinies	1958–1963	*Monstras (girls)	1970
Santos	1960–1963	*Lil Termites	1972–1981
Peewees	1961–?	*Lil Termites (girls)	
*Locos	1964–1968	Locos	1973–1981
*Las Locas (girls)		Lil Locas (girls)	
*Chicos	1967–?	Lil Spiders	1974–1981
*Las Chicas (girls)		Winitos	1974–1976
Ganzos	1969–?		
*Las Ganzas (girls)			
Jokers	1970–?		
Cyclones	1973–?		
Las Cyclonas (girls)			

*Indicates cliques chosen for sampling.

[a]Most of the Vamps lived in El Hoyo Maravilla, which counts them as one of their cliques, even though they were not formally attached either to the neighborhood or to any boys' clique.

[b]Las Monas was an independent girls clique, contemporaneous with but not an auxiliary of the Lil Midgets, the Dukes, and the Tinies. At the outset of our study we believed that it was attached to the [Big] Midgets. See Appendix for details.

FIGURE 2.1 Names and Beginning and Ending Dates for Gang Cliques in East Los Angeles

SOURCE: Moore, 1991:28.

Due partially to the American desire to provide a safe haven to South Viet-namese who wished to immigrate as the Vietnam War escalated, the U.S. im-migration policy was changed. Subsequently, a large number of Asians entered the United States. Many were young, unskilled, and unable to speak English.

Currently the ages of Vietnamese gang members range from mid- to late teens to the early 20s. They have been described as youths who are frustrated by their lack of success in both school and the community and their inability to acquire material goods. These gangs are unlike their African-American or

Hispanic counterparts. They do not claim turf, nor do they adopt particular modes of dress and often do not have a gang name. They tend to be very secretive and loyal, so that it is difficult to obtain good information about them. Fighting is infrequent, while drug dealing, wearing tattoos, and using handsigns are avoided, as attention would be drawn to their activities. They are organized very loosely, and membership changes constantly (Chin, 1990:139; Goldstein and Huff, 1993:15–16; Vigil and Yun, 1990:160). Unlike Chinese gangs, they have few ties to adult groups, although they often develop relationships with protection and extortion operations of the more established organized crime groups (Spergel, 1995:139).

Money is the focal point within these gangs, for they have been extremely entrepreneurial, as have been most other Asian gangs. Their crimes include mostly auto theft, burglary, robbery, and extortion, and they travel rather extensively. They are very pragmatic in that they victimize other Vietnamese citizens because of this group's inability to understand and/or utilize the American legal system. (About half of the strong-arm robberies go unreported; Reiner, 1992:48). Vigil and Yun note that many Vietnamese-Americans "keep large amounts of cash and gold within their homes. Knowing this, the youth gangs will survey a residence and in small groups (usually four or five persons) will enter the home armed with handguns. Victims are beaten and coerced into revealing the location of their valuables" (Vigil and Yun, 1990:157). Many have become very mobile when it comes to the crimes they commit, often traveling from city to city, sometimes going on nationwide crime sprees (Spergel, 1995:139).

The story of one Vietnamese gang member vividly illustrates the often tragic backgrounds they come from.[8] "Huc" was a product of the Vietnam War as he and his family fled the war-torn nation in an old, dilapidated boat that eventually capsized, resulting in the drowning of his mother (who was pregnant at the time), all of his siblings, and an aunt (a common story among the "boat people"). He and his father were lucky to survive. They were coming to America, where they had heard that the streets were "paved with gold." They arrived poor and with little education. (In contrast, the first wave of Vietnamese refugees were much more educated and were thus better prepared to succeed in America.) It was not too long before Huc's relationship with his father became quite strained (his father was absent through most of Huc's childhood because he was imprisoned in one of the government's so-called reeducation camps). The streets of Southern California, where they eventually settled, were not, of course, paved with gold. Huc was placed several grades below his age because of his lack of English (a common experience for these youth). As a result Huc's involvement in school activities was minimal, and he eventually lost interest and dropped out. His relationship with his father became more strained, and his belief in the "American Dream" turned rather cynical. The gang became a way out, a way of fitting in. Huc eventually ran away and spent his nights with his new "family," the gang, "as they traveled from city to city on the West Coast." In due course the gang gave him a "shortcut to his American Dream" and a "new value system" which was "emblazoned on his thigh in the form of a tattoo that depicts four Ts, representing the Vietnamese words for love, prison, crime, and money" (Vigil and Yun, 1996:144–145).

Chinese Gangs

Chinese gangs have strong roots in China, Taiwan, and Hong Kong, tracing back to the famous "tongs" and "triads." They are the most likely to have connections to organized crime groups (Spergel, 1995:139). They can now be found in San Francisco, Los Angeles, Boston, Toronto, Vancouver, and New York City (Chin, 1990; Toy, 1992). In the 1960s and 1970s most Chinese gang members were from Hong Kong. After the passage of the Immigration and Naturalization Act in 1965, thousands of Chinese-Americans sent for family members, who started immigrating to the United States. Thus, a second generation of Chinese youths were either born in this country or brought here at an early age. As with other second-generation adolescents, many formed gangs, often simply to protect themselves from other students in local schools. Most of the youths who are recruited are those who are vulnerable, are not doing well in school, or have dropped out. Their English is usually very poor, and they have few job skills. Many who dropped out of school began hanging out on street corners (like so many other gangs members), whereupon they began to be recruited by adult Tong groups (hiring them to run errands for gamblers and to provide protection for gambling places). Thus, unlike other groups, Chinese gangs already had an existing organized crime network to emulate or operate within (Reiner, 1992:49; Spergel, 1995:139–140). Since the mid-1960s gang members of new Chinese gangs have included not only Chinese immigrants but sometimes Vietnamese-born Chinese and both Korean and Taiwanese youths as well.

Between 80 and 90 percent of Chinese businessmen pay these gangs on a regular or occasional basis for protection. Four distinct types of extortion are common among Chinese gangs: monetary gain, symbolic (used as a display of power to indicate control of a territory), revenge, and instrumental (to intimidate the victim into backing down in certain business or personal conflicts) (Chin, 1990:134, 142).

Several characteristics of Chinese gangs distinguish them from other gangs: (1) They are closely associated with powerful community organizations, (2) they tend to invest in legitimate businesses and spend a lot of their time in these pursuits, (3) many have national and even international networks, (4) they have been heavily influenced by Chinese secret societies, (5) they are involved in serious forms of mostly property crimes and control large amounts of money, (6) monetary profit is their main goal, and (7) they victimize most local businesses (Chin, 1990:137).

Chinese gangs are different from African-American and Hispanic gangs in that (1) they are not based on youth fads or illicit drug use and are closely related to their community's social and economic life; (2) they do not operate in deteriorated, poor neighborhoods; and (3) they are embedded in the legendary Triad subculture and so are able to claim legitimacy in the Chinese community. (Triad secret societies date back several centuries in China;

Chin, 1990:137). Chinese gangs are composed predominantly of males, whose ages range from 13 to 37, with an average age of 22. Each gang has between 20 and 50 hard-core members. Gangs tend to have a hierarchical structure nearly parallel to that of the Mafia or other organized crime groups. Many gang members are used as "muscle" by older gang members and, in this sense, "may be seen as the first rung on the ladder of Chinese organized crime" (Reiner, 1992:48–49). Most gangs have two or more cliques constantly at battle with each other, so that the intergang conflicts are more threatening (gang members are most often killed by other members of the same group) than attacks from external sources, such as rival gangs or the police (Chin, 1990). There are some exceptions, however. A study of Chinese gangs in Vancouver, British Columbia, found that they engaged in a lot of street fighting over such things as status and turf (Joe and Robinson, 1980).

Still another recent study reveals a great deal of violence, heroin trafficking, and even human smuggling (Chin, 1996). This particular study focused on Chinatown in New York City and was based on interviews with 62 males who were either current or former gang members. They represented 10 different Chinese gangs in New York City. Most were between 16 and 21. The majority were born in another country, most commonly in either Hong Kong or China, although 35 percent were born in the United States. Their ethnicity was mostly Cantonese. It was reported that only a slight majority were ever arrested (52 percent) and that only 15 percent were ever in prison. Most reported that their gangs were only somewhat or not at all organized, that most of their gangs had rules, and that almost all (98 percent) had their own territory. They also reported that most had a division of labor within the gang and that a clear majority (three-fourths) of the gangs were involved in legitimate businesses. These gang members were also heavily involved in criminal activities. (More will be said about the criminal activities of these gang members in the next chapter, which covers the subject of gangs and crime).

Filipino Gangs

These neighborhood gangs are similar in structure and operation to Hispanic gangs and so affiliate largely with the latter in the Western United States. They are located mostly in Los Angeles and San Francisco but also in cities in Alaska, Washington, and Nevada (e.g., Las Vegas). The largest gangs include the Santanas, Taboos, and Temple Street Gang. Their crimes include burglaries, muggings, drug sales, and assaults (Jackson and McBride, 1992:50).

Filipino gangs began in the 1940s in the California prison system. However, many came from the Philippines during the 1970s and early 1980s during the height of the political unrest in that country. As the children of these immigrants began to attend school, they met with cultural confrontations and street gangs. In defense, they began to form their own gangs with other members of their families. These family groupings became cliques or sets within each gang (Los Angeles County, 1992:47–49).

African-American Gangs

A study of Chicago's African-American street gangs by Perkins raises the issue of institutional racism as a major role in the development and perpetuation of these gangs. He also suggests that African-American youths are drawn into gangs to develop a sense of belonging, identity, power, security, and discipline, consistent with Maslow's theory (Perkins, 1987:54–55).

According to Lavigne, Crips currently outnumber Bloods by about three to one in Los Angeles. The Crips and Bloods have so influenced African-American street gangs in Los Angeles that the only distinction between the thousands of gang members is the blue and the red colors (Lavigne, 1993:54–55). Crips do not use words starting with the letter *B,* and Bloods do not use words starting with the letter *C.* Crips often refer to themselves as *cuzz,* while bloods often call each other *Piru.* Also, graffiti often includes rival gang abbreviations along with the slant sign and the letter *K,* which means *killers.* Thus the letters *C/K* mean *Crip killers,* and the letters *B/K* stand for *Blood killers.* Typically African-American gang members will ask for an individual's gang affiliation with the question, "What set you from?" (Atlanta Gang Conference, 1992:6).

Dolan and Finney suggest that the gang's clothing borders on the outrageous to attract attention and to advertise gang identity. The style of clothing and an attitude known as hip, capturing the idea of soul and brotherhood, denote African-American gangs. In addition, a street language, which employs a long string of slang words and secret gestures, is referred to as smack. Black T-shirts, controlled or natural hair, bandannas (often either blue or red) hanging from the rear pocket, earrings, jackets (bomber and tanker types), jeans (with rolled-up cuffs), hats (the knitted, floppy types with jewelry attached), canvas shoes, canes, and umbrellas are part of the typical dress of many African-American street gangs (Dolan and Finney, 1984:67–68).

WHITE GANGS

White youths make up only about 10 percent of the nation's gang population (they make up only 2 percent of all gang members in Los Angeles).[9] Since the late 1970s white teenagers have been forming groups based on an interest in punk rock music and the social attitudes it represents, including helplessness, anger, and rebellion. Many of these youths view the world as offering scant opportunity for individual self-expression. Both the listeners and the performers in the punk rock scene exhibit both angry and violent behavior, mostly for shock value. There are, however, groups of punkers who are very involved in drugs and alcohol, which leads to an ever greater involvement in crimes (Atlanta Gang Conference, 1992).

Usually white youth gangs express their delinquent behavior in different ways from those of most other street gangs. White youths typically join gangs of other ethnic groups, such as Hispanic or multiracial groups. Some are involved in the skinhead movement, identified as a militant racist organization.

This organization provides a family link, much the same as with other gangs (Los Angeles County, 1992:33). A closer look at these skinheads follows.

Skinheads

Skinheads have been described by some as "the kiddie corps of the neo-Nazi movement."[10] Youths have belonged to skinhead organizations since the early 1980s. However, skinhead groups are not all avowed racists; they can be divided into both racist and nonracist subgroupings. The racist skinheads advocate white supremacy, but the nonracist skinheads have a multiracial membership. They are rivals and often engage in violent confrontations. These groups are quite scattered, with erratic membership, although in some areas they claim territory and are classified as a street gang (Los Angeles County, 1992:33). One example of a nonracist skinhead gang is a group known as SHARPs (Skinheads Against Racial Prejudice) or SARs (Skinheads Against Racism) (Wooden, 1995:131). A variation is the kind of group known as a separatist group. These youths consider themselves to be "survivalists, concerned only with their own personal welfare and survival in the likelihood of a nuclear holocaust or natural disaster." These groups do not care too much about what is going on around them and try to avoid overt racial violence (Wooden, 1995:136).

A group similar to the racist skinheads is known as political skinheads. These are youths who tend to take orders from such groups as WAR (White Aryan Resistance) or the Aryan Brotherhood. Perhaps the most avowedly racist and very critical of the U.S. government, these groups claim that minorities are given preferential treatment over whites. These skinheads are common in most prisons and frequently join forces with the White Aryan Brotherhood or the Klu Klux Klan (KKK) (Wooden, 1995:136).

Skinhead gangs in the United States have their roots in a similar movement in England during the late 1950s. Those youths, known as *Teddy Boys,* were working-class males who wore distinctive Edwardian coats and tight pants and were viewed by British society "as threatening to everything the traditional family stood for." Some described them as folk devils. However, by the 1960s the Teddy Boys had evolved into a more moderate group, sometimes referred to as "mods" because they wore a type of flashy clothing similar to that worn by young African-Americans (Wooden, 1995:132).

However, according to Wooden, the original skinheads were actually black Jamaican immigrants to England who were called the Rude Boys. Their close-shaven heads and music style were eventually adopted by white working-class youths in Britain. While not avowedly racist, these skinheads adopted a very conservative, working-class view of the world. By 1972, with police harassment and political pressures, the British skinhead movement diminished, only to be replaced with the emergence of punks as the new form of skinheads. These groups were even more flamboyant than the original skinheads, sporting boots, jeans, and suspenders and adding the swastika as a prominent tattoo (Wooden, 1995:133).

The modern American skinheads usually wear a polo shirt or T-shirt, suspenders (often the color matches that of their shoelaces), pants (usually Dickies or Levi's) that are rolled up or tailored so that the entire boot is exposed, flight jackets (often with personalized graffiti), and boots (Wooden, 1995:36–38). If a skinhead's boot has been scuffed on the steel tips, he is considered to be tough; the more scuffs on his boot, the tougher he is considered to be. If he is seen with his suspenders down, this means he is ready to fight. If he wears white laces in his boots, this means that he upholds white pride, while red laces stand for a more aggressive type of white power, and yellow laces signify hatred for the police or a claim that he has killed a police officer.

Skinhead music is as important to these youths as rap is to African-American youths. This music is radical and often reflects the racial and political attitudes of the skinheads. Skinhead graffiti is similar to that of other street gangs, with the addition of a racial and political orientation. Hand-signs are given as well. Tattoos are common, appearing on the face, neck, and inside of the lips. American skinhead gangs have jumping-in initiations for new members, during which the recruit is attacked with fists by between 4 and 12 other members for a certain period of time (Los Angeles County, 1992:39).

Skinheads are highly likely to engage in violent acts and to direct such acts against those they perceive as the most different or a threat to the white majority—homosexuals, racial and ethnic groups, and religious minorities. According to one source, during one period of time in the early 1980s skinheads were responsible for 121 murders, 302 assaults, and 301 cross burnings (Wooden, 1995:134).

Stoners

Youths known as stoners are distinguishable from traditional street gangs by their secretiveness and the difficulty in identifying them. Often referred to as cults, they engage in many ritualistic activities. They are white suburban youths from a higher socioeconomic background than that of most other gangs. According to the California Youth Authority, stoner gangs constitute only about 5 percent of all gangs in the state and an even smaller percentage of all white youths in the correctional system (Wooden, 1995:160–164).

A survey of 52 stoners in the CYA by Wooden found that the majority (62 percent) had an income level in their homes described as either "adequate" or "more than adequate." The majority (72 percent) scored above average on standard intelligence tests, and almost all had some work history prior to their most recent incarceration. Despite their high intelligence, none had yet to graduate from high school, while two-thirds had been placed in special education classes. More than 40 percent dropped out of high school. Most were described as either "low achievers" or "nonachievers." Most had been heavily involved in the abuse of both alcohol and drugs, with the majority (69 percent) beginning their drug use before the age of 13. All except two were white. Their most common offense was burglary (70 percent were incarcerated for this offense). Most (81 percent) came from Southern California (Wooden, 1995:164–165).

Stoner gangs are heavily involved in the use of various kinds of drugs (e.g., speed, LSD, rock cocaine, PCP) and have an especially high rate of toxic vapor use. They are almost always into heavy metal music. They generally do not have any organized leadership, are antiestablishment, and often dabble in Satanism, participating in animal sacrifice and ritual crimes (e.g., grave or church desecrations). These gangs are made up of lower- and middle-class white youths of junior and senior high school age who typically have a higher scholastic and economic status than found in other street gangs (Jackson and McBride, 1992:42–45).

Stoners typically dress in red or black clothing, with athletic jersey tops portraying heavy metal music stars; metal-spiked wrist cuffs, collars, and belts; earrings; long hair; and tattoos. They often wear Satanic relics or sacrilegious effigies. Stoners use graffiti to mark territory, not necessarily geographic, but musical—to claim music groups or types of music (Jackson and McBride, 1992:42–45).

Taggers

It seems that everywhere one travels in urban and suburban areas one sees a form of graffiti known as tagging. Such graffiti is not done to mark turf. Rather it is a way these mostly white middle-class youths call attention to themselves. Wooden, who has studied these groups extensively, quotes one 17-year-old tagger: "It's addictive, once you get started. It's like a real bad habit." Wooden comments that

> the addiction has drawn thousands of teenagers—who call themselves and their rivals "toys," "taggers" or "pieces"—to devote their time to "getting up" to attain "fame" by tagging poles, benches, utility boxes, signs, bridges and freeway signs in the San Fernando Valley with graffiti (Wooden, 1995:115).

Police estimate that in Los Angeles County there are at least 600 tagger crews, with about 30,000 youths. One crew, who call themselves NBT (Nothing But Trouble) claim a membership of 400 or more. These groups are also referred to by such names as graffiti bands, posses, pieces (so called because they believe that they draw masterpieces of art), housers (because they like to tag houses), and snapers. What specifically is tagged varies by age. Younger taggers (10 to 15) usually tag around school grounds. Older youths will go after bigger targets, such as freeway overpasses or bridges, public transportation (especially buses), streetlight poles, and so on. "Less geographically bound to protecting a particular neighborhood turf than are ethnic and inner-city gangs, the taggers spread their marks far and wide on their nightly runs" (Wooden, 1995:117–118).

Taggers, like regular street gangs, have their own slang. For example, a "toy" is someone who is a novice or amateur tagger; to "kill a wall" is to cover a wall completely with graffiti; taggers will go on a "bombing run" whereby members of a crew will go out and try to mark as many places as possible with their "tag names" and the names of their crew; and sometimes crews will "slash" or cross out rival crews' or taggers' names, which is considered an insult or challenge (Wooden, 1995:1190).

Among some of the more common names, or monikers, of taggers in Southern California include AAA (Against All Authority), KNP (Knock Out

Posse), ABC (Artist By Choice), ACK (Artistic Criminal Kings), DCP (Destroying City Property), and CMC (Creating Mass Confusion). Many of the names suggest a form of rebellion typical of many suburban white teenagers (Wooden, 1995:120).

One explanation given for the rise of these tagger groups is that middle-class, suburban white youths have been influenced by the ethnic gangs of the inner cities and their "gangsta rap" and have tried to emulate them or even compete against them. However, taggers did not suddenly appear in the 1990s. There was a crew in New York City in the early 1970s who called themselves Tough Artist Group (TAG). There were even a few tagger crews in Southern California in the 1980s (Wooden, 1995:121).

Wooden's interviews with tagger crews found that they typically do not have much of a formal organizational structure, that most members are not jumped in or otherwise go through a formal initiation process, that members often drift in and out of the groups, and that they often change their names (monikers) when they get tired of the old ones. Often these groups will do "battle" with each other, which is merely a contest to see who can have their name up the most often (Ibid.:124).

Although more and more are carrying weapons, mostly for protection from rival crews, for the most part tagging is a form of fun and play. Most do not choose to call what they do a crime but merely an art form and a way to express themselves. They are insulted when others (e.g., the police) call their work graffiti. On the other hand, many become increasingly destructive in order to achieve some form of notoriety with other taggers. Many are merely trying to outperform their competitors (Ibid.).

Taggers have drawn the ire of many citizens and criminal justice officials. Some citizens, however, have taken matters into their own hands. In Los Angeles recently (winter of 1995), many people applauded the actions of a man named William Masters after he shot two graffiti taggers in the back. One of the youngsters died. There was conflicting testimony about whether the taggers really threatened Masters. A new report containing an interview with Masters (*Chicago Tribune,* February 16, 1995) revealed that he had been in this sort of trouble before and that he apparently is urging citizens to "take matters into their own hands" with the use of weapons. There was a time in this country when such behavior would have been considered an act of cowardice and/or murder. However, the Los Angeles district attorney stated that Masters had acted "reasonably."

SOME COMMON CHARACTERISTICS
OF GANG MEMBERS

Are there any characteristics (personal or social) that distinguish youths who belong to gangs from youths who do not? This is not an easy question to answer, for there are a variety of types of gang members, and often there is little differentiation between the gang member and the typical adolescent urban dweller, both delinquent and nondelinquent. While research into this question is at best incomplete, some tentative conclusions can be drawn about the typical gang member. Jankowski, after seven years of observing gang members in three large urban areas (Boston, New York, and Los Angeles), has concluded that most gang members have developed a social character structure he calls *defiant individualism* (Jankowski, 1990:22–25).

Gang Members as Defiant Individualists

According to Jankowski, gangs emerge within poor inner-city communities because these areas have their own unique form of social organization. They are organized "around an intense competition for, and conflict over, the scarce resources that exist in these areas" (Jankowski, 1990:22). This social order is an alternate social order, a sort of Hobbesian order characterized by Social Darwinist principles.

Jankowski's theory starts with the assumption that people from low-income communities tend to develop a social character known as defiant individualism. He uses the term *character* in the sense that Erich Fromm used it, in contrast to the term *personality*. According to Fromm this social character is a constellation of characteristics common to an entire group that comes about as a result of people's adaptation to various conditions (social, cultural, economic, and so on) unique to that group. The defiant individualist character consists of seven main attributes, outlined as follows:

1. **Competitiveness.** This trait stems from the scarce resources available within low-income communities. Most youths begin to experience this within their own families (typically there are a number of children), where there are not many material items to go around. They also must compete for the affection and general attention of the parents (contrary to popular belief, most of their parents work). In low-income housing, space is also limited, so there is competition for both physical and psychological space.

2. **Mistrust or Wariness.** This trait is the outgrowth of the first trait, especially as it is manifested in the community outside of the home. Youths learn that trust is not something that is given but rather is "something to be calculated."

3. **Self-Reliance.** Because there are so few resources, both within the family and in the outside community, youngsters soon learn that they are going to have to do things on their own because they cannot rely on others due to mistrust.

4. **Social Isolation.** This trait stems from both self-reliance and mistrust as individuals become less emotionally attached to others (including women). Therefore, they become isolated from others, and this reduces their options (and the chances of being emotionally hurt by others). This may be one reason why entire low-income communities have become so isolated, as noted by Wilson (1987).

5. **Survival Instinct.** This trait is the logical result of the first four traits. Life in general within these poor neighborhoods results in youths becoming

like "predators trapping prey." That is, youths often "observe, confront, and negotiate with people whose competitive mode has led them to view young people as prey" (Jankowski, 1990:25). Thus, there are drug dealers and drug users, pimps, armed robbers, and all sorts of people preying on others for scarce resources. Jankowski makes a telling point when he says that within this kind of environment it is those who are the ultimate "failures" that help solidify this survival instinct more than others. This is because the "derelicts, the women and men dependent on public assistance, and the men and women (including possibly their fathers and mothers) who have taken jobs in secondary or informal labor markets that lead nowhere represent to many young people those who have succumbed to the environment" (Jankowski, 1990:25). The result is that these youths become determined, at least in the early stages of their lives, not to fail like all the others they see (especially their own parents). Their goal is to survive, to fight, and to prevail.

6. *Social Darwinist Worldview.* From the perspective of these young people the outside world is characterized by competitiveness, illegal behavior, and corruption, all of which are tolerated and often encouraged. Such behavior can be found even within the upper echelons of society. To these young people even the most successful (e.g., the white upper class) have achieved their success in a manner not unlike that of offenders within their own lower-class world (although not quite as crudely). To them this is the natural order of things, how things are supposed to be. Moreover, they look around them and see what people in more affluent neighborhoods have, they want the same things, and they will obtain these goods through illegal methods, just as "respectable" members of the community do.

7. *A Defiant Air.* This final character trait is a culmination of all the other traits and is a type of demeanor that says to others, "I am going to take what I want and no one is going to stop me!" It is expressed on two levels: public and private. Publicly, when confronting authority (especially the police and the courts) there is little display of fear, deference, or remorse. Privately, it is more subtle and involves a quiet resolve to continue and to resist any attempt to change. In contrast to what some gang researchers have suggested, the hard exterior is not insecure or fearful on the interior but rather is equally as hard.

While most members of low-income communities will display some of these traits, gang members tend to display all of them and do so more intensely. What is important to emphasize is that gang members display these traits not because they are in gangs but rather because they come from low-income communities. Gangs, in order to persist, must attempt to cope with and control these defiant individuals.

Growing up in such communities can also lead to another characteristic, namely, a resignation to one's own death, even at an early age. In the final section of this chapter we will explore a somewhat different perspective on gangs and gang members, a kind of typology that no one else has considered when studying gangs. We contend that gang members can be both victims and victimizers.

Gang Members as Victims and Victimizers

Alex Kotlowitz (1991), in his penetrating book about youths growing up in a Chicago housing project, makes the following observation about nine-year-old Diante McClain, whose older brother, William, was fatally shot at Chicago's Henry Horner public housing project. During the gunfire, Diante remained glued to a playground swing. His friend pleaded with him to take cover. Instead, Diante continued swinging, repeating over and over again, "I wanna die. I wanna die" (Kotlowitz, 1991:54)

A 13-year-old gang member told one of the authors, "Man, I don't give a fuck if I die—it don't mean nothing" (Brown and Shelden, 1994). What is often lacking in recent research on gangs is a close look at the immediate environment of gang youths as they are growing up, long before they even begin to think about joining a gang. This is not to say that researchers never address the social sources of gang delinquency, for indeed most have done this. However, what is the long-term impact of a very violent environment on young children? By a violent environment, we mean both inside and outside the home, where millions of children are exposed to an incredible amount of violence. Whether or not they are directly harmed in a physical sense is not the issue, although many are harmed in this manner. What needs to be looked at is how much indirect harm is done and how this exposure to violence tends to produce, over time, youths who not only act in aggressive ways but also are desensitized to violence.

The typical gang member has been a persistent victim of violence, both directly and indirectly. We also believe, as argued by Deborah Prothrow-Stith (1991) in her book *Deadly Consequences,* that many of these youths have suffered a form of posttraumatic stress syndrome. The statements at the beginning of this section are typical of those who suffer this problem. The statement by the 13-year-old gang member reminds us of what many soldiers in Vietnam experienced. During this war many combat soldiers used the phrase "It don't mean nothing" to reflect a self-defensive mechanism that reduced the impact of disappointment and dangerous situations. This expression was not an indication that the individual was resigning from life, nor did it mean that the individual was going to commit suicide. Rather, it was a response to a set of circumstances in which the individual felt little or no control over the outcome. Many would argue that such an attitude is irrational, and in a normal situation they would probably be correct. However, many Vietnam soldiers frequently found themselves, very much like many inner-city youths, in abnormal settings where such an outlook is very rational. There is still another analogy with Vietnam soldiers that applies to inner-city youths. Some of these veterans have been described as "trip-wire" veterans. This term refers to those who suffered so much from the war that they developed a sort of siege mentality or an "us versus them" outlook on life. They would go far into the woods in the Pacific Northwest, set up trip wires or booby traps, and hide from the world, fully armed and ready to defend themselves.

Alex Kotlowitz (quoted at the beginning of this section) has written extensively about some very young African-American males living in the Henry Horner projects in Chicago in a book with the poignant title *There Are No Children Here.* He describes two youths, one a 12-year-old named Lafayette Walton, the other his nine-year-old brother Pharaoh, as living in a war zone. Lafayette "knows how to fling himself to the ground at the sound of gunfire. He knows how to crawl on his belly through the dirt to safety. He knows how to distinguish a .357 caliber Magnum from a .45 caliber revolver. . . . There is no one to protect Lafayette or his five siblings from violence. To live in the project is to live outside a protected circle. Inside the circle are middle-class people, middle-class neighborhoods, middle-class institutions. Outside are the very poor, the very powerless. . . . During the summer, someone is shot, stabbed, or beaten every three days at Henry Horner Homes." This reality cannot be captured in mere words. Kotlowitz describes one occasion when nine-year-old Pharaoh found himself in the middle of a drug-gang gunfight while walking home from school (aren't children supposed to feel safe walking home from school?). One of the gang members has a submachine gun, and Pharaoh just barely escapes the gunfire, which occurred literally outside the door to his home. But, as Kotlowitz notes, "other kinds of shootings, beatings, stabbings, and rapes occur more frequently. Weapons are ubiquitous, and family disputes often end in violence. Women as well as men resort to physical force, and project residents are often the victims of crime" (quoted in Prothrow-Stith, 1991:66–67).

We believe that every Diante McClain, every Lafayette and Pharaoh Walton, and every other child growing up in such an environment are victims of crime. Yet with few exceptions, their names do not appear on police reports as crime victims, and the environment, such as that described by Kotlowitz, is not typically what people have in mind when they speak of crimes or criminals (more often than not the image of the victims is an innocent middle-class white person, and the perpetrator is an African-American gang member). But the effects are the same as if they had been raped or assaulted.

Prothrow-Stith writes that many "mental health providers have begun to see signs of posttraumatic stress syndrome in crime victims, in the victims of terrorist attacks, and *in the children chronically exposed to violence in their homes and communities*" (Prothrow-Stith, 1991:68, emphasis added). We all know the data on the victimization of young African-American males: The most common cause of death is now homicide, and this group has the highest rate of victimization by violence in general. The fact that this same group has the highest rate of offending is also nothing new to us. But why do so many not see a connection here?

Given the violent environment most of these children grew up in, it should come as no surprise that one of the main reasons they give for joining a gang is for protection. And there is some research that is beginning to show the extent to which gang members have been victims—and we are not talking only of drive-by shootings. Studies have shown that gang members have had plenty of experience with violence while growing up. Such youths have seen and have been victimized by violence in their homes and in their communities. These experiences have shaped the attitudes of these young people toward perpetuating violence. Gang youths have accepted violence as the normal and appropriate way to resolve minor and major disputes. These youths have come to believe that there is no nonviolent method for dealing with daily disputes and other problems of life. Further, as our own research shows, these gangs reinforce what their environment has taught them by encouraging and even praising a gang member's willingness to engage in violence.

Data from 77 Detroit gang members were collected over an 18-month period by Brown through unstructured interviews and observations. Some of the interviews were conducted in the homes of the participants, on street corners, in alleyways, in the backseats of automobiles ("ride-arounds"—the equivalent of "ride-alongs" with police officers), and in crack houses. The concept of interviews is used rather loosely here because many of them were simply recordings of conversations in a variety of situations in which several participants were involved. Although there were specific research questions for this study, an unfettered interview schedule was used to prompt subjects to volunteer information on selected topics.

The majority of the gang members (74 percent) had been involved as a perpetrator in gang-related violence, and an almost equal number (70 percent) had been a victim in some kind of gang conflict. The gang members gave various reasons for why they engaged in the gang-related violence, and some of their responses indicated that many were not altogether willing participants. For example, two members said they faked involvement in the violence, while another four individuals said that they had protested but engaged in the violence anyway. Six members bluntly said that they did not want to be involved at all but did it anyway. The largest number (40 percent) said, in so many words, that they had no choice but to get involved in gang violence because they were members of the gang and felt that this was a basic requirement. Only 5 percent had actually initiated the violence. The remainder were admittedly willing participants in the violence.

It would be safe to say that just about every member of this gang had experienced some form of victimization during his lifetime. For example, more than one-third (36 percent) had the experience of losing someone close to them from a homicide, and an almost equal proportion (35 percent) had actually seen someone dead following a gang-related homicide. However, when asked if they were ever concerned about being killed or seriously injured through violence, the vast majority (84 percent) said no. When asked why they were not concerned, they gave some fascinating reasons. About one-fifth (19.5 percent) said it "doesn't matter"; another 18 percent said, "I don't worry about it"; and 13 percent said, "Who cares?" About one-fourth (24.7 percent) responded that they "don't think about it," while an equal number said, "Someone will get even."

Clearly gang members are not strangers to the world of violence. But to conclude, as many do, that they themselves are violent people is misleading. We wonder how others (including everyone who reads these pages) would respond if they grew up under similar conditions. When so many young men and women accept violence and accept even the inevitability of their own deaths from violence (some as young as 12 or 13), how can anyone say that they have not been victims and that this victimization is not a causal factor in their own violence against others?

We now turn to a consideration of the question, "What do gang members *do* with their time"? The stereotype (constantly reinforced in the media, especially in full-length movies, and by "war stories" told by some police officials, who should know better) is that all gangs do is engage in drive-by shootings, drug deals netting thousands of dollars, robberies, and other crimes. Actually, the life of a typical gang member is rather boring. Our favorite line is from a 30-year veteran of gang research, Malcolm Klein, who writes that during the years of research he and his colleagues have engaged in,

> we learned much about gang member life which, with the occasional exception of a boisterous meeting, a fight, an exciting rumor, is a very dull life. For the most part, gang members do very little—sleep, get up late, hang around, brag a lot, eat again, drink, hang around some more. It's a boring life: the only thing that is equally boring is being a researcher watching gang members (Klein, 1995:11).

However, they do commit crimes—a lot of crimes, compared to the average delinquent. (The reader should not jump to the conclusion that gangs commit the bulk of *all* crimes committed in your typical city. They just tend to commit more than nongang members their age.) The next chapter will be devoted to this subject.

SUMMARY

It is impossible to provide a profile of a gang member that is inclusive; it is equally difficult to identify a gang precisely. From scavenger to corporate gangs, with vertical to horizontal structures, any attempt to identify a typical gang falls short. Similarly, gang members cross gender, racial, and ethnic boundaries. There is evidence only the fairly traditional notion of gangs but also a relatively new phenomenon—taggers—which further expands the parameters of a definition, further challenging the drive of social scientists to capture a universality of theme. Further, gangs in the United States are composed of youths from a wide variety of ethnic origins, including Chinese, Japanese, Vietnamese, Filipino, Korean, Mexican, and Cuban.

Viewing gang members as victims as well as victimizers was suggested. While few researchers probe beyond the surface of this thesis, we are convinced that the overwhelming majority of those youths involved with gangs have indeed been victims themselves, both of specific persons who inhabit their social world and of the environment that surrounds them.

NOTES

1. There is plenty of literature on adolescent groups and subcultures. For a good review, see Schwendinger and Schwendinger (1985).

2. German-born Max Weber (1864–1920) was one of the earliest and most famous sociologists in history. Perhaps most famous for his work *The Protestant Ethic and the Spirit of Capitalism* (1958), he was a very prolific writer and wrote several books covering such wide-ranging subjects as law, economy, and religion. Within the academic world he is also popular for developing the notion of the *ideal type.*

3. These typologies are taken from Huff (1989), Fagan (1989), Taylor (1990).

4. This definition comes from Klein (1995:132).

5. Based mostly on Vigil (1988, 1990), Vigil and Long (1990), and Reiner (1992).

6. For an excellent film on the Latin Kings, see *The Heart Broken in Half,* produced by Dwight Conquergood.

7. Bobrowski (1988:31). Although this reference may seem out of date, information provided at the 1999 National Youth Gang Symposium in Las Vegas (attended by the senior author) confirms that not too much has changed.

8. This story is told by Vigil and Yun (1996:142–145).

9. Reiner (1992:114). As alluded to earlier in this book, such a low estimate may be reflection of both the standard definitions of gangs and a racial bias or stereotype of what gangs are. It is suspected that there would be more white gangs and white gang members if the criteria used to define *gang* were expanded. This would especially be the case if groups known as taggers were included in the definition of *gang.*

10. Wooden (1995:129). Other than Wooden's book cited here, there has been very little systematic research done on the topic of so-called white hate groups such as the skinheads. The bombing at Oklahoma City in the spring of 1995 apparently awakened many people to the existence of these kinds of groups, which may be more prevalent and dangerous that the typical minority gangs discussed in this text. Hopefully more careful research will be forthcoming on this subject.

3

The Gang Subculture

Youth gangs constitute a unique subculture in modern society. Like other subcultures, gangs are not only distinct from, but also part of, mainstream American culture. In other words, while they have much in common with the wider society, they also have their own unique set of values, norms, lifestyles, and beliefs. This chapter explores certain key aspects of the gang subculture, beginning with an examination of its origins (focusing especially on Chicano gangs in Los Angeles and a Puerto Rican gang in Chicago) and how youths growing up within these areas become, in effect, socialized into the gang subculture beginning at a rather early age.

CHAPTER THREE

THE NATURE AND ORIGINS OF AND SOCIALIZATION INTO THE GANG SUBCULTURE

The Chicano gang subculture, often referred to as *cholos* (meaning marginalized), has evolved in Southern California during the past 50 years. This subculture allows youths to adopt clothing styles, slang, hairstyles, and so on that set them apart from adults (Vigil and Long, 1990:56). This subculture is an adaptation to the poverty that surrounds the people in these barrios. Vigil and Long describe it in these words:

> The Cholo subculture of Southern California was born in marginal urban areas where small houses exacerbated the crowded living conditions for large families. Poverty and discrimination in employment generated continual stress within these households. Few parks and playgrounds existed in such areas. The youths who created the Cholo subculture and those who have maintained it have been excluded by distance and discrimination from adult-supervised park programs. They have fared poorly in school because of language and cultural differences and limited encouragement from school personnel who expect little of them and parents who often are preoccupied with day-to-day economic crises. It is no wonder that the streets have held such attraction for these youths (ibid.:60).

Moore has noted that success in the male Chicano world "is an idealized version of male strength and male responsibility that the people around them can rarely approach." Moreover, Moore continues,

> This success requires belonging to the group. Thus the gang represents a means to what is an expressive, rather than an instrumental, goal: the acting out of a male role of competence and of "being in command" of things. With the police quickly defining a separate and identifiable group of Chicano adolescents as a group and as dangerous, the gang will tend to at least partly redefine its competence in terms of increasing violence (Moore, 1978:53).

Vigil and Long (1990:63–66) note how the barrio gang provides an arena for age- and gender-role formations and for role enactment and self-empowerment. For example, gang initiation rites and fighting and drinking behaviors allow young males to prove their manhood (machismo). The gang also includes a "cholo front" (described later in this section), a set of role prescriptions that include certain clothing styles, nicknames, tattoos, speech patterns, styles of walking, and so on. Deviations from these prescriptions exist among gang members, and the gang usually allows these deviations so that all members can be themselves without suffering any strong disapproval.

The term *cholo,* according to Vigil (1988), reflects a unique "cultural transitional situation of Mexican-Americans in the southwestern United States; it is a process strongly affected by underclass forces and street requisites. This subculture has been developed over a period of several decades and includes a social structure and cultural value system with its own age-graded cohorts, institutions, norms and goals, and roles." This subculture "functions to socialize and enculturate barrio youth." It also involves many of the old customs of Mexican-Americans, including the adolescent palomilla tradition that "includes many daring and bravado male patterns, and an anti-authority attitude" (ibid.:3–7). An important part of this heritage is the age-graded clique, which Vigil and Long describe as "the nexus of the gang structure" (Vigil and Long, 1990:92). Chicano barrio gangs consist of individuals of about the same age (hence age cohorts, or klikas), each clique being separated by two or three years.

These gang members tend to be drawn disproportionately from the poorest households within a community. More specifically, they come from households with incomes lower than other inner-city, barrio families and with a much higher incidence of family stressors. In short, they are the poorest of the poor (Vigil, 1988:5; see also Moore, 1993). Also, the lives of the street youths who make up the barrio gang reflect what Vigil calls a status of multiple marginality, which "derives from various interwoven situations and conditions that tend to act and react upon one another." Moreover, the lifestyle within that gang subculture is merely a response to the "pressures of street life and serves to give certain barrio youth a source of familial support, goals and directives, and sanctions and guides" (Vigil, 1988:1–2).

In the urban setting of Los Angeles most Mexican-American families suffer economic problems revolving mainly around unemployment. As Vigil notes,

> Economic struggles taxed the parents' energies and affected the time they could spend monitoring their children's behavior, especially under crowded conditions and in large families. Disruptions in family life, moreover, often brought a high incidence of broken homes, where the mother had to take on the dual role of breadwinner and breadmaker. As a result, children spent more time outside the home, where there was more space to play and cavort. Here they began to learn the ways of the streets under the aegis of older children, with minimal adult supervision. The outcome was often early exposure to and induction into the gang (ibid.:36).

It should be noted in this context that the supervision of children can be seen not merely as an independent variable that causes delinquency but also as a dependent variable. Thus the degree to which children are supervised may vary according to such factors as the number of children in the home, the number of rooms in the home, the type of residence the home is (e.g., government housing project versus single-family residence), the family income, and the presence of a father. In families experiencing multiple stresses, espe-cially those with many children, there is a loosening of control networks. One result of this is that children spend more and more unsupervised time in the streets with other similarly situated youths. As Vigil notes, such "street peers, some slightly older and a few in their early teens (frequently including older siblings), become major agents of socialization. Concomitantly, school behav-ior and performance also tend to suffer when parental guidance is lacking. School problems and the influence of street-based peer groups reinforce one another in a youth's increasingly marginal development; one can witness the same small group together in both schoolyards and the streets" (ibid.:43).

So the street subculture becomes a significant and powerful presence in the lives of barrio youths. Similarly, in Chicago, the Diamonds studied by Padilla grew up in an area where gangs were an ever-present part of the terrain. In fact, the youths studied by Padilla "were unable to recall a day when the gang was not part of the neighborhood." One youth reported to Padilla that the gang was "a natural fixture of his neighborhood." The youth stated that, "Like the apartment buildings, the sidewalks, and trees of the neighborhood, we [the gangs] were all part of the same thing. You can't get the gangs out. They were there when I was a kid, and now we are here for the new kids" (Padilla, 1992:61).

Most of the gang members Vigil interviewed in his study came from fami-lies with a history of stress. One of the main reasons these youths became in-volved in gang life was to get the kind of support they did not get at home. The absence of a father was especially significant (Vigil, 1988:44).[1]

Most of the gang members Vigil studied began their association with the street subculture—that is, they began to hang out in the streets with their peers—between the ages of seven and nine. Interestingly, the majority hung out with a brother, uncle, or other older male role model. These "early associa-tions provided a sense of friendship and mutual trust that later proved useful in gang circles," especially in "backing up" friends (ibid.:48).

The general pattern Vigil found was that most gang members "become in-volved with street life early and additionally spend a great deal of time there, starting off as mischief and adventure seekers. Most of the street habits and customs are normal cohorting behavior, but other deviant activities are also learned. The experiences, good and bad, are bonding events that solidify trust and closer relations among the participants. Learning to back your friends is an early street lesson and, later, a core requirement for gang membership" (ibid.:52–53). Not unlike what happens in the military, such personal qualities as sharing resources with others and backing up one's friends become prereq-uisites of gang membership and, incidentally, are learned early, before becom-ing a regular member (ibid.:82).

The influence of peers in the lives of the gang members Vigil studied can be divided into three types: friendship, direct confrontation, and psychological disposition, with friendship being the most common. The most committed gang member (i.e., the hard core) generally experienced peer pressure in the following way. First, friendships developed during elementary school years, and, if the person remained in the same barrio, such friendships became more solidified during the adolescent years, at the time when the probability of gang involvement is highest. Direct peer pressure (e.g., helping a friend make a decision about joining a gang) was also common, but not as much as friendship. Psychological disposition, such as fear or the tendency toward loco (crazy) behavior, was rarely found among the gang members studied by Vigil (ibid.).

It is important to note that each of the three types of gang members Vigil monitored (regular, periphery, and temporary) have much in common, such as growing up in barrios and adopting a cholo front—that is, the dress, demeanor, talk, and so on of gang members. It is relatively easy to look like a gang member by adopting this front. The regular gang members are distinguished by their earlier and more intense street experiences. What this does is to make them more embedded within the street subculture. Vigil describes what happens as *carnalismo,* or a strong support system among one's peers, which "is sometimes the only human support system they have." Thus it is out of the question for such youths to avoid or reject this peer group, which is why so many have trouble leaving the gang. To them it might be like rejecting and leaving one's own family (Ibid.:84).

In his study of the Diamonds in Chicago, Padilla noted that youths in this neighborhood grew up with the gang culture, learning many aspects of this culture from an early age. One important lesson they learned was that, as one gang member said, "those guys got along so well. . . . They cared for each other. They were brothers. . . . They cared about each other more than a lot of other people who are not in gangs do" (Padilla, 1992:62). In short, the attitude toward these gangs on the part of these youths as they were growing up became more and more positive as time passed. They slowly began to define gang members as straight, cool, and together—in short, "people to be admired and not resented." As one gang member put it, "The gang forces you to always be cool, together. You know, this is your homey, and brother, so take care of him, don't rat on him. That's what makes the whole thing cool, like a family. Everybody is a friend and brother. You treat people like a brother, like family" (Ibid.:67).

School became a problem for many second-generation Mexican-Americans in Southern California (as well as for the majority of gang members in other parts of the country). A great deal of research has confirmed the importance of school and that one of the key variables distinguishing gang members from other youths from similar backgrounds is school failure (Curry and Decker, 1998; Padilla, 1992; Shelden, 1995; Shelden, Snodgrass, and Snodgrass, 1992; Spergel, 1995:118–120). A high incidence of dropping out and/or exclusion or expulsion from school resulted in "a situation in which significant numbers of barrio youngsters are socialized to a considerable degree in the streets" (Vigil, 1988:37). The majority of the gang youths Vigil studied began to withdraw from school life by the third or fourth grade. For many, their "school careers began with skepticism, limited parental encouragement, and early exposure to street experiences that did little to promote self-discipline. It is clear that by the third or fourth grade they had not effectively adapted to the school situation" (Ibid.:57). Long before they officially dropped out (usually around age 16), they had been turned off by school. Some began to have problems as early as kindergarten, with the language barrier being the predominant cause. Many had experienced a great deal of prejudice and discrimination. Most of the problems at school began long before any involvement with a gang (Ibid.:61).

A typical experience in school is related by Padilla. He describes the gang members he studied as being labeled deviants and troublemakers by school officials, usually during their elementary school years (some as early as the fourth grade), long before they joined the gang. These youths responded (as if their labels were a self-fulfilling prophecy) "by joining with others so labeled and engaging in corresponding behavior." These youngsters began to develop various forms of oppositional behavior (fighting, cutting classes, and not doing homework). Many began to develop "a distinctive subculture within which they could examine and interpret what was going on in their lives and in school." In short, very early in their lives these youths began to respond in ways that were almost identical to gang behavior. In effect, says Padilla, "they were undergoing early preparation for a later stage in their teenage years (during high school) when they would finally join the gang" (Padilla, 1992:68–69). It is important to note that these particular youths experienced a form of public humiliation from some of their teachers (and some of their own peers). Such experiences were quite painful, and they quickly sought out others who were similarly branded. (It should be noted that part of their humiliation was from the various negative evaluations of their own Puerto Rican culture on the part of both teachers and peers.) "These youngsters began to recognize the common fate they shared with others like themselves." A quote from one of Padilla's gang members summarizes this problem:

> If the teachers and everyone else thought that we were bad, we started to show that we were. So, we started doing a lot of bad things, like hitting some kids and even talking back to the teacher and laughing at her. In a way, it was kind of fun, because here are these teachers thinking we were nuts and we would act nuts. That made them feel good (Ibid.:74).

Another response to these problems was that most concluded that it was better to simply stay out of school than be victimized by the constant verbal assaults by their teachers, so they began skipping school, most as early as elementary school. This became a regular experience, one in which they found pleasure. Padilla observes that "during their adolescent years the institution of education and its agents, the administrators and teachers, were already experienced as antagonistic elements in their socialization rather than as facilitators of their goals" (Ibid.:78).

As Padilla found with Puerto Rican youths, Vigil notes that there was a conflict between the Mexican-American and white cultures that resulted in the marginalization of many youths. This conflict has created problems for

Mexican–American families, which in turn has meant that these families have lost some of their effectiveness as a social-control institution. As a result, schools and the police have taken over this function.

For gang members, a lack of strong attachment to the home and to the school has created an environment in which the gang provides answers. It is here, in the gang, where they associate and identify with similarly marginalized youths. Vigil comments that

> the gang has constituted a secondary "fringe" organization to resocialize members of the group to internalize and adhere to alternative norms and modes of behavior. Such gang patterns play a significant role in helping mainly troubled youth acquire a sense of importance, self-esteem, and self-identity. In short, rather than feeling neglected and remaining culturally and institutionally marginal, the gang members develop their own subcultural style to participate in public life, albeit a street one (Vigil, 1988:63–64).

Padilla's gang members indicate that one of the turning points in their lives came during high school. Prior to this time most of these youths were marginal members of the gang, engaged mostly in hanging out on the street corners or at school; "turning" (becoming regular and committed gang members) came during their early high school years. Throughout their elementary school years, most of the gang members referred to themselves as "neutrons"—that is, those with no affiliation to any of the many gangs within their neighborhood. However, this status was constantly being challenged by members of the various competing gangs. The punishment that they received from these gangs was aimed not so much to pressure them to turn but rather "to insure that they would remember the importance of remaining neutrons." Among gangs there is constant fear that these neutrons might become informants for another gang or, even worse, be informants for the police (Padilla, 1992:65). The decision to turn came rather informally without much thought. As one of Padilla's gang members put it,

> When I joined, like, four or five other guys that were like my neighbors, right there by the crib, they turned too, and we all joined at one time. Since we were friends we all decided to join—because we used to hang with the gang, but we were neutrons, and we just decided that we might as well become something since we hung out on the corner and gangbanged anyway, and so we just decided to go for it. We just did it just like that. We didn't think about it or think, "Wow, what is this?" We just slid into it (Ibid.:79).

While there are several specific reasons youths give for becoming gang members (to be discussed in the next section), the point here is that the process of becoming a gang member is a gradual learning process that occurs over a considerable period of time as youngsters become embedded in the subculture of the gang. Over time this street subculture has become an institutionalized or permanent fixture within many poor communities. The streets provide youths with networks of support that are not available to them in the family, the school, or the church.

Moore has noted that in cities where gangs have existed for a long time, they have become *quasi-institutionalized* (Moore, 1991:6). In this sense, some gangs have functioned to help "order adolescents' lives. They have provided outlets for sociability, for courtship, and other normal adolescent activities." More importantly, the legitimate institutions of socialization, such as schools and families, have become less important in their lives, and street socialization has begun to compete with, and often replace, these institutions (ibid.). She also found that, whereas in many communities gangs have disappeared as a result of the surrounding populations being integrated into the host culture (this happened with most of the gangs Thrasher studied), in many Chicano communities in Los Angeles constant immigration and the persistent problem of integrating the population into the mainstream mean that "the legitimate institutions remained comparatively marginal and the alternative structure—the gang—could become institutionalized" (ibid.).

Vigil describes the gang subculture as a *lifeway* for youths because early life experiences appear to be the most important determinants of whether one will become a gang member. Also, the existence of age-graded cliques means that "there is a place for everyone, even the youngest member" because this "allows for gang regeneration with the inclusion of each new generation" (Vigil, 1988:87).

About half of the gang members Vigil studied cited the important influence of a male relative who was, or had been, a gang member. This individual provided the youngster with an image or role model to emulate. Many wanted to follow in the footsteps of a relative. Brothers were especially important because they usually had lived under similar background circumstances and "it appeared that very little else was available to them except to follow suit" (ibid.:89). Sometimes youngsters followed a family tradition. Vigil quotes one gang member who related that, since his own father had been a Chino Sinner (the name of the gang), he would be, too, because "it's been in the culture of my family for years. It's kind of like when white boys are brought up to play football or something else" (ibid.).

The gang members Padilla studied gradually learned about different elements of the gang subculture throughout their youth. For example, many witnessed fights and learned that the way youths from different gangs settle their differences is by "throwing down" (fighting), especially if it was over their hood. As one member recalls, "To me the fights were started because some guy was in some neighborhood where he did not belong." What this youth learned was that the most important thing is one's neighborhood. "Youngsters learned to accept the neighborhood as something that was very personal, for its identity and character were believed to originate directly from all of its residents" and that "maintaining neighborhood social harmony was an essential responsibility of gang members" (Padilla, 1992:62–63).

As with any other subculture, the gang has many unique features that distinguish it from other groups. In many ways the typical behavior of gang members is identical to that of adolescents in general, such as hanging out, joking (including playing the "dozens," a game in which youths see who can come

up with the best ways of "putting down" other youths), seeking out the opposite sex, drinking, using drugs, and, of course, partying. Gang members, not
unlike other adolescent groups, want to distinguish themselves with their own
styles of dress, a certain kind of walk, a way of talking, and so on.

JOINING A GANG

There appear to be two major ways of considering the process of joining a
gang. On the one hand, as noted previously, most youths are informally socialized into the gang subculture from a very early age so that they do not so much
join a gang as evolve into the gang naturally. Actually turning or being jumped
is little more than a rite of passage. Conversely, many researchers have found
that there are often more formal mechanisms for joining the gang. In both cases
there is some degree of decisionmaking by the youths along the way. One does
not suddenly wake up on a Saturday morning in June and decide, "Hey, I think
I'll join a gang!" The point here is that it is a process that is very complex.

Jankowski (1990:37–62) offers perhaps one of the most detailed discussions
of the more formal processes whereby an individual is recruited by a gang and
why some individuals choose to join and others choose not to join. Jankowski
argues that kids join gangs for a variety of reasons, and a determining factor is
whether the gang wants a particular youth as a member. Thus there are two rational decisions: one by the potential member and the other by the gang itself.

Reasons for Deciding to Join a Gang

Jankowski notes that because gangs already exist in virtually all low-income
areas, the question facing a youth is not whether to start a gang but whether to
join one. However, many of the reasons why youths join gangs are the same reasons why gangs are initiated. Jankowski lists six main reasons for joining a gang:

1. *Material Reasons.* The most often-cited reason for joining a gang in
   Jankowski's study was that the youths believed that doing so would
   increase their chances of making money. They also believed that being in a
   gang meant not only a steady source of income but also assistance for their
   families in times of need. Thus the gang serves as both a bank and a social
   security system. One gang member stated that "they are there when you
   need them and they'll continue to be" (ibid.:42). Further, in pursuing
   various illegal ventures within the context of gang membership, they
   would not have to work quite as hard to earn money, and, moreover, the
   gang would provide a form of protection.

   In another study, Skolnick (1990:14) noted that "it now seems that
   youths are increasingly interested in joining the gang for the economic
   benefits conferred by such membership," especially the economic benefits
   of dealing in drugs. One of Skolnick's respondents (a prison inmate at the
   time of the interview) used this analogy in explaining the benefits of
   joining a gang: "[Being a gang member] is just an easier way to get in

[to drug dealing]. It's like if you going to get a job and you have a high school diploma. If you don't have one, you ain't goin' to get the job" (ibid.:16).

2. **Recreation.** The gang provides entertainment, not unlike a fraternity or a lodge (e.g., Elks, Masons, and others). While in the gang the individual has plenty of things to do, such as partying and meeting women. One member, talking about the gang he joined, said that "all the foxy ladies were going to their parties and hanging with them" (Jankowski, 1990:43). The gang also provides a source of drugs and alcohol. It must be stressed, however, that most of the gangs frown on members getting hooked on drugs or alcohol because they could then become unreliable to the organization.

3. **A Place of Refuge and Camouflage.** A gang provides its members with a cover and the protection of group identity. Some use the gang to hide from the police or others who may be after them. As one gang member put it, "It [the gang] gives me refuge until the heat goes away" (ibid.:44).

4. **Physical Protection.** Many dangers exist within low-income communities. There are predators everywhere. The gang provides some protection to its members. If one is in a gang, one does not have to be on the alert constantly and therefore can devote more time to pursuing illegal ventures. Vigil notes that the element of fear is paramount in many cases. He quotes a 14-year-old Latino who said, "It was either get your ass kicked every day or join a gang and get your ass kicked occasionally by rival gangs" (Vigil, 1988:154). In a study of the recruitment into African-American gangs in Chicago, Johnstone (1983) found that one of the variables most significantly related to joining a gang was that of being the victim of a crime. In comparing active members, new recruits, and youths who were not connected in any way to gangs, Johnstone found that both recruits and active members were far more likely to have been victims. This fact supports the notion that protection is an important reason for joining a gang, especially because there is so much intergang rivalry. Protection was also cited in a study by Hochhaus and Sousa (1988).

　　　Several of the gang members studied by Padilla reported that while in high school they encountered many rival gangs. Many of these rival gangs were in the same school primarily because of busing (see also Hagedorn, 1988, for a discussion of a similar phenomenon). Thus the school environment was tense. Members of different gangs were constantly harassing those who were neutrons, asking questions such as "Where do you live?" and "What you be?" or "What gang are you with?" Eventually many said, in effect, "If they are going to keep this up, I may as well turn!" (Padilla, 1992:82).

5. **A Time to Resist.** Joining a gang gives members an opportunity to resist becoming like their parents. That is, most members come from families whose parents are either unemployed or underemployed or, if employed, are trapped within the secondary labor market in dead-end jobs. Most

gang members "have lived through the pains of economic deprivation and the stresses that such an existence imposes on a family. They desperately want to avoid following in their parents' path, which they believe is exactly what awaits them." By joining a gang, the youth is able to resist and is able to say to society, in effect, that "I will not take these jobs passively" (ibid.:45). One gang member was quoted as follows: "My parents work real hard and they got little for it. . . . If I don't make it, at least I told the fuckers in Beverly Hills what I think of the jobs they left for me" (ibid.:46).

Jankowski makes an interesting point when he says that many wrongly believe that these youths are having problems forming an identity and that they join a gang to gain this. He states that, more than a new identity, these gang members simply want better living conditions.

6. **Commitment to Community.** In some communities gangs have existed for many generations, and in many ways belonging to a gang is seen as a commitment to one's own community. Such a desire represents a type of local patriotism. This is especially the case for Irish and Chicano gangs. Vigil and Long (1990), along with Moore (1988), have similarly noted that in some communities there are a few households or families with several generations of gang members: "In such households, one or both parents continue to participate more or less overtly in illicit activities while raising their children. Their children are thus virtually preselected to associate and unite with other troubled and disaffected barrio youths in emergent cliques, often at far younger than typical ages" (Vigil and Long, 1991:67). The same is often found in some African-American families (Bing, 1991).

Jankowski concludes that most gang members join gangs for a combination of one or more of the previously stated reasons. Whatever the specific reason(s) for joining, it was a well-thought-out decision, based on what these youths believed was in their own best interest at the time. The literature on gangs has cited other reasons youths join gangs. For example, Hochhaus and Sousa (1988) cite the need for companionship and excitement in addition to the need for protection. There may be several deep-seated, underlying motives for joining gangs: "Those who join gangs are struggling with the classic, desperate needs of adolescence: for an end to childhood; for acceptance as an adult; for sexual, social and economic identity; for status and success; for respect and a sense of belonging" (Reiner, 1992:22). They join gangs simply because the existing institutions of society that are supposed to meet many of these needs or provide opportunities to meet such needs—the family, the school, the church, the community—have become dysfunctional.

Gang Recruitment

Many gangs go through some process of recruitment, whereby new members are sought out. Gangs have their own reasons for accepting a new member.

Gangs also use one of a number of different recruitment strategies. Jankowski cites three of these:

1. **The Fraternity Type of Recruitment.** As a fraternity might do, the gang using this will present itself as an organization that is the "in" thing to belong to, that is hip or cool. It advertises through word of mouth. Usually there is a party, and potential members are invited, at which time gang members and potential members size each other up. The potential member is evaluated according to his potential as a good fighter, his courage, and his commitment to assist other gang members. The most important factor, however, is the potential gang member's ability as a fighter—more specifically, whether he will come through when the gang is threatened or whether he will turn tail and run off. If he is already known as a good fighter, then he will be admitted without further testing. However, if his reputation is not known, then his ability will be put to a test by having a member purposely pick a fight with him to see how he reacts. This becomes an initiation ritual (Jankowski, 1990:49–50). Some gangs also look for other skills, such as military skills (e.g., the ability to build incendiary bombs).

2. **The Obligation Type of Recruitment.** As implied by the term, the gang using this type of recruiting tries to convince the potential member that it is his duty to join. This is especially common in areas where gangs have existed for many generations and therefore where one must "uphold the tradition of the neighborhood." One potential member was told that he had an obligation to "give something back" to the community (ibid.:52). One member told a potential recruit that "I want you to know that your barrio needs you just like they needed us and we delivered" (ibid.). In some cases, if youths join a gang, some members of the community may help them find a job later. They are also told that women in the community look up to gang members; thus the recruit is promised access to many women. The prospective member is also told that if he fails to join, he will lose the respect of others in the community and even perhaps that of his own family (especially true for Chicanos and Irish).

3. **The Coercive Type of Recruitment.** This method of recruitment is used most often when gangs need more members quickly (not unlike a nation instituting a draft during a time of war). Often this is because a gang wants to expand some illegal operation into a new territory or wants to take over control of a new neighborhood not already under control of a gang. Other times it may be because the gang faces possible takeover from a rival gang.

   The types of coercion employed are both physical and psychological intimidation, the latter being the most preferred method. Typically, psychological intimidation involves threats to the individual or members of his family. Physical intimidation involves actual attacks on the individual or family members in addition to the destruction of personal property.

Additional Comments on Gang Recruitment

Fagan (1990) examined the various social processes within gangs that might influence the nature of the gang's structure and the extent of gang cohesion. Specifically, four processes were examined: the process of getting involved in the gang (e.g., being recruited by leaders, partying with members, hanging out), the reasons for joining the gang (e.g., status, protection from other gangs, a family feeling), violations that provoked sanctions (e.g., taking someone's woman, ripping off a fellow gang member), and sanctions (e.g., defending the gang's name, stealing for the gang) for breaking rules.

According to Fagan's research, there were no consistent recruitment patterns within any of these gangs. Few gang members reported that they were actively recruited by gang leaders, and the process of initiation into the gangs took many different forms. The most common reason they joined was that they had friends who were in the gang and they merely hung out with them on a regular basis. No specific reason was associated with any of the four types of gangs (social, party, serious delinquent, and organization—see Chapter 2).

Many gangs have developed somewhat elaborate rites of passage, or initiation ceremonies. Most of these rituals involve some form of physical confrontation with other members. Padilla describes one kind of initiation ritual with the Diamonds, the Puerto Rican gang he studied in Chicago. Known as the V-in, this initiation ritual is described by Padilla as a process that

> most poignantly demonstrates the kind of physical torture these young people are willing to suffer in order to "turn," that is, to become official members of the gang. Youngsters' willingness to undergo and endure this vicious physical onslaught suggests the high appraisal they give to the organization. The agonizing course these youngsters are determined to cross also points to the limited opportunities they believe to exist in the larger society. Members of the Diamonds have come to accept the idea that, since society cannot offer them the means with which they can make something positive of their lives, the physical punishment of the gang's violation ritual is not too big a price to pay. They have taken physical punishment before—it comes with living in the inner city—so, why not take more, particularly when it can open doors that have been shut to them during an entire lifetime? (Padilla, 1992:59).

However, as noted earlier, the initiation is merely a formal procedure and really the final stage of a long process of socialization into the gang subculture. The acceptance of the new members of this initiation rite follows several years of conditioning through a number of contacts with individual gang members. This results in a perception that the gang has something very positive to offer them, so that, as a result, they are willing to walk through the V-in line in order to become official members of the gang (ibid.:59–60).

Who Does Not Join a Gang?

Not everyone who grows up in an area where gangs flourish becomes a gang member. Why is this the case? Jankowski (1990) gives two answers to this crucial question. First, some youths see no advantage to joining a gang. These individuals constitute two groups: (1) those who possess all of the characteristics of defiant individualists but do not believe that being in a gang is to their advantage at the present time (most are already involved in illegal economic activity and see no advantage to joining but will eventually join at some point in the future) and (2) those who not only see no advantage to joining, but also see many disadvantages (e.g., the risks of going to prison would be too great). These individuals have usually developed their own strategies for escaping from their ghetto environment (some will try to escape via sports, get an education, or develop a legitimate skill). Jankowski maintains that these individuals do not possess all of the characteristics of the defiant individualist character structure. The second reason is that gangs do not want everyone who wants to be a member.

Despite popular beliefs, many youths who live in gang territories who are invited to join a gang and refuse for various reasons do not suffer any negative consequences. Huff's (1998) research on a sample of gang and nongang youth in several parts of the country found that of those who refused to join, fully two-thirds suffered no physical harm.

Jankowski suggests that there are seven possible outcomes for those who become gang members: (1) Some stay in the gang indefinitely, (2) some drop out and pursue illegal activities alone, (3) some move on to other organizations (e.g., Irish social clubs, organized crime), (4) some become involved with smaller organizations known as crews and continue to pursue illegal activity, (5) some end up doing long and/or frequent prison terms, (6) some die (e.g., from drugs, from violence, or merely from the risks of being in the lower class), or (7) some drop out of the gang and take the jobs and live the lifestyle they were originally trying to avoid (the most common outcome).

Most gang members will drift in and out of the gang most of their lives. Thus coming and going is a normal part of the gang organization. This leads us to consider some of the reasons why a member leaves or quits the gang and some of the processes of doing so.

LEAVING THE GANG

There has been a trend lately whereby an increasing number of gang members remain with the gang longer than normal, so that leaving the gang is becoming less and less common. Among the factors that account for this include a real increase in the age of the population, the changing structure of the economy resulting in the loss of millions of unskilled and semiskilled jobs, and increasing opportunities to commit crime, especially in the lucrative drug markets (Reiner, 1992:27).

As the study by Reiner notes, there is not a lot known about the process of leaving the gang, but many members do leave. There are any number of specific reasons: the influence of a girlfriend or adults, including parents; frequent arrests and incarceration (leading to burnout, or battle fatigue); a family move to another neighborhood or city; or a job (ibid.:26). The key seems to be the availability of jobs. As Reiner notes, "Nothing can make a young man quit before he is ready. But if no work is available at the critical moment, he may not quit even when he is ready" (ibid.). It is also important to note that the availability of illegal opportunities may cause one to leave the gang to pursue these sorts of activities. This method of leaving the gang is becoming increasingly popular.

Leaving the gang brings increased risks, as there is so much emphasis on loyalty within the gang. Leaving is often seen as betrayal. As noted by Padilla, one can get jumped out just as well as one can get jumped in. As will be described in a later section, the V-out is a common form of leaving the Diamonds (the Chicago gang Padilla studied).

The danger of leaving may actually be the greatest for those who have been the most successful and visible within the gang. As Reiner notes, "They cannot simply fade away unnoticed. Even if their colleagues acquiesce, they remain (not unlike gunfighters in the old west) prestigious targets for rival gangs—especially those looking to build a 'rep' " (ibid.:29). Gang members wishing to get out are often advised to begin engaging in other activities, such as getting a job, going back to school, starting a family, and so on. Such activities can provide a "graceful cover for gradually dropping out" of the gang. Conversely, youngsters can resist joining a gang by participating in such activities. In each case they can legitimately save face by telling gang members they do not have the time to participate (ibid.).

More recent research sheds new light on entering and leaving the gang. Decker and Lauritsen (1996) interviewed a group of 24 ex–gang members, asking them about why they left the gang. The most common reason (given by two-thirds of this group) was because of the level of violence they experienced. Many left because of direct experience as a victim. For many it was a rather sudden realization that, as one ex–gang member put it, "it wasn't my type of life. I didn't want to live that type of life" (Decker and Lauritsen, 1996:109). Another stated that he became concerned because many of his friends were getting killed and he might be next: "When I really woke up was when my friend died because we got in there together. . . . We was in the eighth grade together [and] freshman year" (ibid.:110–111). Another reason given was of "maturational reform," with one stating that he had two children to live for, while another stated that "I wasn't spending time with my daughter." This same person also stated that he obtained a job, which would help him take care of his daughter" (ibid.).

What is perhaps most interesting from the Decker and Lauritsen study was what they discovered when they asked these ex–gang members *how* they left the gang. Contrary to popular conceptions, most just simply quit and said that they did not have to give a reason to anyone. This should come as no surprise to experienced gang researchers, for it has been said all along that most gangs are very loosely organized, with few close ties, few formal rules, very little structure, and few formal leaders. Typical was one gang who responded to the question of "How did you leave?" with "I just walked away" (Decker and Lauritsen, 1996:113). A total of five of these 24 ex–gang members left by moving away. One moved from California to St. Louis.

Another interesting finding (paralleling Huff's research, noted above) is that most of the active gang members, when asked why others left the gang, mentioned the same reasons: violence, maturational reform, and just plain quitting. One respondent told the researchers that an ex-member left the gang because "One of they (sic) friends got killed." Another said an ex–gang member got his girlfriend pregnant and "he said fuck that shit [the gang]. I'm just going to lay low with my gal, I ain't got time for that" (ibid.:116).

These researchers conclude that while violence is a big part of gang life, there are contradictory consequences: "The very activity that often keeps gangs together appears to have provided the impetus for the majority in this sample to leave the gang" (ibid.:117). They suggest that gang prevention programs may want to seize the opportunity that presents itself when a gang member and/or someone close gets killed or seriously injured from an act of violence (ibid:121).

BELIEF SYSTEMS OF GANG MEMBERS

An important part of the gang subculture, as with other subcultures, is the belief and value system. There appear to be several core beliefs and values that tend to be most important in the lives of gang members. These include honor, respect, pride (in oneself and in one's neighborhood), reputation, recognition, and self-esteem. The respected gang member is often one who displays very noteworthy qualities, such as having courage, heart, and loyalty. Not unlike as with soldiers or comrades, one must prove oneself worthy to be a gang member.

Jankowski recognizes the importance of respect and honor among gang members. These two terms are not the same, however. The term *respect* is an active trait, something that needs to be earned by each gang member. Once a person has earned respect, it is up to him to protect it. In contrast, *honor* is a term most closely associated with Chicano gangs and is a passive trait that is automatically bestowed on Chicano gang members and as such is not something to be earned. Every Chicano youth enters the gang with honor, "whereupon they must guard against it being taken away through the actions of others" (Jankowski, 1990:142). Honor is extremely important to a Chicano gang member because it is linked to his entire family. In other words, the gang member must protect both his own honor and the honor of his family.

Horowitz (1983b:22–23) furthers this concept by suggesting that honor is based on others' evaluations of one's actions, especially the style of one's actions. Honor relates to the person's self, and it "sensitizes an individual to violations of his person that are interpreted as derogations of fundamental properties of self" (ibid.). For the middle-class person, an action such as staring (known in gang terminology as "mad-doggin' ") is at best a violation of good manners; from the perspective of the gang subculture, it may be seen as an attempt to demean the individual, thus requiring some form of action (e.g., a fight).

In a study of gangs in Los Angeles, Reiner suggests that, like other subcultures that appeal to young people,

> gangs offer a distillation of the dark side of adolescent rebellion. . . . Their revolt is total; it confronts and confounds adult authority on every level—sex, work, power, love, education, language, dress, music, drugs, alcohol, crime, violence. As icons of popular culture, gangs not only represent a powerful group identity utterly inaccessible to adults, they are surrounded with an appealing aura of outlaw danger. That the boring, brutish reality of gang life rarely matches the fantasy does not diminish the power of the myth (Reiner, 1992:30).

Gang members often emphasize a core of values that "require physical, verbal and behavioral expression. The uniformity of style within most gangs is far from accidental. It reflects deliberate emphasis on group unity and a clear demarcation between those who belong and those who do not" (ibid.:30–31). Other important values for gang members include friendship, manliness, and hedonism. Vigil and Long (1990) note that the cholo subculture emphasizes the importance of friendship. To most gangs, the ideal man is one similar to the gunfighter of the Old West, "a two-fisted, hard-drinking, dangerous man who is quick to avenge any insult; he lives and dies by violence, with his exploits rousing fear and respect in the hearts of men—and, in the hearts of women, fear and desire" (Reiner, 1992:34).

A sense of wildness and locura (craziness) are often admired as ideal characteristics. As Vigil and Long note, most gang members on occasion act in a muy loco (very crazy) fashion in an attempt to deter would-be attacks or to merely intimidate others. Many gangs, however, have a few members who are described as vatos locos (wild and crazy guys), who too often start trouble and therefore become a liability to the gang (Vigil and Long, 1990:64).

Every gang Jankowski (1990) studied had some form of ideology, which consisted of a set of beliefs that gave members (1) a worldview, (2) an interpretation of this world, and (3) a justification for the superiority of this worldview.

There was also an organizational ideology that was concerned with issues of unity and the question of identity. In order to deal with a group of defiant individualists, the gang had to develop a brotherhood ideology that strongly emphasized the idea that all members are brothers, or members of a family. The Chicanos have been the most successful at this with their use of the word *homeboys.* Jankowski did not notice this form of ideology in any of the other gangs. The others, more often than not, paid only lip service to this ideology.

Jankowski found the existence of a great deal of internal social conflict in most gangs. This conflict, argues Jankowski, helps the gang legitimize itself as an organization. Internal fighting, for example, causes others to mediate, which in turn usually leads to closer bonding and also adds to social control. This conflict aids in internal control by providing mechanisms for venting frustrations, often in the form of a scapegoat (e.g., another gang could be blamed for a problem).

Some gangs may operate in a manner not unlike private governments. Whether they operate in a democratic or dictatorial way depends on the type of leadership structure they have. The most democratic is the horizontal/commission style. It resembles the New England town meeting. Few gangs with this type of structure last for very long. The leadership form is adopted as a compromise in an effort to save the gang rather than as a commitment to the model itself.

Jankowski found that the next most democratic was the vertical/hierarchical structure. Leaders of these gangs have good political skills. They have many of the traits described by Machiavelli (1950) as necessary to be good leaders. Once this type of person becomes a leader, three factors are needed for him to maintain power: (1) meeting the needs and desires of the rank and file (e.g., by building a group of loyal supporters [a "court"] and by building a staff to perform routine duties); (2) showing flexibility in handling problems, such as dissent, and doing so without appearing weak; and (3) being prudent in the administration of justice (knowing how much punishment is appropriate).

The least democratic is the influential model. This type of gang is described as dictatorial.

Jankowski concludes by suggesting that if gangs fail to maintain some sort of structure, they will wither away. Groups that have loose structures are in a pre-gang state, and they will not last very long unless they become more structured.

A CASE EXAMPLE: THE CODE
OF THE STREETS

In a fascinating study, Anderson (1994) explores what he calls "the code of the streets," based on his observations of ghetto streets over several years. He echoes Cohen, Thrasher, and many others when he notes that in such poor environments the negative influences are everywhere and have become part of an oppositional culture, which he refers to as "the streets." The street subculture contains norms opposed to those of mainstream society. This culture is in direct contrast to what inner-city residents refer to as "decent" families who are "committed to middle-class values." The existence of such an oppositional culture means that even those youths from "decent" homes "must be able to handle themselves in a street-oriented environment." The parents of such youths actually encourage them to at least become familiar with these norms (ibid.:82). One of the main reasons behind this is that the street culture has created a "code of the streets" or a "set of informal rules governing interpersonal public behavior, including violence. The rules prescribe both a proper comportment and a proper way to respond if challenged. They regulate the use of violence and so allow those who are inclined to aggression to precipitate violent encounters in an approved way" (ibid.).

The heart of the code is respect, which is defined as being treated right, or with proper deference. Unfortunately, the precise definition is not consistent. Moreover, respect is something that is "hard-won but easily lost," and thus one must be ready to guard against its being taken away. If one has respect, then one can go about one's business without being bothered by others. But if one is "bothered" in public, it means that one may not only be in physical danger but be disgraced, or, as in current slang, one has been "dissed," or disrespected. While many of the examples of what constitutes dissin' (e.g., maintaining eye contact for too long) may seem trivial to middle-class people, to those involved in the subculture of the gang these events are of major importance. Why is this so? Anderson suggests that the reason can be found in the fact that so many inner-city African-Americans (especially the young) feel totally alienated from mainstream society and its institutions. The code is nothing more than a subcultural adaptation to the lack of faith in the justice system (especially the police), which they believe does not respect or protect them. Many residents have taken on the responsibility of protecting themselves from those who would violate them. The code of the streets, therefore, takes over where the police and judicial system end.

Anderson distinguishes between two polar extremes among families in the inner city—the decent and the street family, titles used by residents themselves. (They may even exist simultaneously within the same family.) The decent families accept mainstream values and try to instill them in their children. Most are among the working poor, and they place a high value on hard work and self-reliance. They want their children to stay in school and better themselves. They tend to be strict parents and warn their children to be on the lookout for bad people and bad situations.

In contrast, street parents tend to show a lack of consideration for others and are often unable to cope with the demands of parenthood. They strongly believe in the code and try to instill it in their children. Their lives are often disorganized, and they often engage in self-destructive behavior, largely as a result of their lowly status and their frustration over bills, lack of jobs and food, and so on. Many of the women get involved in drugs and abusive relationships with men. They often become bitter and angry, and they have short fuses, causing them to lash out at anybody who irritates them (ibid.:83).

The women (too often at home with children and no man in the house) can be very aggressive with their children, yelling and striking at them with little or no explanation. Such verbal and physical punishment teaches children a lesson: "that to solve any kind of interpersonal problem one must quickly resort to hitting or other violent behavior." These mothers may love their children, but this is the only way they know how to control them. Many of these women believe, for example, that there is a "devil in the boy" and that this must be "beaten out of him" or that "fast girls need to be whupped" (ibid.)

The children are often ignored by their mothers, and so they often learn to fend for themselves at a very early age. They become children of the street, and, as a popular saying goes, they "come up hard" (this has also been noted by Vigil, 1988). Many become employed by drug dealers and learn to fight at an early age. In such environments, says Anderson, these children learn that might makes right and that in order to protect oneself "it is necessary to marshal inner resources and be ready to deal with adversity in a hands-on way. In these circumstances physical prowess takes on great significance" (Anderson, 1994).

In the most extreme cases, a street-oriented mother may leave her children alone for several days. This is most common among women with drug and/or alcohol problems (especially crack addicts). For these children, a very harsh lesson is learned: "Survival itself, let alone respect, cannot be taken for granted; you have to fight for your place in the world" (ibid.:86).

Beginning at a very early age, these children begin to hang out on the streets. After school they will come home, then walk right out the door and spend the afternoons and evenings (often as late as 9 or 10 p.m.—much later for teenagers) on the streets with their peers. Children from decent homes are more closely supervised, with curfews imposed on them and lessons given by their parents on how to avoid trouble. When children from decent families meet children from street families, there is always tension and a social shuffle in which the decent children are tempted. Their choice depends on how well they have already been socialized by their parents. Street children rarely develop the values of decent families; when they do it is almost always from sources in another setting, such as church or school, and often as a result of involvement with a caring adult (ibid.).

In the street these children continually witness disputes, and the resolution of such disputes reinforces the might-makes-right belief already mentioned. They see that "one child succumbs to the greater physical and mental abilities of the other. . . . In almost every case the victor is the person who physically won the altercation, and this person often enjoys the esteem and respect of onlookers." The children learn that "toughness is a virtue, while humility is not" (ibid.).

While growing up, these children get these messages reinforced verbally by other family members, neighbors, and friends. They are told "Watch your back," "Don't punk out," and "If someone disses you, you got to straighten them out." Some parents even impose sanctions if their children do not live up to these norms. "Don't you come in here crying that somebody beat you up; you better get back out there and whup his ass. If you don't whup his ass, I'll whup your ass when you come home." Even some decent parents give similar warnings about the need for self-defense.

Although youths are ambivalent about fighting, they feel pressured to fight by the code. "Looking capable of taking care of oneself as a form of self-defense is a dominant theme among both street-oriented and decent adults who worry about the safety of their children" (ibid.).

The essence of the code centers around the presentation of self. The major requirement is to prove to others that one is willing and able to use violence and that one can take care of oneself. One communicates this message through facial expressions and a certain way of walking and talking (including the words one selects). Physical appearance is also important—jewelry, certain kinds of clothing (jackets, sneakers, and so on), and the way one is groomed. In order to be respected, one must have the right look (ibid.:88).

There are always going to be challenges to one's respect, or "juice" (as it is often called). If one is assaulted or otherwise challenged, one must avenge oneself. According to the code, maintaining one's honor or respect is crucial, and to do this it is necessary to show others one cannot be messed with or dissed.

There is much pressure from peers to wear the right kind of clothing, jewelry, and so on (especially the most expensive items), and if a person displays these things he is likely to be robbed by someone who wants what he has. Yet if he does not wear the right stuff, then he may be teased by others or even assaulted. Not having the right stuff is often translated into being socially deficient (ibid.).

By obtaining material things, one improves one's identity, but such an identity is very delicate, which results in a "heightened sense of urgency to staying even with peers, with whom the person is actually competing." One is able to maintain respect mostly by displaying one's possessions. However, the precariousness of such an identity means one must constantly be involved in maintaining it and is thus very prone to deal violently with even a minor slight or put-down (ibid.).

Stealing from others, the ability to get in someone's face, to dis someone, and to take away another person's honor or someone else's girlfriend are methods of enhancing one's own worth. In other words, according to the code one must often put someone else down in order to feel up. These are trophies showing others one is important (not unlike professional people showing off their awards, degrees, certificates, and so on indicating that they too have made it), and it is important to note that the open display of these trophies can provoke others into challenges. "This game of who controls what is thus constantly being played out on inner-city streets, and the trophy—extrinsic or intrinsic, tangible or intangible—identifies the current winner" (ibid.:89).

There is a widespread feeling that within this environment there is little respect available and thus "everyone competes to get what affirmation he can of the little that is available." These individuals crave affirmations, and a show of deference can enhance one's self-esteem tremendously. If one violates another and there is no response, it merely encourages further violations against that person. Thus one must be constantly on guard against not only direct violations but even the appearance of potential violation. This is especially true among teenagers, whose self-esteem is by definition already vulnerable.[2] There are many young males who so desperately want respect that they are willing to die in order to maintain it (ibid.).

The issue of self-respect is therefore important to understand, for it is related to the extent to which a young person has the potential for violence. Most individuals in mainstream society are able to retreat and not seek revenge against an attack, for they have enough self-esteem from other sources (e.g., education, jobs, and family). For inner-city youths, however, other sources of self-esteem are absent; thus they have to seek revenge (even going so far as to enlist the aid of relatives or fellow gang members).

The concept of manhood within this subculture is defined in terms of concerns over one's identity and self-esteem. To be a man within this subculture is to be concerned with one's level of respect. But the irony (a "chicken-and-egg" aspect) is that a person's safety is more apt to be threatened in public because manhood is associated with respect. Manhood and respect, therefore, are two sides of the same coin—"physical and psychological well-being are inseparable, and both require a sense of control, of being in charge" (ibid.). In short, being a man means being in control, in charge. This is not to say that within middle- and upper-class society being a man does not mean the same basic thing; the main difference (which Anderson does not mention) is that within the inner city it comes down to the physical aspect of this equation and that so much violence is involved (stemming from the fact that there are few nonviolent means to maintain respect and to prove that one is a real man).

One major assumption is that every man should know this code. Thus even the victim of a mugging who does not act according to the code may cause the mugger to feel justified in killing him and feeling no remorse. After all, the mugger reasons, this person "should have known better" (ibid.:89). Because even youths from decent families are familiar with the code, they too may have to resort to violence to defend their honor or respect.

One of the core beliefs associated with this concept of manhood is that one of the best ways of gaining respect (therefore proving one is a real man) is to exhibit nerve. The concept of nerve refers to the ability to take someone else's possessions, mess with someone's woman, get in someone's face, or fire a weapon. The show of nerve, however, is a very forceful method of showing disrespect—it can very easily offend others and result in retaliation (ibid.:92).

SOCIAL CONTROL IN THE GANG

One of the unique functions of gangs is that they tend to provide a great deal of structure for members. Indeed, most gang members get from gangs something sorely missing from their families—consistent rules and sanctions. The effects of various economic hardships experienced by barrio and ghetto inhabitants have undermined traditional social institutions, which are supposed to provide social control. Over time in these barrios and ghettos the streets and older street youths have become primary agents of socialization (Moore, 1991:137–138). According to Vigil (1988:12), the gang has become "a type of street social control institution by becoming in turn a partial substitute for family (providing emotional and social support networks), school (giving instructions on how to think and act), and police (authority and sanctions to enforce adherence to gang norms)."

Jankowski (1990) has argued that gangs are formal and cohesive organizations. Jankowski further argues that they have developed systematic methods of control and recruitment. All but one of the gangs Jankowski studied were very cohesive, largely because of the establishment of mechanisms for control. (The gangs who disappeared had lost these mechanisms.) Control was maintained through the use of both formal and informal codes and by reference to a particular ideology.

Formal codes (22 of the 37 gangs Jankowski studied had such codes) pertain to the following six areas: (1) regulatory behavior (e.g., fighting with one another); (2) personal relations between members and female relatives and lovers of other members (this was the most sensitive issue); (3) behavior of members while in the clubhouse (e.g., violence, use of drugs); (4) heroin use; (5) leaders abusing power; and (6) punishment for various offenses (i.e., what types of punishment are most appropriate). Informal codes consist of unwritten norms everyone is expected to follow, including being respectful to other members and observing dress codes.

Fagan's (1990) study of four types of gangs in Chicago, Los Angeles, and San Diego found that the most common violations that would provoke sanctions were to rip off a gang member and to snitch on a gang member. The two most delinquent gangs (the serious and the organization gang types) were the most likely to have specific sanctions for violating rules. The most common included having to fight another member of the gang and getting beat up by other gang members. Yet fewer than one-half of the respondents agreed with any of these sanctions (the highest percentage was 47.5).

A Puerto Rican gang in Chicago (heavily involved in the selling of drugs) studied by Padilla has developed some very strict rules, and the penalties are often harsh. If an individual ventures out on his own, he risks avoidance by the gang if he should get arrested—in this case, they will not come to bail him out, as they would if he were still part of the gang. One of the penalties involved what they called the violation ceremony, or simply the V. This involves using violence against members as a form of punishment for rules violations. One specific ceremony is the V-out penalty, which is used when a member who is leaving the gang knows a lot about the gang's drug-dealing operations. The V-out is also used against those "who have been nothing but trouble for the gang"—that is, they have been constant troublemakers and have not been committed team players (Padilla, 1992:56–57). There is also a V-in ceremony, used as part of the initiation ritual for new members (see Padilla, 1992:105).

GANG MEMBERS AND THEIR FAMILIES

A study by one of our coauthors (Brown, 1998) provides some rare glimpses into the complex world of gang members and their families. The data are taken from interviews, discussion, and observations of 79 African-American gang members and 68 of their parents/guardians, in Detroit.

Most of the participants in Brown's study lived in apartments (77 percent) and houses (18 percent) that would be targets for condemnation in many of Detroit's surrounding suburbs. Only 29 percent of the gang members lived in households where both parents were present. About 40 percent lived in family environments characterized by the presence of a female single parent, 13 percent lived with their grandparent(s), and the remainder lived either with their father, sister, brother, or friend. Four gang members lived, as one participant described, "wherever I can." Often, this means, "today a friend's house, and tomorrow a drug house."

In about three-fourths of the dual-parent households, both parents were employed. In these households, the parent's combined, "before-taxes," weekly incomes amounted to less than $475. Part-time jobs, paying minimum wages without benefits, were common among the participants. They are what Harrington (1984) called the "working poor." Of the 31 female single-parent households, 58 percent of those women were unemployed. Considering all of the single- and dual-parent households participating in this study, 63 percent had only part-time jobs.

The families in this study had no material luxuries. One father of four, wearing the scars of rejection and humiliation, stated:

> We ain't got much of anything anymore, but maybe we're luckier than some I guess. I worked at Chrysler for eight years, but they laid me off four years ago. They never did hire none of us back. I tried finding another job like that one but I never did get one. There just weren't none to be had. Now I'm just good for laboring I guess.

Holding his wife's hand (she works in a laundry for minimum wages), he looked up and said, "Me and this old woman is about wore down now." His wife in an attempt to lighten the subject and offer inspiration for her husband, said, "When they build that new stadium (Detroit Tigers' baseball stadium) here you can make some money then. Well," he replied, "they is just going to hire us niggers for the laboring jobs, so don't go counting on that new stadium to help us none."

The father of another gang member has two full-time, minimum-wage jobs. His wife works part-time; they have three children. "I've tried to get me a full-time job," she stated, "but they ain't none around here. We only got one car, and he's (husband) got to use it because his other job is a long way from the shop."

One mother of four, whose husband had abandoned her and the children several years earlier, lives in a deteriorating two-bedroom apartment with an inefficient heating system. During one visit I heard gun shots very close by. I jerked my head toward the window. Obviously accustomed to the sound, she never moved. We began talking about the subject of "hope." This woman revealed,

> I used to think about the future all the time; that was before my husband lost his job. He started drinking heavy when he couldn't find no work. Then one day he just got up and left me and these kids. I used to think someday I'd have me a house and plant a garden. I love fresh tomatoes. I wanted my kids to get what I never got—a house of their own and a good education. Well, those times is gone now. I don't think much about what they ain't got because the biggest trouble is just feeding them mouths and having them a place to sleep . . . . We mange though, but it sure ain't easy none. I ask the Lord for some help everyday. Guess He is listening because we still got a roof over our head and something to eat.

Thus there is a sense of resignation and a feeling that her life could be worse. When asked why she never left the neighborhood, she said:

Where do you want me to go live? I ain't got no other place to live. I ain't got no skills to get no job—at least one that can pay the bills. The only real job I ever had was working downtown once, but downtown is all gone now. Do you know someone who's going to help some old black woman with no education and has four kids? I sure don't. I live here because this is all there is.

Ten gang members live in households where a grandparent is the primary breadwinner. In eight of these cases, most of the family income comes from social security and/or very modest retirement benefits. Rather than the elderly being assisted by their children, many grandparents find themselves in a position where they must raise a second family. One elderly woman, who has lived in the same neighborhood for more than 40 years, shares her two-bedroom house with her daughter-in-law, three grandchildren, and Boots, the family feline. Rags are stuffed around the windows to fill gaps that run her heating bill "through the ceiling." The middle step leading to the front door is broken. She leans back in an overstuffed chair, once belonging to her husband who died more than 10 years ago, and started to talk about her "boys" who are both in prison.

Both my boys is in prison, and Bobby's[3] [name of one son] wife and kids stay here with me because they can't live no other place. What they going to do? I can't work no more because I got a bad leg, and besides, who's going to hire an old black woman anyhow? I get my check [social security]. Kathy gets some money from the state; it sure ain't much. She can't work because she's got these kids to take care of. I help take care of them, but I'm old and can't do it by myself. Besides there ain't no jobs around here and we ain't got no car. We are doing the best we can do. I don't know what's going to happen to us. Engler [governor of Michigan] say he's going to cut welfare some more. If he do then I don't know what's going to happen. Sometimes I think that dying is about all that's left to do. But who is going to help Kathy with them kids if I ain't here? That oldest boy is a handful now. He's good to me and his mother though. He runs wild but I understand. He ain't got much else to do. There ain't no job for him. I worry about him all the time. He going to end up like his daddy—in prison some day. It's going to happen I tell you.

Bobby, who once was a member of a gang in this neighborhood, was prosecuted and convicted on auto theft and drug charges. He received 5 years and 15 years (consecutive) sentences. Brown asked the woman about her husband and she replied:

Them boys' daddy was a good man. He bought this house for us when he worked at General Motors. We had a real good life then. Well, he killed himself off working all kinds of jobs when he got laid off from the plant. He managed to pay for this house before he died—God, bless him. My boys was always mad about what happened to their daddy. Now I see

Johnny mad about his daddy being taken away from him. He's running with the same crowd his daddy ran with.

All adult family member participants expressed concern about their children's, or grandchildren's, involvement in youth gangs. Most attempted to control their children's activities. "I tell him all the time to stay away from them kind of kids," says one mother. A father states, "I don't like him running wild out there, but we [including his wife] both got jobs. We just can't watch him all the time." Another concerned parent said,

> I do the best I can do to get him stay in school. I work hard, but, as you can see, I don't seem to get nowhere. He's not dumb. He can see that this family is never going to get ahead. He respects me and his little sister, but he knows that what I am doing ain't getting his family nowhere.

One father admitted, "I beat the hell out of him when I found out he was banging. But he keeps right on doing it. I can't just keep beating him—then they'll come and arrest me." Another father stated, "I try to tell him that he's going to end up dead or in prison some day. He just won't listen. I want him to get a job, but there ain't none around. I'm lucky to be working myself." One grandmother said,

> I know he is in a gang. I ain't dumb. But I also know that until all them kids lay down them guns then he's got to protect himself somehow. The police sure ain't going to protect him none. Those who is blaming the parents for these here gangs don't know much about life down here. We have to survive however we can. Them kids is surviving the only way they knows how to survive. They're just kids you know.

The parents and guardians who participated in Brown's study did not want their children to join youth gangs, nor did they encourage their children to sustain membership in the gang. Many parents actively attempted to discourage their children's gang involvement. They were, however, attempting to raise their children under conditions with gross limitations. Like their children, they too are realists. They realize their children's life chances outside the gang and outside the inner city are limited. This realization comes, in part, from their own futile attempts to forge a better life. Their children join gangs for a variety of reasons, and there are an equal number of reasons why those children sustain their memberships.

Racial discrimination is a crucial factor that must be addressed in any analysis of inner city youth gangs; the impact of racism affects not only the parents/guardians but their children as well. Racism ensures that many of these families will remain confined to the poverty-stricken areas of Detroit. Whether it is the not-so-subtle redlining that has plagued much of Detroit or the overt demonstrations of racial discriminations by suburban police officers, one thing is clear—most will not escape the poverty of this city. The responses to racial

discrimination by parents/guardians and their children may differ, but the pain
of racism remains the same.

GANG GRAFFITI AND TATTOOS

As unique subcultures, gangs can be described as exaggerated versions of normal adolescent groupings. As every parent knows, adolescents have a need to
create their own unique world, separate and distinct from the adult world. In so
doing they often devise elaborate methods of distinguishing themselves and devise their own methods of communication. Modes of dress and the words used
to communicate help them draw the line between themselves and adults. With
gangs there is the added attraction of two unique forms of communication—
graffiti and tattoos.

Graffiti is the primary form of communication used by gangs today, although historically a wide variety of groups have used graffiti. Not all graffiti is the product of gangs. As several studies have shown, many respectable
artists began with graffiti. The goal of such artwork (e.g., that displayed in
many New York City subways) is to establish an individual artist's reputation
and to display one's own style of art (Hutchinson, 1993:139). In contrast, the
purpose of gang graffiti is usually (but not always) to expand the reputation
of the gang rather than that of an individual. Gangs use graffiti to identify
their existence (to tell others who they are), to mark a specific area as their
turf (e.g., by writing on a wall, a building, or other structure), to challenge
rival gangs, and to commemorate members who have died in battles (it is
common for gang members to draw the letters "RIP" [rest in peace] on a
wall or other structure, along with the name of the deceased). Graffiti can be
used as a "newspaper of the street" (Fradette, 1992:1) or a "poor people's
memo."

Gang graffiti may be viewed as a form of artistic expression because it follows established styles and makes use of sophisticated principles of graphic design (Hutchinson, 1993:139–140). There is a consistency in style in much of
the gang graffiti today. The style of gang graffiti in Los Angeles, for example,
especially the form of lettering used, is quite similar to the styles used in the
1960s. Much of it, in fact, has been appropriated by commercial artists and the
adolescent subculture in general (ibid.).

Tattoos serve a similar purpose. The use of tattoos is ancient in origin and
is not limited to gang members or even to criminals in general. It is very popular among many segments of the population (at the present time it can be
seen on many youths who are not in any way affiliated with gangs or any other
deviant group). For years it has been used by men in the military. In gangs tattoos are a form of identification and communication, mostly to indicate to
others the gang or set to which one belongs. In addition to the gang name or
initials (or perhaps in place of the gang name) may be the gang logo (usually
some type of symbols, such as a pitchfork, crown, stars, dots, and so on).

FIGURE 3.1 Graffiti of the Cash Flow Posse (left). The teepee (middle) signifies the Folks nation.

Photo by William B. Brown

Purposes and Styles of Graffiti

Modern gang graffiti takes on a variety of styles and serves several different purposes. One of the most common styles is the use of large block lettering. This is especially common when writing the name or initials of the gang. Figure 3.1 contains a photograph of gang graffiti in Detroit, Michigan.[4] This photo represents graffiti of a gang called the Cash Flow Posse (part of the Folks nation). Their initials (CFP) are shown on the left, the drawing in the middle that looks like a teepee stands for the Folks nation, and the words *Cash Flow* appear in block letters on the far right.

Graffiti can be classified into several different types, which include the following:

1. ***Identifying the Neighborhood of the Gang.*** Usually graffiti will identify a neighborhood, or varrio (*barrio* is Spanish for neighborhood; *varrio* is slang for *barrio*), often by merely the letter *V* or *B*.

    One example was found in a suburb of Los Angeles, the city of La Puente, where *VP-13* was used to identify a local gang. The *13* refers to the 13th letter of the alphabet, or *M,* and within the gang subculture has normally referred to Sur, or Southern, California. This method of gang reference is believed to have originated with prison gangs in California as a way to distinguish gangs in the southern part of the state from those in the northern part. (The number *14* stands for the 14th letter of the

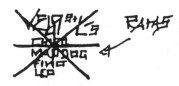 

FIGURE 3.2 Crossed-out graffiti in Los Angeles, indicating intragang conflict.
National Law Enforcement Institute, 1992:28.

alphabet, or *N,* and refers to Norte, or Northern, California.) A variation of this usage is to place the word *barrio* or *varrio* before, after, or in the middle of the gang name. For example, a gang in south-central Los Angeles located in the area of Grape Street is known as Watts Varrio Grape. Another example is illustrated as follows:

BHGR
POS
-13-
L's

In this illustration, on the first line the *B* stands for Barrio, the *HG* stands for the name of the gang (in this case Hawaiian Gardens City), and the *R* is street slang for Rifa, or to rule, control, or reign. In other words, this gang is making a statement that they control or rule this specific area. (In reality this is typically an exaggerated boast, as they do not literally control every aspect of the entire area. They are claiming to be the only gang in this area and declaring that other gangs should stay out.) On the second line the letters *POS* stand for the actual clique from this gang, in this case the Pequeños. The *13* stands for Southern California (as noted previously) and the *L's* stands for another gang slang—Vatos Locos— meaning crazy ones or brave ones (the Spanish term *loco* is often used to mean wild and crazy).

2. ***Making Certain Pronouncements.*** Gangs use graffiti to communicate with one another. One of the most common messages is to use the letter *R* (see previous example) or to simply write out the words *Rifa, Rifan,* or *Rifamos,* followed or preceded by the name of the gang. One of the most common pronouncements is to challenge or to show disrespect for a rival gang. Often gang members will travel into a rival's territory and cross out graffiti of the rival. (The police study this process to measure the extent of conflict between gangs or to predict a pending battle.) An example is noted in Figure 3.2.

A variation of this is the targeting of a rival gang for retaliation. Figure 3.3 illustrates this (the number *187* stands for the California Penal Code number for murder and is often used by gangs in their graffiti to target a rival).

FIGURE 3.3 Targeting a specific gang for retaliation.
National Law Enforcement Institute, 1992:28.

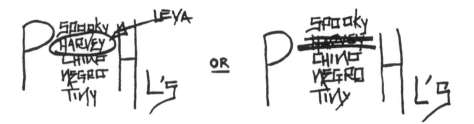

FIGURE 3.4 Putting down one of your own members for violating a gang rule.
National Law Enforcement Institute, 1992:28.

Sometimes a gang will put down one of their own members, as when they write the word Leva next to a member's name. This means that the member is being given the silent treatment because of associating with another gang, talking bad about the gang, or some other infraction. (As noted in a previous section, gangs have some very strict rules, and violators are punished.) An example of this is shown in Figure 3.4.

3. ***Commemorating the Dead.*** Gangs often provide methods of grieving for fellow members who have died. Death is an ever-present reality for gang members, and much of their graffiti is used to commemorate their fallen brothers. Figure 3.5 shows an example of this, as the Cash Flow Posse of Detroit is commemorating Lil'Joe. Printing the letters RIP (rest in peace) is a common method of honoring the dead on walls and buildings in their neighborhood. Also common is the drawing of a flower (shown here in the middle of the photograph).

4. ***Using Numbers.*** Much gang graffiti involves the use of various kinds of abbreviations, typically letters or numbers that stand for something related to the gang. The numbers may be in English, in Spanish, or roman numerals or a combination of these. Numbers usually refer to a specific street where most of the gang members live. This becomes part of the actual gang name, such as 18th Street or XVIII Street. A variation is to replace numbers with words, especially common among African-American gangs. Thus, the numbers *1, 2,* and *3* are replaced by *Ace, Deuce*

FIGURE 3.5 Commemorating the dead. The Village Boyz. Detroit, Michigan.
Photo by William B. Brown.

(often written as Duce), and *Trey* (or Tray). In Los Angeles, for example, 73rd Street is written as 7 Trey St., and 101st Street is written as 10 Ace St. Specific examples are Eight Tray Gangster Crips (found on 83rd Street), Eleven Deuce Crips (located on 112th Street), and Ace Deuce Crips (found on 12th Street).

5. ***Subgroups, Cliques, and Sets.*** Gangs are often subdivided into age-graded cliques or sets, and graffiti often reflects this. For example, *TDS* would stand for the Tiny Dukes (a younger version of the Dukes gang), *MLS* would refer to the Midget Locos, and *LL* or *LxL* would stand for Little Locos. Also, Spanish names differentiate male from female gangs—thus *Chicos* = male, and *Chicas* = female.

6. ***Location.*** The location or turf of a gang is often extremely important. Gangs often identify with either a small area (e.g., a housing project or a park) or a very large area within a city. Typically they use names like *West, Westside, South, Southside, North,* and so on to refer to a wide area of a city. Then they will follow this location with the actual name of the gang itself. A common method is to use letters to stand for the location, or the side, of the area within which they are located. Thus the symbol *n/s* or *n* will stand for the northside, and *s/s* or *s* will stand for the southside. This notation will be followed by an abbreviation of the gang name. Some

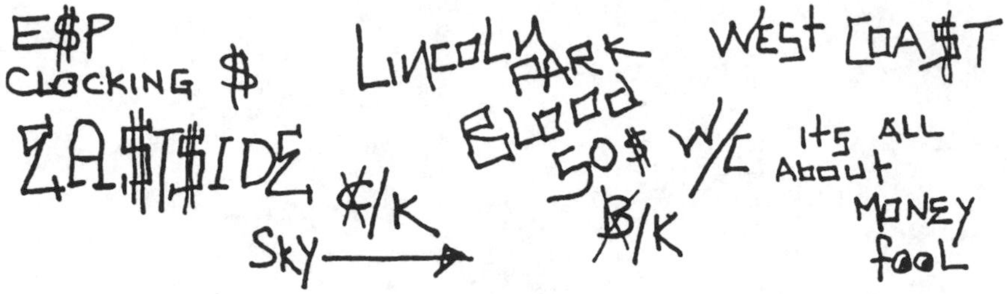

FIGURE 3.6 Examples of African-American gang graffiti.

National Law Enforcement Institute, 1992:29

examples are as follows: w/s V13 = Venice 13, a gang on the westside of Los Angeles within the city of Venice near 13th Street; e/s BP (Eastside Baldwin Park) and n/s BP (Northside Baldwin Park) are two rival gangs within the same city. Often, as in the Baldwin Park example, landmarks are used to differentiate east and west and north and south. These can be streets, canals, rivers, freeways, railroad tracks, and, in Los Angeles, washes (dry riverbeds). For example, the Harbor Freeway in Los Angeles separates east from west for African-American gangs. In Las Vegas, I-15 separates the West Coast Bloods from the East Coast Bloods.

7. *African-American Gang Graffiti.* Gangs of different racial and ethnic groups have their own unique style of graffiti. In the case of African-American gangs, there are noteworthy differences between the Crips and the Bloods. Crip gangs often use the word *Cuz* or *Cuzz* as a salutation. They also use the letters *BK* (often written as B/K), which stand for Blood Killer. Blood gangs will use the letters *CK,* which stand for Crip Killer. Both gangs often refuse to use the letters that stand for their rivals. Thus, for example, a Blood gang from the Citrus Heights suburb of Sacramento will call themselves Bitrus Heights (replacing the *C,* which stands for Crips, with a *B*). Sometimes a gang will include a rival's name followed by a *K* (which stands for Killer). For example, the Lime Hood Bloods (LHB), whose rivals are the Broadway Gangster Crips (BGC), may write on a wall the letters *BGC/K*. The Broadway Gangster Crips may in turn write *LHB/K*. These gangs may simply write *C/K* or *B/K,* respectively. African-American gangs often use the dollar sign in their graffiti, which is reflection of their emphasis on making money (what they describe as clocking dollars). Figure 3.6 shows some examples of African-American gang graffiti.

8. *Taggers.* The phenomenon of tagging has been growing rapidly in most urban areas in recent years (see Chapter 2 for a more detailed discussion). This form of graffiti is not usually associated with specific gangs, although some people refer to groups of youths who do this as gangs. Tagging is usually a method of announcing who they are (typically by using a nick-

FIGURE 3.7 Examples of tagging.

National Law Enforcement Institute, 1992:29.

name. Some common examples in Las Vegas include the following names: ACME, BNEE, ASTRO, DAZE, POUR, TRASH, LEEN, REAM, and SMIRK. Figure 3.7 illustrates some tags on walls in San Diego (ibid.).

9. **Chicano Gang Graffiti.** Chicano gangs use a lot of Spanish words in their graffiti. The graffiti used by these gangs is often referred to as *placas* (literally translated as *plaques*) and is a form of public tattoos (Vigil, 1988:113). Placas typically give the name of the gang member, his or her gang, and the location of the gang. Hutchinson (1993:141–158) provides the following example, written in large letters on a wall in Los Angeles: Lil Bobby SS 38 St. CXS. Lil Bobby is the name of the gang member writing the graffiti. The SS 38 St. stands for the Southside 38th Street gang. The CXS stands for "con safos," or "the same to you," which serves as a threat to anyone who might want to deface this message.

   Within Chicano gangs graffiti is a way of gaining attention and recognition from the public. Vigil quotes one gang member, who said, "I always wonder what people think of when they ride by and see the name 'Puppet' (his nickname) there. Do they think of me?" Another stated, "I know the guys from that barrio know who I am. They've seen my placas in their neighborhood" (ibid.). Some of the more common words used include: *Puro* (pure), *VNE* (Varrio Nueva Estrada, a local gang), *P/V* (meaning "for life," as in "I'm in the gang for life"), *R* or *Rifa* (meaning "control," "We control the neighborhood," or "We're number one"), *C/S* ("con safos," which means "back to you" or, more commonly, "there's nothing you can do about it," as in "we are in control and you can't do anything about it," an obvious challenge to another gang), *TOL* or *TO* (meaning united or total), and *CONTROLLA* (control). Some examples are shown in Figure 3.8.

10. **Graffiti of the People and Folk Nations.** Figure 3.9 provides some examples of the various forms of graffiti used by the *People and Folk* gang nations. Note the six points used by the *Folk* gangs and the five points used by the *People* gangs. Note also the use of the pitchforks for both. Each representative of these two nations have their own forms of graffiti (Sachs, 1997:87–88).

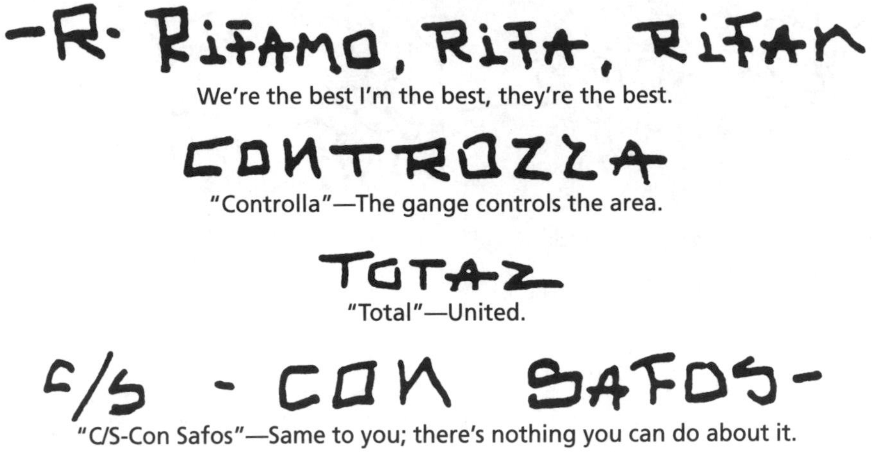

-R· RiȚAMO, RiȚA, RiȚAN
We're the best I'm the best, they're the best.

CONTROZZA
"Controlla"—The gange controls the area.

TOTAZ
"Total"—United.

C/S - CON SAFOS-
"C/S-Con Safos"—Same to you; there's nothing you can do about it.

FIGURE 3.8 Illustrations of Chicago graffiti.

National Law Enforcement Institute, 1992:30.

SUMMARY

This chapter has attempted to capture the characteristics of the gang subculture—from dress style to graffiti to membership requirements.

The beliefs of a gang and the commitment to a gang are quite similar among gang members despite the differences in race and/or ethnicity. There are no greatly significant differences for African-American, Hispanic, or white gangs. Taggers (a fairly recent youth-group phenomenon) reflect the same commitment and loyalty to the group as do members of long-established gangs. Asian gang members exhibit somewhat less loyalty to the group. This is not particularly surprising because their reasons for joining the gang center around economics rather than personal relationships.

Much of the discussion in this chapter has focused on the works of Moore and Padilla and their detailed observations of the structure, style, and language within Chicano gangs. This language includes the very artistic graffiti employed by these individuals.

Attention has also been given to Jankowski's theories of gang recruitment and membership. While the reasons for joining a gang may vary somewhat, one compelling factor appears to be universal—the sense of self-worth and belonging. The authors believe self-worth and the need to belong are so intertwined that it is not possible to separate the two concepts. These concepts indeed may define the entire identity of the individual, making the gang member not so different from the rest of humanity.

Black Gangster Disciples

Satan Disciples

GRAFFITI OF THE FOLK NATION

Orchestra Albany

Maniac Latin Disciples

Maniac Latin Disciples (showing disrespect to the Latin Kings)

Simon City Royals

GRAFFITI OF THE PEOPLE NATION

Undertaker Vice Lords

PR Stones

Mickey Cobras "All is Well"

Future Stones

Conservative Vice Lords

Latin Kings

Insane Unknowns

El Rukns

FIGURE 3.9 Graffiti from the *People and Folks* nations.

(Sachs, 1997:87–88).

NOTES

1. Prothrow-Stith (1991:159) notes that the presence of fathers is of critical importance in determining the extent to which a child becomes involved in antisocial activities. Specifically, she notes that "children who spend a great deal of time with their fathers are more likely than other children to grow up to be highly empathetic adults. This is important because empathy is such a socially desirable trait: People who feel for others tend to be good parents, good citizens."

2. Shelden heard a good example of this that occurred at a local alternative school. A gang member attacked someone else merely because he heard a rumor that this other person was out to get him for some reason, and the code he lived by dictated that he attack this person before he was attacked in order to not be embarrassed or dissed.

3. All names of participants in Brown's study are pseudonyms to ensure confidentiality.

4. All photos of gang graffiti from Detroit were taken by coauthor Brown.

4

✦

Criminal Activities
of Gangs

INTRODUCTION: AN OVERVIEW
OF GANGS AND CRIME

The stereotype of the gang member and the gang revolves around criminal activity, as if they do nothing else. This is in part perpetuated by both the media and the police. In the case of the media this is no doubt because the daily activities of the typical gang member are rather boring with little or no crime occurring (much less the stereotype of the "drive-by") and thus not newsworthy. As for the police, their historic role in this society is to catch people who have committed crime, and they usually could care less what the person does the rest of the time. Moreover, largely because of this role, information from the police about gangs (printed up and handed out at literally hundreds of "gang workshops" throughout any given year) tends to focus almost exclusively on the criminal activities of gangs and methods of identifying gang members (e.g., graffiti, dress styles, hand-signals, gang slang) in order to help officers make arrests or engage in "proactive policing" (i.e., keeping "tabs" on gang members). It is important to keep this in mind as we discuss the various crimes committed by gang members. Most of their time is spent doing other things—sleeping, eating, going to school, "hanging out," and so on—that occupy the time of adolescents everywhere.[1]

The criminal activities of gangs vary according to the type of gang (as noted in Chapter 2), with some committing little crime and others heavily involved in criminal activity, some committed serious crimes, and others committed minor crimes. Overall, however, the typical crimes committed by gangs have consistently been a "garden variety" or "cafeteria style" of offenses (e.g., burglaries, petty theft, vandalism, fighting, and truancy). The major victims of gang violence are other gang members. Innocent bystanders are rarely the victims despite claims from law-enforcement and other officials to the contrary (Klein, 1995:22).[2]

Gang violence, however, does differ in significant ways from nongang violence. An analysis by Klein and Maxson of over 700 homicides in the Los Angeles area found that gang violence is much more likely to occur in the streets (in contrast, most other homicides occur inside people's homes) and tends to be associated with the use of guns and less often associated with a robbery. Gang-related homicides are more likely to involve a larger number of participants and involve strangers, and the suspects are more often youths (Klein and Maxson, 1989:223–224). However, when considering the overall rate of involvement in criminal behavior, there is little question that gang members commit a disproportionate amount of crime, as several studies have shown (Shelden, Snodgrass, and Snodgrass, 1992).

A study of a sample of youths from neighborhoods (both high school students and dropouts, mostly African-American and Hispanic youths) in three parts of the country (Chicago, Los Angeles, and San Diego) is instructive. The offending (or participation) rates (of involvement in such offenses at least once during the past year) were higher among gang members for all behaviors (felony, minor assault, robbery, and extortion) except violence. However, for all offenses (including drug possession and drug sales), gang members committed these crimes more frequently than nongang members. Specifically, gang members were about five times more likely than nongang members to commit a crime during a given year, and more than half of the gang members had committed more than one offense during the year (Fagan, 1990).

Among the Chicago gangs, most of the crimes committed during the period under study by Bobrowski (January 1, 1987, to July 31, 1988) were intraracial and involved Part II offenses[3] (it must be stressed that these data are based on those known to the police and are therefore subject to underreporting). Crimes were about equally divided between personal and property crimes (49.7 percent were personal). The largest category was vice offenses (mostly drugs), which accounted for almost 30 percent. The next most common offense was aggravated battery (22 percent), with simple battery ranking third (15.6 percent).

What is most interesting is that Part I gang offenses[4] constituted less than 1 percent of all Part I crimes in the city of Chicago. However, when considering homicides and serious assaults, gang offenses accounted for as much as 18 percent of the homicides during certain months. Furthermore, in certain neighborhoods this percentage was even higher, with gang homicides accounting for 28 percent in one particular area (Bobrowski, 1988:42–44).

A study by McCorkle and Miethe (1998, 2001) further illustrates the myth that gangs are responsible for most of the crimes in a given jurisdiction. Examining court records in Las Vegas, Nevada, for the years 1989–1995, they discovered that the proportion of defendants charged with index crimes who were identified as gang members was quite low. For violent index crimes, for example, the proportion who were gang members ranged from 2 to 6 percent. Gang members were most often involved in murder cases, but even here their percentage of the total murder cases ranged from 10 to 23 percent during this period of time. As for property offenses, gang members constituted from 2 to 7 percent of the total; they were most likely to be involved in motor vehicle theft (ranging from 4 to 12 percent). The myth that gangs dominate the drug scene was shattered by this study, as the researchers found that gang members constituted from 2 to 8 percent of all felony drug defendants. These figures were in stark contrast to local media and law-enforcement reports that gangs had "taken over" the drug market.

The use of weapons is common in many gangs. In Chicago, for example, handguns were used in about 16 percent of all crimes and in about one-fourth of all crimes against the person (murder, rape, robbery, and assault); but they were used in 93 percent of all the homicides and 42 percent of all the serious assaults. Other kinds of weapons were used in the majority (55 percent) of all the other crimes reported. It should be noted that included within the term *weapon* was "hands/feet." The use of hands or feet accounted for 29 percent of all the crimes in which a weapon was used; hands or feet were used in 86 percent of the simple batteries involving a weapon, and hands or feet were involved in 93 percent of the strong-arm robberies involving a weapon. In fact, hands and feet were the most commonly used weapon (constituting 15.9 percent of all cases, compared to 15.7 percent for handguns), according to the Chicago data (Bobrowski, 1988:42–44; Appendix D, Table 21).

It should be emphasized that for most gangs the bulk of their time is not spent committing crimes. Hagedorn's gangs spent most of their time partying and hanging out (Hagedorn, 1998:94; a similar finding was reported by Huff, 1989:530). Noted gang researcher Malcolm Klein (who has been studying gangs for more than 30 years) has observed that gang life "with the exception of a boisterous meeting, a fight, an exciting rumor, is a very dull life. For the most part, gang members do very little—sleep, get up late, hang around, brag a lot, eat again, drink, hang around some more." Klein notes that it is a rather boring life and in fact "the only thing that is equally boring is being a researcher watching gang members" (Klein, 1995:11). When they "hang out" it is usually by a park or a taco stand, and they are "smoking, drinking, roughhousing, playing a pickup ball game, messing with a few girls, or sauntering up a street in a possessive, get–outta–our–way fashion" (Klein, 1995:22). When they do get involved in crime, it is either fighting (mostly with other gangs) or hustling, which included petty theft and drug sales. Drugs will be discussed in a later section, but it should be noted here that, as Hagedorn found for Milwaukee gangs, selling drugs "for most gang members is just another low-paying job—one that might guarantee 'survival,' but not much else" (Hagedorn, 1998:103; see also Padilla, 1992; Klein, 1995). The minimal amount of violence actually engaged in by gangs has been corroborated by other studies (Horowitz, 1983a, 1987; Keiser, 1969; Miller, 1975). Property crimes remain the major type of offense committed by gangs.

Having said this, however, it should be noted that gang members do in fact commit more crime than nongang members. This has been demonstrated in numerous studies, the most comprehensive of which was done by Huff (1996, 1998) as part of a project funded by the National Institute of Justice that included gang and nongang but "at risk" youth in three parts of the country (Colorado, Ohio, and Florida). Not surprisingly, the gang members were found to be more involved in criminal activity. Gang members were significantly more likely to engage in drug selling, assault, theft, weapons-related offenses, shoplifting, and a host of other crimes. One of the most interesting findings was that the first arrest for gang members typically came *after* becoming a gang member. In fact, in each of the areas where the research was conducted, the pattern was as follows: The youths began hanging out with the gangs at around age 12 or 13, joined the gang around 6 to 12 months later (between 13 and 14), and incurred their first arrest at around age 14. Typically they experience their first arrest about 6 months after they join the gang (Huff, 1998). These findings are corroborated by other researchers (Battin et al., 1998; Ebsensen and Huizinga, 1993; Thornberry et al., 1993).

Why do gang members commit more crimes than nongang members? According to research by Reiner, part of the reason is that gangs tend to attract individuals who are in the highest at-risk group in society—adolescent males who live in urban areas. However, Reiner also notes that there are "three realities of life in the gang subculture which drive the crime rate: fighting, partying and unemployment" (Reiner, 1992:55).

In the first instance, most gang homicides are the result of "gang fights over turf, status and revenge." They "are the results of traditional gang codes which require members to fight to prove their honor, manhood and loyalty" (ibid.). Reiner further notes that

> boys who are toying with the gang lifestyle—hanging around with friends, perhaps, and timid or slow about speaking out—may suddenly, and unintentionally, become targets or accessories to drive-by shootings. There is a finality to such episodes, even when they do not end in death. For

they can drag young men over the line and leave them there—exposed to arrest and imprisonment; fearful of retaliation from other gangs; wary of any action which would trigger rejection by friends they need now more than ever. Each attack thus creates a chain reaction of complicity, vengeance and commitment (ibid.).

Partying tends to increase the likelihood of crime because, first, it corresponds with heavy drinking and drug use, both related to crime. Also, there is a need to obtain drugs for parties, costing money, which in turn brings gang members into contact with the illegal drug world. Because most gang members are without work (either because it is unavailable or because they have never been socialized into good work habits), crime becomes a part-time job. The most common crimes tend to be robberies (because they can produce money fairly quickly) and drug dealing.

It is important to note that the commission of these crimes is rarely a gang activity as such but rather the product of a small group of gang members. The gang, it should be noted, does not condone such activity, and in fact most discourage it. Moreover, "the crimes themselves are not committed on behalf of the gang, nor are proceeds shared. The individuals (or groups, which may include non-gang members as well as homeboys) who commit such crimes do so for their own reasons and by their own rules—and that includes drug dealing" (ibid.:58–59). This fact is important to underscore because it contradicts the theory underlying most gang-enhancement statutes (which increase the punishment if the crime is gang related), which suggests that gang crimes are committed on behalf of the gang.

ENTREPRENEURIAL ACTIVITIES OF GANGS

Jankowski's (1990) study of gang members in three large cities suggests that the behavior of gang members differs from the prevailing view that they are merely parasites and do not have any of the skills necessary to be productive members of society. In contrast, Jankowski found that they had a strong entrepreneurial spirit. The gang members possessed five attributes that reflected such spirit: (1) competitiveness—they were very self-confident and had a strong drive to succeed; also, their Social Darwinist worldview was reflected in their belief that there were no rules in business, that anything goes; (2) a strong desire and drive to accumulate money and material possessions; (3) status seeking—most members, not unlike other Americans, seek to achieve some sort of status; (4) the ability to plan—a lot of time is spent figuring out ways to make money; and (5) the ability to take risks.

The entrepreneurial spirit present in many gang members encompasses a set of favorable attitudes toward accumulating money. Jankowski suggests four major sources of these attitudes. The first source is the traits associated with the defiant individualist character, especially lack of trust and the Social Darwinist view (survival of the fittest). The second source of these attitudes is tensions between the consumer culture and the scarcity of resources in low-income neighborhoods. One message these youths receive is that activities not requiring cash are unsatisfying; therefore, they need to take advantage of any opportunity. This scarcity causes them to act in creative ways to obtain money.

The third source is the belief that a member can improve himself if he comes up with a new idea. Gang members often think of several ideas that seem to be con jobs, but this is simply a variation of the American entrepreneurial spirit. The fourth source of these attitudes is a desire to resist the resignation to poverty and failure, which their parents accept.

The most important of these entrepreneurial traits is risk-taking. Gang members, not unlike others, make choices among ventures that are high risk, moderate risk, and low risk. Those who most often fail are those who typically take risks that are at either extreme. In other words, the more successful individuals take moderate risks most of the time.

Gang leaders have developed two main strategies to control entrepreneurial activities of members and to direct them toward the general goals of the gang. First, members are persuaded to devote some of their time and energy to the gang. Second, members are encouraged to donate some of their earnings to the gang coffers, similar to an income tax.

Gang members largely concentrate on how to make money. Many of their discussions involve the investment of money, time, and resources. There are two areas in which members get involved: planning and implementation. Relatively few are involved in actually planning activities; therefore, being asked to participate in the planning effort brings a high level of prestige.

At the planning stage are found significant differences among gangs of different cities and ethnic groups. For example, Jankowski found that gangs in New York (especially Irish gangs) spend a lot more time planning criminal activities than do Chicano gangs in Los Angeles and non-Irish gangs in New York (for these gangs, having a lot of money in their treasury is not so important).

Many gang members do not want to take risks, so not all volunteer to participate in implementing plans. Often they have to be coaxed to do so. Many feel that there may be a strong possibility of being arrested and going to jail if they participate in a certain activity. However, fear of incarceration varies. Chicano gangs are far less likely to have such a fear because going to jail enhances their status. "So many Chicano gang members have gone to jail that imprisonment has ceased to be something feared and has become something expected" (Jankowski, 1990:116). Moore's study of Chicano gangs in East Los Angeles corroborates this. In fact, her data strongly suggest that for most gang members the prison is experienced as a climax institution. In other words, going to prison is not a dramatic departure from their prior existence in the real world. Moore notes that "prison is no very big change for a man who walks a lifelong slack-wire between the highly personalized and emotionally consuming worlds of the barrio and of the institutional agencies" (Moore, 1978:105–106).

Gangs as organizations must also maintain contacts with other individuals and organizations. These include (1) contacts the gang as a whole has and (2) the contacts of individual members. Gang members adhere to the common view that it is who one knows rather than what one knows that results in success.

Most gangs obtain at least some money through legitimate business activity (this occurred in 27 of the 37 gangs Jankowski studied). Illegal activities involve mostly goods, services, and recreation, as follows:

1. *Goods.* These include drugs, liquor, and stolen property items such as guns, auto parts, and electronics equipment (some engage in the manufacturing of homemade drugs and moonshine liquor). Almost every gang tries to sell drugs because this is the biggest moneymaker. The sale of stolen guns is also profitable.

2. *Services.* The most common are protection, demolition of property (usually arson), and prostitution. The most common form of protection involves extortion (typically from store owners in the form of protection from being robbed). Gangs also provide services to clients who need someone else to be punished. For example, certain hustlers or loan sharks may hire gangs to coerce borrowers who are delinquent. (The El Rukns gang in Chicago was allegedly hired by Libya to engage in terrorist acts against the United States.) Torching property is a common activity in which the gang is paid by a landlord who wants to collect insurance. Sometimes tenants ask gangs to deal with landlords who do not provide them with needed basic services. Prostitution is something in which gangs get indirectly involved. Examples of this include protecting pimps and their women for a fee.

3. *Recreation.* The most common is establishing numbers games in their neighborhoods, setting up gambling rooms, and renting old buildings and using them for cockfights (Jankowski, 1990:120–126).

According to Jankowski (1990:126–131), whether gangs are successful depends on four factors: (1) the control of competition, (2) the type of organizational structure, (3) the stability of the division of labor within the gang, and (4) the extent to which they avoid antagonizing the community.

Gangs must view their competitors as people who are the lowest form of human life and must therefore attempt to wipe them out, often with the use of extreme force. The second factor has to do with how effective the members are in carrying out their plans. The vertical/hierarchical structure works best. Establishing a consistent division of labor is difficult. One of the main obstacles is that so many individual members spend so much time on their own economic ventures. Finally, the gangs must try to avoid getting members of their own community upset. Therefore, they must engage in activities elsewhere, which presents greater risks for them.

Jankowski found that a great deal of criminal activities engaged in by gangs are what he describes as crude economic activity. Most of this is done by gang members on their own, acting in their own interests. It is often reported by police as gang-related crime but is really done independently and is a direct result of the defiant individualist character (ibid.:132–133). When the gang as a whole engages in this kind of activity, it is usually a symptom of some type of organizational breakdown. This, says Jankowski, is a product of four factors: (1) mismanagement in times of economic crises; (2) leaders siphoning off the profits, which in turn encourages the gang to replenish the treasury; (3) inability of gang leaders to convince the members to work for the good of the gang; and (4) covering costs until the dues or income taxes are paid.

Almost all of the gang's economic activities are undertaken for the purpose of consuming various goods, engaging in recreation, and acquiring basic resources (both material and psychological). The first category is largely drugs and alcohol. Recreation takes the form of activities such as parties and picnics. Finally, some of the money is used to help members of their own family.

In a similar vein, Taylor (1990a, 1990b) argues that drugs have become a unifying economic force for today's gangs, just as alcohol was during Prohibition. The intense demand for drugs has created an economic opportunity for gangs to act as suppliers. The gangs of the 1990s are no longer the same as those of the 1950s or 1970s, says Taylor. Today's gangs are entrepreneurs engaged in a corporate, albeit illegal, enterprise. They are, continues Taylor, the illegal counterparts of IBM and other legitimate corporations. As a result, a great number of today's gangs are highly organized and extremely deadly.

The entrepreneurial activities of gangs are perhaps best illustrated by a gang studied by Padilla (1992) called the Diamonds. According to Padilla, the activities of this relatively small Puerto Rican gang in Chicago illustrate what he calls a business enterprise, not unlike any other such enterprise within the capitalistic marketplace.

THE GANG AS A BUSINESS: A CASE STUDY OF THE DIAMONDS

The Diamonds were originally a musical group, but the killing of one of their members by a rival gang was the catalyst for changing them into a violent gang. This act occurred in 1971, and for the ensuing six years this gang engaged in violent confrontations with rival gangs. The gang gradually became more of a business in the mid-1970s. The Illinois Controlled Substance Act of 1971 increased the penalties for adults who sold heroin and cocaine, making the sanction for such selling a mandatory 20-year prison term. The adults in the area, aware that juveniles received light sentences, began to use them in their drug-dealing ventures. In effect, these youngsters became an instant source of cheap labor for adult drug dealers. Several members of the Diamonds were hired. It was not too long before several members of the gang began to think about starting their own drug-dealing business. So, like a new company issuing stock, they asked other members to donate money to start the business (ibid.:95–97).

During the 1970s there was an increasing demand for drugs, especially cocaine. In fact, the demand was greater than the supply. "There was simply too much money to be made to forgo this economic opportunity, as more and more people began to use drugs; it was almost a natural act for the youth gang, which already controlled the streets of different neighborhoods, to become involved in this type of business. Youngsters realized that, by taking control over street-level drug dealing, they would have a long-lasting clientele desiring to purchase their goods" (ibid.:15). What helped the Diamonds, first, as suggested previously, was that they already had control of their own neighborhood. Second, gang alliances that brought about the People and Folks nations were aimed at reducing intergang violence. The alliance resulted in a better environment in which to conduct business. "Each gang was permitted to operate its business from a relatively safe turf or marketplace, selling only to those customers who voluntarily frequented there" (ibid.:101).[5] After all, with so much demand for drugs, it made good business sense. (This is similar to what occurred as a result of the passage of the 18th Amendment, prohibiting the sale of alcoholic beverages—namely, the rise of organized crime.)

Part of the motivation for these youths was their belief that traditional jobs did not pay enough to enable them to purchase the goods they wanted. These youths were also very pessimistic about the future of the economy. They rejected the traditional middle-class norm of success and, because of the strain from the lack of legitimate opportunities, became, in effect, innovators, as Merton predicted they would (ibid.:101–103). "The youth gang as an ethnic enterprise came to represent an economic strategy with which they would create a niche for themselves outside a system that denied them equal participation. In brief, the youth gang became these youngsters' reply to a system of opportunity they believed to be closed" (ibid.:14).

The gang became a sort of counterorganization or counterculture. The most important part of this culture was a collective ideology that bound them together as a whole, much like a family, and somewhat like a partnership in a business venture. Their business was analogous to a local mom-and-pop grocery store, as they catered to a "base of local consumers or people who are referred by friends." As one gang member told Padilla, "People from the neighborhood know that they can get smoke, cane, and other things from us" (ibid.:107–108). They also believed that they could not succeed individually but could succeed if they acted together as a group.

The gang business of the Diamonds is run like any other business with a bureaucratic structure. At the top of this structure are the cocaine and marijuana suppliers or distributors. These are the leaders of the gang, often called the "older guys" or "mainheads." The distributor, says Padilla, "embodies the dream which the larger society had denied Puerto Rican youngsters." The distributors resemble an exclusive club and are not unlike the superstars of the NBA. But, like these superstars, only a few make it that far (ibid.:112).[6]

This business enterprise is also typically capitalistic in another sense. Most of the workers within the gang hierarchy are street-level dealers. The goal of these individuals is to become independent businessmen, but success is rare. The average profit is only about $100 to $150 per week. However, the profit for the distributor is from $1,000 to $2,000 per week (ibid.:135).

At the bottom of the hierarchy are youths who make money stealing. They are called Pee Wees or Littles. Most often this stealing is a way to prove loyalty to the gang (ibid.:113). These individuals are the youngest members of the gang, generally between 13 and 15 years of age. Older gang members take advantage of these youngsters because they realize that, if they are caught, the juvenile justice system will be lenient toward them. Also, the Pee Wees are perceived by older members as a little crazy—that is, with little regard for their actions and a desire to demonstrate their commitment to the gang. Some of these individuals already have a reputation for stealing and want to display their talent. Most of the stealing is done in groups or crews (ibid.: 118–119). It is important to note that it is the policy of the gang to never steal in its own neighborhood, so they burglarize homes and businesses in other areas (ibid.:124).

Stealing cars is a common crime the gang commits. Quite often they steal specific types of cars as requested by those who operate "chop shops." Gang members become familiar with several of these operations in the Chicago area. Many times chop shop operators tell members of the gang where a specific car is located. Contrary to popular stereotypes, however, the amount of money the car thieves earn is rather small, usually between $20 and $50 per car. Most of the time the money is spent on each other or on girlfriends (ibid.:126–127).

Eventually those who have proven themselves good at stealing will be given an opportunity to take on jobs as street-level drug dealers working for the drug distributors. This job is in many ways like any job in the legitimate world of work. Padilla writes that "street-level dealers are not independent workers; rather, they are employed by the gang's distributors, or mainheads, and perform their jobs in accordance with job rules established by their superiors" (ibid.:129). They become street-level dealers with the ultimate goal of becoming distributors, but this turns out to be a dream few realize.

Most of them begin working as "runners" or "mules." The job description for these individuals entails making deliveries, or drops, of merchandise for various customers of the distributors, not unlike someone who drives a beer truck for a distributor and delivers to bars and restaurants (ibid.:130). As with any other job, the employers are looking for people who can be trusted and who are hard workers. Unlike legitimate work, however, this work is often irregular, with many downtimes when the "heat is on." Many of the gang members interviewed by Padilla continued stealing to supplement their income while working as runners.

Working as a runner provides a person with some valuable training in good business skills. For example, they learn how to manage customers, not letting them take advantage of their youthfulness and inexperience, and learn how to show who is in control. They also learn that most of the profits go to the distributors and that as long as they remain runners their wages will be low. Yet, like wage earners in the legitimate business world, most of these runners do not realize they are being manipulated and kept as part of an "army of reserve workers" that Marx once wrote about (Marx, 1964). Padilla notes that these youngsters believe what the distributors tell them—that their low wages are due chiefly to the fact that not enough people are buying or are not buying in

large enough quantities. The runners believe that "this form of labor exploitation could be best resolved once they had achieved the occupation of street-
level dealer" (Padilla, 1992:132).

The job of street-level dealer is the next stage in the occupational hierarchy, in which runners become hired dealers for the distributors and work on a
consignment basis—that is, they are given the drugs on credit, not unlike salesmen in legitimate businesses. Those who have worked their way up to this position have proven themselves to be competent and trustworthy workers. Still,
the money they make is small compared to the money made by independent
dealers or distributors. One gang member interviewed by Padilla stated that
his biggest profit in a week's time was between $100 and $200, while the distributor he was working for made as much as $1,000 to $2,000 off his sales
(ibid.:135).

The method of operations is quite sophisticated, again not unlike in legitimate businesses. Usually street-level dealers claim a specific block or corner (called their "turf" or "marketplace") and ply their trade at this location.
This is, of course, quite risky, for they always face the possibility of being
invaded and taken over by rival gang members. Little wonder violence is
often common as competitors try to take over a marketplace (ibid.:137).
One of the main differences between this scenario and legitimate businesses
(aside from the obvious legal difference) is that competitors in the legitimate world have lawyers who do battle in a courtroom rather than in the
streets.

There are times when the police attempt to break up their marketplace,
and the gang members, knowing that they have customers to satisfy, will learn
of this beforehand and establish their turf at a different location.

After they have established a turf, the next order of business is establishing
a clientele. As customers continue to consume the drugs, they become, in effect, salespeople for the product because they tell others where to purchase
good drugs (not unlike in the legitimate business world when one customer
tells another where to buy a certain product). But actually it is more accurate
to use the phrase "controlling the customer" because the dealers never know if
the individual is a legitimate customer or working for the police. Also, dealers
usually work in groups on the various street corners and blocks to provide
protection not only from the police but also from customers who may want to
rip them off.

Another common practice is to "control the law." What this means is that
the gang members "must contend with the ever-present possibility of police
detection," for there is the danger of becoming a victim of a "buy-bust," when
the police working undercover will buy drugs from one of the street-level
dealers and then proceed to arrest them. Many of the street-level dealers
learn that certain police officers can be "bought" for the right amount of
money (ibid.:146). One method of avoiding getting busted is to simply ask a
suspicious-looking customer to step out of the car and test the merchandise,
for example, by smoking a joint. They also find several good hiding places for
their drugs within their neighborhood.

The labor within the gang is highly exploitative, with few moving into their own businesses as independents. Not unlike in the mainstream labor market, the pay is low. They earn mostly survival income. One gang member told Padilla that, after working from about 4:00 in the afternoon until around 10 p.m., he earned between $250 and $300 for his employer but only $70 to $80 for himself and sometimes less than this (ibid.:171). Another said he often earned around $25 out of $200 worth of sales. Despite hard work, dealers rarely venture beyond their own little corner in the neighborhood. Most believe they will become distributors, just like most playground basketball players believe they will be in the NBA. The street-level dealers are a cheap and permanent supply of labor. The distributors help keep it this way. In short, it is pure capitalism. The money is sporadic, with peaks and valleys. The majority of the youths Padilla studied spent most of the day and well into the night "working the block" or standing on the corner because a sale could occur at 6 a.m. or at midnight. Such a scenario is similar to that of a car salesmen who stands around all day long waiting to make a sale.

After a period of time, disillusionment set in for many members of the Diamonds. As Padilla concludes, "For these youngsters the gang did not serve as the leverage necessary for improving their life chances in society, as they had earlier envisioned. Instead of functioning as a progressive and liberating agent capable of transforming and correcting the youngsters' economic plight, the gang assisted in reinforcing it" (ibid.:163). They soon learned that the business of the gang was established to benefit mostly the chiefs and mainheads. As one gang member put it, "I used to see guys with the big cars and the ladies, and I thought everyone was like that. But those guys are the mainheads. You know, they are the suppliers, and there are only a few of them around" (ibid.:165). The gang members interviewed by Padilla dreamed of one day establishing their own business and could never anticipate (perhaps because as they were growing up they got only bits and pieces of the whole story) "being relegated to the status of a dependent class of workers" (ibid.:166).

GANG VIOLENCE

According to Klein and Maxson (1989:202–203), membership in youth gangs can increase the probability of violence in two ways. First, being in a gang increases the probability of offending in general, so that violent offending will merely be a part of overall offending. Second, certain features of gangs may facilitate violence. Additionally, as already noted in this chapter, fighting, partying, and unemployment contribute to the high potential for violence. Research indicates that frequent or chronic offenders do not generally specialize in one specific type of crime and that the greater the number of offenses one commits over one's lifetime, the greater is the possibility that more of these offenses will be violent (Wolfgang, Figlio, and Sellin, 1972).

Fagan's study found that gang members are far more likely than nongang members to engage in violent acts. Yet, at the same time, it should be understood that violence among gang members is a relatively rare activity, compared to nonviolent crimes (Fagan, 1989). On the other hand, there is little disagreement that gang violence is on the rise, especially in Los Angeles. The belief among many is that gang violence is rising faster than the overall level of violence in American society.

Moore's follow-up study of East Los Angeles gangs (1991) is instructive and warrants discussion in some detail. She begins by noting that gang violence has been on the rise in the Los Angeles area. Whereas between 1970 and 1979 gang homicides accounted for 16 percent of all Hispanic homicides, gang homicides accounted for only 7 percent of the homicides among other ethnic groups (ibid.: 57–58).

Moore cites the following reasons for gang fights: invasion of gang territory by a rival gang, rivalry over dating, fights related to sporting events, and personal matters in which the gang is brought in to support someone. During the 1970s there were more deaths among gang cliques than in the 1950s. Moore offers two explanations for this. The first has to do with weapons. Not only were there more guns available in the 1970s, but those who used them were more likely intending to hurt someone rather than just intimidating them. Second, a greater degree of impersonality entered the picture, especially with the emergence of the drive-by shooting. This is related to the demise of the fair fight, whereby when the fight ends, the fighters shake hands and go their separate ways.

Moore comments that "younger members often want to match or outdo the reputation of their predecessors. Respondents from the more violent cliques were significantly more likely to believe that their clique was more violent than its immediate predecessor" (ibid.:60).

It may be tempting to explain the increase in gang violence by pointing to exaggerated masculine behavior, or machismo. However, this term, says Moore, refers just as much to control as it does to aggressiveness. Increased violence by the younger cliques has been described as a reflection of members being loco (crazy) or muy loco. Moore states that "locura is the 'craziness' or wildness that is stereotypically associated with Chicano gangs and their vatos locos (crazy guys)" (ibid.:62). It is especially related to unrestrained conduct on the part of a member. But even the definitions of locura have changed over time, often becoming linked to violence among the younger members.

Also, more of the recent clique members described themselves as either loco or muy loco (81 percent versus 65 percent of the older members); they also were more likely than the older members to emphasize violence in describing themselves. And it is the more extreme locos in a gang who are most likely to start fights.

Moore concludes by saying, "In general the elevated level of violence over time had some relationship to each clique's sense that it must outdo its predecessor and also with some elements of the changing definitions of locura. Violence also puts the gang under considerable strain. This is a consequence of the 'code of the barrio.' In part, this translates into a norm that homeboys back one another up in all situations, especially fights. . . . This 'code of the barrio' is one of the prime sources of lethal violence, especially in more recent times when guns replaced one-on-one fighting to establish a pecking order" (ibid.:65).

There is little question that the level of violence is related to the increasing availability of guns, especially the high-powered, semiautomatic weapons that, in the words of Reiner, "have profoundly altered the balance of power on the streets" (Reiner, 1992:87). Much of this is a direct result of more money being made selling drugs, so that there is a decreasing need to steal guns. As one gang member put it, because of involvement in drug selling, "now you can just go buy a Mac 10 [an assault weapon] if that's what you want, instead of burglarizing somebody's house to get a weapon" (Bing, 1991:223, quoted in Reiner, 1992:87–88). The more weapons that are available, and the more powerful the weapons are, the more violence there will be. An increasing number of gang members carry guns with them all the time. One result of this is an increase in spur-of-the-moment shootings. Finally, with many of the new weapons, poor marksmanship is no longer a problem. Reiner concludes that "fewer constraints on violence, more shootings, fewer misses, and a greater chance of killing bystanders—that's a sure-fire recipe for accelerating the classic action/reaction cycle of gang attack and revenge" (Reiner, 1992:89).

The violence committed by gang members is often shocking in its ferocity and is incomprehensible to ordinary citizens. Reiner notes that many rival gang members grew up in the same general area (perhaps a block or two is all that separated them) and went to elementary school together. But upon entering early adolescence, when the gang becomes more salient in their lives, they begin to drift apart. "Perhaps it is this very familiarity which yields such intensity of feelings. It also explains, incidentally, why gang members are usually very accurate (bystander casualties notwithstanding) about who they attack. These battles take place within small, fairly intimate local communities. In that sense, they are reminiscent of blood feuds from other cultures" (ibid.:57– 65). As with violence among acquaintances in general, violence can erupt over minor insults. One ongoing conflict, so far involving the deaths of at least two dozen people, is between two Crip gangs: the Rollin' 60s and the Eight Tray Gangsters. It allegedly started over a junior high school romance (ibid.).

Gang violence is also enhanced because gangs often attract young men who, frankly, enjoy violence. Reiner makes the following assessment: "The stark reality is that Los Angeles is producing an extraordinary number of dangerous, alienated young men—and, one way or another, there is a price to be paid for that in terms of crime. It may even be that gangs should be seen as symptoms rather than causes. After all, if gangs disappeared tomorrow, there is no reason to believe their members would join the Boy Scouts" (ibid.:59). We may not agree with the rather pessimistic conclusions offered by Reiner, but there is no question that there are a lot of angry, alienated, and violent young males, not only in Los Angeles but throughout the country.

As Jankowski has observed, gang membership increases the tendency toward violence because gangs attract youths (especially males) whom he describes as defiant individualists. Violence among gang members is often used to enhance one's status and reputation and in general to assert one's masculinity (e.g., by using violence to control people and/or territory).

Jankowski criticizes previous research by noting that violence has been treated as a dependent variable to be explained by a number of independent variables. Previous research has emphasized two factors regarding the causes of gang violence: (1) It stems from leadership composed of disturbed people, where the source of the illness is typically claimed to be drugs (Yablonski, 1962), and (2) it stems from status deprivation, where the violence is used to establish a rep or higher status (Jankowski, 1990:138–140). Both views have a similar logic—certain kinds of deprivations produce frustrations and hence violence.

Jankowski argues that from the view of the defiant individualist the surrounding environment is plagued by scarce resources and that violence is a natural state of affairs. Yet gang violence is limited (although not eliminated) by various restraining mechanisms, such as fear of reprisal and the pain that often results, and internal gang codes.

If fear of physical harm is important, then why do gang members persist in community violence? The answer, according to Jankowski, is that this fear inhibits them from violent acts but does not eliminate the possibility of committing such acts. The main reason for participation in community violence is that injuries can serve as commendations; scars are often proudly displayed as if they were medals (ibid.:139).

The anxiety about death is mediated by a belief (common among soldiers in war) that the gang members are invincible and, in turn, immortal. Gang members are socialized within the gang to appreciate their fallen brothers.

Much of what is officially labeled as gang violence is not gang violence per se. Rather, a great deal of violence is committed by gang members acting on their own and is not part of the gang's objectives.

According to Jankowski, four factors cause both individual and collective gang violence: fear, ambition, frustration, and personal/group testing of skills (ibid.). Also, there are six contexts within which violence is likely to occur: (1) a fellow gang member is the target, (2) members of a rival gang are targeted, (3) the residents of a gang's own neighborhood are the target, (4) violence occurs against people in another community, (5) violence involves attacks on property within the gang's own community, and (6) attacks occur on property outside the gang's own community.

Individual Violence by Gang Members

Acts of violence committed by gang members acting on their own do not represent gang violence and also do not occur because they are members of a gang. These acts are related to gangs only in the sense that the individuals involved have defiant individualist character traits. Violence results from the connection between the emotions of fear, ambition, frustration, and testing of skills and the encounters during which such emotions are apparent.

Violence Between Members of the Same Gang Fear is one emotion that instigates this specific kind of violence. It is manifested through the concepts of respect and honor, concepts that are particularly relevant within the Chicano culture, according to Jankowski (as noted in Chapter 4). Jankowski found that violence occurred most often against those who showed a lack of respect or challenged the gang's honor, at least as perceived by the gang. This is very important because gang members firmly believe that if there is not respect, honor, and reputation, there is nothing (and the gang member comes to believe that he is a nobody). Also, attacking a member of one's own gang may be a way of helping one advance in the organization.

Violence is often associated with frustration and anger, which emerge from three main sources. First, violence may be a result of verbal combat, also referred to in street language as the "dozens." A common occurrence is that the dozens routine simply gets out of control, and someone's honor or respect is challenged or offended. A second source is over women. From the perspective of the gang members Jankowski studied, the women are often viewed as property, and sexual advances to someone else's woman will result in violence. The women he studied had apparently resigned themselves to a level of subordination. A third source is the result of physiological reactions to the deprivation of food, inadequate rest, and the taking of drugs. A poor diet, consisting of too much fat and carbohydrates and low protein plus the ingestion of drugs and lack of good sleep and rest (they usually stay up most of the night and therefore have to sleep in the day, which is difficult because others are up and about making noise), often caused them to be tired and irritable. Moreover, the buildings in which they live are poorly insulated or have poor climate control (either too hot or too cold).

The fights between members of the same gang are often more intense and serious than fights with others. Jankowski suggests that fellow gang members are not really viewed as brothers. They are "loners who have chosen to participate not because the gang represents a family (with brothers) but because they perceive it to be, at least in the short run, in their best interests" (ibid.:148).

Horowitz (1983b:81) succinctly summarizes the important relationship between insults, honor, and violence. She suggests that public humiliation causes a person to question his own competence or weakness. This is especially important for young men without many personal accomplishments or valued social roles to protect their own self-worth when they are insulted. In a culture (such as the Chicano one about which both Horowitz and Jankowski have written) that emphasizes machismo and "defines violations of interpersonal etiquette in an adversarial manner, any action that challenges a person's right to deferential treatment in public . . . can be interpreted as an insult and a potential threat to manhood." This situation demands that the offended male be able to respond. Horowitz states that this situation is particularly acute for youths because of their lack of educational and occupational success (ibid.:247). Further, dishonor is something that is perceived as a loss of manhood, and the response to this, according to this subculture, must be physical.

In short, "violence is triggered by the norms of the code of personal honor" (ibid.:82; see also Anderson, 1994).

Attacks on Members of Other Gangs Fear is an important trigger for one gang attacking another. This usually happens in a neutral area (e.g., members of rival gangs happen to be at the same mall, football game, or party). Most often the gangs who have the smallest numbers present are the attackers.

Another reason is personal ambition. Attacking members of other gangs is used to try to advance within the organization. Yet another reason is to test how strong they and others really are, often to test the reputation of another gang (e.g., if that gang has a reputation for being tough).

Frustration and anger are typically related to an ongoing conflict between two gangs. Sometimes gang members are really angry with their own gang and attack other gangs to vent or deflect such anger.

Attacks on Residents in Their Own Community This usually involves gang members acting on their own. There are most often two reasons for this: (1) fear of being reported to the police and (2) a threat to one's respect or honor by a resident (e.g., an insult) or by someone going after one's woman or someone trying to restrict the gang member's activities.

Violence Against People Outside Their Community Sometimes this is a result of being threatened in some way that produces fear. Also, any behavior that is perceived as a threat to honor, respect, reputation, and so on will be met with violence.

Ambition is also a factor when a gang member is trying to do business and someone tries to curtail him. Sometimes a fight is staged with a stranger to test respective abilities. Also, attacks may occur because the victim is vulnerable and "this reminds them of their own vulnerability. Their attacks on others are a way of displacing the self-contempt inspired by their own feelings of vulnerability" (Jankowski, 1990:156).

Attacks on Property in the Community Stemming largely from ambition, this can be a means to achieving a personal goal without attacking an individual; the most common attack is through the use of arson.

Attacks on Property Outside the Community This can be attributed mainly to a combination of ambition and frustration/anger. Money appears to be the major cause. Individual members often attack the property of those who have refused to do business with them. Also, in cases where gang members have gone into the prostitution business, they may attack the property (e.g., cars) of competing pimps.

Often, they will attack someone's car or house if they have been offended (i.e., their honor or respect has been offended). Sometimes mere frustration will lead them to attack the property of someone who is wealthy. By attacking this person they are able to vent anger about denied opportunities; therefore, this type of violence becomes therapeutic.

Organizational Gang Violence

Jankowski (ibid.:160–168) outlines five major types of violence engaged in, by, or on behalf of the gang itself:

Collective Violence Against Members   This is done only in extreme situations, and the cause is fear. The gang is fearful that it is disintegrating as a result of internal problems. This kind of violence occurs for two reasons: (1) to establish legitimacy and authority (to establish authority in a general, abstract level and at a more immediate level for those in positions of authority within the gang to justify the current leadership and to counter challenges from within) and (2) to punish violators of gang codes.

Violence Against Members of Other Gangs   There are three factors that seem to cause intergang violence. The first relates to the ambitions of the gang, especially that of accumulating capital. More often than not this involves attempts to take control over a particular geographical area.

Another factor is that the gang may be merely testing the loyalty of its members. The leaders of a gang may initiate a plan to attack another gang "for no reason other than to see whether a specified group of their own members is serious about its commitment to the organization" (ibid.:162).

Finally, there is the element of fear. In some situations the leader of a gang may fear he has lost some status or authority with his gang; in order to regain this he subsequently calls for an attack on another gang. In other situations, the gang is in decline and experiencing a crisis, so an attack on another gang may be an attempt to create more group cohesion. In some situations an attack may merely be an outgrowth of a first-strike mentality (perhaps stemming from a form of paranoia).

Violence Against Residents of the Community   This is mostly an outgrowth of the fear that the gang is in decline as an organization. In this case it is an indication that the gang is experiencing a crisis because the last thing a gang wants is to unnecessarily antagonize members of its own community.

Attacks Against People Who Live Outside the Community   This is relatively rare. When it does occur, it is usually for one of three reasons. The first reason is ambition. A gang may enter into a contract in return for money (e.g., the El Rukns gang in Chicago was allegedly hired by Libya to engage in assassinations). Second, it may stem from a combination of both ambition and frustration. For example, the gang may be part of a business deal, and the others involved fail to live up to the agreement. The gang has therefore been frustrated in achieving its ambitions, and it seeks revenge. Third, there is the element of fear, specifically of organizational decline and frustration. One example is when the gang is being harassed by the police and such harassment is interfering with its activities. In this case the gang will attack the police.

Sometimes there is a case of mistaken identity—the victim was just at the wrong place at the wrong time. Gangs try to avoid this because it brings forth calls for a police crackdown. This occurs often among African-American gangs in Los Angeles, which indicates that they may be in a state of decline (ibid.: 345).

Attacks on Property in the Community Gangs try to avoid this, but when they do resort to this, it is usually related to organizational ambition. They may attack a house to drive out undesirables (e.g., crack houses or someone who refuses to pay for protection).

The research conducted by Jankowski on violence emphasizes the following points: (1) Gang violence is not one-dimensional—it is both organizational and individual; (2) gangs are practical and cautious in punishing their members; (3) policymakers must understand the root causes of fear, ambition, testing, and frustration; and (4) contrary to popular myth, gang members do not like to fight—in fact, they try to avoid it.

Violence by gang members is, as already noted, more prevalent than violence among nongang members of the same general age-group and similar socioeconomic backgrounds. There are no known jurisdictions where gang homicides outnumber nongang homicides, however, since most homicides are committed by adults in totally different contexts. Klein's research documents the many differences between gang and nongang homicides. For example, homicides committed by gang members are more likely to be committed on the streets, with the use of guns, with a greater number of participants, to involve victims with no prior contact with their assailants and where both the suspects and the victims are considerably younger (Klein, 1995:114–115).

Gang-related homicides in Los Angeles are an interesting case because of the fluctuations during the past 20 years. Malcolm Klein and Cheryl Maxson collected data covering the years 1980 through 1997 (figures through 1992 found in Klein, 1995:120; figures from 1993 to 1997 from Maxson, 1999). Gang-related homicides really "took off" in the mid-1980s, exactly during the time when "crack" was introduced into the streets of Los Angeles. There was also a noteworthy increase in the availability and lethality of weapons during this time (Klein, 1995:116). The number of gang-related homicides went from 212 in 1983 to more than 800 by 1992; the percentage of all homicides that were gang related went from 10 to around 45 during that period of time. A more detailed analysis revealed that part of this increase was directly related to the increase in "drive-by shootings." Between 1989 and 1991 the number of these incidents went from 1,112 to 1,543, with the number of victims increasing from 1,675 to 2,222 and the number of deaths going from 78 to 141. The average number per day went from 3.0 in 1989 to 4.2 in 1991 (Klein, 1995:118).

The good news is that there was a drop from 1992 to 1993, followed by a slight increase to 1995, which in turn was followed by a very significant decrease after 1995. Several possible explanations have been offered to account for this sudden drop, with the most plausible centering around the decrease in crack dealing, the improvement in the overall economy, and an increase in gang truces in the wake of the rioting following the Rodney King decision (Maxson, 1999).

GANGS AND DRUGS

There is little question that drug usage and violent crime are closely related. What is still in doubt, however, is the relationship between drugs (both usage and sales) and gangs. Research on this issue has produced conflicting findings. Skolnick (1990:4) argues that drug distribution is not synonymous with gangs and that we cannot assume "that just because gang members participate in the sale or use of controlled substances, they have some preestablished arrangement to distribute drugs."

The rate of involvement in drug sales among gang members is highest among those who have been arrested and convicted. In San Diego County, for example, out of 276 gang members on probation, 75 percent had been convicted of drug offenses at one time or another (Spergel, 1990:43).

Gang members are about twice as likely as nongang members to use drugs and to use them more often (Fagan, 1989). Many researchers have found that patterns of drug use are quite variable within and among gangs (ibid.). Drug use is not only normal among gang members but may have many different meanings. For example, Vigil (1988) has found that, among Chicanos in East Los Angeles, drug use is mostly for pleasure and is confined to drugs that enhance status and acceptance among gang members. The use of heroin, says Vigil, is scorned because these gangs believe that this is a betrayal of both the gang and the barrio. In some gangs, drug use is simply not allowed, while in others only recreational use is allowed (Fagan, 1989; Mieczkowski, 1986). On the other hand, Moore found that "the marketing of heroin is a significant entrepreneurial opportunity for a number of barrio-based dealers in East Los Angeles" (Moore, 1978:76).

A study by Klein, Maxson, and Cunningham (1988) of the sales of rock cocaine in the Los Angeles area during the years 1983 to 1985 found that while arrests for crack sales rose dramatically, the involvement of gangs in these arrests did not. Also, there were no significant differences between gang and nongang involvement in arrests for the possession of weapons (arrests for gang members for possession actually decreased during this time), and sales of crack were "small-time," while the well-publicized rock houses were the exception rather than the rule (perhaps this is why the media plays it up so much—because it is news). In short, arrest data from this study show that selling crack is not an exclusive domain of gangs.

Bobrowski's study in Chicago found that vice offenses (which are about 90 percent drugs) accounted for about 30 percent of all gang crimes during the period studied. The most common drug involved was cocaine, which accounted for 44 percent of the cases. The next most common was barbiturates (29 percent), followed by PCP (11 percent) and heroin (9 percent). The largest amount of drugs seized involved cannabis (11,852 kg), followed by PCP (4,020 kg) and cocaine (3,533 kg) (Bobrowski, 1988:45).

Fagan's study (1989) of drug use/sales and other offenses among gangs in three cities (Los Angeles, San Diego, and Chicago) found that rates of drug use and sales as well as most other offenses were generally much higher among gang members than nonmembers. The most commonly used drug was alcohol, both by the gang itself and among individual members, while marijuana was ranked second. Other drugs, including PCP, cocaine, and heroin, were used at least once by 40 percent of the gangs and individual gang members. The most frequently committed crime (committed 12 or more times during the past year) among gang members was use of alcohol (40.8 percent), followed by marijuana use (33.6 percent), with minor theft, robbery, felony theft, and extortion ranking closely behind (23.6, 22.0, 22.0, and 21.1 percent, respectively).

As noted in Chapter 3, Fagan found that the extent of drug use, drug sales, and general criminal behavior varied according to the type of gangs to which these youths belonged. As noted, the organization gang type was found to have a very strong linkage between serious crime and drug use/sales.

What we can conclude from Fagan's data is that drug involvement "is not inextricably linked to violence." More specifically, says Fagan, "a strong relationship exists among violence, serious crime, frequent intoxication, and drug dealing among gang members, just as there is among other inner-city adolescents. The relationship between gang violence, nonviolent crimes, drug selling, and drug use is complex. Violence occurs in gangs with distinct drug use patterns, but rarely among gangs that also are not involved with drug use and drug selling" (ibid.:652).

Fagan's study also examined the extent of drug use and other forms of delinquency among individual gang members according to the type of gang they belonged to (i.e., the four types noted in Chapter 3). Regular drug use and offending (regular was operationalized as "a few times" or more often during the previous year) varied significantly according to the type of gang. In general, those in the serious and organization gangs had the highest rate of delinquency involvement but differed significantly in terms of drug usage. The serious delinquent gang members were significantly less likely to use such drugs as PCP, psychedelics, speed, barbiturates, cocaine, and heroin and are somewhat less likely to engage in the selling of drugs (ibid.:654).

Fagan also examined the social organization of each gang type. The serious and organization type gangs had the most formal structures, as measured by such variables as the presence of established leaders, the extent of rules or codes, specified roles for members, and specified roles for girls. Because these two types of gangs had much different levels of involvement in drug usage and drug sales, Fagan concluded that there is little relationship between the structure of a gang and involvement in drugs (ibid.:655–656).

Fagan concludes that there exists "a positive association between drug involvement and serious collective gang acts" that is similar to the behavior of urban youths who are not in gangs. Also, "substance use and delinquency among gangs occur in gangs with well-developed organizational structures and social norms." Yet, at the same time, the use of drugs occurs "both independently of other crimes and also as part of a general pattern of deviant behavior." Further, whereas delinquency among gang members "did not occur in the absence of drugs," nevertheless crime and violence of a serious nature "occur regardless of the prevalence of drug dealing within the gang," and "involvement in use and sales of the most serious substances does not necessarily increase the frequency or severity of violent behavior." Also, there are some gangs heavily involved in the use of drugs but not involved in violence (ibid.:660).

There is some evidence that in recent years some gangs have gained control of a good proportion of the drug trade. Fagan reported that gang members are far more likely to engage in drug selling than are nongang members. Most of them, however, sell drugs on a relatively infrequent basis (less than one-fourth in Fagan's sample sold drugs three or more times during the previous year). Generally, most gang members who sell drugs can be described as small-time dealers (Reiner, 1992:61). This is not to say that some members of some gangs do not get heavily involved in the drug trade. Gang involvement in the drug-dealing business increased tremendously after the introduction of crack cocaine in Los Angeles in the mid-1980s. As Reiner (ibid.:62) notes, the change was most dramatic in the African-American community. From a "trendy but expensive specialty," it shifted "to a low-cost, high-volume product for the mass market. Suddenly, a greatly expanded market had room for countless local 'franchises.' Almost overnight, a major industry was born—with new outlets in every neighborhood, tens of thousands of potential new customers and thousands of available jobs in sales." The selling of crack has become one of the major forms of profit making. There are at least two reasons for this. First, crack can bring a return of from 300 to 400 percent. Second, the high from crack is short-lived, and it is very psychologically addictive, thus creating a lot of repeat business. Therefore, it is not surprising to find drug distribution and sales are appealing alternatives to the inner-city poor, especially African-Americans (Kitchen, 1995:28).

Some reports give a rather exaggerated account of the gang-drug involvement. One report, for example, argued that the Crips and Bloods "have gained control of 30 percent of the crack cocaine market in the United States" (Spergel, 1990: 46). However, the spread of the crack problem as a gang-related problem "is generally attributed to market forces and normal migration patterns of individuals and families seeking economic opportunities [rather] than to a centralized, bureaucratic franchising campaign" (ibid.:48).

Klein and Maxson (1990:6) also take exception to the gang-drug linkage. They offer several reasons why the gang-drug sales connection is not as strong as media reports would have us believe. First, the greater degree of cohesiveness and organization that would be required for a sophisticated drug trafficking network does not normally exist in the typical gang. Also, such a business venture would require a gang "to overcome its own age-group compartmentalization, inter-member suspicions, inter-clique rivalries, age-specific leadership, and a focus on inter-gang rivalries." Second, if a gang were to specialize in profiting from drug sales, it would have to compensate its members. However, because membership fluctuates so much, such compensation would "require far more altruism, fellowship, and organization than is typical for street gangs." Third, strong and effective leadership would be required. The leadership within the typical gang "tends to be age-related and specialized for different functions." Fourth, because drug use and sales are generally combined and because users cannot be trusted (and trust is essential for any efficient business), it seems unlikely that most gangs could be successfully involved in the drug trade. Fifth, and finally, is the issue of violence. A successful drug trade requires instrumental violence, the kind that involves the "enforcer role, or takeover of rival territories," which is quite different from normal gang violence, which tends to be sporadic, retaliatory, unplanned, and expressive. As Klein and Maxson note, "It is no mean trick to convert 'normal' gang violence to that said to be demanded by drug distribution" (ibid.:6).

There is also little evidence that there is a strong connection between drug selling and violence. Most gang-related homicides are not motivated by drugs but rather are motivated more by such things as revenge, defending the hood, or any number of reasons totally unrelated to the drug business (Bing, 1991:121 –123; Reiner, 1992:64).

Skolnick (1990) questions the conclusions reached by Klein and Maxson. His study, based on detailed interviews with more than 100 inmates (in both adult and juvenile correctional facilities in California), concluded that only a certain type of gang—the entrepreneurial gang—is likely to become heavily involved in drug dealing.

THE DRUG-DEALING BUSINESS
OF GANGS: SKOLNICK'S STUDY

The study by Skolnick (1990) was based on over 100 interviews with inmates in five correctional institutions in California. Skolnick wanted to focus on, among other things, the conflicting perspectives of Southern California convicts and the findings of Klein and Maxson on the extent of gang involvement in drug dealing. Law-enforcement sources claim that it is increasing, while Klein and Maxson say such claims are exaggerated.

The foundation for this disagreement may be that gang members are reluctant to admit they are in a gang. Therefore, the common belief among law-enforcement officials is that only 50 to 60 percent of all Los Angeles gang members have been identified. In 75 percent of the cases examined by Klein and Maxson, no gang member was arrested on a drug charge. Skolnick (ibid.:4) argues that this would mean that "the remaining 40–50% of unlisted gang members do not sell drugs." His data suggest that belonging to a gang decreases the probability of being apprehended on drug-selling charges because the gang has many advantages over nongang sellers. These advantages include "easy control and access to territorial markets; exclusion of others from territorial markets; shared marketing information; and reliance on gang member lookouts to protect against intruders, including the police" (ibid.). Gang members, in short, are more efficient in selling drugs and avoiding detection.

Another research question resulted from the problem of explaining the migration of gangs out of California to other parts of the country and how this relates to drugs. Two criminological perspectives have been previously offered to explain this migration. First, there is the "organized crime infiltration or 'mafia' theory." The second is the symbolic association theory. The first essentially argues that street gangs evolve into very sophisticated criminal organizations. The second argues that young men (who may or may not have been involved in gangs) move away from their old neighborhoods and establish new gangs, using the names of Los Angeles gangs (ibid.:6).

Skolnick argues that neither theory is totally accurate. He offers a cultural resource theory instead. To Skolnick there is a gang culture that "generates values, understanding and trust relationships which facilitate, but do not direct, drug selling or the migration of members. Cultural gangs are initially organized horizontally, stressing values of neighborhood, loyalty, and the equality that obtains among members of a family" (ibid.:7). This applies particularly to Southern California gangs.

The Northern California gangs are organized vertically, "with status in the gang dependant upon role performance" (ibid.:7). As with any other capitalist organization, the organization of these gangs "is motivated by profits and the control of a particular market or markets. But unlike many capitalist enterprises, not all drug organizations strive for growth or expansion. They often perceive themselves as local businesses. Some may merely seek to control drug sales and distribution within delimited territorial boundaries, such as part of the city or housing project" (Skolnick, 1990:5). (Padilla's [1992] study of a Puerto Rican gang in Chicago arrived at similar findings.) This may help explain why the gangs in the San Francisco Bay Area rarely travel (not even to Sacramento), while the Bloods and Crips of Los Angeles travel extensively. Skolnick claims that his research has discovered the paradox that those gangs originally organized for social purposes have more resources at their disposal to support their travels, more than entrepreneurial groups organized to sell drugs.

Skolnick also argues that among the African-American gangs of Los Angeles there has been a shift from a cultural kind of gang toward a more entrepreneurial type of gang. As this has occurred, the development of the drug business has been "supported by the resources of traditional gang membership." Such a foundation helps to develop "migratory selling" (Skolnick, 1990:8). Whereas the cultural gangs of Los Angeles (especially Chicano gangs) are involved in criminal activities only in a relatively minor way, the entrepreneurial gangs "are businesses focused with financial goals paramount," and youths join the gang because of the economic opportunities offered. Traditional neighborhood or cultural gangs, especially Chicano gangs, do not organize specifically for the purpose of drug dealing. Rather, this type of gang "is strongly grounded in a neighborhood identity which may extend through generations. . . . We designate these gangs as 'cultural' to distinguish them from opportunistic groups of young men who also may call themselves 'gangs' or 'mobs' and are organized primarily for the purpose of distributing drugs" (Skolnick, 1990:4–5).

The two types of gangs use violence differently. The cultural gang uses it largely symbolically to reinforce gang loyalty and identity. In contrast, the entrepreneurial gang uses violence in an instrumental way—to control drug markets or to enforce loyalty norms.

Part of the reason for the shift from cultural to entrepreneurial gangs has been the increasing importation of cocaine into the Los Angeles area. This has caused a decrease in price from $60,000 a kilo to as low as $9,000. An increase in the number of drug dealers and an increase in violence (more competition) have occurred simultaneously. Additionally, law enforcement has become increasingly stringent. The business of drug dealing has become more difficult and dangerous (ibid.:12–13).

One strong indication of the recent changes is in the ambitions of youths wanting to join gangs. They are joining because of the perceived economic benefit (ibid.:14). A new criteria for membership has become one's ability to sell drugs. Specific benefits of being a member of a gang include (1) shared marketing information (who sells what drug for what price); (2) homeboys provide protection and retribution if anything happens; (3) easy access to, and control of, markets within one's territory (a sort of territorial monopoly); and (4) a sense of trust in the "homeboy relationship so that gang members are expected not to betray other members to the police or rival gangs" (ibid.:16).

One gang member used the analogy of getting a high-school diploma: without one you cannot get a job. Similarly, if you are a gang member, it provides an "easier way into the drug dealing business" (ibid.:16). The shift from cultural to entrepreneurial gangs is evidenced in the following ways.

First, there appears to be an apprenticeship system within some gangs "for those just entering the drug trade." Some of the older gang members will "often not only introduce younger members to drug dealing but also routinely offer these younger members pre-packaged drugs on consignment, to be sold for easy 'double-up' profit" ("double-up" is a street term for doubling the amount that the suppliers want returned to them) (ibid.:17). In effect, the older gang member acts as a sort of general manager or area supervisor as in any sales organization (as, e.g., in a new car dealership). In return for his tutelage of the novice drug-dealing gang member, the supervisor has a steady share of the recruits' business (again, as in a car dealership).

Second, gangs provide information on out-of-town markets. Third, support for fellow members has gone beyond mere protection and has become more economically oriented. Provisions include cash or loans and "fronting" drugs, weapons, clothes, and even cars. Some of these items are gifts for a job well done (like a Christmas bonus for salesmen in legitimate businesses). Also included is bail money, help when one gets into prison, or a steady supply of good-quality drugs.

The traditional gang-banging activities that used to get respect and positions within the gang are slowly being replaced (although not completely eliminated) by the use of violence as a means of enhancing drug dealing. Good drug dealing now gets as much, if not more, respect within many gangs as violent activities.

Because of police crackdowns in Los Angeles, many gangs who are involved in drugs have expanded their networks to other cities. The respondents in Skolnick's survey reported that Blood or Crip crack cocaine operations can now be found in 22 states and at least 27 cities (e.g., Alabama; Alaska; Phoenix, Arizona; Arkansas; Denver, Colorado; Indianapolis, Indiana; Iowa; Kansas; Shreveport, Louisiana; St. Louis and Kansas City, Missouri; Las Vegas, Nevada; New York City, New York; Cleveland, Ohio; Portland, Oregon; Seattle, Washington; and Milwaukee, Wisconsin).

Skolnick's respondents indicated that many gang members travel extensively as part of their normal drug business; this appears to have begun in 1986 or 1987.

One reason for travel is competition. The Los Angeles drug market is becoming saturated with new dealers. There are now an estimated 80,000 gang members in this area, creating a reduction in prices of drugs and therefore profits. Another explanation for lower prices is the increase in the quantity of drugs. The ability to command a higher price in areas other than Los Angeles has made these drug markets more attractive. As one gang member said, "Here you can sell an ounce for $600, over there you can sell it for $1500" (ibid.:25).

Another reason to leave the Los Angeles area is intensified policing policies. Whenever drug sales increase rapidly in a particular neighborhood, the police soon are present, making mass arrests. Gangs then move elsewhere. Despite such crackdowns, none of Skolnick's respondents gave even a hint "that anyone committed to selling drugs is about to seek out an honest job. Instead they look for business elsewhere" (ibid.:26).

Aside from the higher prices that can be charged in out-of-town markets, there are four main advantages to migration: (1) Gang members get more respect because of the reputation of Los Angeles as a crazy place with crazy gang members; their reputation for violence follows them; (2) they have great resources, are more sophisticated, and are more technologically advanced than those in smaller areas; (3) they can get more drugs more easily; and (4) they can more easily avoid arrests because of their experience in California (ibid.: 26–29).

Despite these advantages, most gang members choose to stay at home and rarely travel outside of the state, if they travel at all (ibid.:29–31), for the following reasons: (1) fear of doing time in prison in other states, especially because they already have contacts (other gang members) within California prisons; (2) sentence severity—they fear that in other states (and in the federal system) sentences may be more harsh; (3) distance from friends and family; this is mostly fear of the unknown, that is, separation from the "security, familiarity and recognized relationships of the neighborhood" (ibid.:30), and many are disinclined to be away from their hood; and (4) satisfaction—some are satisfied with the money they make in the California area.

For most, the sudden wealth they possess from selling drugs enables them to travel to other places for the first time. They may also be motivated to leave because they have relatives or friends in other areas. When they finally decide to travel, they select an area either because a trusted homeboy is already there or because they are informed that a lot of money can be made there. Often they will simply learn about a place out of state from news they have heard on the street. Others are simply recruited to sell drugs by someone out of state; a few will just be adventurous, as if seeking the promised land, and will simply get on a plane and go.

In order to engage in any sort of extensive traveling, these gang members must develop a careful plan to get drugs into their out-of-town markets. Some will pay runners or couriers as much as $10,000 a month, which allows some Los Angeles gang members to sell drugs in places as far removed as Nebraska.

Some have developed very elaborate systems of drug selling by working with the latest technology, such as beepers and cellular phones. Some have begun to make peace with rural gangs and drug dealers in the Los Angeles area; they are progressing from gang-banging to cooperation, where out-of-state drug sales are concerned. In short, new rules are being established by these gangs, and younger gang members have to be resocialized to them.

According to Skolnick, the Northern California vertical gangs have the following features: (1) Members consider themselves a business organization, (2) the business is drug dealing, and (3) as a consequence, "the use of violence is limited to intentional harm and directed towards protection or promotion of business interests" (ibid.:38–39).

The vertical organizational characteristics are as follows: (1) A single person controls who sells drugs within a turf, (2) this person determines who sells drugs in the turf and who becomes a member, and (3) several roles are created and filled within such an organization based on the expertise and age of the member. This type of organization results in a great deal of competition within the gang, which further results in distrust, betrayal, and violence among members. Leaders, too, often resort to extreme violence to enforce order.

Both Northern and Southern California gangs sell drugs curbside and in crack houses. Both types rely on violence; the main differences concern intra-gang relationships. Within the Southern California gangs, a sense of trust is more likely to be developed in addition to loyalty and a strong identity with the gang. Members are more likely to feel a sense of belonging. Also, it does not matter whether one sells drugs; one is a member anyway. Gangs do not sell drugs per se; individual members sell drugs. Southern California gangs do not have many designated leaders.

Skolnick investigated why some old markets attract gangs to do business while others do not. The effectiveness of local police does not seem to be a factor. Arrests for drugs have increased dramatically in all major cities; simulta-neously, the price of cocaine has dropped (ibid.:46). Gang migration tends to occur most often among Jamaican, Haitian, and Dominican gangs in the East Coast area and among African-American gangs in Los Angeles. Only the African-American gangs of Southern California and the Jamaicans travel to the Midwest.

Skolnick concludes that it is the "cultural and structural organization of gangs, rather than law enforcement or market pressures" (ibid.:47), that best explains why some gangs migrate and some do not. The horizontal gangs tend to migrate the most because of the greater loyalty and trust that are developed within this structure and because these gangs furnish their leaders with more resources to conduct their drug business.

It should be noted that the Skolnick study has some limitations. The most important of these limitations is the fact that the data come from interviews with a small and unrepresentative sample of prison inmates. The gang-drug connection discussed in this study has so far not been supported by most other research (with the exception of Padilla's [1992] work). However, as Reiner (1992:70) notes, the Skolnick study "may document the rise of inde-pendent drug gangs rather than the transformation of traditional turf gangs." Even so, as Reiner suggests, some police officials believe that the drug-gang connection is more valid for African-American gangs than for Chicano gangs. It may be too early to tell the extent to which African-American gangs will make a transition to drug-dealing gangs. Reiner arrived at several conclusions regarding the drug-gang connection (ibid.:70–75): (1) Gangs are highly likely to exercise at least indirect control over the selling of drugs in their own neighborhoods; yet, it is incorrect to say that gangs control the supply of drugs; (2) many original gang members (O.G.s) may take on major roles in drug selling, although most gradually drift away from the gang; (3) large-scale operations are generally conducted by "individuals and small groups acting on their own rather than for the gang" (ibid.:72); (4) gangs often recruit younger members as street-level dealers, and these members continue to engage in other gang-related activities simultaneously; (5) most gang members do engage in some amount of drug dealing, mostly of a lim-ited nature and on their own rather than on behalf of the gang; (6) as with other kinds of businesses, a few gang members make a lot of money dealing drugs, while the majority either make a small amount or fail altogether; (7) gang members who sell drugs usually do not use them and even look down on those who do; and (8) some members of Los Angeles gangs have formed national drug-distributing networks; one report suggests that some ex-members of Crip sets have been identified as selling drugs in a total of 46 states (ibid.:76).

The gang-drug connection will continue to be a topic of disagreement among both researchers and law-enforcement officials. One thing is certain: As long as there is such a high demand for drugs in our society, someone will supply the product. And some of these individuals will be affiliated with gangs because so many gang members are from the most disadvantaged segments of society and are therefore seeking methods of making money outside of the traditional labor market, which has been closed to them for so long.

Still another recent study reveals a great deal of violence, heroin trafficking, and even human smuggling (Chin, 1996). This particular study focused on Chinatown in New York City and was based on interviews with 62 males who were either current or former gang members. They represented 10 different Chinese gangs in New York City. Most were between 16 and 21. The majority were born in another country, most commonly in either Hong Kong or China, although 35 percent were born in the United States. Their ethnicity was mostly Cantonese. It was reported that only a slight majority were ever arrested (52 percent), and only 15 percent were ever in prison. Most reported that their gangs were only somewhat or not at all organized, that most of their gangs had rules, and that almost all (98 percent) have their own territory. They also reported that most had a division of labor within the gang and that a clear majority (three-fourths) of the gangs were involved in legitimate businesses. These gang members were also heavily involved in criminal activities, with fully 82 percent being involved in one or more robberies and over half using guns in their offenses. A goodly number of these youths had been involved in crime on a "frequent" basis (defined as 12 or more times): assault (67 percent), theft against business (87 percent), protection (78 percent). Not too many were involved in the sale of drugs (17 percent did this at least once, but none did it frequently), and few were regular users of drugs (except for alcohol and marijuana).

SUMMARY

Gang members commit a variety of crimes, although the extent to which they contribute to the overall crime problem is not known with any degree of certainty. The crimes they tend to commit are similar to the kinds of crimes committed by other delinquent individuals—that is, mostly property and drug offenses. The extent of the violence committed by gang members is not nearly the level portrayed by the media, and, in fact, gang members' contribution to the overall rate of violence is relatively small. There is little question that the presence of drugs also accounts for increased criminal activity of youth gang members.

Drug dealing on the part of gang members is significant, but not to the extent that is portrayed by the media. As has been noted in this chapter, the extent of their involvement is in dispute, as is the claim that gangs are involved as an organized business. For the most part, drug dealing is a small-time activity in which the majority of dealers work long hours and receive little money. Most of the profits go to the suppliers and distributors.

NOTES

1. The stereotypes have often become so ludicrous that there are many times when adolescents are mistaken for gang members simply because they "look like one." Much gang attire, plus slang, tattoos, and so on, have been borrowed by millions of teenagers all over the country, perhaps trying to "mimic" the rebellious image of gangs. Each of the authors has had students in their classes who "looked like" gang members—for that matter, many really once were gang members! Shelden gets many from Southern California who have moved to Las Vegas with their families and will tell him that they were once in this gang or that gang. Likewise, Tracy gets former gang members from Atlanta, while Brown gets them from Detroit. In all likelihood, the reader is sitting in a class with a few ex–gang members! These observations reinforce one of the key findings from gang research: Many gang members leave the gang eventually and lead normal lives, including going to college and majoring in criminal justice!

2. Data collected by Klein and Maxson found that only 2 to 5 percent of gang homicides involved innocent, nongang victims (Klein and Maxson, 1989:231).

3. Based on categories in the FBI's annual report, Part II offenses include fraud, drugs (sales and possession), vandalism, driving under the influence, possession of stolen property, and minor assaults, among others.

4. Based on categories in the FBI's annual report, Part I offenses include murder,

rape, robbery, aggravated assault, burglary, larceny, motor-vehicle theft, and arson.

5. Padilla notes that, in the area where the Diamonds operated, drug dealing was "the most widespread and visible informal business establishment" with "nearly a dozen gangs and/or sections of the same gang carrying out drug-dealing operations in the community. . . . Drug dealing can be found on most street blocks, corners, and schoolyards" of this part of Chicago (Padilla, 1992:48).

6. It goes without saying that the illegal drug business is not only one of the largest businesses in the United States but also an international business. And, like legitimate international businesses, a few garner the bulk of the profits, operating seemingly without fear of government prosecution. This fact did not escape the attention of one of the members of the Diamonds, who told Padilla, "I don't know, but it seems like a setup. We work selling drugs, but have you ever stopped to wonder why it's people like, you know, people like Latinos, Puerto Rican people, and black people that are selling the drugs? I know that these drugs come from places far away from here. We don't grow this shit here. Maybe we should so we can keep all of the profit. You know, maybe all the money could belong to us. Have you thought about how the smokes and the cane get into the country, into our community, into the community of black people? You know, the government talks about the

guards who patrol the borders and shit like that. And on television, yeah, you see people talking about how the government made a large bust. And they say that's because of those guards on the borders. That's all bullshit. They are letting all the shipments of drugs come in because it's all political. People are making huge amounts of cash. But, then, we are the ones that pay. We can't get jobs, but we can certainly get our hands on as much reefer and cocaine that we want" (Padilla, 1992:54).

5

Girls and Gangs

Beginning in the early part of the 1990s there was a resurgence of interest in female offenders who engage in nontraditional, masculine crimes, particularly their involvement in gangs. The purpose of this chapter is to critically assess whether girls are becoming more like their male counterparts in relation to gang activities.[1]

Girls' involvement in delinquent gangs has never been of the same magnitude as boys'. Indeed, the stereotype of the delinquent in general is that of a male. The subject of girl delinquents in general, and girl gang members in particular, has been largely ignored. When girls and women are mentioned, it is often through media stereotypes of bad, evil, or even overly masculine girls, ignoring the social context, especially that for young minority women (Joe and

Chesney-Lind, 1993:3; see also Chesney-Lind, 1993). Traditional discussions of gang delinquency, from Thrasher's work in Chicago in the 1920s (1927) to more recent accounts (Cohen, 1955; Cloward and Ohlin, 1960; Dawley, 1992; Keiser, 1969; Short and Strodbeck, 1965); stress the image of girls as playing auxiliary roles to boys' gangs, if they are involved in gang activity at all. In fact, in his study of over 1,000 gangs in Chicago, Thrasher discovered only six female gangs, and only two of these he called true gangs. The stereotypical gang role for girls was "to conceal and carry weapons for the boys, to provide sexual favors, and sometimes to fight against girls who were connected with enemy boys' gangs" (Mann, 1984:45). Most of the earlier accounts of girls' roles in gangs were based on data given by male gang members to male researchers and then in turn interpreted by male academics, which no doubt reinforced traditional stereotypes (Campbell, 1990:166). More often than not, girl gang members have been portrayed "as maladjusted tomboys or sexual chattel who, in either case, are no more than mere appendages to boy members of the gang" (Joe and Chesney-Lind, 1993:8).

Such impressions are often reinforced by male studies of girl gang members. Miller's nationwide study of gangs in the mid-1970s, for example, found fully independent girl gangs to be rare, constituting less than 10 percent of all gangs. He also noted that about half the male gangs in the New York area had female auxiliary groups and that, of all the gangs known to exist in the Bronx and Queens areas of New York City, there were only six independent female gangs. Further, he reported that the crimes committed by girl gangs were far less serious than those committed by boy gangs and were no more violent than in the past (Miller, 1975). In contrast, Moore's research on gangs in East Los Angeles estimated that about one-third of the gang members were female (Moore, 1991:8).

Given the range of estimates, one might wonder whether girls and their involvement with gang life resembles the involvement of girls in other youth subcultures, where they have been described as "present but invisible" (McRobbie and Garber, 1975). Certainly, Moore's higher estimate indicates that she and her associates saw girls that others had missed. The long-standing "gendered habits" of researchers has meant that girls' involvement with gangs have been neglected, sexualized, and oversimplified.[2] So, while there have been a growing number of studies investigating the connections between male gangs, violence and other criminal activities, there has been no parallel development in research on female involvement in gang activity. As with all young women who find their way into the juvenile justice system, girls in gangs have been invisible.

This pattern of invisibility was undoubtedly set by Thrasher and carried on by many subsequent, mostly male, researchers. Jankowski (1991), for example, sees gangs as a distinctly male phenomena, and females are discussed in the context of "property" and "sex." Curiously, when female gang members have been studied by female researchers, a different perspective emerges, one that suggests that girl gang members do *not* fully accept such conceptions of their roles and positions. This will become evident when we review some of these studies.

Taylor's (1993) work marks a complete reversal in themes where girls are the central focus, but from a male centered perspective. His work, like Thrasher's and Jankowski's, is a reflection of a general tendency to minimize and distort the motivations and roles of female gang members and is the result of the gender bias on the part of the male gang researchers, who describe the female experience from the male gang member's viewpoint or their own stance (Campbell, 1990).

Taylor's study provides a facade of academic support for the media's definition of the girl gang member as a junior version of the liberated female crook of the 1970s. It should be noted that it is difficult to determine exactly how many girls and women he interviewed for his book (and there are many methodological shortcomings that seriously call into question his findings), but his introduction clearly sets the tone for his work when he writes, "We have found that females are just as capable as males of being ruthless in so far as their life opportunities are presented. This study indicates that females have moved beyond the status quo of gender repression" (Taylor, 1993:8).

Other studies of female gang members stress the image of girls as having auxiliary roles to boy gangs (Brown, 1977; Flowers, 1987; Miller, 1975, 1980; Rice, 1963). Miller (1980) also conducted an in-depth analysis of a Boston gang known as The Molls. This gang consisted of a core membership of 11 girls whose ages ranged from 13 to 16. They were white and Catholic (mostly Irish). These girls seemed to fit the stereotype of inner-city working-class girls, as they spent most of their time "hanging out" around street corners and looking and talking tough. They were known in the neighborhood as "bad girls." Their illegal activities included truancy, theft, drinking, property damage, sex offenses, and assault, in order of decreasing frequency. Truancy was by far their most common offense, occurring about three times as often as the next most common offense, which was theft (predominantly shoplifting).

Similar findings have been reported in Philadelphia (Brown, 1977) and in New York City (Campbell, 1984). In general, while there have been some changes and some indications that girls are becoming more independent and aggressive, overall these studies portray that girls who are part of gangs are either the girlfriends of the male members or "little sisters" subgroups of the male gang (Bowker, 1978:184; Hanson, 1964). Further, they suggest that the role for girls in gangs is "to conceal and carry weapons for the boys, to provide sexual favors, and sometimes to fight against girls who were connected with enemy boys' gangs" (Mann, 1984:45).

Girl gangs typically emerge after a male gang has been established, and it "often takes a feminized version of the male name" (Campbell, 1990:177). Examples of the latter include the Egyptian Cobrettes (related to the male gang called Egyptian Cobras), the Lady Rocketeers (affiliated with the male Rocketeers) and the Vice Queens (related to the Vice Kings) (Bowker, 1978:144). One group was known as The Dagger Debs, a female Puerto Rican gang in New York City, which was associated with a male counterpart known as the

Daggers. This group, consisting of about 14 full-time members, was described as a tough gang that exhibited typical "male" behavior. It was observed that they were aggressive and took an active role in gang wars (Hanson, 1964; see also Fishman, 1988; Prothrow-Stith, 1991).

According to Campbell (1984:9), in New York City there are as many as 400 gangs with a membership of about 40,000. About 10 percent of the gang members are female. Their ages usually range from 14 to 30. Some are married with children and all are from working- or lower-class backgrounds. The earliest gangs in the New York City area date back to 1825 with a gang called the Forty Thieves, located in lower Manhattan (Campbell, 1984). This gang consisted mainly of Irish youth and originated from a drinking spot owned by a woman. Soon other gangs formed, again mostly Irish. The earliest gang wars lasted two or three days without interference by the police. Women were not excluded from the fighting. Gangs were diversified even then, with some fighting for the group and some who were interested only in financial gain. Women were involved in each type of gang. They were usually viewed as instigators of activities. They were generally seen as auxiliary to the male gangs. They functioned as weapons holders, alibi givers, and spies and lures and to provide sex for the male members.

The area of East Los Angeles provides a fascinating glimpse of how gangs emerge and change with the times. As noted in Chapter 1, gangs in this area first emerged during the late 1930s and early 1940s; girl gangs came along with male gangs. Many gangs started in an area known as El Hoyo Maravilla (translated roughly as "the hole" in Spanish). The girl gangs in Maravilla (going by such names as Black Legion, Cherries, Elks, Black Cats, and others) were small groups not tightly bound to the boy gangs and not as closely bound to a specific barrio as were the boys. They often partied with boys from different gangs (Moore, 1991:27–28).[3]

In the mid-1940s there were some girl gangs that were auxiliaries to the boy gangs (e.g., Jr. Vamps, who were associated with the Cut-downs). The girl gangs from the White Fence area were more like the traditional auxiliary girl gangs. Many offshoots of these gangs continue to flourish today, some 70 years later. The fact that they have existed so long may contribute to the continued fascination with girl gangs by the media. It is unfortunate that the vast research on these and other girl gangs (showing the incredible diversity of these groups) is too often ignored by the mass media. Instead, we are too often presented with stereotypic images (for a fuller treatment of the media's treatment of girl gangs, see Chesney-Lind and Shelden, 1998: 45–47).

TRENDS IN GIRL GANG MEMBERSHIP

Media portrayals of young women suggest that they, like their male counterparts, are increasingly involved in gang activities. The following discussion includes a number of these sources that merit attention.

Girl Gang Membership and Their Crimes

Official estimates of the number of youth involved in gangs have increased dramatically over the past decade, as noted in Chapter 1. But what is the role of gender in gang membership? Let us look more closely at the characteristics of youth labeled by police as gang members. One report in the early 1980s noted that in New York City police estimated that about half of all gangs now have female members (Dolan and Finney, 1984). In Los Angeles, for each male gang, there is one or more female group. However, these claims may be highly exaggerated. According to the "GREAT" database program (Fall, 1991), only about 6 percent of all gang members in Los Angeles County were female (Reiner, 1992:111). A 1992 survey showed the exact same percentage (Howell, 1998). Esbensen and Huizinga (1993) found in their Denver gang study that 25 percent of all gang members were females; Moore estimated that gang membership in Los Angeles included one-third females (Moore, 1991). Some self-report studies put the percentages much higher, such as the 38 percent figure reported in an 11-city survey of eight-graders (Esbensen and Osgood, 1997).

Bjerregaard and Smith (1993) found that in every offense category, female gang members had a higher rate of delinquent offenses than nongang females. Fagan (1990) also found high levels of involvement in serious delinquency among female gang members in Chicago, Los Angeles, and San Diego; in fact, in all delinquent categories, including violent acts, female gang members committed more offenses than nongang males (Howell, 1998). Curry and his associates found that girls are three times more likely than boys to be involved in "property offenses" and about half as likely to be involved in violent offenses. Looking at these statistics differently, only girls' involvement in property offenses exceeded 1 percent of the total number of offenses tracked nationally. Contrary to popular conceptions about "violent girls," only 8 (0.7 percent) of the 1,072 gang-related homicides in this data set were attributed to girls. Homicides by girls differ significantly from those committed by boys. According to one study, girls' homicides are more likely to grow out of an interpersonal dispute with the victim (79 percent), while homicides committed by boys are more likely to be crime related (57 percent); that is, they occurred in the commission of another crime, such as robbery (Loper and Cornell, 1995).

Many argue that law-enforcement agencies tend to minimize female gang membership. Curry (1998:20) has suggested that law enforcement might not view female gang involvement as serious enough to be considered a problem. Chesney-Lind, Shelden, and Joe (1996) believe that earlier researchers and law enforcement have had "gendered habits." These critics argue that females have been invisible as gang members, as they had historically been invisible as potential crime fighters and firefighters (see also Sikes, 1997).

A study by Curry, Ball, and Fox (1994) noted that some cities reported that as a matter of policy, females were not counted as gang members; a few cities counted them as "associate gang members"; of those law-enforcement agencies with gang problems, no statistics on females were kept, and nine more felt confident in reporting no female gang members.

Sikes (1997) posits that investigating females in gangs is of low priority to law-enforcement agencies. Many gang girls are minors; thus, police have less inclination to deal with these girls, as they believe that the juvenile justice agencies will simply ignore the problem or release the girls immediately. They view females as less a threat than males, and so, Sikes believes, this preserves an attitude that "leads to both an over-identification of those boys only on the fringes of gang activity as bona fide gang members and an under-representation of girls" (Sikes, 1997:66).

A more detailed look at differences between male and female gang members in police databases can be obtained from a study that analyzed files maintained by the Honolulu Police Department (HPD). Examining the characteristics of a sample of youth (N = 361) labeled as gang members by the HPD in 1991 (Chesney-Lind et al., 1994), this study specifically examined the total offense patterns of those labeled as gang members, and it also compared a juvenile subsample of these individuals with nongang delinquents.

The study found patterns consistent with the national data. For example, only 7 percent of the suspected gang members on Oahu were female, and, surprisingly, the vast majority of these young women were legally adults (70 percent); the median age was 24.5 years for the young women and 21.5 years for the men in the sample.

Virtually all the youth identified as gang members were drawn from low-income ethnic groups in the islands, but these ethnic differences were also found between male and female gang members. The men were more likely than the women to come almost exclusively from immigrant groups (Samoan and Filipino); the women, by contrast, were more likely to be native Hawaiian and Filipino.

Most importantly, women and girls labeled as gang members committed fewer offenses than men and also committed less serious offenses. Indeed, the offense profile for the females in the gang sample bears a very close relationship to typical female delinquency. Over one-third of the "most serious" arrests of girls (38.1 percent) were property offenses (mostly larceny-theft), followed by status offenses (19 percent) and drug offenses (9.5 percent). For boys, the most serious offense was likely to be "other assaults" (27 percent), followed by larceny-theft (14 percent). In essence, this profile indicated that while both the males and the females in this sample of suspected gang members were chronic but not serious offenders, this was particularly true of the girls. These offenses patterns correspond closely overall national arrest patterns, especially for the girls (see Chapter 2). Serious violent offenses accounted for 23 percent of the most serious offenses of males suspected of gang membership, but *none* of the girls' most serious offenses.

Finally, it is important to note that once police identified a youth as a gang member, they apparently remained in the database regardless of patterns of desistance; for example, 22 percent of the sample had not been arrested in three years, and there was no gender difference in this pattern.

These patterns prompted a further exploration of the degree to which young women labeled by police as "suspected gang members" differed from young women who had been arrested for delinquency. To do this, a comparison group was created for those in the Oahu sample who were legally juveniles. Youth suspected of gang membership were matched on ethnicity, age, and gender with youth who were in the juvenile arrest database but who had not been labeled as gang members. A look at offense patterns of this smaller group indicates no major differences between girls suspected of gang membership and their nongang counterparts. The most serious offense for gang girls was status offenses, and for nongang girls it was other assaults.[4]

These quantitative data do not provide support for the rise of a "new" violent female offender. Yet we still have an inadequate understanding of the lives of girl gang members. There have been a small but growing number of excellent ethnographic studies of girls in gangs that suggest a much more complex picture in which some girls solve their problems of gender, race, and class through gang membership. As we review these studies later in this chapter, it will become clear that girls' experiences with gangs cannot be framed simply as "breaking into" a male world. They have long been in gangs, and their participation in these gangs, even their violence, is heavily influenced by their gender.

Types of Female Gangs

There are three types of female gang involvement: (1) membership in an independent gang, (2) regular membership in a male gang as a coed, and (3) as female auxiliaries of male gangs. Most girls are found within the third type.[5]

Auxiliaries usually form after a male gang comes into existence and usually take a feminized version of the boys' gang name. They often reflect the age grouping found in male units. They have no formal leader but usually have some members with more clout than others. Girls are not coerced to join. Rather, they come into the gang through regular friendships and families. Wannabes are informally screened for acceptability. Initiation usually involves an intense fistfight with a regular (girl) member of the gang to prove that the wannabe has courage. Initiation ceremonies are not unlike those experienced by sororities or fraternities or even country clubs (Campbell, 1993:136). "The gang will not accept just anyone, and this fact alone augments the members' self-esteem, which has taken such hard knocks from teachers, social workers, police, and families. . . . The gang rejects 'prospects' whose aim is merely to avail themselves of the gang's fighting ability for their own ends" (ibid.).

Even these auxiliary gangs are more than mere appendages of the male gangs, for many of the girls have some control over their own gang. They collect dues, hold meetings, expel members for violating rules, and so on. Strong normative control is exerted over members of the gang. For example, once a girl becomes involved with a boy, she must remain loyal while the relationship lasts. Remaining loyal to the boy is important because suspicion and jealousy are extremely disruptive, and a norm of fidelity seeks to prevent this.

Girls usually fight other girl gangs (sometimes even boy gangs). However, girls generally do not use guns; rather, they fight with fists or knives. There is recent evidence that this may be changing for some gangs as more guns become available and as fewer legitimate opportunities become available for underclass women.

Many of these young women are becoming less and less attached to male gangs. Campbell's (1984a) study of independent female gangs in New York illustrates this. She found that these gangs exist as their own unique subculture in an attempt to survive within the larger capitalist society. Similarly, Taylor's most recent study of Detroit gangs focused on female gangs that he describes as much more independent and more willing to use force than earlier girl gangs. Much of the violence, especially utilizing weapons, is an effort at survival in a difficult and cruel world. Taylor quotes one gang member: "Look, it's easy for somebody that lives in some quiet place to talk 'bout violence. But, come and live with us and you'll be carrying a gun or two yourself." Another stated, "Call it violence if you want, but I say it's just taking care of yourself" (Taylor, 1993:100). Kitchen (1995:43) notes that many female gang members "are rejecting the roles as mere extensions of male gangs, and working for males as drug runners and prostitutes. These females see the only way out of the ghetto life, while keeping their self-respect, is through the creation of their own crews, with their own rules and values."

Kitchen's ethnographic study of seven female gang members (and three nongang members) in Fort Wayne, Indiana, provides additional documentation of the economic deprivation underclass women, especially African-American women, face today. The specific area she studied (south-central Fort Wayne) had a poverty level that was higher than that of the city as a whole and higher than the national average (almost 40 percent of all individuals and 27 percent of all families were below the poverty level). For African-Americans the percentages were even higher (38.5 percent of all African-American individuals and 39.5 percent of all African-American families). African-American females in this part of Fort Wayne fared even worse: Over half (54.2 percent) of African-American female-headed households lived under the poverty level (Kitchen, 1995:84). The gang members whom Kitchen studied had some job experience, but most were in low-paying service industries.

MOVING BEYOND THE STEREOTYPES: THE SOCIAL CONTEXT OF GIRL GANGS

During the past two decades several firsthand accounts of girl gangs have been conducted in a wide variety of settings, literally covering the breadth of the United States, from Hawaii to New York. Several themes emerge from these studies, as follows: (1) the importance of class and race, (2) crimes and drug use, (3) reasons for joining the gang (including some benefits), (4) their relationship with male gangs and males in general (including being victimized),

(5) family-related issues, and (6) school and work issues. We will cover each of these issues in the following sections.

Class and Race

Kitchen's study in Fort Wayne, Indiana, revealed some strong feelings about race and racism. Her respondents had some very strong feelings about the society they lived in, expressing the belief that racism was fundamental. One gang member expressed her feelings this way: "I think people are racist, because they always stop and look at me funny, and think I'm going to rob them or beat them up. Everyone is scared of you if you black." Another complained that "every time I go to the store with my friends the managers, or security, are always following us around. Like they think 'cause we black we couldn't afford to buy nothin' so we must be stealing" (Kitchen, 1995:100).

Kitchen's study demonstrates the dual problems faced by African-American women: racism and sexism. The world that they inhabit does not afford many legitimate opportunities to succeed. It is a world filled with poverty on the one hand and the ready availability of drugs on the other. Selling drugs becomes an accepted part of an informal economy that has become institutionalized over many years. It is capitalism in its purest form—a product is in demand, and there are many willing to provide the goods. Whereas African-American women face many barriers in the legitimate world of work, including the consternation of males who do not approve of women who are in any way tough and assertive, they find acceptance and respect in the world of drug dealing.

A study by Joe and Chesney-Lind of girl gang members in Hawaii found that these gang members come from many different ethnic backgrounds from those normally found on the mainland. Honolulu, its major city, currently has around 171 different gangs, with an estimated membership of 1,267. The majority of the girls were either Filipino or Samoan, whom the authors describe as part of the "have-not" ethnic groups (Joe and Chesney-Lind, 1993:14).

A study of 65 female gang members in San Francisco (Lauderback, Hansen, and Waldorf, 1992) found that race was of critical importance, as the majority of the seven gangs studied were Latinas (78.5 percent), with African-Americans (15.4 percent) and Samoans (6.2 percent) constituting the remainder. Some noteworthy differences were found when comparing Latina and African-American gang members. The African-Americans were less likely to be affiliated with male gangs, while Latinas were more likely. Latina gang members were also more likely to be involved in activities with their male counterparts, while the African-American female gang members were more likely to engage in activities (e.g., drug sales) on their own. All of the African-American gang members were actively involved in selling drugs. For the total sample, however, less than one-half were involved in selling drugs.

A study of Hispanic girl gangs in Southern California shows that there are few economic opportunities within the barrio. As a result, families are disintegrating and do not have the ability to provide access to culturally emphasized success goals for young people about to enter adulthood. Not surprisingly, almost all activities of young people occur within the context of gang life, where they learn how to get along in the world and are insulated from the harsh environment of the barrio (Quicker, 1983).

The importance of social class was demonstrated in a study by Harper and Robinson (1999). Those girls who identified themselves as current (7.1 percent) or past (14.3 percent) gang members had the following characteristics: 96 percent of their families were receiving unemployment or welfare benefits, 56 percent were receiving food stamps, 71 percent received reduced-cost or free lunches at school, and 48 percent were from single-parent families.

The economic context of gangs in general, both male and female, cannot be ignored, especially the occupational structure of America. A quote from a "crew" member by Taylor (1990:57) illustrates this. She flatly stated that "better paying jobs ain't in this world for bloods, especially young bloods. I been kicking it with a crew since I was thirteen. . . . Some of the fellahs after that got busted, had to join job training fake-ass programs. Train you for what? A cook? Bullshit janitor job? A security guard that pays $3.65 an hour?"

A study by Laidler and Hunt (1997) found that most of the girl gang members either grew up in the same housing project or knew a relative associated with their group. The majority of these females were immigrants. Thirty-five percent of the fathers were absent; others were semiskilled or unskilled laborers. Their mothers were in the service industry or in unskilled jobs; 25 percent were homemakers/babysitters.

What is important to emphasize is the social context of poverty within which girl gangs exist and to examine what it means to be a young girl growing up in such an environment. Campbell (1990:172) notes that female gang members "seek to resolve the intractable problems of class by simultaneously rejecting and opposing some aspects of community and mainstream values while incorporating and internalizing others. Their resulting identity is often apparently contradictory or incoherent." Campbell argues that, at least for the young female gang members she studied in New York, there are five major problems that such poverty-class girls face and try to seek answers from within the gang (ibid.:172–173):

(1) "A future of meaningless domestic labor with little possibility of educational or occupational escape." Indeed, most are from welfare families and have dropped out of school and thus have few marketable skills.

(2) "Subordination to the man in the house." Especially within the Hispanic culture, the woman must submit to the man and has no say in the matter.

(3) "Responsibility for children." This job is hers and hers alone and this further restricts her options;

(4) "The social isolation of the housewife." She becomes trapped within the home with, at best, a few friends who are also housewives.

(5) "The powerlessness of underclass membership." As a member of this class, she is not only removed from the social and economic world, but is potentially a victim of crime within her own neighborhood.

Crime and Drugs

A study by Esbensen, Descheses, and Winfree (1999) found that gang girls, while to a significantly lesser degree in number of incidents, are very similar to gang boys in the types of illegal acts they commit. These researchers concluded that their findings did not support the idea that gang girls are only ancillary members or that they are excluded from the illegal and violent activities to which male gang members are exposed. "They are involved in assaults, robberies, gang fights, and drug sales at substantial rates" (ibid: 48).

Being "bad," "crazy," or "wild" earns respect and status within the gang. Harris found that there were four motives for engaging in gang violence: honor, local turf defense, control, and gain. "Machismo, even for girls, is involved in the value system that promotes the ready resort to violence upon the appearance of relatively weak provoking stimuli" (Harris, 1997:158).

The same "macho themes" emerged in a study of the female "age sets" found in a large gang in Phoenix, Arizona (Moore, Vigil, and Levy, 1995). In these groups, fighting is used by the girls, as well as the boys, to achieve status and recognition. Even here, though, the violence is mediated by gender and culture. One girl recounts that she established her reputation by "protecting one of my girls. He [a male acquaintance] was slapping her around and he was hitting her and kicking her, and I went and jumped him and started hitting him" (ibid.:39). Once respect is achieved, these researchers found that girls relied on their reputations and fought less often. One interview conducted by Sikes (1997) concluded that "in this world, the strongest . . . (gangbanger), the one 'crazy' enough to take the dare—snipe at the cop, deal the big bucks, wipe out the enemy—survived. So you found a guy who was crazy or became crazy yourself" (ibid.:21).

Most females, researchers (e.g., Harris, 1997; Sikes, 1997) have noted, do not seek out violence; it is simply a part of the girls' existence, as acceptable as any other behavior, such as drinking, taking, or selling drugs, in their society. Sikes, for example, found that many girls had become ruthless and able to act violently without limits. This behavior was prompted by the overarching need to survive in the environment in which these girls saw themselves. "The more you could feel, the more you cared, the greater chance of self-destruction. It was not coincidental that many of the kids in gangs took drugs or drank. Drugs helped protect them from things that would, if fully perceived, drive them crazy." (Sikes, 1997:27).

Kitchen (1995) explored the issue of violence and the question of whether female gang members were as tough and aggressive as their male counterparts. All of her subjects stated that the use of violence was often necessary if one was going to sell drugs. One respondent flatly stated that "anyone who sells drugs has to be violent, even if they female. It is part of doin' business." Another stated that people would take advantage of the female not willing to use force. "Someone think you weak, they goin' take from ya'. Even if you female you got to be willing to shoot." And another responded that these women "fight each other, they fight guys, sell drugs, wear colors, they do everything the guys do." Another stated that "females who are soft won't make it" (Kitchen, 1995:93). Another researcher noted that "being 'bad' provides an outlet, a diversion from the monotony of her life and that of her friends. Possessions and partying are major preoccupations. Authority figures provide opportunities to prove toughness and control in challenging situations" (Davis, 1999:254).

Kitchen (1995) noted that joining a gang seemed to be fueled by the desire to make money and by the lack of good jobs in the area. Selling drugs was the main method of obtaining money for gang members, both male and female. One of her subjects expressed the problem this way: "They ain't no jobs out here. No one goin' hire someone like me. I ain't never had a job, and ain't no one goin' to give me a chance. Most people around here have to collect welfare or sell drugs, or both." Another female gang member stated, "I don't have enough education or experience to get nothing but a minimum wage job. That's bullshit workin' for minimum wage. It ain't worth it. That's why these cats are out there sellin' drugs" (ibid.:90). The selling of crack cocaine was the most lucrative business in this area. As another female gang member put it, "Most are selling crack cocaine 'cause that is where you make the most money. You can find crack on any corner. You have to ask who sellin' marijuana, but both males and females can be found selling crack on any street corner in this area" (ibid.:90–91). Another female stated that by selling drugs more money can be made than by working at minimum-wage jobs. She said that "there's a lot of young people around here who are living on their own and takin' care of their mothers only because of selling crack. They couldn't make that kind of money workin' no minimum wage job. . . . It's sad that you can make more money selling drugs, but that's the way it is" (ibid.:91).

Kitchen notes that toughness, meanness, and aggressiveness are qualities that women must possess in order to succeed in the informal economy. On the other hand, when African-American women possess these qualities within the formal economy, they "are seen as too aggressive and threatening to the male structure." However, such qualities "are necessary, and contribute to your success in business and respect from peers in an underclass community, whether you are operating legitimately or not" (Kitchen, 1995:93). It is clear that most of Kitchen's respondents believed that, in order to succeed, they had to take on certain masculine characteristics or behaviors. One responded, "Most women if they actin' like men get the same respect as men. It's the same as in legitimate businesses. Those women who act aggressive and will do anything to get to the top, get to the top, and get respect. Those who sleep their way to the top, or are too soft, ain't goin' to get the same respect" (ibid.:108).

Sikes (1997:12) found that the female gang members in Los Angeles were "hypnotized by the equating of money with power and fashioned gang hierarchies on things like clothing, gold-plated AK-47 pendants and, expensive Nike air shoes." Interestingly, the qualities that gang girls tend to have for materialistic things creates tension. This "tension exists not only between deviance and respectability but also between old-fashioned and modern values, between poverty and glamour" (Harris, 1997:131).

A somewhat different interpretation is presented by Laidler and Hunt, who note that female gang members are often characterized as being "wild, hedonistic, irrational, amoral and violent." These girls challenge the traditional gender roles and are therefore deemed to be more troublesome than male gang members. They suggest that there exists a "punitive policy response to the grimness of street life, like the stiffening of sentences, criminalizing drug addiction among pregnant women, remanding juveniles to adult courts, and reducing monies for diversion" (Laidler and Hunt, 1997:148).

Laidler and Hunt found that "gang-banging is an ideal arena for studying the way in which gender is accomplished because the streets—like mainstream society—are typically organized along patriarchal lines." As Messerschmidt succinctly put it, "gender is a critical organizing tool in gangs" (quoted in Laidler and Hunt, 1997:148–149).

An African-American female gang known as the Vice Queens provides yet another glimpse of the relationship between gangs and criminal behavior. This gang was a female auxiliary gang to a male gang, the Vice Kings, that existed in Chicago during the early 1960s (Fishman, 1988). As other studies have found, the bulk of their time was spent hanging out on the streets with the Vice Kings, which usually included sexual activities and the consumption of alcohol. Contrary to popular opinion, most of their time was not spent in delinquent activities. Their delinquent activities, however, were quite varied. They committed such traditional female crimes as shoplifting and running away from home, along with such minor offenses as driving without a license, disturbing the peace, and loitering. They also committed traditional male crimes, such as auto theft and grand larceny, although these were not as frequent.

Drug use is quite common among girl gang members, as it is for males. In the San Francisco gang study (Lauderback et al., 1992), drug use was reportedly widespread among these young women, although marijuana was the most popular drug. They are not generally bothered by the police (half of those interviewed had no arrest record), primarily because they do not wear the usual gang attire. One member stated, "Basically we just wear our little beads and braids and stuff so they [the police] just think we are some girls hanging out." Another member stated, "We not in the gang bang shootings and all of that" (ibid.:63). The Potrero Hill Posse gets its supply of drugs from their own homegirls (usually a senior member of the gang), while the Latina gang members get their drugs from both homegirls and homeboys. Most of their crack sales are conducted in rock houses. These houses are usually a neighbor's residence that is rented in exchange for drugs.

In the Hawaii study the majority of both male and female gang members had extensive arrest records, with about one-fourth of each group having 10 or more arrests. Their offenses were mostly property offenses, but many (about one-third of the girls) had been arrested for violent offenses. Not surprisingly, girls were about equally as likely to have committed status offenses[6] as any other type of offense. Peer pressure was cited by both groups as a reason for their criminal behavior, but boys were more likely to cite economic reasons (e.g., they needed money) (Joe and Chesney-Lind, 1995).

It is important to note, once again, that the bulk of a gang member's time is not spent committing crimes. Furthermore, most crimes happen rather spontaneously, usually because of just plain boredom. In the Hawaii study, Joe and Chesney-Lind found that to fill the time, gang members join together to hang out and have fun and develop makeshift strategies to fill the time void. They engage in sporting activities and various activities on the state's many beaches. The solution to the boredom of their lives is handled somewhat differently by the girls in contrast to the boys. Many of their activities correspond to traditional gender roles—the girls often engage in singing, going to dances, and learning the hula from their families, while the boys spend a lot of their time cruising. This cruising is not unlike similar teenage activities in any city or town in America. As is typical for males, such activity often includes such expressions of masculinity as drinking, fighting, and petty theft (e.g., ripping off the tourists). A typical day of a male is described as follows by an 18-year-old Samoan:

> After school there is nothing to do. A lot of my friends like to lift weights, if there was someplace to lift weights. A lot of my friends don't know how to read, they try to read, but say they can't, and they don't have programs or places for them to go. . . . There are no activities, so now we hang around and drink beer. We hang around, roam the streets. . . . Yesterday we went to a pool hall and got into a fight over there (Joe and Chesney-Lind, 1995:20).

In contrast, girls are not usually involved in much drinking or fighting, although this occasionally happens. When it does happen, it is due either to unsubstantiated rumors (e.g., that someone in a rival gang threatened a girl gang member) or to the boredom in their lives. A 15-year-old Samoan girl explained it this way: "Sometimes we like cause trouble, yeah, 'cause boring, so boring, so we like make trouble eh, to make a scene" (Joe and Chesney-Lind, 1995:21).

The Hawaii study found significant gender differences in the nature and extent of crime. Generally speaking, the girls were found to be much less involved than the boys in most areas of criminal behavior. It is interesting to note that one of the major activities of the boys was fighting, but when the girls were in their presence, they did not engage in much violence. Drug dealing was another major difference between the boys and the girls. The involvement among the boys in drug using and selling was far more frequent than among the girls. However, even among the boys, only a few were involved in the selling of drugs. Mostly it was using drugs and drinking that occupied the time of both boys and girls.

For girls, arrests for running away and other status offenses (e.g., staying out beyond curfew) were more common. Usually such arrests stemmed from the double standard of enforcement—boys were allowed to engage in this sort of behavior.

Moore's study of girl gangs in East Los Angeles reveals drugs to be a major problem. She noted that heroin has been a consistent feature of Chicano life for many years. Moore commented that in the 1980s there was a heroin epidemic that was barely noticed in the press, no doubt because of the focus on crack cocaine. The lifestyle that revolved around the use of heroin was known as the *tecato* lifestyle. As the life history of one gang member revealed, this was a life filled with a sporadic work history and characterized by frequent jail and prison terms. By the age of 20 about half of the male gang members studied, but less than 25 percent of the females were using heroin. By this age most had already been labeled tecatos by their gang and had withdrawn into their own subculture. To give an idea of the importance of heroin in their lives, Moore reported that 39 percent of the men and 16 percent of the women mentioned "heroin, drugs, narcotics" as being "the major happening during their teens," and "it was during their teens that they were initiated into the world of heroin and its usually disastrous life consequences" (Moore, 1991:107).

These individuals did not differ significantly from nonheroin users so far as family characteristics were concerned. However, they were significantly more likely to have grown up in a family where an addict lived in the home. Also, they were significantly more likely than nonusers to answer yes to the question, "Are you all for your barrio now?"

There were significant differences between men and women tecatos. Men were more likely to begin heroin and to continue the tecato lifestyle within the context of the gang. Also, the men were more likely to spend a greater part of their lives in and out of jails and prisons.

The women were more likely to be preoccupied with their children, while the men tended to lose contact with their children, a not altogether surprising finding. Also, the women were more likely to grow up in a family with another addict in the home and were most likely to begin using heroin with a boyfriend or husband. The world of the streets dictated that "a tecata's next boyfriend will also be a heroin user" (Moore, 1991:109). The women tended to continue using heroin for longer periods of time than did the men. Being arrested was a common occurrence, and most grew up in households where other members had an arrest record. Men were more likely than women to have been arrested, however (ibid.:111).

Reasons for Joining the Gang

Girls in gangs are not generally "recruited" in the normal sense of the term, nor are they pressured or coerced. Members come from normal friendship groups in the neighborhood and through family ties (Harris, 1988). The reasons girls join a gang are much the same as their male counterparts: a sense of belonging (family-like), power, protection, respect, fear, and sometimes paranoia. In addition, with membership comes prestige and identity, guidance, and ample access to drugs and cash. Sikes notes that

> although most girls in gangs are poor and members of minorities—being cut off from mainstream society is among the reasons kids join gangs—I met white girls from middle class homes who packed 9-millimeter semiautomatics. It's precisely the gang girls similarity to other teenagers that makes their cruel behavior so haunting" (Sikes, 1997:xxiv).

The Hawaii study by Joe and Chesney-Lind illustrates a common theme among both male and female gang membership: Many, if not most, gradually "grow into" gangs rather than merely "join." For the Hawaii youths, gangs had been a constant presence in their neighborhoods while growing up, and the majority of both boys and girls had another family member (usually a sibling) who had belonged to a gang. Girls tended to join at an earlier age (12) than the boys (14). Few reported having been jumped in or otherwise initiated into the gang. The boys' gangs were generally larger than the girls' (45 percent of the boy gangs had 30 or more members, whereas about half of the girl gangs had between 10 and 20 members).

The gang becomes a sort of "family." Indeed, Brown (1977) found that friendships with fellow gang members were of utmost importance for girl gang members. Giordano's (1978) study arrived at the same conclusions, with an additional reason that gangs also provided opportunities for mate selection, with many boys and girls in the same gang (i.e., boys in the main gang and girls in the auxiliary gang) eventually marrying and having their own families (Campbell, 1984; Flowers, 1987:137). Girls in gangs observed by Campbell very often engaged in the same behavior as the boys, such as smoking pot, drinking, fighting, committing theft, and "partying." Also, most of the fights the girls got into arose from domestic or romantic disputes (Campbell, 1984:33).

The "pseudo community" of a gang "provides a haven for sexually abused and battered girls who, having no genuine sense of safety, of being significant, or of the promise for a better life away from their neighborhood or community" seek security (Davis, 1999:257). However, in joining the gang, she is becoming more apt to be subjected to cruel treatment, injury, or death. Expected to do the bidding of the gang, activities that are for the most part criminal, she may find herself even more isolated if she is arrested and incarcerated.

The current generation of girls started to join gangs in the late 1980s and early 1990s. Some were steady girlfriends of gang members, says Sikes, adding that "almost any pair of kids who stuck together for more than six month informed me they had a 'common-law marriage' " (Sikes, 1997:102).

Females, like males, generally go through some form of initiation, not unlike initiations into other groups in society (e.g., fraternities and sororities, military boot camps, and social clubs). Some of these initiations may include being beaten and kicked by gang members, participating in a robbery, drive-by shootings, getting tattoos, having to fight 5 to 12 gang members at once, or having sex with multiple male gang members. In addition, stealing sprees, muggings, or mental tests administered by other gang members are common requirements for initiation.

Laidler and Hunt found that one other type of initiation was that girls might be required to fight with a male, unlike in the independent female gang. They were also targets for violence by other male gangs and/or the females in similar gangs (male-dominated). The Latinas self-reported fighting among themselves, usually because of disrespect from another girl or because of a male; much of the conflict arose after drinking heavily. These fights were fistfights and did not include weapons (Laidler and Hunt, 1997:160).

Some gangs have what are called *roll-ins* whereby a female initiate rolls a pair of dice and whatever number appears determines how many males have sex with her. In addition, there is an HIV initiation in which females have sex with an HIV-infected male—there are, however, no data to support this claim; all reports and tests have been negative. Sex is one of the ways to use and/or abuse girls in an auxiliary or coed gang (Sikes, 1997:102–103). Psychiatrist Robert Jiminez of Los Angeles told Sikes that of the many girls he has interviewed, only 15 were gang-raped as part of an initiation. Females are most often psychologically coerced. "A girl wouldn't have sex if she had a choice, but if it means being left out, she'll do it—giving in to her boyfriend for as much sex as he wants, when he wants it, and how he wants it—sodomy or whatever." More common is gang sex, "pulling a train" on a drunken girl at a gang party—"the boy's rank in the gang determined whether he was the engine, the caboose, or somewhere in between" (Sikes, 1997:103).

Moore found that a clear majority of the males (89 percent) lived in the gang territory and sort of drifted into the gang through friends in the neighborhood and at school. For the girls, whereas 65 percent lived in the neighborhood and naturally drifted into the gang like the boys did, a significant number got into the gang through relatives and close friends, including boyfriends. One of the most common differences between the male and female gang members was the existence of problems within the home, which served as a major reason for joining a gang. One of the major problems that the girls had that the boys did not was the experience of being sexually abused (Moore, 1991).

Fishman's study of the Vice Queens in Chicago noted that they lived in a predominantly African-American, low-income community characterized by poverty, unemployment, deterioration, and a high crime rate. Joining the gang came quite naturally and participation in the gang functioned to give them companionship, status, and protection (Fishman, 1988). Fishman concluded that the Vice Queens deviated somewhat from the traditional female gang that has been portrayed in the literature. The key to understanding this difference may be that this group was African-American and had experienced socialization practices distinctly different from those of their white counterparts. Specifically, they were "socialized to be independent, assertive and to take risks with the expectations that these are characteristics that they will need to function effectively within the black low income community. . . . As a consequence, black girls demonstrate, out of necessity, a greater flexibility in roles." The girls in this study used their participation within this gang "as a means to acquire some knowledge of such adaptive strategies as hustling and fighting in order to be prepared to survive as independent adult women within their community" (Fishman, 1988:26–27).

Harris's study of female gangs in Southern California found that females join gangs much the same as they would any other group of their peers but that the gang becomes a way of life, "a total institution, much like a commune or military unit completely absorbing the individual into the subculture" (151–152). She found that certain values become internalized in a gang girl and that any girl who exhibits the qualities of being willing to fight, to be "bad" and/or "crazy," to have great stamina and fortitude, and to use drugs is a welcome addition to the group (ibid.:152). Also, in Mexican-American female gangs, which are perhaps the most uncommon within the varied ethnic groups, the requirements for joining a gang are to be of Mexican-American descent and to live in or near the barrio (ibid.:152–153).

Harris found that the reasons for joining a gang were centered around belonging and seeking an identity. Their perception of the gang was that with these other girls, they had "a common destiny . . . a need for group support and cohesiveness, and a need for revenge. (Ibid.:154–155). The violent nature of their own lives also appeared as a commonality among the Mexican-American female gang members. The abusive relationships they had witnessed or experienced themselves created the necessity for an outlet for their emotions—often their anger and their rage.

As a member of the gang, the girl will be willing to exhibit risk-taking behavior in order to maintain her status and to prove her loyalty. "Supporting the 'hood' and identification as a gang member are two norms of great consequence, with strong sanctions applied if a girl is shown to be disloyal" (ibid.:156–157).

The everyday lives of girl gang members and the neighborhood context of marginalization made joining or forming gangs an answer to their problems. Joe and Chesney-Lind put it this way:

> At one level, the boredom, lack of resources, and high visibility of crime
> in their neglected communities create the conditions for turning to others
> who are similarly situated, and consequently, it is the group that
> realistically offers a social outlet. At another level, the stress on the family
> from living in marginalized areas combined with financial struggles
> created heated tension, and in many cases, violence in the home. It is the

group that provides our respondents with a safe refuge and a surrogate family (Joe and Chesney-Lind, 1993:17).

These young people lived in areas without recreational activities, no jobs, no vocational training opportunities, no money to pay for what entertainment was available, and "nowhere to go and nothing happening for long stretches of time." Many of the respondents said, "there is nothing to do" (ibid.:19).

For both the boys and the girls the gang serves as an alternative family. Some of these youths come from families in which the parents are overemployed (working at two working-class or service jobs) just to make ends meet in an area with an extremely high cost of living. Many youths are on their own much of the time, without any supervision, mostly due to being in a single-parent household where that parent (usually the mother) is working full time. In other cases there are family stresses due to frequent periods of unemployment or underemployment. Thus the gang takes the place of their families in terms of having someone to share problems with and give support. One girl, a 15-year-old Samoan, stated it this way: "We all like sistas all taking care of each other." Another girl belonged to a group called JEMA, which stands for Just Every Mother's Angel. She describes the origins of this group as follows: "We chose that because all the girls I hang out with, yeah, all their mothers passed away, and during elementary days, we all used to hang and all our mothers were close, yeah, so that's how we came up with that name" (ibid.:23).

Campbell's study of an Hispanic gang in New York concluded that for these girls the gang represents "an idealized collective solution to the bleak future that awaits" them. These girls have a tendency to portray the gang to themselves and the outside world in a very idealized and romantic manner (Campbell, 1990:173). Like their male counterparts, the gang offers girls solutions to two important human needs as have been noted by Maslow (1951) acceptance and safety (Campbell, 1993:136). These girls develop an exaggerated sense of belonging to the gang. In reality, they were loners prior to joining the gang, having been only loosely connected to schoolmates and neighborhood peer groups. The gang closeness, as well as the excitement of gang life, is more of a fiction than reality. Their daily street talks are filled with exaggerated stories of parties, drugs, alcohol, and other varieties of fun. However, as Campbell notes:

> These events stand as a bulwark against the loneliness and drudgery of their future lives. They also belie the day-to-day reality of gang life. The lack of recreational opportunities, the long days unfilled by work or school, and the absence of money mean that hours and days are whiled away on street corners. "Doing nothing" means hanging out on the stoop; the hours of "bullshit" punctuated by trips to the store to buy one can of beer at a time. When an unexpected windfall arrives, marijuana and rum are purchased in bulk and the partying begins. The next day, life returns to normal (ibid.:176).

Instability in these girls' lives plays an important part in understanding their membership in street gangs. Frequent moves and failure to form real ties to school friends make rebelling easier and more attractive. Perhaps because of this instability, female gang members bond so strongly that they will risk their own safety to help another female. Gilligan (1991) believes that female adolescent crises pose difficulties for girls through the sacrifice of childhood idealization (in relationships) in exchange for stronger self-identity. When they are asked, they say that their aspirations are typically unrealistic, with the girls expressing desires to be rock stars or professional models. Campbell cites recent data revealing a very bleak future indeed, as 94 percent will have children, and 84 percent of these will have to raise their children without a husband. Most will be dependent on some form of welfare (ibid.:182). Their lives, in effect, reflect all the burdens of their triple handicaps of race, class, and gender. "Gang life becomes girls' religion, giving courage and faith and teaching one how to live. It gives the sense of something greater than the individual, of some higher purpose" (Sikes, 1997:37).

Girls not only "age in" but also "age out" of gangs at earlier ages than do boys. According to Harris, girls are most active in gangs between 13 and 16 years of age. She suggests that "by 17 or 18, interests and activities of individual members are directed toward the larger community rather than toward the gang, and girls begin to leave the active gang milieu" (Harris, 1994:300). Others "mature out" of gang activity when they have children or go to jail.

However, for many girls, leaving the gang life constitutes much the same activity as initiation into the gang. It is not uncommon for female gangs to "beat out" members, with other members taking turns beating each girl who has asked to quit the gang. In some instances, members kill those who want out or force the girl to kill a member of her family in order to leave the gang, but these instances are rare (McNaught, 1999).

McNaught (1999) suggests that some girls who are drawn into gangs through sexual relationships and become pregnant are especially problematic. Often the children's fathers are incarcerated and cannot provide assistance, and their fellow gang members, their only friends, indeed, their family, often reject them. In addition, these girls have no skills or education to help themselves and their children. These girls realize that their gang membership can no longer help them, and so they drift away from the gang.

In the Laidler and Hunt study, the girls joined gangs for the "family-like" relationships; however, they found that these feeling were different for girls in the independent female gang and the other female gangs. In the independent gang, the group "served as a surrogate family; providing a fictive kinship network and resource to draw upon for emotional and economic support." The females also joined together to make money. This was done largely through drug sales and shoplifting; viewing their actions as a way to make life better for themselves and their children (Laidler and Hunt, 1997:153–154).

The conclusions reached by Joe and Chesney-Lind echo the words of Thrasher and many others (see chapter 7) and can be used to summarize the other studies noted above. They state that, for both the girls and the boys,

> The gang is a haven for coping with the many problems they encounter
> in their everyday life in marginalized communities. Paradoxically, the sense

of solidarity achieved from sharing everyday life with similarly situated others has the unintended effect of drawing many gang youth—both boys and girls—into behaviors that ultimately create new problems for them. . . . The gang provides a needed social outlet and tonic for the boredom of low income life. The gang provides friends and activities in communities where such recreational outlets are pitifully slim. Gender, though, shapes these activities. For girls, the list of pro-social activities is longer than boys. For boys, getting together in groups quickly moves into cruising instead of hanging out and that, in turn, leads to fights and confrontations with other groups of boys (Joe and Chesney-Lind, 1993:29–30).

For the girls, the abusive relationships within their families and in their communities lead them to seek protection within the gang, which in turn gives them skills for fighting back. But the violence the girls do engage in, which violates traditional notions of femininity, is hardly evidence of any sort of liberation from patriarchal controls. As Joe and Chesney-Lind note, the life of girls in gangs is not an expression of liberation but rather "reflects the attempts of young women to cope with a bleak and harsh present as well as a dismal future" (ibid.:32).

Relationship with Males and Male Gangs

Sexism was a topic that Kitchen (1985) explored with her respondents. Women (especially African-American women) do not appear to get much respect within the legitimate business world, but in the informal economy of drug dealing, they command respect as long as they are tough and do not sell themselves. As one put it, "The only girls not respected around here are the ones that are givin' it up for drugs, or are selling themselves to buy. Most women get respect if they sellin' drugs, but not if they using. It's ok for guys to use, but not us" (ibid.:104). This double standard did not go unnoticed among some of the female gang members Kitchen interviewed. One commented, "I think it is harder for girls to earn respect than guys. Guys just beat someone up, or carry a gun, and they got respect. But girls, if they mess up, they get treated like a ho [whore]." Another stated that, "Guys get more attention, and women do not get the same amount of respect on jobs. Males have better opportunities. The bosses think 'cause they guys they will do a better job." Still another said, "Guys around here don't respect women much. I think it is because of all the rap music bashin' women. I listen to some of this music calling women bitches and ho's and it upsets me. I think the guys around here think sex is all we're good for" (ibid.:104).

Quicker's study of female Chicano gang members in East Los Angeles found evidence that these girls, although still somewhat dependent on their male counterparts, were becoming more and more independent. These girls identified themselves as homegirls and their male counterparts as homeboys, a common reference to relationships in the barrio (Quicker, 1983).

Campbell (1995:70) states, "These types of roles tend to suggest a no-win situation for gang girls. As Sex Objects, they are cheap women rejected by other girls, parents, social workers, and ironically often by the boys themselves. As Tomboys, they are resented by boys and ridiculed by family and friends who wait patiently for them to 'grow out of it.'"

Fishman's study of the Vice Queens found that the relationship these girls had with the boys in the Vice Kings was primarily sexual. "Vice Queens had sexual relations with members of the gang in the process of 'going with' the boys and they bore the boys' illegitimate children." Moreover, their relationships were very open and lacked the subtle discretion consistent with middle-class values. That is, rather than engage in flirtatious behavior, they "unabashedly placed themselves at the boys' disposal and openly encouraged them to fondle and to have sexual relations with them." There was little actual dating in the usual sense, and the boys tended to pay attention to the girls only when they wanted sex. Typically, the males tended to "handle them, curse them and beat them." While they did "go steady," neither "perceived each other as future marriage partners." The Vice Kings viewed the Vice Queens "as useful for premarital sexual relations but not as steady girlfriends" (Fishman, 1988:17–19).

Females are increasingly encouraged to consider themselves equal to males, yet most of their experiences with males are those of abuse, both physical and sexual and violence (Davis, 1999). One survey, conducted in Seattle's juvenile detention center found that 98 percent of the females incarcerated were sexual abuse victims (Mendez, 1996:A7). Similarly, Sikes (1997) found that the girls she studied had many problems of this nature. She found that they were victims of physical brutality in gangs and in domestic situations as well.

According to a U.S. Department of Justice (1998:14) report, "Many female groups are no longer simply extensions of male gangs. Female gang members manage their own affairs, make their own decisions, and often engage in a system of norms that is similar to that of male gangs."

Harris's study of the *Cholas,* a Latino gang in the San Fernando Valley (in Southern California), echoes this theme. She notes that while the *Cholas* in many respects resemble male gangs, the gang did challenge the girls' traditional destiny within the barrio in two direct ways. First, the girls reject the traditional image of the Latino woman as wife and mother, supporting instead a more macho homegirl role. Second, the gang supports the girls in their estrangement from organized religion, substituting instead a form of familialism that "provides a strong substitute for weak family and conventional school ties" (Harris, 1988:172).

Kitchen (1995:43) notes that many female gang members "are rejecting the roles as mere extensions of male gangs, and working for males as drug runners and prostitutes. These females see the only way out of the ghetto life, while keeping their self-respect, is through the creation of their own crews, with their own rules and values."

Fighting protects female gang members from this victimization. The gang provides a "number of discrete functions" that serve as a "bulwark against a very hostile environment" (Davis, 1999:256). The girls are most often from families that pay little, if any, attention to them, and they are starved for familial relationships, for having a close circle of people on which they can depend and trust.

Harris found that while girls try to maintain an independence from males, they often allow the males to dominate; in gangs, the males exhibit an attitude of territoriality toward the girls. Girls are more likely to interact frequently, "together, all the time, everywhere," than boys. Informally they "hang out" together, and formally they hold policy discussions and planning sessions (Harris, 1997:157).

The girls in the Laidler and Hunt study described their boyfriends as "possessive, controlling, and often violent." This differed from the relationship with their other members with whom they kept a close and supportive relationship and did not fight but rather "talked out" their problems (Laidler and Hunt, 1997:157). While the males in these gangs were often protective of the females, they also victimized them, unlike the independent female gang members. This victimization took the form of verbal, physical, and sometimes, sexual abuse. Their boyfriends used similar actions to control their girls; many of these males did not approve of the girls "hanging out" on the streets (ibid.:161). Laidler and Hunt concluded that any type of female gang affiliation presents girls with violence-prone situations and places them at high risk for abuse.

Most of the girls in Moore's (1991) study denied that the gang boys treated them like possessions. However, 41 percent of the older men and 56 percent of the younger men agreed that the girls were indeed treated as such. Three themes emerged from the male views. First, they believed that the gang was a male preserve and that "any girl who joins is worthless and deserves whatever happens to her." A second theme centered around male dominance over women. As one young man said, "When you're young you want to be on top. You don't want no girls telling you what to do" (ibid.:54). The third theme had to do with sexuality, one of the developmental imperatives of adolescent males. One male gang member stated that 90 percent of the girls were "treated like a piece of ass. . . . We just used them as sexual need things, and companions." In more recent cliques, sexual activity began at an earlier age—14.5 years was the median age of the first sexual experience of younger cliques, whereas it was 15.2 years for older cliques (ibid.:55).

Moore also notes that the practice of dating partners from other gangs (which the majority of both boys and girls do) often caused gang fights. One gang member said that "many wars started with other neighborhoods because of a love affair" (ibid.:56). On the other hand there were times when the women helped prevent a fight with a rival gang.

In the earlier cliques it was not unusual for gang members to have friends outside of the gang; in fact, Moore found that 65 percent of the earlier gang members had such friends. However, in more recent cliques, this percentage dropped to only 34. Additionally, significant gender differences were found. Girls were more likely to date boys from gangs; in contrast, boys were more likely to date girls who were not in gangs, that is, who were "squares." The boys reported that they enjoyed dating nongang girls and believed that these square girls "were their future," as they would be a stabilizing influence. One male gang member said, "You know that they were going to be good. You know they going to take care of business and in the house, be a good house-wife, you know what I mean" (ibid.:75). Another change noted by Moore was that the men from more recent cliques were more likely to report that their girlfriends disapproved of their gang membership.

Latino gang girls have had to negotiate within a Mexican-American cul-ture that is "particularly conservative with regard to female sexuality" (Moore, Vigil, and Levy, 1995:29). In their neighborhoods and in their relations with the boys in the gang, the persistence of the double standard places the more assertive and sexually active girls in an anomalous position. Essentially, they must contend with a culture that venerates "pure girls" while also setting the groundwork for the sexual exploitation by gang boys of other girls. One of their respondents reports that the boys sometimes try to get girls high and " 'pull a train' [where a number of males have sex with one girl], something she clearly rejects for herself—even though she admits to having had sex with a boy she didn't like after the male gang members 'got me drunk' " (ibid.:32; see also Portillos and Zatz, 1995).

In the San Francisco study (Lauderback et al., 1992), most of the girl gang members have children of their own, who are brought along to many of the picnics. The fathers of their children are not involved in their children's lives, nor are many other members of their families. Also, their experiences with the men in their lives have been mostly negative. The men in their lives "are gen-erally abusive, verbally and physically, and controlling." One member com-mented on her child's father: "They just get you pregnant and they go on about their business with somebody else" (ibid.:69). However, they would like to have a man in their lives, one that would be working and would be a fam-ily man.

Campbell suggests a close connection between gender relationships, vio-lence, and victimization. She asks, if gangs represent the "zenith of untamed masculine hostility" (as so many male gangs do), then why should young girls be attracted to gang life? She notes that the typical male gang member's an-swer is that girls join gangs because they "want tough men and gravitate to gangs in pursuit of them." Campbell, however, responds by noting that many observers (including many researchers) assume that "violence equals masculin-ity" and ignore the distinction between instrumental and expressive violence (Campbell, 1993:125–126). For the girls who join gangs, says Campbell, their fear and loneliness drive them toward an instrumental view of violence. Fur-ther, their use of violence is mostly for the sake of their reputation. Campbell writes that these girls

> know what it is to be victims, and they know that, to survive, force must be met with more than unspoken anger or frustrated tears. Less physically strong and more sexually vulnerable than boys, they find that the best line of defense is not attack but the threat of attack. The key to this is the development of a reputation for violence, which will ward off opponents. There is nothing so effective as being in a street gang to keep the message blaring out: "Don't mess with me—I'm a crazy woman" (ibid.:133).

For most gang girls, and indeed most girl delinquents in general, being a victim and/or witnessing victimization within their own home is something they have grown used to (ibid.:133–135; see also Chesney-Lind and Shelden, 1998). Much like their male counterparts, they experience a great deal of indirect violence in the sense that they see so much around them in their neighborhoods. As Campbell notes,

> The neighborhoods in which gangs thrive are among the poorest and most crime-ridden in the city. Burglaries and robberies are commonplace. Assaults in bars and on the streets are frequent. Drug dealers and pimps own the sidewalks. No one is safe there, not even a gang girl when she is walking alone (ibid.:135–136).

Thus, within such a context, it is easy to understand how girls can be attracted to a gang.

Family-Related Issues

Females most at risk for gang involvement come from homes in crisis. Easton (1991) finds that these homes most often are those that have marital discord, that are headed by a single parent, that display prevalent alcohol and drug abuse, in which physical and/or sexual abuse occurs, and that have sibling or parental gang involvement.

Girls usually become active in gangs in early adolescence. Many have children, and some are married. Girls are most commonly identified as either "good girl" with "typically middle class values (love, marriage, better social and life situation)" or "bad girl" with no "illusions about her socioeconomic status and the lack of opportunities it affords . . . likely to have performed poorly in school . . . struggle for money is relentless" (Davis, 1999:254).

Moore has noted that "neighbors, family and—for the men—girlfriends all tended to have been more actively opposed to gang membership in recent cliques as compared with older cliques. The gangs of the 1970s, then, were operating both with less involvement with square friends and in a climate of disapproval: They were defined as deviant groups, and conventional neighbors, parents, and girl/boyfriends tried to discourage membership" (Moore, 1991:76). Not surprisingly, girls had more restrictions placed on them. Whereas all of the respondents reported that their parents were strict, the female gang members were more likely to report this, especially those from earlier cliques.

Moore reports that 29 percent of the women said that someone in the family had molested them. Incest was more common among the earlier cliques than in more recent ones. Not surprisingly, incest was associated with the patriarchal family system. Fathers who molested their daughters were also more likely to assault their wives, who were more likely to be strict with, and to devalue, their daughters. The victims of incest were more likely to report that their fathers were alcoholics (ibid.:96). Another finding, not unexpected, was that most of the girls never told anyone about the incest and received no help (ibid.:98).

Moore also reports that girls were more likely to run away from home than boys, which is not surprising given the fact that they were more likely to be the victims of incest. Boys from more recent cliques were more likely to run away than those from earlier cliques. For the girls no difference was found between the two generations.

There was a lot of stress in the families of these gang girls, which caused many problems in childhood (as noted by Werner and Smith, 1982). Alcohol was one of several concerns. In one-fourth of the men's homes and in almost half of the women's homes, someone was either physically handicapped or chronically ill. In most homes some member of the family died when the gang member was growing up, usually a grandparent, but in 30 percent of the homes it was the father (ibid.:101).

Moore also discovered that there was the additional problem of deviance of other family members. A heroin addict (usually a brother) lived in the home of 20 percent of the men and 45 percent of the women. Also, the majority of the respondents (57 percent of the men and 82 percent of the women) reported that they witnessed a member of their family being arrested when they were growing up. In over half it was a brother, while in 28 percent of the homes it was the father (ibid.:101).

Moore concludes that, first, the problems in these families were varied, and there were few significant differences between earlier and more recent cliques. Second, it is clear that more of the women came from troubled families than the men. They were more likely than the men to come from families with an alcoholic, a chronically ill relative, someone who died, someone who was a heroin addict, or someone who had been arrested. For the girls, the gang may have been more of a refuge or escape than was the case for the boys (ibid.:101; see Jankowski's list in Chapter 3 of reasons for joining a gang, one of which is to provide refuge).

Some of these earlier family problems were repeated in the girls' own relationships with men. Almost all of the girls Moore studied (both addicts and nonaddicts) had been married at least once. But the marriages did not last very long, especially for men who had used heroin early in life. A term in prison usually ended the marriage (ibid.:111).

Heroin users began living with a mate at an earlier age than others. There were gender differences here, as the heroin-using women were twice as likely as the men (42 percent versus 21 percent) to live with someone at age 16 or younger, in contrast to only 7 percent of the nonusing men and 8 percent of the nonusing women (ibid.:112).

Even among nonusers, marriage (and relationships in general) was unstable. One main reason was that so many of the men continued to hang out with their gang after getting married. Hanging out with the gang led to problems for the family because the gang remained of central importance to the man, even more than the marriage. Also, when there were problems in the marriage, the gang became a convenient escape. (Many men escape to their circle of friends—for example, drinking buddies at the bar, golfing partners, business partners, and so on—whenever their marriages are rocky or even when there is nothing wrong.) A third source of problems was that so many marriage partners were both gang members; thus there were two people, not one, unwilling to give up the gang (ibid.:112–113). (It may be like an addiction, in that the addicted person is unwilling to give up the addiction to save a relationship or his or her family.)

Most of them had children, with men having fewer than the women (an average of 2.9 for the men versus 3.4 for the women); heroin users had the fewest. Whereas the majority (85 percent) of the women raised their children, less than half (43 percent) of the men did. Heroin users were even less likely to raise their children. Women were much more likely than the men to mention parenthood as a turning point in their lives (43 percent versus 19 percent) (ibid.:114).

Most of the women the men married were not in a gang; thus most of their children were brought up by square mothers. In contrast, the gang tradition (whatever this may be) was more likely to be found in the gang woman's household because she was more likely to marry a gang member. Most of the respondents said they did not want their children in gangs (ibid.:114).

Similar findings were reported in the Hawaii study (Joe and Chesney-Lind, 1993). Here the majority of both girls and boys live with both parents. Also, most of them reported being physically abused (55 percent of the boys and 62 percent of the girls). A key difference is that 62 percent of the girls reported having been either sexually abused or sexually assaulted.

School and Work

It should not be too surprising that gang members have had problems in school. Indeed, numerous studies of delinquency in general have found that school problems are strong predictors of chronic delinquency (for a good review, see Bartollas, 2000:chap. 9). We have noted in Chapter 3 how school problems were of critical importance for male gang members. Thus we have still another illustration of the common themes among both male and female gang members.

Kitchen's (1995) gang members had very negative reactions toward the school system. Even though 7 out of 10 graduated from high school, they all felt unprepared to compete in the legitimate economy. A typical response was as follows: "Mostly school is a waste. The teachers don't care nothing about us. . . . It has nothing to do with the real world." Another said, "School doesn't teach you about real life. All it prepares you for is a minimum wage job" (ibid.:119). Most believed that once one begins to sell drugs, one gets used to the money, and it becomes harder and harder to enter into the regular workforce. One respondent stated, "Most kids know that they don't need school to sell drugs" (ibid.:120).

Gang members, as a general rule, are highly likely to drop out of school. For example, the study of San Francisco gangs by Lauderback et al. (1992) found that the median number of years of education was 10, and only about one-third were actually in school at the time of the interviews. Lauderback et al.

conclude, in a statement that echoes Campbell, that "the prospects for these young women, unmarried, with children, less than a high school education, and few job skills, can only be considered bleak" (ibid.:70). Fishman's study of the Vice Queens in Chicago found that most attended school only sporadically because they experienced much conflict with school officials. Most eventually dropped out of school. Only 2 of the 19 hard-core members had jobs at the time the study ended. Most did not have any interest in working, as they generally expected "that their old man will take care of them" (Fishman, 1988:10).

Many have noted that school is often deemed as totally irrelevant to the lives of gang members and presents a motivation to drop out and become part of a gang. Davis, for example, has concluded, "In lives filled with boredom, the gang interjects excitement and "something" happening." For most girl gang members, success is elusive: "School is a road that leads to nowhere, and emancipation and independence are out of reach, given their limited family and community networks . . . avenues of opportunity for urban underclass girls are blocked by several sobering realities" (Davis, 1999:257). These include lack of education, training, access to meaningful employment, and few, if any, career possibilities.

Harris's study of the *Cholas* found that the bonds to both family and to school were weak (see our discussion of the "social bond" theory in Chapter 6). None of the females in her study completed high school. The gang therefore became the source of status and identity; "the most prevalent peer group association in the barrio, the one most readily available, and [it] provides a strong substitute for weak family and lack of conventional school ties" (Harris, 1997:156).

Closely related to school problems are, quite naturally, work-related problems. As a general rule, gang members of both sexes have not had good work records. However, contrary to popular myths, most gang members, especially girls, have had plenty of experience in the workforce, although mostly in the very low-wage service economy. Moore found that there were several differences between earlier and later gang cliques concerning employment. In the earlier ones (before downsizing), 61 percent of the men and 44 percent of the women had jobs; in the more recent cliques, the figures were 48 percent and 61 percent, respectively. Those who used heroin were the least likely to have a job.

Of those working, about one-third (both men and women) worked in semiskilled factory jobs; about one-third of the women but a fraction of the men were unskilled workers. Neither the men nor the women earned much— the median was $1,200 per month, although some earned more than $1,800 per month. Most found jobs through personal connections, such as friends, relatives, and gang members. Most were reasonably happy with their jobs, and, interestingly, most recognized that they would need more education and/or training to advance themselves (ibid.:116).

In most households at least one person was working. Roughly one-third of the men had received some form of government assistance (welfare, unemployment compensation, and so on), whereas women were less likely to receive it. Approximately one-fourth (no gender differences) got income from illegal sources, mostly from small-scale drug sales and hustling (ibid.:117).

SOME CONCLUDING THOUGHTS

What emerges from a review of research on girl gangs is a portrait of young women who, just like their male counterparts, find themselves trapped in horrible social conditions characterized by widespread poverty and racism. Fishman's closing statement in her study of the Vice Queens places African-American girl gangs like them in a larger context, as she writes that

> There has been little improvement in the economic situation of the black community since 1965. As black females growing up, the Vice Queens' situation was bleak. They lived in a black lower income community characterized by high chronic unemployment and intermittent employment as well as high homicide, crime, drug addition and alcoholism rates. . . . The situation for teen-age black girls today is even bleaker than it was for the Vice Queens during the early sixties. The findings suggest that as black girls are increasingly exposed to the worsening conditions within their low income neighborhoods where legitimate opportunities become increasingly restricted, then they will increasingly turn to black female auxiliary gangs which provide these girls with the opportunity to learn the skills to make adaptations to poverty, violence and racism. Thus black girls who join gangs today are no different than their sisters, the Vice Queens, but they have gone one step further. In response to the economic crisis within their communities, black female gangs today have become more entrenched, more violent and more oriented to "male" crime. These changes in the content of the black female gang appear not to be related to the women's liberation movement but to forced "emancipation" that stems from the economic crisis within the black community (Fishman, 1988:28–29).

Fishman's dismal speculation about the situation of girl gangs in contemporary poverty-stricken neighborhoods can be easily transferred to the conditions in the areas already cited: Campbell's Hispanic gangs in the New York area; Moore's Chicano gangs in East Los Angeles; the gangs in Potrero Hills in San Francisco; the gangs in Fort Wayne, Indiana; and the various ethnic girl gangs in Hawaii.

Moore makes a very interesting statement that should be carefully considered. She notes that the stereotypic gang is "quintessentially male, with no place for women." This image is held by both gang and nongang males. It is interesting to note that gang boys acknowledge the presence of the girls by referring to the gang as a family. This idea is missing from the media stereotype. Moore makes a valid point when she says that if the image of a gang included girls, it would "humanize the gang too much, to force the audience to think of domestic relationships as well as pure male brute force. It might also challenge the simplified and comfortable notions about women" (Moore, 1991:136–137).

The closing statement in Moore's study is instructive and reminiscent of what Thrasher said nearly 70 years ago (see Chapter 6): "Institutions develop when there are gaps in the existing institutional structure. Gangs as youth groups develop among the socially marginal adolescents for whom school and family do not work. Agencies of street socialization take on increased importance under changing economic circumstances, and have an increased impact on younger kids, whether they serve as beeper-driven flunkies for drug-dealing organizations or are simply recruited into an increasingly adult-influenced gang" (Moore, 1991:137–138).

SUMMARY

Girls' involvement in gangs has never been as frequent as that of their male counterparts. When they have been involved, it has usually been as so-called auxiliaries to male gangs. However, the extent to which girls have been involved in gang life may be understated because of the vague definitions of *gang, gang member,* and even *gang involvement.* As has been stated in this chapter, most male gang members have relationships with females, and this, almost by definition, makes every such female at least an associate gang member.

Media images of girl gangs continue to reflect the common stereotypes typical of how the media work in general. The images are exaggerations of "violent women" who have reached the level with males in just about everything. Largely ignored is the larger social context of poverty, class inequality, and racism that pervades their lives.

There is a general consensus in the research literature that girls become involved in gang life for generally the same reasons as their male counterparts—namely, to meet basic human needs, such as belonging, self-esteem, protection, and a feeling of being a member of a family. The backgrounds of these young women are about the same as those of male gang members—poverty, single-parent families, minority status, and so on.

The case studies of girl gang members in many different parts of the country reveal the common circumstances in their lives. The crimes that they commit are for the most part attempts to survive in an environment that has never given them much of a chance in life. Most face the hardships that correspond to three major barriers: being a member of the underclass, being a woman, and being a minority. The gang, while not a total solution, seems to them a reasonable solution to their collective problems.

NOTES

1. Portions of this chapter are taken from Chesney-Lind and Shelden (1998).

2. For exceptions see Brown (1977); Bowker and Klein (1983); Campbell (1984, 1990); Ostner (1986); Fishman (1988); Moore (1991); Harris (1988); Quicker (1983); Giordano, Cernkovich, and Pugh (1978).

3. Moore's (1991) study was a follow-up to her original study completed in the 1970s (Moore, 1978). The more recent study compared an earlier generation of gangs (those growing up in the 1940s through the 1950s) with a more recent generation (1960s and beyond). This is what we mean when we refer in this chapter to "earlier" and "later" gang cliques.

4. In addition, similar studies, using comparison groups in Arizona (Zatz, 1985) with Hispanic gangs and in Las Vegas (Shelden, Snodgrass and Snodgrass, 1993) with African-American and Hispanic gangs, while not focusing on gender, found little to differentiate gang members from other "delinquent" or criminal youth.

5. In the first edition of this book, we noted that there is another type of gang involvement on the part of girls and young women. We noted at that time that, as far as we could determine, this had not been noted in the literature. This remains true with the second edition. This involvement is in the everyday relationships of girls with males who happen to be in gangs, either as steady girlfriends, occasional dates, lovers, wives, or just friends. Should these girls also be called auxiliary gang members? Is this not similar to the situation of many young males who, because they happen to know regular gang members or are occasionally seen in the company of them, are therefore labeled as gang members (associates, wannabes, and so on) by the police? If we want to extend the often-vague definition of a gang member to its logical conclusion (e.g., to include everyone who knows a gang member or is seen with them), then there are probably just as many female gang members as there are male gang members.

6. Status offenses are applicable to juveniles only, such as running away, truancy, and curfew violation.

6

Why Are There Gangs?

Explanations of why there are gangs are really part of a much larger concern with explaining crime and delinquency in general. In fact, some of the most popular sociological theories of crime and delinquency have actually been attempts to explain *gang* delinquency or crime (e.g., the theories of Cohen, Cloward, Ohlin, and Miller to be discussed here). Thus, in a sense, this chapter is really a summary of some of the major theories of *crime and delinquency.*

Multiple theories have been offered to explain crime, delinquency, and gangs. Some have taken a strictly sociological perspective, others have come from a purely psychological point of view, while others have been a combination of both of these perspectives. Space does not permit a complete review of all the theories of crime and delinquency and gangs, although the most common theories are included here, and these take a mostly sociological approach to the problem. The theories to be reviewed here can be grouped into eight general categories: (1) social disorganization/social ecology, (2) strain/anomie, (3) cultural-deviance, (4) social bond (also known as control theory), (5) social learning, (6) labeling, (7) rational choice, and (8) critical/Marxist perspectives. Figure 6.1 provides a general summary of each of these perspectives. In this chapter we will provide a general overview of each of these perspectives, followed by a more detailed discussion of specific representations of these theories.

SOCIAL DISORGANIZATION/SOCIAL ECOLOGY THEORY

Social disorganization theory has been one of the most popular and enduring sociological theories of crime and delinquency. Variations of this theory have been called the *social ecology* perspective, since it has a lot to do with the *spatial or geographical distribution* of crime, delinquency, and gangs (Lanier and Henry, 1998: chap. 9; Stark, 1987). Modern versions of this perspective began with the work of several sociologists at the University of Chicago during the first three decades of the twentieth century. The original idea behind the spatial distribution of crime can be traced back to the mid-19th century to the work of two rather obscure scientists, Adolphe Quetelet (1796–1874), a Belgian astronomer and mathematician, and a French lawyer and statistician named Michel Guerry (1802–1866). These two were actually the first scientists who collected and analyzed various crime data and examined the residences of offenders, matching them with various socioeconomic variables, such as poverty, infant mortality, unemployment, and other social indicators. This began what became known as the *Cartographic School* of criminology—in other words, "mapmaking," which involved merely plotting on a city map the location of criminals and various social indicators (e.g., with colored dots, as police departments still do today when, for example, they plot the locations of certain crimes, such as a serial rapes, or the locations of a series of muggings, auto thefts, and so on).[1]

This idea of mapmaking and the more general notion that crime is *spatially* distributed within a geographical area became one of the hallmarks of what came to be known as the *Chicago School* of sociology (named after the many researchers in the sociology department at the University of Chicago during the early twentieth century). Within the city of Chicago (and other major cities of the era) these researchers noticed that crime and delinquency rates varied by areas of the city (just as Guerry and Quetelet had done 50 years earlier). The researchers found that the highest rates of crime and delinquency were also found in the same areas exhibiting high rates of multiple other social problems, such as single-parent families, unemployment, multiple-family dwellings, welfare cases, and low levels of education.

Theory	Major Points/Key Factors
1. Social disorganization	Crime stems from certain community or neighborhood characteristics, such as poverty, dilapidated housing, high density, high mobility, and high rates of unemployment. *Concentric zone theory* is a variation that argues that crime increases toward the inner city area.
2. Strain/anomie	Cultural norms of "success" emphasize such goals as money, status, and power, while the means to obtain such success are not equally distributed; as a result of blocked opportunities many among the disadvantaged resort to illegal means, which are more readily available.
3. Cultural deviance	Certain "subcultures," including a "gang subculture," exist within poor communities, which contain values, attitudes, beliefs, norms, and so on that are often counter to the prevailing middle class culture; an important feature of this culture is the absence of fathers, thus resulting in female-headed households which tend to be poorer; youths get exposed to this subculture early in life and become *embedded* in it.
4. Control/social bond	Delinquency persists when a youth's "bonds" or "ties" to society are weak or broken, especially bonds with family, school, and other institutions; when this occurs a youth is apt to seek bonds with other groups, including gangs, in order to get his/her needs met.
5. Learning	Delinquency is *learned* through association with others, especially gang members, over a period of time. This involves a *process* that includes the acquisition of attitudes and values, the instigation of a criminal act based on certain stimuli, and the maintenance or perpetuation of such behavior over time.
6. Labeling	Definitions of "delinquency" and "crime" stem from differences in power and status in the larger society, and those without power are the most likely to have their behaviors labeled as "delinquency"; delinquency may be generated, and especially perpetuated, through negative labeling by significant others and by the judicial system; one may associate with others similarly labeled, such as gangs.
7. Rational choice	People freely choose to commit crime based on self-interest because they are goal oriented and want to maximize their pleasure and minimize their pain. A variation is known as *routine activities theory,* which suggests that criminals plan very carefully by selecting specific targets based on such things as vulnerability (e.g., elderly citizens, unguarded premises, lack of police presence) and commit their crimes accordingly. However, choices are often based not on pure reason and rationality.
8. Critical/Marxist	Gangs are inevitable products of social (and racial) inequality brought about by capitalism itself; power is unequally distributed, and those without power often resort to "criminal" means to survive.

FIGURE 6.1 Perspectives on delinquency, crime, and gangs.

One of the key ideas of the social ecology of crime is the fact that high rates of crime and other problems persist within the same neighborhoods over long periods of time *regardless of who lives there.* As several gang researchers have noted, some gangs in certain neighborhoods have existed for as long as 50 or more years, often spanning three generations. This has been especially the case in East Los Angeles.[2] Thus there must be something about the *places* themselves, perhaps something about the *neighborhoods,* rather than the people per se that produces and perpetuates high crime rates (Stark, 1987).

The social ecology perspective borrows concepts from the field of plant biology, specifically studying human life and problems using notions derived from studies of the interdependence of plant and animal life. From this perspective, people are seen as being in a relationship to one another and to their physical environment. Further, just as plant and animal species tend to *colonize* their environment, humans colonize their "geographical space."[3] One of the most important ideas originating from these Chicago sociologists (specifically Robert Park and Ernest Burgess) was the *concentric zone* model of city life (Burgess, 1925). This perspective on city life and land use patterns identified specified zones emanating outward from the central part of the city. Five zones were identified: (1) central business district, or the "Loop"; (2) zone in transition; (3) zone of workingmen's homes; (4) residential zone; and (5) commuter zone.

According to this theory, growth is generated (from mostly political and economic forces) outward from the central business district. Such expansion occurs in concentric waves, or circles. Such expansion and movement affects neighborhood development and patterns of social problems. Studies of the rates of crime and delinquency, especially by sociologists Henry Shaw and David McKay, demonstrated that over an extended period of time, the highest rates were found within the first three zones *no matter who lived there.* These high rates were strongly correlated with such social problems as mental illness, unemployment, poverty, infant mortality, and many others.[4]

Such a distribution is caused by a breakdown of institutional, community-based controls, which in turn is caused by three general factors: industrialization, urbanization, and immigration. People living within these areas often lack a sense of community because the local institutions (e.g., schools, families, and churches) are not strong enough to provide nurturing and guidance for the area's children. It is important to note that there are important political and economic forces at work here. The concentration of human and social problems within these zones is not the inevitable "natural" result of some abstract laws of nature but rather the actions of some of the most powerful groups in a city (urban planners, politicians, wealthy business leaders, and so on).

Within such environments there develops a subculture of criminal values and traditions that replaces conventional values and traditions. Such criminal values and traditions persist over time regardless of who lives in the area. (This is part of the "cultural deviance" theory, to be discussed shortly.) One of the classic works about gangs coming from a social disorganization perspective was that by Frederic Thrasher. His book *The Gang,* published in 1927, seems to be as relevant today as it was when originally published. For Thrasher, gangs originate from

> the spontaneous effort of boys to create a society for themselves where none adequate to their needs exists. What boys get out of such associations that they do not get otherwise under the conditions that adult society imposes is the thrill and zest of participation in common interests, more especially in corporate action, in hunting, capture, conflict, flight, and escape. Conflict with other gangs and the world about them furnishes the occasion for many of their exciting group activities (Thrasher, 1927:32–33).

Thrasher's view of gang causation was consistent with the social disorganization perspective. Specifically, gangs develop within the most impoverished areas of a city. More specifically, Thrasher noted that gangs tend to flourish in areas he called *interstitial*. These areas lie within the "poverty belt" within a city, "a region characterized by the deteriorating neighborhoods, shifting populations, and the mobility and disorganization of the slum. . . . Gangland represents a geographically and socially interstitial area in the city" (Thrasher, 1927:20–21). Such an area has been called many names, such as the zone in transition, the slum, the ghetto, and the barrio.

Thrasher found evidence of at least 1,313 gangs in Chicago, with an estimated 25,000 members. No two of these gangs were alike; they reflected the great diversity characteristic of the city of Chicago in the 1920s (even today Chicago itself and the gangs of Chicago reflect this diversification). Much like today, gang delinquency in Thrasher's day ranged from the petty (such as truancy and disturbing the peace) to the serious (serious property crime and violent crime).

His theory of why gangs exist and what functions they perform can be summarized in the following quotes:

> The failure of the normally directing and controlling customs and institutions to function efficiently in the boy's experience is indicated by the disintegration of family life, inefficiency of schools, formalism and externality of religion, corruption and indifference in local politics, low wages and monotony in occupational activities; unemployment; and lack of opportunity for wholesome recreation. All these factors enter into the picture of the moral and economic frontier, and, coupled with deterioration in the housing, sanitation, and other conditions of life in the slum, give the impression of general disorganization and decay.
>
> The gang functions with reference to these conditions in two ways: It offers a substitute for what society fails to give; and it provides a relief from suppression and distasteful behavior. It fills a gap and affords an escape (ibid.:228–231).

According to Thrasher, by being in a gang a young man acquires a personality and name for himself; he acquires a sort of status and has a role to play. Without the gang the individual would lack a personality in the sense used

here. The gang "not only defines for him his position in society . . . but it becomes the basis for his conception of himself." The gang becomes the youth's
reference group, that is, the group from which he obtains his main values, beliefs, and goals. In a sense the gang becomes his family. Moreover, these groups
of youths tend to progress from what Thrasher called "spontaneous play
groups" to gangs when they begin to bring on disapproval from adults. When
this occurs, particularly if coupled with legal intervention, the youths become
closer and develop a "we" feeling.[5]

Thrasher clearly believed that gangs provided certain basic needs for growing boys, such as a sense of belonging and self-esteem. This perspective is consistent with Abraham Maslow's hierarchy of needs. Maslow's views will be
discussed in a later section of this chapter.

Several subsequent studies have focused on the community or neighborhood as the primary unit of analysis. Such a focus begins with the assumption
that crime and the extent of gang activities vary according to certain neighborhood or community characteristics. In a study called *"Racketville, Slumtown
and Haulberg,"* Spergel found that the three neighborhoods he studied varied
according to a number of criteria and had different kinds of traditions, including delinquent and criminal norms. For example, Racketville, a mostly Italian
neighborhood, had a long tradition of organized racketeering. Gangs in this
neighborhood were mostly involved in the rackets because this was where the
criminal opportunities were to be found (Spergel, 1964).

In contrast, the area Spergel called Slumtown was primarily a Puerto Rican
neighborhood with a history of conflict and aggression. The gangs in this area
were mostly involved in various conflict situations with rival gangs (usually
over turf). Haulberg was a mixed ethnic neighborhood (Irish, German, Italian,
and others) with a tradition of mostly property crimes; thus a theft subculture
flourished.

A more recent variation of this theme can be seen in the ethnographic
fieldwork of Sullivan. His study of three neighborhoods in Brooklyn provides
important new information about the relationship between social, cultural,
and economic factors and gangs.

The three neighborhoods studied by Sullivan varied according to several
socioeconomic indicators. These neighborhoods also had significantly different
patterns of crime. Hamilton Park had the lowest rate of all three neighborhoods, whereas Projectville ranked first, and La Barriada ranked second. La
Barriada ranked the highest for crimes of violence.

La Barriada was a mixed Latino and white area; Projectville was a largely
African-American neighborhood. The third area, Hamilton Park, was predominantly white. The two neighborhoods with the highest crime rates (Projectville and La Barriada) also had (1) the highest poverty level, with more
than half the families receiving public assistance; (2) the highest percentage of
single-parent families; (3) the highest rate of renter-occupied housing; (4) the
highest rate of school dropouts; and (5) the lowest labor-force participation
rates (and correspondingly highest levels of unemployment) (Sullivan,
1989:21–27, 98).

Sullivan suggests that these differences can be explained by noting;

> The concentration in the two poor, minority neighborhoods [La Barriada and Projectville] of sustained involvement in high-risk, low-return theft as a primary source of income during the middle teens. The primary causes for their greater willingness to engage in desperate, highly exposed crimes for uncertain and meager monetary returns were the greater poverty of their households, the specific and severe lack of employment opportunities during these same mid-teen years, and the weakened local social control environment, itself a product of general poverty and joblessness among neighborhood residents (ibid.:203).

A key to understanding these differences, argues Sullivan, is that of personal networks rather than merely human capital. He explains that these

> personal networks derived from existing patterns of articulation between the local neighborhoods and particular sectors of the labor market. These effects of labor market segmentation were important for youth jobs both in the middle teens and during the ensuing period of work establishment. The Hamilton Park youths found a relatively plentiful supply of temporary, part-time, almost always off-the-books work through relatives, friends and local employers during the middle teens, most of it in the local vicinity (ibid.:103).

When these youths reached their late teens, they were able to make use of these same contacts to get more secure and better-paying jobs. The minority youths from Projectville and La Barriada never developed such networks.

Sullivan found that among the precursors to a criminal career among most of the youths studied was involvement in some gang or clique of youths. It typically began with fighting with and against other youths. Street fighting was motivated mostly by status and territory. Beginning in their early teens, these youths would spend a great amount of time within what they considered to be their own territory or turf. The cliques and gangs these youths belonged to "were quasi-familial groupings that served to protect their members from outsiders" (ibid.:110).

STRAIN THEORY

Strain theory originated with Robert Merton, who borrowed the term *anomie* from the nineteenth-century French sociologist Émile Durkheim and applied it to the problem of crime in America.[6] The concept of *anomie* refers to inconsistencies between societal conditions and opportunities for growth, fulfillment, and productivity within a society (the term *anomia* has been used to refer to those who experience personal frustration and alienation as a result of anomie within a society). It also involves the *weakening of the normative order* of society—that is, norms (rules, laws, and so on) lose their impact on people.

The existence of anomie within a culture can also produce a high level of flex-ibility in the pursuit of goals, even suggesting that it may at times be appropri-ate to deviate from the norms concerning the methods of achieving success.

Durkheim, writing during the late nineteenth century, suggested that under capitalism there is a more or less chronic state of "deregulation" and that industrialization had removed traditional social controls on aspirations. The capitalist culture produces in humans a constant dissatisfaction resulting in a never-ending longing for more and more. And there is never enough—whether this be money, material things, or power. There is a morality under capitalism that dictates "anything goes," especially when it comes to making money (it certainly applies to the modern corporation).

What Durkheim was hinting at (but never coming right out and saying it—this was said very forcefully by Karl Marx) was that a very strong social structure is needed to offset or place limits on this morality. In other words, strong institutions, such as the family, religion, and education, are needed to place some limits on us. But the failure of these institutions can be seen in our high crime rates and the fact that the economic institution is so powerful that it has sort of "invaded" and become dominant over other institutions. (More will be said about this shortly.)

The basic thesis of strain theory is this: Crime stems from the lack of artic-ulation or "fit" between two of the most basic components of society: *culture* and *social structure*.[7] Here we refer to culture as consisting of (1) the main value and goal orientations or "ends" and (2) the institutionalized or *legitimate means for attaining these goals*. Social structure, as used here, consists of the basic *social institutions* of society, especially the economy, but also such institutions as the family, education, and politics, all of which are responsible for distributing *access* to the legitimate means for obtaining goals.

According to Merton, this "lack of fit" creates *strain* within individuals, who respond with various forms of deviance. Thus people who find them-selves at a disadvantage relative to legitimate economic activities are motivated to engage in illegitimate activities (perhaps because of unavailability of jobs, lack of job skills, education, and other factors). Within a capitalist society like United States, the main emphasis is on the "success" goals, while less emphasis is on the legitimate *means* to achieve these goals. Moreover, these goals have become *institutionalized* in that they are deeply embedded into the psyches of everyone via a very powerful system of corporate propaganda.[8] At the same time, the legitimate means are not as well defined or as strongly ingrained. In other words, there is a lot of discretion and a lot of tolerance for deviance from the means but not the goals. One result of such a system is high levels of crime.

Another important point made by strain theory is that our culture con-tributes to crime because the opportunities to achieve success goals are not equally distributed. We have a strong class structure and incredible inequality within our society, which means that some have extreme disadvantages over others.[9] Another way of saying the same thing is that *culture promises what the social structure cannot deliver,* that being equal access to opportunities to achieve success. People faced with this contradiction (one of many under capitalism) face pressures, or "strains," to seek alternatives.

According to Merton, there are several possible alternatives, which he calls "modes of adaptation." In his now famous typology of adaptations (reproduced in almost every criminology textbook), Merton suggested several alternatives, which include the following: (1) *conformity*—accepting both the legitimate means and the success goals; (2) *ritualism*—accepting the means but rejecting the goals (one just goes to work every day but has given up the goal of "success"); (3) *innovation*—where the person accepts the *goals* of success but rejects the legitimate *means* to obtain them; (4) *retreatism*—where one rejects both the goals *and* the means and more or less drops out of society (e.g., to become part of a drug subculture); and (5) *rebellion*—where one rejects both the goals and the means but, instead of retreating, begins to substitute *new* definitions of success and means to obtain them. Obviously, the adaptation known as *innovation* directly relates to criminal activity, including gang activities. Thus anomie/strain theory would suggest that participating in gang-related activities would be an example of being *innovative* in the pursuit of success.

According to Messner and Rosenfeld, in a recent revision of anomie theory, such strain explains high rates of crime not only among the disadvantaged but also among the more privileged since they are under "strains" to make more money, often "by any means necessary." This theory can certainly help explain the large amount of "corporate crime" in this country (Messner and Rosenfeld, 1997). Messner and Rosenfeld's revision of strain theory contains an important component that has usually been missing from writings on this particular theory. We are referring here to their emphasis on the importance of *social institutions* and the relationship with what is normally called the *American Dream*. The next section pursues this idea in more detail.

Strain Theory and the Institutional Structure of Society: Crime and the American Dream

The "American Dream" is a sort of "ethos" that is deeply embedded into our culture. Generally, it refers to a commitment to the goal of material success that is to be pursued by everyone. Within a capitalist society everyone is supposed to act in their own self-interest (part of the creed of "rugged individualism") in this pursuit (this has been part of the mythology of the "free enterprise" and the "free market"), and this, in turn, will automatically promote the "common good." Somehow, the fruits of individual pursuits in this "free market" system will eventually "trickle down" to benefit others.

The American Dream contains four "core values" that are deeply embedded within American culture. These are summarized in Figure 6.2. There is, however, a "dark side" to the American Dream, that stems from a contradiction in American capitalism: The same forces that promote "progress" and "ambition" also produce a lot of crime since there is such an incredible pressure to

1. *Achievement*—Often expressed by the phrase "Be all that you can be" (contained in a popular advertisement for the U.S. Army). According to this value, one's *personal worth* is typically evaluated in terms of one's monetary success and/or how "famous" one has become. This stems from a culture that emphasizes "doing" and "having" rather than "being." Failure to achieve is equated with the failure to make a contribution to society. This value is highly conducive to the attitude "it's not how you play the game; it's whether you win or lose." A similar attitude is "winning isn't everything; it's the *only* thing."

2. *Individualism*—According to this value, people are encouraged to "make it on your own." This value discourages one value that could (and has proven to successfully) reduce crime, namely cooperation and collective action. The so-called rugged individualist is perhaps the most famous representation of this cultural value. A corollary to this value is that "I don't need any help." Messner and Rosenfeld comment that "the intense individual competition to succeed pressures people to disregard normative restraints on behavior when these restraints threaten to interfere with the realization of personal goals."

3. *Universalism*—According to this value, everyone is supposed to strive for the "American Dream." And, of course, everyone has the same opportunity to succeed, as long as you "work hard." Part of this stems from the famous "Protestant work ethic."

4. *Fetishism of Money*—Money is so important in our culture that it often overrides almost everything else. It is often worshiped like a God. Money is the *currency* for measuring just about everything. Moreover, there is no end, "no final stopping point," for it is relentless. It has created what many call a *consumerist culture,* where everyone is being socialized, almost from the day they are born, to be first and foremost a *consumer.* (Witness the emergence of corporate-sponsored programs within elementary schools, including the ever-present McDonald's.)

FIGURE 6.2 Core values of American culture (Messner and Rosenfeld, 1997:62-64).

succeed "at any cost." The emphasis on competition and achievement also produces selfishness and drives people apart, weakening a collective sense of community. The fact that monetary rewards are such a high priority results in the fact that tasks that are noneconomic receive little cultural support (e.g., housewives and child-care workers). Even education is seen as a means to an end—the end being a high-paying job or any secure job (an advertisement for a local university that the senior author saw on a Boston subway encourages people to "go back so you can get ahead"). The existence of such a high degree of inequality produces feelings of unworthiness. Those who fail are looked down on, and their failure is too often seen as an *individual failure* rather than a failure attributed to institutional and cultural factors.

One of the keys to understanding the linkage of the American Dream and crime is understanding the meaning and importance of the term *social institution.* Social institutions can be defined as a persistent set of organized *methods* of meeting basic human needs. If you think of fundamental human needs, then there are relatively stable groups and organizations, complete with various norms and values, statuses, and roles, that over time gradually have become the human equivalent of "instincts" in lower forms of animal life (because humans do not have such instincts). The human needs that these institutions seek to meet revolve around the need to (1) "adapt to the environment," (2) to "mobilize and deploy resources for the achievement of collective goals," and (3) to "socialize members to accept the society's fundamental normative patterns" (Mesner and Rosenfeld, 1997:65). The most important of these institutions include (1) the economy, (2) the family, (3) education, and (4) politics. Other important institutions include health care, media, religion, and legal (many would place the legal within the much larger political institution).

It is important to understand that when these institutions fail to provide the needs of the members of society (at least of a sizable proportion of the population), then alternative institutions will begin to develop—not the "institution" per se but different forms, or *methods* of meeting needs. For example, if the prevailing economic system is failing, more and more people will engage in alternative means of earning a living; if organized religion is not meeting such needs as answers to fundamental life questions, then people will seek out unorthodox religious forms (e.g., cults like the Branch Davidians or Heaven's Gate); if the legal institution is not perceived as providing "justice," then people may "take the law into their own hands"; and if the mainstream media provide too much disinformation and do not allow dissenting views, then we will see alternative media emerge. Given that our major institutions are not providing the needs of everyone, it is our contention that one of the functions of gangs is to provide what our social institutions have failed to deliver. This view is depicted in Figure 6.3.

As Messner and Rosenfeld suggest, what is unique about American society is that the economic institution almost completely dominates all other institutions. This was once expressed by the famous American philosopher and educator John Dewey who said something to the effect that "politics [or government] is the shadow that big business casts over society" (Chomsky, 1996:29). American capitalism, unlike capitalism in other countries, emerged with virtually no interference from previously existing institutions. Unlike other societies, there were no other existing institutions that could tame or offset the economic imperatives. European and Japanese cultures, in contrast, place almost equal importance to the family, religion, education, and other institutional concerns. Under American capitalism, these other institutions become subordinate to the economic one (which is why in Figure 6.3 we have placed it in the middle). The goal is to make a *profit,* and everything else becomes secondary. Over time this has become a "market society" in contrast to a "market economy." In the former the pursuit of "private gain" dominates all other pursuits (e.g., the arts or family support).[10]

As depicted in Figure 6.3, gangs fit into this scheme by providing some alternatives to the dominant institutions. Note that in this diagram all of the major institutions shown here are connected by straight lines. This suggests what should be considered a truism, namely, that every institution is in some way connected with all the others; problems in one causes problems in another. And all the lines lead, eventually, to the center since the economic institution dominates all others.[11] As suggested in an earlier chapter, gangs function as sort of *quasi-institutions* in many ways. For example, many gang members feel that their "homies" are like a "family." Gangs provide methods and incentives to seek alternative methods of earning

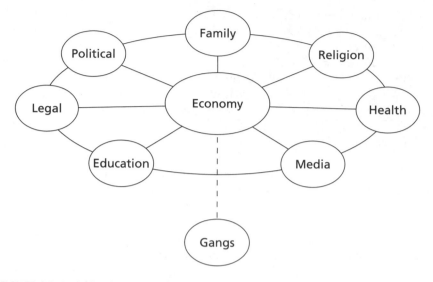

FIGURE 6.3 Social institutions and gangs.

money. They also provide an alternative media (graffiti) and an alternative religion (putting "RIP" style of graffiti on walls). They even have their own informal legal system. In short, gangs provide many of the needs that are supposed to be provided by mainstream institutions.

Differential Opportunity Structures

A variation of strain theory comes from the work of Cloward and Ohlin in *Delinquency and Opportunity* (1960). These authors argued (1) that blocked opportunity aspirations cause poor self-concepts and feelings of frustration and (2) that these frustrations lead to delinquency, especially within a gang context. A key concept here is *differential opportunity structure,* which is an uneven distribution of legal and illegal means of achieving economic success, especially as they are unequally divided according to class and race. Cloward and Ohlin argued that while legitimate opportunities are blocked for significant numbers of lower-class youths, the same cannot be said for illegitimate opportunities (e.g., selling drugs and other crimes). Their major thesis was that

> the disparity between what lower class youth are led to want and what is actually available to them is the source of a major problem of adjustment. Adolescents who form delinquent subcultures, we suggest, have internalized an emphasis upon conventional goals. Faced with limitations on legitimate avenues of access to these goals, and unable to revise their aspirations downward, they experience intense frustrations; the

exploration of nonconformist alternatives may be the result (Cloward and Ohlin, 1960:86).

Among the specific assumptions of this theory is that blocked opportunities (or aspirations) create feelings of frustration and low self-esteem, which in turn often lead to delinquency and frequently gang behavior. Cloward and Ohlin postulate that three different types of gangs emerge and that these types correspond with characteristics of the neighborhoods (which affect opportunities to commit different types of crimes) rather than of the individuals who live there. The three types of gangs are (1) *criminal gangs*, which are organized mainly around the commission of property crimes and exist in areas where there is already in existence relatively organized forms of adult criminal activity (thus adult criminals are seen as successful role models by youths who live there); (2) *conflict gangs*, which engage mostly in violent behavior, such as gang fights over turf, and exist in neighborhoods where living conditions are for the most part unstable and transient, resulting in the lack of any adult role models, whether conventional or criminal; and (3) *retreatist gangs*, which engage mostly in illegal drug use and exist in those neighborhoods dominated by a great deal of illegal drug activity. These youths are described as double failures by Cloward and Ohlin.

Social Embeddedness

One of the most interesting new variations of strain theory comes from Hagan (1993:465–491). Hagan borrows the term *social embeddedness* from economist Mark Granovetter (1992) to describe a developmental view of involvement in delinquency. Because much of the literature Hagan cites in support of this view pertains to gangs, it is obviously highly relevant here.

Hagan notes that instead of unemployment preceding involvement in criminal behavior (a common view in criminology), for young offenders the reverse is actually the case. For these youths, involvement in crime begins well before they can legally be involved in the labor market. According to Granovetter, becoming a regularly employed person involves much more than an individual's skills and education. It involves being connected to a social network of contacts that accrue over time and usually begins at a relatively early age. In other words, in order to become involved in the labor market, one needs to be socialized into this market starting at an early age. This means, among other things, that a youth begins to earn money doing odd jobs such as mowing lawns, babysitting, washing windows, shoveling snow, delivering papers, and so on long before turning 16. Through such activities a youth begins a process of social embeddedness rather early in life. For those youths who do poorly in school and/or drop out, such contacts become difficult to establish.[12]

Hagan argues that, just as one can become socially embedded in the world of regular job contacts and the world of work, so too can one become embedded in a network of crime and deviance. In most of the high-crime, inner-city neighborhoods, the odd jobs of middle-class youths noted above do not exist in large number (.e.g., in the projects there are no lawns to be mowed). He notes that parental involvement in crime will integrate youths into networks of criminal opportunities. Likewise, association with delinquent peers or contacts with drug dealers can also integrate youths into criminal networks. Moreover, delinquent acts tend to cause youths to become further isolated from networks of employment. A sort of snowballing effect takes place whereby each delinquent act and/or contact with the world of crime further distances a youth from the legitimate world of work. Thus the perspective of social embeddedness identifies "a process of separation and isolation from conventional employment networks" that has a time sequence with a "lagged accumulation of effect that should build over time" (Hagan, 1993:469).

Hagan goes on to cite several examples of recent ethnographic research on delinquency (mostly work on gangs) that support this view.[13] Hagan quotes Anderson, who noted; "For many young men the drug economy is an employment agency. . . . Young men who 'grew up' in the gang, but now are without clear opportunities, easily become involved; they fit themselves into its structure, manning its drug houses and selling drugs on street corners" (Anderson, 1990:244). Similarly, Padilla noted that gang youths he studied "began turning to the gang in search of employment opportunities, believing that available conventional work would not sufficiently provide the kinds of material goods they wished to secure." Padilla also noted that these youths became involved in the gang world between the ages of 13 and 15. Increasing involvement in the gang further embedded them, and entry into the legitimate world of work became a serious problem for them later in life (Padilla, 1992:101–102).

The process of estrangement from the legitimate world of work and consequent embeddedness in the world of criminal opportunities are further documented in Moore's study of Hispanic gangs in East Los Angeles, Hagedorn's work on Milwaukee gangs, Sullivan's study of three neighborhoods in New York (as reviewed in the previous section), and MacLeod's study of youths in a Chicago housing project. All of these studies found evidence of the socialization of inner-city youths (especially minority youths) into the world of criminal opportunities and their subsequent isolation from the social networks of legitimate work.

CULTURAL DEVIANCE THEORIES

Cultural deviance theory proposes that delinquency is a result of a desire to conform to cultural values that are to some extent in conflict with those of conventional society. In part, this perspective is a direct offshoot of social disorganization theory because part of that theory (as noted previously) suggests that criminal values and traditions emerge within communities most affected by social disorganization.

Cohen's Culture of the Gang

One of the most popular versions of cultural deviance theory was Albert Cohen's work, *Delinquent Boys: The Culture of the Gang* (1955). Cohen's view incorporates the following assumptions: (1) a high proportion of lower-class youths (especially males) do poorly in school; (2) poor school performance relates to delinquency, (3) poor school performance stems from a conflict between dominant middle-class values of the school system and values of lower-class youths; and (4) most lower-class male delinquency is committed in a gang context, partly as a means of meeting some basic human needs, such as self-esteem and belonging.

There are two key concepts in Cohen's theory: (1) *reaction formation,* meaning that one openly rejects what he wants, or aspires to, but cannot achieve or obtain, and (2) *middle-class measuring rod* or evaluations of school performance *and* behavior within the school based on norms and values thought to be associated with the middle class, such as punctuality, neatness, cleanliness, nonviolent behavior, drive and ambition, achievement and success (especially at school), deferred gratification, and so on. Cohen argues that delinquents often develop a culture that is at odds with the norms and values of the middle class, which they turn upside down and rebel against.

Lower Class Focal Concerns

Still another variation of this perspective comes from the work of Walter B. Miller, an anthropologist from Harvard University, who has published extensively on the topic of gangs for the past 30 years. His theory includes an examination of what he calls the *focal concerns* of a distinctive lower-class culture (Miller, 1958:5–19). Miller argues specifically that (1) there are clear-cut focal concerns (norms and values) within the lower-class culture and (2) that *female-dominated households* are an important feature within the lower class and are a major reason for the emergence of street-corner male adolescent groups in these neighborhoods.

Two key concepts here are (1) *focal concerns,* which include trouble, toughness, smartness, excitement, fate, and autonomy; and (2) *one-sex peer units,* which serve as alternative sources of companionship and male role model development outside the home. Such concerns are often at odds with mainstream middle-class society. The one-sex peer group is important to Miller's theory in the sense that gangs provide male members opportunities to prove their own masculinity in the absence of an adequate male role model within their family of origin. The principal unit in lower-class society is an age-graded, one-sex peer group constituting the major psychic focus and reference group for young people. The adolescent street-corner group is one variant of the lower-class structure, and the gang is a subtype distinguished by law-violating activities. For boys reared in female-headed households, the street-corner group provides the first real opportunity to learn essential aspects of the male role—by learning from other boys in the group with similar sex-role

1. *Trouble* is a dominant feature of lower-class life. The major axis is law-abiding/ non-law-abiding behavior. Unlike the middle class, where judgment is usually based on one's achievements (e.g., education, career advancement), the lower-class concern is whether one will pursue the law-abiding route or its reverse. Further, membership in a gang is often contingent on demonstrating a commitment to law-violating behavior, acts that carry much prestige.

2. *Toughness* is associated with stereotypical masculine traits and behaviors, featuring mostly an emphasis on a concern for physical prowess, strength, fearless daring, and a general macho attitude and behavior (or machismo). It also includes a lack of sentimentality, a disdain for art and literature, and a view of women as sex objects. Concern over toughness may derive from being reared in a female-headed household and lack of male role models. The concern with toughness precludes males from assuming roles that might be seen as feminine, such as caring for one's children and acting responsibly toward fathering children out of wedlock.

3. *Smartness* revolves around the ability to *con* or outwit others, to engage in hustling activities. Skills in this area are continually being tested and honed, and the really skillful have great prestige. Many leaders of gangs are more valued for smartness than toughness, but the ideal leader possesses both qualities.

4. *Excitement* refers to the lifestyle within the lower class that involves a constant search for thrills or kicks to offset an otherwise boring existence. Alcohol, sex, and gambling play a large role here. The night on the town is a favorite pastime involving alcohol, sex, and music. Fights are frequent, so "going to town" is an expression of actively seeking risk and danger, hence excitement. Most of the time between episodes of excitement is spent doing nothing or hanging around—common for gang members.

5. *Fate* involves luck and fortune. According to Miller, most members of the lower class believe that they have little or no control over their lives, that their destiny is predetermined. Much of what happens is determined by luck, so if one is lucky, life will be rewarding; if one is unlucky—then nothing one does will change one's fate, so why bother working toward goals?

6. *Autonomy* is reflected in a contradiction of sorts. On the one hand there is overt resentment of external authority and controls ("No one is going to tell me what to do!"), and on the other hand there are covert behaviors that show that many members of the lower class do want such control. They recognize that external authority and controls provide a somewhat nurturing aspect to them. So, if one is imprisoned and subjected to rigid rules and regulations, one may overtly complain while locked up but on release may soon behave in such a way as to ensure reimprisonment and its corresponding nurturance. Rebellion over rules is really a testing of the firmness of the rules and an attempt to seek reassurance that nurturing will occur. Youngsters often misbehave in school because they do not get such reassurance.

FIGURE 6.4 Miller's "focal concerns" of lower-class culture.

identification problems. The group also acts as a selection process in recruiting and retaining members. These concerns are illustrated in Figure 6.4.

Echoing Thrasher's work, Miller states that two central concerns of the adolescent street-corner group are belonging and status. One achieves belonging by adhering to the group's standards and values and continues to achieve belonging by demonstrating such characteristics as toughness, smartness, and autonomy. When there is conflict with other norms (e.g., middle-class norms), the norms of the group are far more compelling because failure to conform means expulsion from the group. Status is achieved by demonstrating qualities adolescents value (e.g., smartness, toughness, and others, as defined by lower-class culture). Status in the adolescent group requires *adultness,* that is, the material possessions and rights of adults (e.g., a car, the right to smoke and drink, and so on) but *not the responsibilities of adults.* The desire to act like an adult and avoid "kid stuff" results in gambling, drinking, and other deviant behaviors and compels the adolescent more than the adult to be smart, tough, and so on. He will seek out ways to demonstrate these qualities, even if they are illegal.

There is also a pecking order among different groups, defined by one's "rep" (reputation). Each group believes its safety depends on maintaining a solid rep for toughness compared with other groups. One's rep refers to both law-abiding and law-violating behavior. Which behavior will dominate depends on a complex set of factors, such as which community reference groups (criminals or police) are admired or respected or the individual needs of the gang members. Above all, having status is crucial and is far more important than the means selected in achieving it.

CONTROL THEORY

The essence of *control theory* (sometimes called *social bond theory*) is that the weakening, breakdown, or absence of effective social control accounts for delinquency. A unique feature of this perspective is that instead of asking "Why do they do it?" it asks "Why *don't* they do it?" In other words, this theory wrestles with what it is that keeps or prevents people from committing crime. In this sense, control theory is really a theory of prevention.

The basic assumption of control theory is that proper social behavior requires socialization. Thus proper socialization leads to conformity, while improper socialization leads to nonconformity. Delinquency is one consequence of improper socialization.

The essence of control theory is that delinquent behavior occurs because it is not prevented in the first place. There are several different versions of this theory. One states that the delinquent lacks either strong inner controls and/or strong outer controls (Reckless, 1961). The former refer to things such as a positive self-image or strong ego, while the latter refer to strong family controls, community controls, legal controls, and so on. Another version maintains that many youths commit delinquent acts because they rationalize deviance before it occurs—that is, they neutralize the normal moral beliefs they have learned while growing up. For example, they deny that there is a victim by saying things like "He had it coming," or they deny that there was any real harm by saying something like "No one was really hurt" or "They won't miss it" (Sykes and Matza, 1957).

The most popular version is the one put forth by sociologist Travis Hirschi (1969). According to Hirschi all humans are basically antisocial, and all are capable of committing a crime. What keeps most of us in check (i.e., prevents us from deviating) is what he calls the "social bond to society," especially the

1. *Attachment*—This refers to ties of affection and respect between kids and parents, teachers and friends; attachment to parents is most important because it is from them that they obtain the norms and values of the surrounding society and internalize them (very similar to Freud's superego but more conscious than his term).

2. *Commitment*—Similar to Freud's concept of ego, except it is expressed in terms of the extent to which kids are committed to the ideal requirements of childhood, such as getting an education, postponing participation in adult activities (e.g., working full-time, living on your own, getting married), or dedication to long-term goals; if they develop a stake in conformity, then engaging in delinquent behavior would endanger their future.

3. *Involvement*—Similar to the conventional belief that "idle hands are the devil's workshop"; in other words, large amounts of unstructured time may decrease the ties to the social bond; those busy doing conventional things, such as chores at home, homework, sports, camping, working, or dating, do not have time for delinquency.

4. *Belief*—This refers simply to the belief in the law, especially the morality of the law (e.g., belief that stealing is just plain wrong).

FIGURE 6.5 Hirschi's four elements of the *social bond.*

norms of society that we have internalized. There are four major elements of this bond, as shown in Figure 6.5 (Hirschi, 1969:16–34).

This theory is very popular (although many do not express it as "control theory"), as most people believe these traditional values about what is and is not appropriate role behavior for young people. Furthermore, juvenile justice workers practice this every day as they try to, in a sense, *reattach* delinquents to family, school, and so on; to get them to *commit* themselves to the demands of childhood; to *involve* them in conventional activities; and to help them acquire a *belief* and respect for the law. This theory becomes an important starting point for the social development model and the risk-focused approach of delinquency prevention.

Johnstone, quoted earlier concerning strain theory, suggests that purely ecological explanations of gangs are limited "and cannot account for why gangs influence only some of the boys who live in gang neighborhoods. . . ." Continuing, he notes that the opportunity to join a gang "is established by the external social environment, but the decision to do so is governed by social and institutional attachments and by definitions of self. . . . The transition from unaffiliated to gang-affiliated delinquency occurs at the point that a boy comes to believe that he has nothing further to gain by not joining a gang" (Johnstone, 1983:297).

One recent study confirms control theory. Extensive studies of various ethnic gangs by Vigil and Yun led them to conclude that the common theme for all these gangs is that the weakening of the bonds identified by Hirschi sort of "frees" these youths "from social control and encourages deviant behavior." The study by Vigil and Yun, based on interviews of 150 incarcerated gang members from four ethnic groups (Vietnamese, Chicano, African-American, and Hispanic), confirms the social control thesis (Vigil and Yun, 1996).

SOCIAL LEARNING THEORY

According to this theory people become delinquent or criminal through the same kind of process as learning to become anything else. One learns behavior, as one learns values, beliefs, and attitudes, through one's association with other human beings. One of the earliest variations of this theory as it applies to delinquency was the theory of *differential association* originally developed by Edwin Sutherland (Sutherland and Cressey, 1970). According to this theory, one becomes a delinquent not only through contact with others who are delinquent but also through contact with various values, beliefs, and attitudes supportive of criminal/delinquent behavior in addition to the various techniques used to commit such acts. One of the central points of this theory is the proposition that one becomes a delinquent/criminal "because of an excess of definitions favorable to violation of law over definitions unfavorable [to violation] of law" (Shoemaker, 1996:152–153). In other words, a young person will become delinquent through his or her association with delinquent youths. Together they reinforce beliefs, values, and attitudes that lead to and perpetuate delinquency.

Social learning theory suggests that there are three related processes that lead one to become a delinquent or criminal. These are (1) acquisition, (2) instigation, and (3) maintenance (Goldstein, 1991: 55–61).

Acquisition refers to the original learning of behavior. The key to this process is that of reinforcement through the modeling influences of one's family, the immediate subculture (especially the peer subculture), and symbolic modeling (e.g., via television). In the case of learning aggression, a child who witnesses violence within the home is apt to engage in violence later in life. This is especially true if such violence within the home is rewarded or no sanctions are applied. Important here is the fact that children tend to acquire behaviors they observe in others and to see that these behaviors are rewarded.

Instigation refers to the process whereby once a person has acquired the behavior, certain factors work to cause or instigate a specific event—in this case, an act of delinquency. Learning theory suggests five key factors as major instigators. One is known as *aversive* events, which include such characteristics as frustration, relative deprivation, and, of particular importance in gang violence, verbal insults and actual assaults. For those who are especially violent, threats to one's reputation and status, especially those occurring in public, are very important instigators of violent acts.

A second factor is *modeling influences,* which refer to the possibility that actually observing delinquent or criminal behavior by someone who serves as a role model can be an immediate instigator. A third factor is referred to as *incentive inducements,* or the anticipated rewards. One can be motivated to commit a crime by some perceived reward, usually monetary.

A fourth is *instructional control,* which refers to simply obeying orders from someone in authority. A gang member, for example, may obey a direct order from a leader within the gang. A fifth factor is known as *environmental control.* This refers to factors in one's immediate environment, which include crowded conditions (including traffic), extreme heat, pollution, and noise. Each of these can cause someone to "lose it" and act out, sometimes in a violent manner.

In order for delinquent or criminal behavior to persist, there needs to be consistent reinforcement or *maintenance.* Social learning theory suggests four specific kinds of reinforcement: (1) direct reinforcement, (2) vicarious reinforcement, (3) self-reinforcement, and (4) neutralization of self-punishment.

Direct reinforcement refers to extrinsic rewards that correspond to an act (e.g., money, or recognition). *Vicarious reinforcement* includes seeing others get rewards and/or escape punishment for delinquent or criminal acts (e.g., a youth sees someone carrying a lot of money obtained by selling drugs). *Self-reinforcement* simply means that a person derives his self-worth or sense of pride as a result of criminal acts.

Finally, *neutralization* is the process whereby one justifies or rationalizes delinquent acts. One long-standing sociological theory is commonly referred to as *techniques of neutralization* (Sykes and Matza, 1957). The authors of this perspective suggest that delinquents often come up with rationalizations or excuses that absolve them of guilt. Thus, for example, a youth may say that no one was harmed or that the victim deserved it ("He had it coming to him"), or he may condemn those who condemn him (e.g., by saying that adults do these kinds of things, too), appeal to higher loyalties (e.g., "I'm doing it for the 'hood"), or merely put the blame on various external factors. An important aspect of such techniques of neutralization is that during the process the victim is dehumanized, and there is a gradual desensitization regarding the use of violence or other means of force to get one's way.

GANGS AND MASLOW'S
HIERARCHY OF NEEDS

Consistent with social learning theories is the view that humans pass through various stages in their lives. Relatedly, this view suggests that human problems do not emerge overnight, seemingly out of nowhere. Rather, life is a process, and humans go through life developmentally, through various stages of growth. There are numerous theories relating this process to human growth and fulfillment (e.g., those of Freud, Piaget, and Erikson), but space does not permit a complete summary of these views.[14] While all of these views can be used to better understand the development of gangs, one perspective seems to relate to gangs better than most—namely, Maslow's *hierarchy of needs* (Maslow, 1951).

According to Maslow there are five basic human needs that evolve in the following order: (1) physiological/biological, (2) safety and security, (3) love and belongingness, (4) self-esteem, and (5) self-actualization. Satisfying these needs is an essential part of everyday human struggles. Initial needs are those for basic survival, such as food and shelter, which should be met by one's parents during early childhood. The need for safety and security refers to stability, protection, freedom from fear, freedom from anxiety and chaos, and the need for structure, order, and limits.

The need for love and belongingness refers to the need to belong to some group or some individual, especially a family. If all three basic levels of needs are met, especially through the family, then the adolescent will be able to get along well with others and be motivated to satisfy the next level of need in the hierarchy. It should be noted that the need for love and belongingness becomes more problematic in an industrialized society with high geographic mobility, leading to the breakdown of traditional groupings. This often results in the formation of artificial groups, such as religious cults and gangs. (This is consistent with the social disorganization perspective.)

Self-esteem needs include self-respect, feeling good about oneself, and being held in esteem by others. It also includes the need for strength, achievement, adequacy, confidence, and a positive reputation. These needs can best be fulfilled by learning a skill, pursuing a profession, or otherwise engaging in conduct that elicits positive regard from others. Looking closely at youth gangs today we can see how important reputation, or rep, is and why an attack against one's reputation, often called "dissin'," is a serious offense calling for severe sanctions against the offending party.

Finally, self-actualization needs are those that can be satisfied only when all the others are satisfied. Here the individual strives to become everything he or she is capable of becoming, to fulfill his or her potentiality. Self-actualized people can keep pessimistic doubts, wishes, fears, and so on from bothering them. They are very spontaneous and creative people. They accept themselves and others and are reasonably independent.

Clearly, gangs provide many of these developmental needs of adolescents, especially those from disadvantaged neighborhoods. Perkins suggests that some gangs (especially African-American gangs) provide members with housing, food, clothing, and other essentials (Perkins, 1987:59). They are given a sense of security and power, a sense of belonging, identity, and discipline. Moore has noted that some gangs have functioned to help "order" adolescents' lives. They provided outlets for sociability, courtship, and other normal adolescent activities. More important, the legitimate institutions of socialization, such as schools and families, have become less important in adolescents' lives, and "street socialization" has begun to compete with, and often replace, these institutions (Moore, 1991:6). In still another statement reminiscent of Thrasher, Moore further suggests that "institutions develop where there are gaps in the existing institutional structure. Gangs as youth groups develop among the socially marginal adolescents for whom school and family do not fill socialization needs." Moreover, gangs "persist as young-adult institutions in a changed society, in which the labor market is not filling the needs of the transition from adolescence to young adulthood. It is not that they are rebels, rather it is that they are left out of the credentialed, ordered society" (Moore, 1991:9).

Bing provides an insightful look at what gangs provide for youths. A. C. Jones, a counselor at a youth camp in Southern California, puts it this way:

> What do you think happened when that kid there first began to seek out his masculinity? What happened when he first tried to assert himself? If he lived in any other community but Watts there would be legitimate ways to

express those feelings. Little League. Pop Warner. But if you're a black kid living in Watts those options have been removed. You're not going to play Pop Warner. Not in Watts. Maybe if you live in Bellflower, maybe if you live in Agoura, but not in Watts—it's just not there, there's no funding for it. But you're at that prepubescent age, and you have all those aggressive tendencies and no legitimate way to get rid of them. And that's when the gang comes along, and the gang offers everything those legitimate organizations do. The gang serves emotional needs. You feel wanted. You feel welcome. You feel important. And there is discipline and there are rules (Bing, 1991:12).

RATIONAL CHOICE THEORY

A theory that became popular in the 1970s and 1980s took the position that crime was merely a product of "rational" choices and decisions that people made in their daily lives. Various terminology has been used, almost interchangeably, with this idea, such as *criminal opportunity theory* and *routine activity theory*.[15] Actually, these recent developments are merely a kind of "old wine in new bottles" since this kind of thinking originated with what has come to be called the *classical school of criminology,* starting with the writings of Cesare Beccaria and Jeremy Bentham in the late eighteenth and early nineteenth centuries.

From the perspective of the classical school an unwritten "social contract" emerged roughly during the period known as the *Renaissance* (1300–1600), which was a vast social movement that swept away old customs and institutions and old feudal estates and made for gains in intellectual development and paralleled the emergence of capitalism throughout the Western world. According to the emerging view of the social contract (perhaps best illustrated by such famous philosophers as Thomas Hobbes and Jean Rouseau), man had originally lived in a state of nature, grace, or innocence, and his escape from this state involved the application of *reason* as a *responsible* and *rational* person. In other words, humans were essentially rational people whose reasoning powers placed them far above animals. Also, this perspective stressed that man has *free will* and theoretically that there was no limit to what he could accomplish. Furthermore, it was asserted that humans were essentially *hedonistic,*—that humans, by their very *nature,* will choose, freely, actions that *maximize pleasure and minimize pain.* More importantly, social contract thinkers claimed that the main instrument of the control of human behavior is *fear,* especially fear of *pain.* Thus punishment, as a principle method of operating to create fear, is seen as necessary to influence human will and thus to control behavior. Also, society had a right to punish the individual, and to transfer this right to the state for executing this right. Finally, some code of criminal law, or better, some system of punishment was deemed necessary to respond to crime.[16]

The classical school of thought derives mainly from the work of an Italian publicist known as Cesare Beccaria (1738–1794), who wrote a book called *On Crimes and Punishment,* first published in 1764.[17] For Beccaria and other liberal thinkers the major principle that should govern legislation was that of "the greatest happiness for the greatest numbers" (this supports the view that government should be "of the people, by the people, for the people"), which is the basic philosophical doctrine known as *utilitarianism,* the idea that punishment was based on its *usefulness* or *utility* or *practicality.* One of Beccaria's most famous statements in his book was as follows: "For a punishment to attain its end, the evil which it inflicts has only to exceed the advantages derivable from the crime." In other words, punishment should not be excessive; *it should fit the crime* (this is a key phrase, most commonly expressed as "let the punishment fit the crime," actually attributed to Bentham).

Jeremy Bentham (1748-1832) was one of Beccaria's contemporaries. He suggested that criminal behavior (like all human behavior) is a rational choice, born of man's free will. In order to prevent crime we must make the punishment (i.e., pain) greater than the criminal act.

Fast-forward to the last half of the twentieth century, and we have the reincarnation of the classical approach to crime. However, modern versions have usually learned from the mistakes of the original classical school. The original statements from Beccaria and Bentham erroneously assumed that all humans behave "rationally" all the time, that they carefully calculate the pros and cons of their behaviors. More recent examples of this view—including the *rational choice theory*—recognize that choices are often not based on pure reason and rationality but rather are determined by a host of factors. There are constraints on our choices because of lack of information, various moral values, the social context of the situation, and other situational factors. In short, not everyone acts logically and rationally all the time, which may be especially true for young offenders.[18]

Modern rational choice theory still makes the assumption that people freely choose to commit crime because they are goal oriented and want to maximize their pleasure and minimize their pain. In short, they are acting mostly out of self-interest. One modern variation, known as *routine activities theory,* suggests that criminals plan very carefully by selecting specific targets based on such things as vulnerability (e.g., elderly citizens, unguarded premises, lack of police presence) and commit their crimes accordingly. Thus people who engage in certain "routine activities" during the course of their daily lives place themselves at risk of being victimized, such as being out in high crime areas at night, not locking your doors, leaving keys in your car, working at certain jobs during certain hours of the day (e.g., late night clerk at a 7-11 store), and so on. Active criminals select such targets carefully, weighing the odds of getting caught accordingly. One flaw, among others, in such thinking is that there is an assumption that people should stay home more often to avoid being a victim when in fact certain groups (especially women and children) seem to be much more vulnerable at home than anywhere else (Maxfield, 1987; Mesner and Tardiff, 1985).

As we saw in our discussion on socialization into the gang, there are many logical reasons why a youth may want to join a gang. Thus rational choice theory may be quite suitable in explaining this. On the other hand, however, it does not logically follow that the threat of punishment (e.g., so-called enhancement statutes that increase the penalty for the commission of a crime if a person is a gang member) will deter such a youngster. One of the best comments on this problem comes from one of the most respected gang researchers, Malcolm Klein. Klein used a crackdown on gangs by the Los Angeles Police Department known as *Operation Hammer* to illustrate the problem of deterrence. This operation resulted in mass arrests of almost 1,500 individuals who were subsequently booked at a "mobile booking" unit next to the Los Angeles Memorial Coliseum. About 90 percent were released with no charges filed; there were only 60 felony arrests, and charges were eventually filed on about half of these. Klein uses a hypothetical situation of a gang member arrested and booked during such an operation. There are one of two possible scenarios as the gang member, immediately following his release, returns to his neighborhood and his gang. Klein writes as follows:

> Does he say to them [his homies], "Oh, gracious, I've been arrested and subjected to deterrence; I'm going to give up my gang affiliation." Or does he say, "Shit man, they're just jivin' us—can't hold us on any charges, and gotta let us go." Without hesitation, the gangbanger will turn the experience to his and the gang's advantage. Far from being deterred from membership or crime, his ties to the groups will be strengthened when the members group together to make light of the whole affair and heap ridicule on the police (Klein, 1995:163).

In other words, human behavior is far more complex than the rather simplistic notion that "we all make choices" with our "free will."

Most of the perspectives summarized previously have a tendency not to seriously question the nature of the existing social order (possible exceptions are social disorganization and strain theories, which to some extent provide at least an indirect critique of the existing order). Beginning with the labeling perspective, some recent perspectives have focused on questioning the nature of the existing social order, specifically the social order of advanced capitalism in the late twentieth century. One result of the next two perspectives covered here is that instead of focusing on how offenders and potential offenders or at-risk youths can be made to accommodate to the existing social order, these views call for changing the nature of the existing social order so that fewer people will be drawn into criminal behavior in the first place.

THE LABELING PERSPECTIVE

The labeling perspective (also known as the *societal reaction* perspective) does not address in any direct way the causes of criminal/deviant behavior but rather focuses on three interrelated processes: (1) how and why certain behaviors are defined as criminal or deviant (in the case of gangs, why some groups and not others are labeled as gangs and why some crimes but not others are labeled as gang related), (2) the response to crime or deviance on the part of authorities (e.g., the official processing of cases from arrest through sentencing), and (3) the effects of such definitions and official reactions on the person or persons so labeled (e.g., how official responses to groups of youths may cause them to come closer together and begin to call themselves a gang) (Schur, 1971). The key to this perspective is reflected in a statement by Becker, who wrote, "Social groups create deviance by making the rules whose infraction constitutes deviance, and by applying those rules to particular people and labeling them as outsiders" (Becker, 1963:8–9).

One key aspect of the labeling perspective is that the criminal justice system itself (including the legislation that creates laws and hence defines crime and criminals) helps to perpetuate crime and deviance. For example, several studies during the late 1960s and 1970s focused on the general issue of how agents of the criminal justice system (especially the police) helped to perpetuate certain kinds of criminal behavior.[19] In short, this perspective focuses on how gangs and gang-related behavior may be perpetuated by the criminal justice system's attempts to control the problem.

One of the most significant perspectives on crime and criminal behavior to emerge from the labeling tradition was Quinney's theory of the *social reality of crime*. In a truly landmark textbook on crime and criminal justice, Quinney organized his theory around six interrelated propositions, which are as follows (Quinney, 1970:15-25):

1. Crime is a definition of human conduct that is created by authorized agents in a politically organized society.
2. Criminal definitions describe behaviors that conflict with the interests of the segments of society that have the power to shape public policy.
3. Criminal definitions are applied by the segments of society that have the power to shape the enforcement and administration of criminal law.
4. Behavior patterns are structured in segmentally organized society in relation to criminal definitions, and within this context persons engage in actions that have relative probabilities of being defined as criminal.
5. Conceptions of crime are constructed and diffused in the segments of society by various means of communication.
6. The social reality of crime is constructed by the formulation and application of criminal definitions, the development of behavior patterns related to criminal definitions, and the construction of criminal conceptions.

An important component of Quinney's theory is four interrelated concepts, which include (1) process, (2) conflict, (3) power, and (4) action.[20] By *process*, Quinney is referring to the fact that "all social phenomena . . . have duration and undergo change." The *conflict* view of society and the law is that in any society "conflicts between persons, social units, or cultural elements are inevitable, the normal consequences of social life." Further, society "is held together by force and constraint and is characterized by ubiquitous conflicts that result in continuous change." *Power* is an elementary force in our society. Power, says Quinney, "is the ability of persons and groups to determine the conduct of other persons and groups. It is utilized not for its own sake, but is the vehicle for the enforcement of scarce values in society, whether the values are material, moral, or otherwise." Power is important if we are to understand public policy. Public policy, including crime-control policies, is shaped by groups with special interests. In a class society, some groups have more power than others and therefore are able to have their interests represented in policy decisions, often at the expense of less powerful groups. Thus, for example, white upper-class males have more power and their interests are more likely to be represented than those of working- or lower-class minorities and women. Finally, by *social action,* Quinney is referring to the fact that human beings engage in voluntary behavior, which is not completely determined by forces outside of their control. From this perspective, human beings are "able to reason and choose courses of action" and are "changing and becoming, rather than merely being." It is true that humans are in fact shaped by their physical, social, and cultural experiences, but they also have the capacity to change and achieve maximum potential and fulfillment.

An important aspect of this perspective comes from the distinctions between *primary and secondary deviance* (Lemert, 1951). *Primary deviance* includes acts that the perpetrator and/or others consider alien (i.e., not indicative, incidental) to one's true identity or character. In other words, an act is "out of character" (commonly expressed by others as "this is not like you"). These acts have only marginal implications for one's status and psychic structure. They remain primary deviance as long as one can rationalize or otherwise deal with the behavior and still maintain an acceptable self-image and an image acceptable to others. *Secondary deviance,* on the other hand, refers to a process whereby the deviance takes on self-identifying features; that is, deviant acts begin to be considered as indicative of one's true self, the way one "really" is. Deviance becomes secondary "when a person begins to employ his deviant behavior or a role based upon it as a means of defense, attack, or adjustment to the overt and covert problems created by the consequent societal reaction to him" (Lemert, 1951:76).

This perspective eventually led some scholars to begin to question not only the criminal justice system but also the very social structure and institutions of society as a whole. In particular, some research in the labeling tradition directed attention to such factors as class, race, and sex in not only the formulation of criminal definitions (including the definition of *gang*) but also as major causes of crime itself. This in turn led to a critical examination of existing institutions of American society and to a critique of the capitalist system itself. A critical/Marxist criminology emerged from such efforts.

CRITICAL/MARXIST PERSPECTIVES

Quinney and Wildeman place the development of a critical/Marxist line of inquiry in the historical and social context of the late 1960s and early 1970s. They note that

it is not by chance that the 1970s saw the birth of critical thought in the ranks of American criminologists. Not only did critical criminology challenge old ideas, but it went on to introduce new and liberating ideas and interpretations of America and of what America could become. If social justice is not for all in a democratic society—and it was clear that it was not—then there must be something radically wrong with the way our basic institutions are structured (Quinney and Wildeman, 1991:72).

In *Class, State, and Crime,* Quinney outlined his own version of a critical or Marxist theory of crime. Quinney linked crime and the reaction to crime to the modern capitalist political and economic system. This viewpoint suggests that the capitalist system itself produces a number of problems that are linked to various attempts by the capitalist class to maintain the basic institutions of the capitalist order. These attempts lead to various forms of accommodation and resistance by people who are oppressed by the system, especially the working class, the poor, and racial and ethnic minorities. In attempting to maintain the existing order, the powerful commit various crimes, which Quinney classified as crimes of control, crimes of economic domination, and crimes of government. At the same time, oppressed people engage in various kinds of crimes related to accommodation and resistance, including predatory crimes, personal crimes, and crimes of resistance (Quinney, 1977:33–62).

Much of what is known as gang behavior, including gang-related crime, can therefore be understood as an attempt by oppressed people to accommodate and resist the problems created by capitalist institutions. Many gang members, as noted in Chapter 4, adapt to their disadvantaged positions by engaging in predatory and personal criminal behavior. Much of their behavior, moreover, is in many ways identical to normal capitalist entrepreneurial activity.

A critical/Marxist perspective goes even further by focusing on "those social structures and forces that produce both the greed of the inside trader as well as the brutality of the rapist or the murderer. And it places those structures in their proper context: the material conditions of class struggle under a capitalist mode of production" (Quinney and Wildeman, 1991:77). The material conditions include the class and racial inequalities produced by the contradictions of capitalism (which produce economic changes that negatively affect the lives of so many people, especially the working class and the poor).

According to Lanier and Henry, there are six central ideas common to critical/Marxist theories of crime and criminal justice. These are as follows (Lanier and Henry, 1998:256-258):

1. *Capitalism shapes social institutions, social identities, and social action.* In other words, the actual "mode of production" in any given society tends to determine many other areas of social life, including divisions based on race, class, and gender plus the manner in which people behave and act toward one another.

2. *Capitalism creates class conflict and contradictions.* Since a relatively small group (a "ruling class" consisting of perhaps 1 to 2 percent of the population) owns and/or controls the "means of production," class divisions have

resulted, as has the inevitable class conflict over control of resources. The contradiction is that workers need to consume the products of the capitalist system, but in order to do this they need to have enough income to do so and thus increase growth in the economy. However, too much growth may cut into profits. One result is the creation of a *surplus population*—a more or less steady supply of able workers who are permanently unemployed or underemployed (also called the "underclass").

3. *Crime is a response to capitalism and its contradictions.* This notion stems in part from the second theme in that the "surplus population" may commit crimes to survive. These can be described as crimes of *accommodation* (Quinney, 1980). Crimes among the more affluent can also result (see next point) in addition to crimes of *resistance* (e.g., sabotage and political violence).

4. *Capitalist law facilitates and conceals crimes of domination and repression.* The law and legal order can often be repressive toward certain groups and engage in the violation of human rights, which are referred to as *crimes of control and repression*. Crimes of *domination* also occur with great frequency as corporations and their representatives violate numerous laws (fraud, price-fixing, pollution, and so on,) that cause widespread social harms but are virtually ignored by the criminal justice system.

5. *Crime is functional to capitalism.* There is a viable and fast-growing *crime control industry* that provides a sort of "Keynesian stimulus" to the economy by creating jobs and profits for corporations (e.g., building prisons, providing various products and services to prisons, jails, police departments, and courthouses) (Shelden, 2001; Shelden and Brown, 1997).

6. *Capitalism shapes society's response to crime by shaping law.* Those in power (especially legislators) define what is a "crime" and what constitutes a threat to "social order" and, perhaps more importantly, *who* constitutes such a threat—and this usually ends up being members of the underlcass. Various "problems" that threaten the dominant mode of production become "criminalized" (e.g., the use of certain drugs used by minorities rather than drugs produced by corporations, such as cigarettes, prescription drugs, and of course alcohol).

The importance of the capitalist system in producing inequality and hence crime is apparent when examining recent economic changes in American society and the effects of these changes. In recent years particularly, many scholars have begun to seek an explanation of gangs (and crime in general) by examining changes in the economic structure of society and how such changes have contributed to the emergence of what some have called an "underclass," which in many ways represent what Marx called the "surplus population" in addition to the "lumpenproletariat."[21] In many ways, this perspective is an extension of some of the basic assumptions and key concepts of social disorganization/ecology, strain, and cultural deviance theories in addition to critical/Marxist perspectives.

SUMMARY

This chapter has reviewed several different theoretical explanations for the question "Why are there gangs?" Several key themes can be discerned from this review. First, with few exceptions (e.g., social learning theory) these theories stress the importance of the external socioeconomic environment in explaining gangs. Beginning with social disorganization/ecology (especially the early work of Thrasher), these theories link gangs to such environmental factors as poverty, social inequality, lack of community integration, and lack of meaningful employment and educational opportunities, along with the larger economic picture of a changing labor market and the corresponding emergence of a more or less permanent underclass mired in segregated communities.

A second theme is that adolescents who grow up in such environments are faced with the daily struggles for self-esteem, a sense of belonging, protection from outside threats, and some sort of family-type structure. These and many other basic human needs are not being met by such primary social institutions as the family, the school, the church, and the community. Clearly, for significant numbers of youngsters the gang fills many of these needs.

A third theme developed in this chapter is that becoming a gang member is a social process that involves learning various roles and social expectations within a given community. It involves the reinforcement of these expectations through various rationalizations or techniques of neutralization in addition to the perpetuation of various lifestyles, attitudes, and behaviors on the part of the significant others in the lives of these youths. Over time a youth (actually beginning at a very early age) becomes embedded in his or her surrounding environment and cultural norms so that it becomes more and more difficult to leave the world of the gang.

A fourth theme is that delinquency in general and gang behavior in particular are shaped to a large degree by the societal reaction to such behavior and to the kinds of individuals who engage in such behavior. Such a response helps to perpetuate the very problem that the larger society is trying to solve.

A fifth theme is that gang behavior is often a quite "rational" response to the surrounding social conditions within one's environment. Rational choice theory, however, suggests that such a response might be offset by increasing the risks of being apprehended and punished by the juvenile or criminal justice system and specifically by increasing the degree of punishment. Given the context of gangs in American society, the deterrent effect of punishment is minimal, if not counterproductive. In fact, as punishments have become harsher during the past 20 years, the gang problem has escalated.

A sixth and final theme that emerges in this chapter is that one cannot possibly explain the phenomenon of gangs without considering the economic context of capitalism. As we have discussed in earlier chapters, most criminal activity of gang members is consistent with basic capitalist values, such as the law of supply and demand, the need to make money (profit), and the desire to accumulate consumer goods. And, like the larger capitalist system, there are many failures in the world of crime and gang activity.

NOTES

1. For a more detailed discussion of the work of Guerry and Quetelet, along with the "Chicago School," see Lanier and Henry (1998:183–192); see also Quinney and Wildeman (1991:48-50).

2. See Moore (1978, 1991) for documentation of this phenomenon.

3. Lanier and Henry (1998:182). Lanier and Henry also note that the term *social* or *human* ecology comes from the Greek word *oikos* which translates roughly into "household" or "living space."

4. This is especially documented in Shaw and McKay (1972).

5. In a more recent study Vigil concludes that the gang provides many functions a family does. "The gang has become a 'spontaneous' street social unit that fills a void left by families under stress. Parents and other family members are preoccupied with their own problems, and thus the street group has arisen as a source of familial compensation." Vigil notes that about half of those he interviewed mentioned how important the group was to them, that the gang was something they needed, and that it gave them something in return. Close friends become like family to the gang member, especially when support, love, and nurturance are missing from one's real family (Vigil, 1988:89–90.).

6. This is spelled out in Merton (1957).

7. The reader is encouraged to merely browse through any introductory sociology textbook to find numerous references to these two terms. In fact, one definition of *sociology* itself could easily be "the study of culture and social structure."

8. For an excellent discussion of the role of corporate propaganda see the following: Herman and Chomsky (1988), Chomsky (1989), Fones-Wolf (1994), and Carey (1995).

9. For a quick and easy-to-read look at inequality see Folbre and the Center for Popular Economics (1995); see also Domhoff (1998) and Rothman (1999).

10. Messner and Rosenfeld (1997:73) note that the United States lags far behind other countries (whose economic institutions are not nearly as dominant) in paid family leave.

11. A good illustration of this dominance is shown in Derber (1998).

12. Although not mentioned by Hagan, to become embedded in the labor market one also needs social or cultural capital. This term is discussed at length by MacLeod and is included in the next section. In summary, for those who lack the necessary social or cultural capital, being involved in the labor market with steady employment is quite difficult.

13. See, for example, the following: Anderson (1990), Hagedorn (1998), Moore (1991), Padilla (1992), MacLeod (1987), and Sullivan (1989).

14. For a good summary, see Santrock (1981:35–88).

15. Some illustrations of this approach can be found in Cook (1986) and Cohen and Felson (1979).

16. Social contract theorists based their theories on some unproven assumptions about "human nature," yet their views were taken as given by the new bourgeois governments in the seventeenth and eighteenth centuries and "social contract" became a convenient ideology justifying a strong central government, or state, that is ultimately concerned with protecting the interests of private property and profits. The social contract theory in turn justified the buildup of police forces and other formal methods of handling conflicts and disputes, in short, a formal criminal justice system (also included a definition of crime as a harm to the state and the "people," often used interchangeably). Ironically Rousseau wrote that the ultimate source of inequality was man taking a plot of ground and claiming it as his own; and this is exactly what happened during the infamous *Enclosure Movements* in England during the sixteenth century when powerful landlords built fences around common ground (land formally used by all and not legally "owned") and claimed it as their own or charged rent in the name of "private property." This resulted in thousands of vagrants (homeless people)

literally invading European cities in search of work and eventually being labeled the "dangerous classes" or worse by the privileged. The *Elizabethan Poor Laws* were passed during the sixteenth century and declared two kinds of poor: (1) the worthy, which are those who can be reformed and be useful to society, and (2) the unworthy, which are those who are unreformable, useless, and requiring sentence to the poorhouse/workhouse (early forms of jails and prisons). The prevailing view of crime was that it is a *voluntary* violation of the social contract became an essential idea in much of the subsequent thinking about crime, especially classical views. Such a view largely ignored the gross inequalities existing at the time; with such inequality came illiteracy, leading us to question whether "the people" in these new social orders unanimously agreed on the social contract since so few could read or write.

17. This classic book is available in many bookstores and libraries. One edition was published by Bobbs-Merrill in 1963.

18. For a good discussion of this issue see Bartollas (1993:111–112).

19. Examples can be cited endlessly. A few are Chambliss (1975), Chambliss and Seidman (1971), Werthman (*1967*), and Werthman and Piliavin (*1967*).

20. The following quotes are taken from Quinney (1970:8–15).

21. It is important to emphasize that Marx did distinguish between these two terms. The "lumpenproletariat" was seen by Marx as the bottom layer of society, the "social junk," "rotting scum," "rabble," and so on. In short, they were described as the "criminal class." The "surplus population" referred to working-class men and women who, because of various fluctuations in the market (caused chiefly by contradictions within the capitalist system), were excluded, either temporarily or permanently, from the labor market.

7

Gangs in Context:
Inequality in American
Society

I n the previous chapter we reviewed some theories, such as strain and
critical/Marxist, that suggest the importance of the economic institution in
generating not only crime but helping to create and sustain gang activity.
Strong emphasis was placed on the salience of American capitalism in producing certain "strains" on its citizens. The changing economic structure of American capitalism and how this relates to crime in general and gangs in particular
is the subject of this chapter.

RECENT CHANGES IN THE U.S. ECONOMY

We are presently in the midst of an important era in history, the last stage of the Industrial Revolution (Eitzen and Zinn, 1998:188–192). Like previous transformations (e.g., from agriculture to manufacturing) several forces are operating to produce this change. These are (1) technological, (2) the globalization of the economy, (3) the movement of capital, and (4) the overall shift of the economy away from manufacturing to information and services.

Among the most important technological changes is the computer chip, which has led to the replacement of many workers by computers and robots. This has, in turn, resulted in a loss of millions of unskilled and semiskilled jobs. The second force is the globalization of the economy. Presently the U.S. economy is part of a much more competitive world economy. To increase their profits in this competitive world economy, U.S. corporations have had to cut costs, usually by laying off workers or closing plants. The decline in manufacturing has been especially pronounced (see below).

The third force involves the movement of capital, or "capital flight." This is a process whereby companies have invested overseas, relocated plants within the United States, or engaged in mergers with other corporations. All of these efforts have had the effect of eliminating the jobs of many workers. In fact, multinational corporations that are based in the United States have huge investments in foreign countries, and many pay few if any income taxes.[1] More and more U.S. corporations are finding it very profitable to move most of their manufacturing to Third World countries, where labor is cheap, there are no unions, and there are no restrictions on child labor (and most of this labor is reminiscent of "sweatshops" in the nineteenth century) or on worker safety. More than 1,100 American factories (e.g., Ford, General Motors, RCA) are in northern Mexico (Eitzen and Zinn, 1998:190).

As already noted, the movement from manufacturing to service has been significant. Whereas in 1960, 31 percent of the labor force was employed in manufacturing industries, by 1994 this percentage had shrunk by half to a mere 15.9. In contrast, the percentage employed in "service-producing" industries (e.g., transportation, public utilities, retail trade, and services) went from 62 percent to almost 80 percent, with the specific category of "services" accounting for the largest increase (from 13.6 to 28 percent) (Sklar, 1998). From 1973 to 1989 about 35 million jobs were created, and most of these were in the service sector and about half involved few skills and were low paying. Between 1988 and 1993, 1.7 million high-wage, mostly blue-collar manufacturing jobs were lost, while about a million were created in the lowest-paid service sectors. Today the United States could be described as a "low-wage society." The average weekly earnings of workers (in 1997 dollars) went from $494 in 1973 to $424 in 1997. As of 1990 an estimated 18 percent of full-time workers were classified as living under the official poverty line, compared to 12 percent in 1979 (Eitzen and Zinn, 1998:200).

The average wage in constant dollars for full-time workers declined in the late 1970s following a steady increase from the early 1950s. Since the late 1970s wages have leveled off. In short, in terms of what the dollar can purchase, the wages of the typical worker have not changed in 20 years! The effects on the typical *male* worker has been especially negative. The average *male* worker has been most affected by these changes. The median earnings of males have decreased, while wages for females have increased, which is partly explained by the rise in "low-wage" workers from 7.4 percent of the labor force in the mid-1970s to 13.9 percent in 1990. In fact, many male workers have in effect *disappeared* from the labor force. While in the early 1950s almost 90 percent of the men in America were "in the labor force" (meaning they were either working or actively seeking work), by the mid-1990s this percentage had shrunk to about 75 percent.

During this same time, the percentage of women in the labor force went from just over 30 percent to about 60 percent. A portion of the gains for women may be accounted for by the incredible increase in the proportion of workers employed as *temporary* workers. In fact, the number of temporary workers increased by 211 percent between 1970 and 1990. A report from the National Association of Temporary and Staffing Services (the mere existence of this organization is itself most significant) reveals that in the last quarter of 1998 there were 2.94 million temporary workers, up from 1.17 million in 1990. Three-fourths of these workers are employed in two major categories: clerical (40.5 percent) and industrial (34.5 percent). Manpower, Inc., and Kelly Temporary Services are among the leading employers in America today, with profits in recent years increasing much faster than most other companies (Folbre and the Center for Popular Economics, 1995:tables 2–4 and 2–5; Gilbert, 1998:chap. 3; see also Cleeland, 1999).

Another way of describing this process is what Bluestone and Harrison have called *deindustrialization,* which is the reduction in our nation's rank in the world economy (Bluestone and Harrison, 1982). A specific example of this occurred in New York City. Between 1970 and 1984 approximately 500,000 jobs, which were in industries that *did not require a high school diploma,* were lost. These were mostly unskilled and semiskilled jobs typically filled by minorities and young people. During this same period of time the city gained about 240,000 jobs in industries that *required more than a high school diploma* (Schorr, 1989:301).

While all of this has been going on, the share of the total wealth going to the top wealthholders has increased, with the top 5 percent getting 61 percent of all household wealth in 1997, up from 56 percent in 1983. During this same period, all other households received proportionately less (Sklar, 1998). Overall inequality, measured by what is known as the *Gini Index of Inequality* (a scale where 0 means everyone earns the same amount and 1 means one person earns all), has gone up since the late 1960s. Whereas in 1970 the index for the United States was 0.353, in 1996 it was at 0.425, larger than any other industrialized nation (Miringoff and Miringoff, 1999:105). During this same period, the proportion of total income received by the top 5 percent of the households went from 16.6 percent to 20 percent. The "super-rich" reaped the most benefits from "trickle-down economics" of the 1980s as the wealthiest 10 percent of the population received 85 percent of the stock market gains between 1989 and 1997. Indeed, the rich are getting richer, and practically everyone else is getting poorer,[2] and most of the increase has been the result of the "tax reforms" of the Reagan–Bush years in the 1980s, resulting in an estimated $1 trillion going to the very rich.[3] One study found that between 1977 and 1994 the share of after-tax income of the top 1 percent of all families increased by 72 percent, compared to a decrease of 16 percent by the bottom 20 percent of all families (Shapiro and Greenstein, 1997).

In terms of net worth, while the top 1 percent of households held about 20 percent of all the net worth in the late 1970s, by the end of the 1980s their share had risen to more than 35 percent. Also, whereas the mean family income of the top 5 percent of all families was 11 times greater than the bottom 20 percent of the population in 1978, by 1994 the ratio had increased to 19 to 1 (Gilbert, 1998:107). As of 1993, 42 percent of all households had a net worth of less than $25,000, while 25 percent had a net worth of less than $5,000 (11.5 percent had a net worth of either negative or zero), while about 10 percent had a net worth in excess of $250,000, and this latter segment of the population held two-thirds of all the wealth in the country (including over 90 percent of the value of all bonds, about 86 percent of all stocks, more than 80 percent of all nonhome real estate, more than 90 percent of the total business equity, and 88 percent of the value of all trusts).

THE DEVELOPMENT OF THE UNDERCLASS

One obvious result of these changes has been the development of a category of people commonly referred to as the *underclass*. It should be emphasized that this term has been the subject of a considerable amount of debate. As one of the leading critics puts it, the term "underclass" has become merely a form of "new wine in old bottles" in that it has replaced some of the old terms like "dangerous classes," the "undeserving poor," the "rabble," and so on. While it is synonymous with "persistent and extreme poverty," it is more like a "behavioral term invented by journalists and social scientists to describe poor people who are accused, rightly or wrongly, of failing to behave in the 'mainstream' ways of the numerically or culturally dominant American middle class" (Gans, 1995:2). Usually this term is used to, in effect, stigmatize those who fall within the general category of the "underclass"—the homeless, those who live in "the projects," addicts, young poor women with babies, and of course gang members. Needless to say, the term is often used interchangeably with racial minorities.

As noted above, inner cities have been the most negatively affected by these changes. The movement of capital out of the inner cities (capital flight) corresponded to the phenomenon of "white flight" and the exodus of many middle-class-minorities and the decline of the tax base for these areas while the increasing concentration of the poor were left behind. There has also been a corresponding decline in federal funding for social programs, particularly those targeting the urban underclass. This largely occurred during the 1980s with the dawn of a "privatization" movement, a system aiming to replace federal assistance with private-sector methods of solving urban problems. Among the specific types of programs that suffered included aid to disadvantaged school districts, housing assistance, financial aid to the poor, legal assistance to the poor, and social services in urban areas in general (Cummings and Monti, 1993:306).

There has been a marked decline in job opportunities, especially for minorities. Many jobs have shifted to the suburbs, as have many basic services and the tax base as well. It used to be common for many minority youth to be able to find unskilled and semiskilled jobs. Today these jobs are disappearing and being replaced by either low-wage service jobs or high-wage jobs requiring advanced skills and education.

A closely related development has been described as the *feminization of poverty*. This refers to the increase in female-headed households that are most likely to be living in poverty. This has been especially true for African-American women, for according to the 1990 census 43 percent of all African-American families are headed by women, and 45 percent of these families are living under the poverty level (U.S. Bureau of the Census, 1990); Zopf, 1989). Within inner cities these percentages are even greater (Wilson, 1987, 1996). the number of children living in "extreme poverty" (family incomes less than one-half the official poverty level) doubled from 1975 to 1993 (from 5 to 10 percent). In 1996 (the latest figures available) about 40 percent of all African-American children lived in poverty (of the African-American children under 6, 45 percent live in poverty). International comparisons shows the United States ranked number one in terms of the overall child poverty rate among industrialized nations, with an overall rate of 25 percent.[4]

The "welfare reform" movement ushered in during the Clinton administration in 1996 significantly reduced the number of citizens on the welfare rolls. Specifically, as of 1999 about seven million were receiving welfare, compared to just over 12 million in 1996. There has been a negative impact, however, as millions of single mothers who have left welfare are working at poverty wages. One study found that the average wage of these mothers was $6.60 per hour. More than one-fourth were working nights, while two-thirds have jobs without health insurance. Also, more than half of them are having trouble getting decent and affordable child care and paying for such necessities as food and rent. Still another report noted that whites were leaving welfare at a much faster pace than minorities. One example was in Ohio, where in 1995 just over half of the welfare recipients (54 percent) were white and 42 percent were African-American, by 1999 theses percentages were reversed: 53 percent African-American and 42 percent white. In Nevada, between 1994 and 1999 the proportion of whites receiving welfare went from 56 to 47 percent, while the percentage of African-American increased from 30 to 38 percent and Hispanics went from 11 to 13 percent. Research has also shown that it has been much easier to leave welfare for those living away from the inner cities, which obviously helps whites since they are most likely to live in the suburbs (Associated Press, 1999).

The declining social and economic position of African-Americans, especially as this relates to young African-American males, whom one author has called an "endangered species." is significant (Gibbs, 1988). The impact on one particular city, Louisville, Kentucky, is described by Cummings and Monti. They describe the underclass in this city as being "comprised largely of minorities who are increasingly marginal to the city's economy. The neighborhoods populated by the underclass are characterized by high rates of crime, institutional instability, and impoverished households headed by females. . . . Louisville's new urban poverty is exacerbated by severe dislocations in the manufacturing and industrial sectors of its regional economy." The unemployment rates among African-Americans in Louisville rose from 6.9 percent in 1970 to more than 20 percent by the end of the 1980s. Also, in 1970, 45 percent of births by African-American women were out of wedlock, whereas in 1988 it was 70 percent (Cummings and Monti, 1993:312–313).

Or consider the city of Rochester, New York, a city that typifies the deindustrialization process. Mike Males, in his book *Framing Youth,* offers the following description:

> I spent two spring days walking Rochester's formerly prosperous neighborhoods, once well fed by its chief employer, Eastman Kodak, and other topside industries. On North St. Paul sits the 10-story Bausch & Lomb plant, abandoned, windows broken. From the bridge, vacant, silent factories flank the roaring Genesee River. To the right is the Kodak Tower, where corporate cutbacks chopped the labor force from 65,000 in past heydays to fewer than 30,000 today.
>
> Rochester's north and westside formerly-working-class neighborhoods are shabby. In another decade they will fall into the bombed-out look of Camden, Baltimore, Richmond, and Philadelphia. It is mostly a white city, one-sixth black. Among black youths, poverty has risen from 31 percent in 1970 to 48 percent today. Among white youth, poverty tripled from 8 percent in 1970 to 22 percent now (Males, 1999:183).

A similar walk or drive through boarded-up, closed-down former factory towns and cities in cities like Boston, Detroit, Atlanta, Memphis, and Los Angeles reveal identical patterns (as witnessed personally by the authors of this book). Little wonder gangs flourish, as evidenced by the graffiti everywhere, among other indicators.[5]

One of the most important studies pertaining to the underclass theory has been produced by William Julius Wilson in his *The Truly Disadvantaged,* along with his follow-up *When Work Disappears.* Wilson has noted that many of today's inner-city ghettos are unlike an earlier era. During the 1940s and 1950s and much of the 1960s, these areas were inhabited by *different classes* of African-Americans (lower-class, working-class, and middle-class professionals). These different classes provided much stability and reinforced dominant cultural norms and values (e.g., hard work, stability, importance of family, obeying the law). Youths growing up in these areas had a variety of stable role models: They saw that there were people who got up every day and went to work, some of whom were quite successful (e.g., doctors, lawyers).

Today, however, these neighborhoods. as Wilson notes, "are populated almost exclusively by the most disadvantaged segments of the African-American urban community" (Wilson, 1987:8). They lack the training and skills necessary to have long-term job stability. They are not even part of the official "labor force."[6] They exist through various forms of crime and deviance and are more or less persistently living in poverty and/or welfare dependency. This is a relatively new social subgroup that can be distinguished from the traditional "lower class" by its lack of mobility. The individuals who make up the underclass are mostly "the sons and daughters of previous generations of the poor" whose own children will remain poor. Many of them have more or less permanently dropped out of the lower class and lack skills and education to ever "make it" in conventional society.[7] These neighborhoods are qualitatively different from what they used to be. With the departure of stable working- and middle-class African-Americans, the modern ghetto has become *isolated* from mainstream society. Inhabitants of these areas interact and live with similarly situated people.

Consider the following data. First, in 1965 about 25 percent of all births among African-Americans occurred outside of marriage; in 1980 this was 57 percent (more than doubling), and in 1992 it was 68 percent. Second, in 1960 about 22 percent of all African-American families were headed by a female; by 1980, 40 percent were; by 1987 this percentage had increased to almost 42 percent, and in 1994 it stood at 60 percent.[8] More importantly, the *gap* between white and African-American families *increased*. During this period, urban violent crime increased, with homicide now among the leading causes of death of young African-American males.

What has also happened is a continual influx of African-Americans into urban areas, which has kept the average age of metropolitan areas young. Generally speaking, the higher the median age of a group, the higher the income; since African-Americans are on the average younger than whites, one finds higher unemployment rates, lower income, and higher crime rates (since crime is much higher among the younger age-groups).[9]

RECENT CHANGES IN THE LABOR MARKET

Young African-Americans and other minorities have suffered the most from recent *structural economic* changes. Along with the shift from a goods-producing to an information and service-producing economy, other significant changes include plant closures in the Northeast and Midwest (many products are now imported), technological changes (e.g., labor-saving devices and robots), and, perhaps most important, the movement of manufacturing plants outside of the innercities (Duster, 1987). One result of this has been an increasing polarization of the labor market into a low-wage/high-wage dichotomy (helped no doubt by the tremendous increases in "temp" jobs, as noted above). All of this has resulted in a drastic change in educational requirements for employment in those industries paying the most money (job growth has generally been in areas requiring the most education) (U.S. Department of Commerce, 1995:472).

Young African-American males are in that group that has the least amount of education. Thus, they are the least likely to be equipped with the education necessary to compete for the newly created jobs in areas such as finance, computer technology, and other professional and technical careers (e.g., engineering, law, the sciences).

African-Americans have fared a little better in the West since this area has added more jobs with lower levels of educational requirements. Even so, most of this growth in economic opportunity has occurred in the suburbs, far removed from the largest concentration of African-Americans.

These factors have resulted in changes in the labor force participation rates. These rates have declined significantly among young African-Americans. For example, among the under-24 age-groups for nonwhites (the age-groups with the highest crime rates), the declines have been dramatic since 1960; in contrast, the rates for whites have remained virtually the same.

During the 1970s labor productivity remained fairly stable, while real wages remained at the 1973 level. The biggest changes came in the manufacturing sector of the labor force, where African-Americans had historically maintained employment. One thing is very clear: African-Americans as a group lost ground to whites as their median income declined. Also, the proportion of African-American households earning less than $5,000 (the *extreme* poverty level) went from 14.8 to 17.9 percent during the 1970s, compared to a drop from 7 to 5.4 percent for whites. Whites made significant gains in the upper income category ($35,000 or more), as they increased by about 11 percent; for African-Americans there was a more modest increase of about 6 percent. By the 1990s the proportion of all families under $5,000 had dropped considerably, but the racial differences were still pronounced: 10.9 percent for African-Americans and 3.6 percent for whites. The proportion of African-American families within the lowest fifth of the income distribution stood at 37 percent, compared to 18 percent for whites. African-American families were also more than three times as likely than white families to live under the poverty level (31 vs. 9 percent).

The nature of work has changed as well. The proportion of workers (especially young workers) employed in high-paying mining and manufacturing industries has declined. Meanwhile, the largest increases in the job market have been in the industries of retail trade, finance, insurance and real estate, and services. For these latter industries, we find the largest increase in female workers (earning relatively low wages). Young African-Americans have found jobs in industries that generally pay the least. Those industries and occupations that pay the most require increasingly more education and skill levels (e.g., computer skills, knowledge of math and English), thus eliminating many young African-Americans who have dropped out of school and/or experienced a decline in the basic skills level.

In short, the lot of minority youth (especially African-Americans) has grown progressively worse during the past two decades. One cause has been the decline in unskilled and semiskilled jobs, especially jobs in the manufacturing sector of the economy. It is within this sector that one used to find a sizable proportion of young minorities. Plant closings, the movement of capital out of the central cities, the growth of suburbs, and many other changes have, in effect, made many young African-American males "superfluous" within mainstream society. Within the major urban centers during the past two decades, minority unemployment rates for males has doubled; in some cities, such as Detroit and Philadelphia, it has tripled. One study found that among African-Americans aged 16–24, almost half had no work experience at all (Gibbs, 1988:6).

While more African-Americans finish high school today than ever before and the gap between African-American and white dropouts has narrowed, this unfortunately does not often translate to success. A late 1980s survey found that more than one out of every five African-Americans aged 18 to 21 "do not have either the basic certificate or basic skills" necessary for "most entry-level jobs, apprenticeship programs, military service, or post-secondary education (Gibbs, 1988:6). This sad state of affairs prompted one writer to comment as follows:

> If black youth are unable to find jobs, they will not develop the work skills, attitudes, and habits that are appropriate and necessary in a competitive, highly technological economy. Moreover, recent studies have indicated that chronically unemployed black males constitute a disproportionately high percentage of those workers who become "discouraged" and completely drop out of the job-seekers' market. Without gainful employment, black youth are increasingly tempted to participate in the underground alternate economy of the urban ghettos— that is, the illegal system of barter in stolen goods, drugs, gambling, and prostitution (Gibbs, 1988:8).

A commission that studied the "riots" following the Rodney King beating verdicts (the term "riot" seems to always be used when such events are described by the white majority, whereas from the perspective of minorities it is often noted as a "rebellion" or "civil disobedience"[10]) noted the declining investments in the inner city on the part of the federal government. For example, between 1981 and 1992 the amount invested in job training fell from $23 billion to $8 billion, from $21 billion to $14 billion for local economic development, and from $6 billion to zero for "general revenue sharing"; federal support for housing was cut by 80 percent.[11]

Jeremy Rifkin, in his book with the ironic title *The End of Work,* takes a close look at how recent economic changes have affected the African-American community. Significant changes began shortly after the end of World War II, as millions of African-Americans migrated to the North (as well as the West) in search of new job opportunities in the post–World War II boom. On arriving in the North, most African-Americans found limited employment in the auto, steel, rubber, chemical, and meat-packing plants—they were usually used as strikebreakers or to fill slots left by the decline in immigrant workers. Until 1954 the lot of the typical African-American worker steadily improved, but after this time automation began to change that and began a 40-year decline in the fortunes of the African-American population. When automation began to hit, it hit the hardest where the African-American workers were most heavily concentrated: the unskilled jobs. Between 1953 and 1962, 1.6 million blue-collar jobs were lost in manufacturing industries. While unemployment among African-American workers never went higher than 8.5 percent between 1947 and 1953 (vs. 4.6 percent for whites), by 1964 the rate was 12.4 percent (vs. 5.9 percent for whites). Since this time the unemployment rate for African-American has consistently been twice that for whites (Rifkin, 1995:73–74).

A really significant change began in the 1950s with the growth of suburbs, where companies started to build new plants, especially in so-called industrial parks. As Rifkin notes, the "old multistoried factories of the central cities began to give way to new single-level plants that were more compatible with the new automation technologies." Limited land and rising tax rates in the cities began to force businesses into the new suburbs. The interstate highway system helped hasten this change as it favored truck over train transportation. Perhaps more importantly, employers found that moving to the suburbs they could create some distance away from the concentration of plants and militant union members (which eventually was the same incentive for moving plants to foreign countries and the South) (Rifkin, 1995:74).

The first industry to feel the effects of these changes was the auto industry. The big Ford River Rouge plant in Detroit was the "flagship" of their operations and the location of the heaviest concentration of union power. Ford decided to move most of the production to the suburbs, where the new automated plants were located, even though there was plenty of room in the old site. Whereas in 1945 this plant had 85,000 workers, by 1960 it had just 30,000, and it was not just Ford, as GM and Chrysler made similar moves to the suburbs.

It was not just the auto plants but almost equally important the many satellite businesses that served the auto industry: machine tools, tires, car parts, and so on. These companies also began to move their operations to the suburbs. The bulk of the African-American population was left behind in the inner cities. Whereas in the 1950s African-American workers accounted for about one-fourth of the workers in GM and Chrysler, by 1960 there were merely 24 African-American workers out of a workforce of 7,425 skilled workers at Chrysler and only 67 African-American among the 11,000 skilled workers at GM. In fact, between 1957 and 1964 the manufacturing output doubled, while the number of blue collar workers declined by 3 percent (Rifkin, 1995:75).

As businesses flocked to the suburbs, millions of white middle- and working-class families (mostly white) moved too, so that the inner cities became concentrated with poor, unemployed minorities. By 1975 large proportions of urban minorities were unemployed and receiving public assistance (the percentage in New York City in 1975 was 15, while in Chicago it was 19). Essentially, the move to the suburbs corresponded to the emergence of knowledge-based, high-tech industries, requiring advanced education and/or skills, something African-American lacked. The only area where African-American improved was in the public sector: More than half of the net increase in employment for them occurred in this area. In 1960, 13.3 percent of the employed African-American population worked in this sector, while by the next decade 21 percent were employed. In fact, by 1970 the government employed 57 percent of all African-American male college graduates and an astounding 72 percent of all African-American female college graduates. This group became the new "black middle class" of the 1970s and 1980s (many became employed within the Great Society programs of the Johnson administration) (Rifkin, 1995:76–77).

The drive to increase profits within corporate America created a split within the African-American community. The first group consists of the displaced unskilled workers and their families, who became what many call the "underclass"—really just another word for the "surplus labor force." The labor of this group is simply no longer needed, as they are "superfluous" as far as profit is concerned. The second consists of a relatively small group of middle-class professionals who are on the public payroll to administer the various "public assistance" programs. Rifkin notes that this represents a form of "welfare colonialism" where African-American in effect, are called on to "administer their own state of dependence" (Rifkin, 1995:77). In a somewhat similar way, the police often provide this function.

Rifkin also notes that this growth in "technological unemployment" has had a drastic impact on the crime rate and the disintegration of the African-American family. The criminal justice system has stepped in to control this population, and very effectively since one-third of all African-American males in their 20s are somewhere in the system. Also, almost two-thirds (62 percent) of African-American families are single-parent families. Little wonder since African-American workers constituted one-third of the 180,000 manufacturing jobs lost in 1990 and 1991 alone. They also lost heavily in the white-collar and service jobs during the early 1990s. This was largely because they were concentrated in jobs that were the most expendable: office and clerical and skilled and semiskilled laborers. One expert is quoted as saying that "what the whites often don't realize is that while they are in a recession, blacks are in a depression" (Rifkin, 1995:78).

ISOLATION IN THE INNER CITIES

Among the most significant changes in the inner cities has been the extent of poverty. In the 50 largest U.S. cities the number of people living within poverty areas increased by more than 20 percent during the 1970s. Within the five largest cities the total population decreased by almost 10 percent during the

1970s, but the number of poor people living in these cities went up by 58 percent. More important is the fact that the African-American population in what Wilson calls the "most extreme poverty areas" (defined as an area where 40 percent or more are below the poverty level) went up by 148 percent, in contrast to a 45 percent increase for whites (Wilson, 1987:46).

The movement out of the inner cities by middle- and working-class African-American families has removed what Wilson calls an important "buffer." By this he means that this class of people could have been able to "deflect the full impact of the kind of prolonged and increasing joblessness that plagued inner-city neighborhoods in the 1970s and early 1980s." Continuing, Wilson writes,

> Even if the truly disadvantaged segments of an inner-city area experience a significant increase in long-term spells of joblessness, the basic institutions in that area (churches, schools, stores, recreational facilities, etc.) would remain viable if much of the base of their support comes from the more economically stable and secure families. Moreover, the very presence of these families during such periods provides mainstream role models that help keep alive the perception that education is meaningful, that steady employment is a viable alternative to welfare, and that family stability is the norm, not the exception.
>
> Thus, a perceptive ghetto youngster in a neighborhood that includes a good number of working and professional families may observe increasing joblessness and idleness but he will also witness many individuals regularly going to and from work; he may sense an increase in school dropouts but he can also see a connection between education and meaningful employment; he may detect a growth in single-parent families, but he will also be aware of the presence of many married-couple families; he may notice an increase in welfare dependency, but he can also see a significant number of families that are not on welfare; and he may be cognizant of an increase in crime, but he can recognize that many residents in his neighborhood are not involved in criminal activity (Wilson, 1987:56).

Unfortunately, this "social buffer" has practically disappeared; relocating in "better" neighborhoods. The remaining residents of these inner cities have become more and more *isolated* from the rest of society. Such isolation includes being excluded from an informal job network that is found in other areas. One result of this is the growth of alternatives to the mainstream labor force, including welfare and crime, both of which have become more or less permanent alternatives in these areas. Wilson further notes that "the social transformation of the inner city has resulted in a disproportionate concentration of the most disadvantaged segments of the urban African-American population, creating a social milieu significantly different from the environment that existed in these communities several decades ago" (Wilson, 1987:58).

Today, African-Americans who are poor are far more likely than in earlier years to live in areas where just about everyone else is poor. In contrast, whites who are poor are far more likely to be surrounded by nonpoor and therefore retain the "social buffer." These poor African-Americans are isolated from mainstream society. Most of their daily interactions are with similarly situated poor African-Americans. Such isolation makes it more difficult to obtain steady employment, especially since so many good jobs have left the inner cities (Wilson, 1987:60–61).

A somewhat different interpretation has been offered by Massey and Denton. In the view of these authors, the origins and perpetuation of the African-American urban underclass can be linked to specific patterns of *segregation*. They write that

> residential segregation has been instrumental in creating a structural niche within which a deleterious set of attitudes and behaviors—a culture of segregation—has arisen and flourished. Segregation created the structural conditions for the emergence of an oppositional culture that devalues work, schooling, and marriage and that stresses attitudes and behaviors that are antithetical and often hostile to success in the larger economy (Massey and Denton, 1993:8).

Because of segregation (especially within the housing market), African-Americans have been far less able that other minorities (e.g., Mexican-Americans, Jews, Italians, Poles) to escape. Historically, note Massey and Denton, until about 1900 most African-Americans lived in areas that were largely white. Massey and Denton document the changes through the use of an "isolation index": the percentage of African-Americans who live in black-only neighborhoods dominated by African-Americans. Whereas in 1930 the isolation index stood at 31.7 in Northern cities (data for Southern cities unavailable), by 1970 this percentage had increased to 73.5 (Massey and Denton, 1993:48).

Continuing, Massey and Denton note that about one-third of all African-Americans presently live in areas they call *hypersegregated,* or under conditions of "intense racial segregation." That is, they are *highly segregated* in at least four of the five dimensions of segregation (unevenness, isolation, clustering, concentration, and centralization). By "unevenness" Denton and Massey mean that within an urban area African-Americans may be overrepresented in some areas and underrepresented in other areas. "Isolation" is in reference to African-Americans rarely sharing the same neighborhood with whites. "Clustering" occurs when African-American neighborhoods are grouped together so that they either form one continuous enclave (occupying a large area of land) or are scattered about the city. Or they may be "concentrated" in one small area or sparsely settled throughout a city. Finally, they may be either located within the central core of a city or spread out along the periphery. Massey and Denton conclude that

> a high score on any single dimension is serious because it removes blacks from full participation in urban society and limits their access to its benefits . . . blacks . . . are more segregated that other groups on any single dimension of segregation, but they are also more segregated on all

dimensions simultaneously; and in an important subset of U.S. metropolitan areas, they are very highly segregated on at least four of the five dimensions at once, a patter we call hypersegregation (ibid:74).

Massey and Denton conclude that quite often this isolation affects one's lifestyles and life chances:

> Typical inhabitants of one of these ghettos are not only unlikely to come into contact with whites within the particular neighborhood where they live; even if they traveled to the adjacent neighborhood they would still be unlikely to see a white face; and if they went to the next neighborhood beyond that, no whites would be there either. People growing up in such an environment have little direct experience with the white culture, norms, and behaviors of the rest of American society and few social contacts with members of other social groups. Ironically, within a large, diverse, and highly mobile post-industrial society such as the United States, blacks living in the heart of the ghetto are among the most isolated people on earth (ibid:74).

In his continuing research on the ghetto underclass in Chicago, Wilson notes that whereas in 1959 less than one-third of those living in poverty lived in central cities, this percentage increased to almost one-half by 1991. In some areas it is even more concentrated. In the 10 areas of Chicago that represent the majority of African-Americans in that city, eight had poverty rates in 1990 that exceeded 45 percent, with three that surpassed 66 percent. Yet in 1970 only two of these areas had poverty rates greater than 25 percent. It is no accident that Wilson's latest book is called *When Work Disappears*, for in areas of concentrated poverty, the percentage of adults working in two specific neighborhoods, Woodlawn and Oakland, were 37 and 23 percent, respectively. Little wonder that citizens in these areas rank crime as a *major problem* (Wilson, 1996:11–23). It is also perhaps no coincidence that both these areas have a high concentration of gang activity, especially Woodlawn, home of one of the oldest and largest gangs in Chicago, the *Black Gangster Disciples Nation* (Block and Block, 1993).

POVERTY AND FAMILY STRUCTURE

Nearly every criminologist agrees that the family is probably the most critical factor related to crime and delinquency. In fact, for over 50 years research has shown that three or four key family-related factors best distinguish the habitual delinquent from the rest of his or her peers. These factors include the affection of the parents toward the child (the lower the level of affection, the higher the rate of delinquency), the kind of discipline the parents use (those who use consistently harsh and physical discipline will produce the most habitual and violent delinquent), the prolonged absence of one or both parents (those from single-parent households are more likely to become delinquent), and the degree of supervision provided by the parents (the lesser the amount of supervision, the higher the rate of delinquency).

We have already noted that African–American families are far more likely to be headed by a female than are white families. The percentage has increased for both racial groups since 1950; the gap between the two races has also increased. In addition, there has been a dramatic rise in the percentage of African–American children living with their mother only: 29.5 percent in 1970 to 50.4 percent in 1987; the proportion of African–American children under 18 living with a mother who *has never been married* went from a mere 4.4 percent in 1970 to 26.3 percent in 1987.[12] In Chicago's inner-city neighborhoods, about 60 percent of the African–American adults have never been married. In extreme poverty areas, only around 15 percent of African–Americans are married. This is a direct outgrowth in the gradual disappearance of work in these areas. Not surprisingly, as of 1993, the median income of single-parent families in which the mother was divorced was around $17,000, while in single-parent families where the mother had never been married it was around $9,000 (Wilson, 1996:89–92).

The effects on children have been devastating, contributing in large part to the increase in cases of abuse and neglect. Wilson found that by the time children born into single-parent families reach the age of six, nearly two-thirds will have moved into different living arrangements. For African-American children, however, about two-thirds of these moves will be into female-headed families with no fathers; for white children, an almost identical percentage will move into families with two parents (ibid:71).

Of all poor families in the nation, almost half are headed by a female; for poor African-American families, 71 percent are headed by a female (1982 figures). Within the inner cities, 60 percent of all poor families and 78 percent of all poor African-American families are headed by a female. Moreover, female-headed families *remain poor* for *longer* periods of time. Little wonder so many young African-Americans seek the relative comfort of gangs as a substitute family.

One major reason for the rise in African-American female-headed families, says Wilson, is the "increasing difficulty of finding a marriage partner with stable employment." In other words, there is a "poor marriage market" for these young women. Wilson concludes that male unemployment is *the leading cause* of the rise in female-headed households (ibid:72–75).

In recent years, girls from single-parent households are far more likely than those from two-parent households to become unwed mothers. One of the main reasons for this is that it is more difficult to supervise the children's activities if there is only one parent in the household. Wilson's study in Chicago found that the highest rates of pregnancy among teens were in single-parent households living in very poor and highly segregated neighborhoods (ibid:75).

Still another interesting fact is the differences between white and African-American women when they become separated or divorced: 70 percent of white female-headed families were *above* the poverty line in 1982, compared to 44 percent of the African-American women. The reason for this is that white women have greater access to extra money (e.g., ex-husbands who earn more money, more money from the sale of a house, or better education and/or greater skills that enable them to find work). In the final analysis, unemployment among males has been the most important factor. In recent years there has been a growing decline in labor force participation among African-American males under 25, while the rates for whites has remained about the same.

It would be misleading to conclude that the "underclass" is synonymous with African-Americans and other minorities. Clearly this is not the case, just as it is not the case that every "gang" and "gang member" is African-American or some other minority group. In sheer numbers alone, the majority of the underclass and the poor in general are whites. A report in the *Wall Street Journal* reveals that in 1991 more than 700,000 babies were born to single white women, which represented 22 percent of all white births in that year (Murray, 1993). In poor communities this rate is probably much higher. This recent trend will no doubt have a very negative impact, not the least of which might be an increase in white youths joining gangs.

HOW THESE CHANGES RELATE
TO THE GROWTH IN GANGS

It would also be misleading to conclude that the emergence of the underclass is the leading cause of crime. Clearly, there are some areas of the country that have suffered some of these same economic changes noted above but have not shown a significant rise in crime. Nevertheless, the recent changes noted above have played a critical role in the perpetuation of the high rate of crime in many areas of the country. Moore has suggested that part of the problem stems from the existence of what is known as a *segmented labor market*. The theory behind this breaks sharply with conventional economic theory and popular conceptions. According to this view the American labor market is *structurally segmented* according to such factors as job security, pay, and career opportunities. Jobs with good pay, security, and opportunities for advancement are relatively scarce. This is the *primary labor market*. Barrio and ghetto residents do not have ready access to these kinds of jobs. Instead, the majority are most likely to be found within the *secondary labor market,* which consists of unstable jobs with low wages (which are often only part-time jobs) and with little or no career advancement opportunities (Moore, 1978).

It is noteworthy that the geographic distribution of jobs tends to eliminate many minorities, as they become part of the "surplus population" (Shelden, 1999; Shelden and Brown, 1997). Most live within areas where industry has left (in search of greater profits), and hence long commutes are often required not only to obtain jobs but to go to work. This is especially true in the Los Angeles area.

In the Los Angeles area two changes created problems. First, an increase in immigration (especially from Mexico) and, second, changes in the job market.

As new Mexicans moved into the barrios they displaced older Mexicans who were able to escape. High-tech jobs started to replace manufacturing jobs, and the unionized, good-paying steel and auto industries all but disappeared, leaving many minorities jobless. At the same time, the good white-collar jobs were taken mostly by white, educated classes.

Even so, many Mexican-Americans were working, except that the jobs paid wages that placed many below the poverty level. Moore states that in 1980, in Mexican-American husband-wife households in California, 16 percent (with full-time working husbands) fell below the poverty line, and 48 percent earned incomes that fell at less than twice the poverty level. Comparable figures for African-Americans were 5 and 27 percent and for Anglos 4 and 15 percent. And nationally, one out of every 15 Hispanics who worked year-round and full-time fell below the poverty level in 1985, compared to one out of every 22 African-Americans and one out of every 40 whites (Moore, 1991:20, 152).

During the 1960s many community programs emerged to deal with the problems (e.g., the War on Poverty, programs for dropouts, gangs, heroin users, and so on). Also, bilingual education increased. However, by the end of the 1970s and early 1980s these programs had disappeared, even though the problems persisted (ibid:21–22).

By the 1980s the gang members and their families, compared with earlier generations, faced much greater competition for jobs. The good jobs of an earlier generation had been replaced by low-wage jobs with little security and no fringe benefits. In other words, the secondary labor market (ibid:22–23).

One consequence of this system is the existence of *supplemental economic structures,* specifically a welfare economy and an illegal economy. Each has become more or less institutionalized within the barrio. These economic structures serve to supplement the more marginal or peripheral sectors of the secondary labor market. Individuals may move back and forth between the secondary market and this peripheral market. In many instances the welfare and illegal economy "subsidizes" the marginal industries of the secondary labor market. These are "fall-back" sources of income since minimum wages are not enough to support a family. This is the world of very limited opportunities, except for the opportunities to join gangs and engage in all sorts of criminal activities, especially drug selling and gang activity (Moore, 1978:30).

In Moore's study of Chicano gangs of the barrio, this is essentially the world within which gangs exist. Moore concludes that

> this is a world of limited opportunities, with legitimate jobs offering little prospect for lifetime satisfaction. In this respect, the segmented labor market becomes an essential concept for understanding the structure and context of the Chicano gang, the use and marketing of illegal drugs and stolen merchandise, and the prison involvements of the residents of the Los Angeles barrios (ibid:33).

A study by Jackson documents the relationship between demographic and economic changes in the United States and the growth of gangs. Jackson writes that demographic and economic transition seem to have some influence on crime and the presence of youth gangs in U.S. cities, even in the presence of controls for possibly competing explanations: opportunity factors related to the ease and profit of crime, age structure, racial and income heterogeneity, and economic and relative deprivation (Jackson, 1991:393).

Jackson's research suggests that crime and youth gangs "are likely consequences of the patterns of sociodemographic change recently experienced by urban areas in the United States . . . Urban decline, with its associated economic stress and social disorganization, may weaken the social cohesion and social control processes of cities . . . As a result, higher crime rates and more youth gangs may be among the unintended consequences of the nation's postindustrial growth and development" (ibid:395).

A similar process was at work in the area of Chicago where the gang studied by Padilla lived. The change here was the movement of key manufacturing jobs away from the inner city to the suburbs, rural areas, the Sunbelt regions of the United States, or even into Third World countries. Concomitant with this development was the growing militancy of the working class, which began winning some of its battles with the business owners. In response, many business owners simply moved to areas where there would be less worker resistance (Padilla, 1992:32–33).

Adding to this process was a significant shift in the population, namely the so-called white flight into the suburbs, leaving behind the poor, the unemployed, the unemployable, and, in disproportionate numbers, the minorities. In the area studied by Padilla, Latinos represented the majority of the residents in virtually all the census tracts in the area. Within this relatively small area of Chicago, the unemployment rate went from 10 percent in 1970 to 18.7 percent in 1980; in some census tracts the rate was as high as 30 percent (ibid:37–38). With these changes came the emergence of illegal opportunities to make money, in particular drug dealing, which is what occurred with the gang studied by Padilla (see Chapter 3).

Malcolm Klein's research on gangs reinforces the above interpretations. He commented that "the effect of the increasing urban underclass, remains in my mind the foremost cause of the recent proliferation of gangs and the likely best predictor of its continuation" (Klein, 1995:194). The effects of poverty is especially relevant here, and it is summarized nicely but crudely by a gang member Klein quotes, who bluntly states, "Bein' poor's a mother-fucker" (ibid:195). The effect of the changing labor market, as we have discussed here, does not escape the attention of Klein's conclusions, as he writes,

Uneducated, underemployed young males turn to the illegal economies enhanced by gang membership, including selling drugs in some instances. Older males who in earlier decades would have "matured" into more steady jobs and family roles hang on to the gang structure by default. The newer gang cities like Milwaukee thus emerge, looking much like the traditional gang cities (ibid:196–197).

It does not take much of a leap in logic to conclude there exists a strong correlation between the growth of gangs in the inner cities on the one hand and the growth in the gap between the rich and the poor on the other. While the following conclusion may be denied by some, to us it seems rather obvious: trillions of dollars have "trickled up" to the top 5 percent of the population during the past 20 years largely because of "corporate welfare," while millions suffer and join gangs to cope.[13]

SUMMARY

In this chapter we have discussed the role of American capitalism in relation to such important issues as poverty, inequality, and gangs. It was noted that under American capitalism, the "free market" is largely a myth, and a "surplus population" is constantly being created and reproduced. Most criminal activity of gang members is consistent with basic capitalist values, such as the law of supply and demand, the need to make money (profit), and the desire to accumulate consumer goods. And like the larger capitalist system, there are many failures in the world of crime and gang activity.

The term "underclass" was discussed, with the emphasis on how this term has become a sort of moral condemnation of various groups not falling within the mainstream of American society. Closely correlated with this term was the phenomenon of the "feminization of poverty" and the general economic decline of the inner cities. Important labor market changes have helped to perpetuate these problems, especially such processes as deindustrialization and capital flight.

Also discussed was certain specific labor market changes and the increasing segregation of minorities, especially African-Americans. This has led to increasing isolation of this segment of the population—isolated from mainstream society and the contacts that lead to a good education and decent jobs.

Finally, it was stated that there are many ways these changes are related to gangs and gang activity. Unemployment, poverty, and general despair lead young people to seek out economic opportunities in the growing illegal marketplace, often done within the context of gangs.

NOTES

1. Of all American-based multinationals with assets over $100 million, more than one-third (37 percent) paid *no* federal taxes in 1991, while the average tax for those who did pay was around 1 percent. Zepezauer and Naiman (1996:70).

2. Sklar (1999). See also the following studies for further confirmation of the increase in inequality: Wolff (1995), Phillips (1990), and Domhoff (1998).

3. Bartlett and Steele (1992). Bartlett and Steele note that as a result of the 1986 "Tax Reform Act" the average 1989 tax savings for those earning $1 million or more came to $281,033 (a tax cut of 31 percent), compared to $37 to those earning less than $10,000 (11 percent tax cut). They also found that during the 1980s the increase in salaries of people earning more than $1 million per year came to 2,184 percent.

4. Child poverty rates taken from Miringoff and Miringoff (1999:83–84).

5. The reader is encouraged to do your own "drive-through" or walk-through"

where you live or attend college. We are certain you will find a similar area of town that has experienced this form of deindustrialization. Even in the "boomtown" of Las Vegas, Nevada, where the senior author lives, a drive through the very segregated African-American community here reveals that the tremendous growth and the enormous wealth of this city have not "trickled down" to this part of town. Compared to 1977, when Shelden first arrived in Las Vegas, not too much has changed in this community, save for a few token businesses, which significantly are located at the outer fringes of the African-American community. Little wonder that most "gangs" are concentrated here.

6. A cursory look at the "labor force participation rates" over the past 50 years reveals that fewer males are in the labor force in the 1990s than in the 1950s, especially African-American males. This has been largely because of deindustrialization. U.S. Department of Commerce (1996:399–402).

7. Ibid. Another writer has commented that they survive mainly through options "ranging from private entrepreneurial schemes to working the welfare system. Hustling, quasi-legitimate schemes, and outright deviant activity are also alternatives to work." Glascow (1980:8–9).

8. Statistics on female-headed households and unmarried birthrates among African-Americans in most recent years taken from U. S. Department of Commerce (1995:62,73); earlier years taken from Wilson (1987).

9. Between 1960 and 1970 the number of inner-city African-Americans aged 14 to 24 increased by 78 percent compared to a 23 percent increase among whites within this age-group. From 1970 to 1977, African-American in this age-group increased another 21 percent, but whites *decreased* by 4 percent. Wilson (1987:Chap. 2).

10. For a rare insightful analysis of the Watts riots, see the rather obscure book by Conot (1967), rarely cited. For an exception and a brilliant review of the Los Angeles Police Department's response to gangs and riots, see Davis (1992), especially chapter 5. The senior author regularly shows what he would describe as a very "disturbing" historical film contrasting the Rodney King "riots" with the Watts uprising 25 years earlier, called *The Fire This Time.* It is "disturbing" because it implicates the federal and local government, especially law enforcement, in perpetuating the conditions that lead to rebellion and even to create and sustain gangs.

11. These figures are from Klein (1995:196).

12. U.S. Department of Commerce (1994:52). In 1955, 41 percent of the births among African-American women were out of wedlock; in 1991, this percentage had risen to 68 (ibid:80).

13. Verification of the extent of "corporate welfare" and how this occurred can be found in Bartlett and Steele (1992), Zepezauer and Naiman (1996), and Chomsky (1998).

8

Community-Based
and National
Intervention Strategies

INTRODUCTION

It should be stressed at the outset of this chapter that gangs are not strictly a law-enforcement problem or, for that matter, a criminal justice problem. Rather, they are a problem that needs to be addressed at both the community and the societal level. As Cummings and Monti (1993:310) note, economic issues are paramount because "the prevalence of gangs in nearly every American city is related to the same recessionary and industrial changes transforming urban and public policy." Indeed, there is little question that unemployment and underemployment are the residuals after industry has abandoned a community. Many of our cities have suffered from the loss of industry, which has impacted minorities more than any other group. As the industries depart, middle-class workers move from the cities, leaving behind those who cannot afford to follow the job market, for at least a portion of these businesses relocate in outlying areas. As poverty begins to encompass whole neighborhoods, urban blight and decay occur, providing a fertile breeding ground for the underclass youths to form gangs in answer to their despair, both economic and personal.

Further complicating the economic scenario is the adoption by many metropolitan areas of a gentrification policy. In these cases, the poor are further displaced as the middle class and wealthy return to the inner city and begin to restore and rehabilitate property. As the real estate values increase, the poor are driven farther from the core of public services designed in large part to accommodate them. The lack of resources to compete for the improved properties drives a solid economic wedge into poverty-ridden families, causing additional despair and frustration for the young people in these families. It is no wonder that these same youths resort to the sale and distribution of illegal drugs as a response.

Within the past decade, the prevalence of guns in the hands of children, the apparent randomness of gang violence and drive-by shootings, the disproportionate racial minority role in homicides, and media depictions of callous youths' gratuitous violence have inflamed public fear. Politicians have exploited those fears, decried a coming generation of "superpredator" suffering from "moral poverty," and demonized young people in order to muster support for policies under which youths can be transferred to criminal court and incarcerated. Some analysts predict a demographic "time bomb" of youth crime in the near future to which minority juveniles will contribute disproportionately (Fox, 1996; Zimring, 1998:208). However, this contention has been refuted by subsequent research (Elikan, Males, 1999).

As we noted in the first edition of this book, the punitive model for dealing with gangs enjoys widespread support. However, it is evident that within this model there is not only little rehabilitation occurring but also no significant positive change. This is particularly true in one of the most recent fads within the correctional industry-boot camps. As some camp directors have themselves commented, "The effectiveness of the boot camp lasts about as long as the haircut." These camps have not proven to be any more successful at eliminating the criminal activities of those individuals in the program than any other correctional sanction (Walker, 1994:286).

In Georgia, where the first "boot camps" in the country started, funding is substantial. However, with the criticisms voiced and the recidivism rate of 80 to 85 percent, the state department of juvenile justice is taking a more modified approach in several of its camps. Private companies, such as Three Springs, are being contracted to provide this program. The philosophy of such private organizations is somewhat different than an "in your face," "barking orders" approach. While still patterned on the military, in uniforms and lineups for movement (e.g., classrooms, dining hall), a sense of respect for the individual and a more "family-like" atmosphere prevails. The recidivism rate is significantly better than the "state-run" institutions.

This modification to the more harsh "boot camps" is still not well received in some arenas. Even so, all over the country policymakers (including the Clinton administration) are supporting increases in funding for such programs. Such blind faith in the face of contrary evidence has prompted Walker to comment, "Most crime control program proposals rest on faith rather than on facts. People of all political persuasions seem to prefer comforting illusions and unexamined assumptions rather than the unpleasant facts about crime and justice" (Walker, 1994:285).

Part of the problem, as Miller notes, is the absence of any sort of national policy addressing the gang problem. Indeed, argues Miller, this country "has failed to develop a comprehensive gang control strategy. The problem is viewed in local and parochial terms instead of from a national perspective. Programs are implemented in the absence of demonstrably valid theoretical rationales" (Miller, 1990:274). While this remains a source of concern, Spergel and Grossman (1994) noted that there is little systematic independent evaluation to measure the effectiveness of the programs; the federal government has initiated and completed a number of evaluations to measure program effectiveness and has established a National Youth Gang Center under the direction of noted gang researcher, Irving Spergel. Attempts to draft a national policy are being made, but there is still much work to be done—a strategic plan must be developed, budgets must be adequately reflective of the funds needed for the plan, lawmakers must be convinced, and key facilitators of these strategies must be involved in their implementation if they are to be successful.

Later in this chapter we will bring together a collection of general recommendations on the national level that address some of the issues raised by Miller. As has been noted at several junctures throughout this book, the problem of gangs cannot be addressed without dealing with much larger social issues facing American society as we enter the twenty-first century. Before dealing with these more general issues, an overview will be presented of the varied gang intervention strategies that have been offered historically.

TYPES OF INTERVENTION STRATEGIES

The discussion of intervention strategies will be divided into two chapters. The first section begins with a general overview of several major categories of responses to the gang problem. The first typology to be discussed is based on the research conducted by Spergel and Curry during the 1980s. Following the outline of Spergel and Curry's typology, community-based responses—or what Spergel and Curry call community organization, social intervention, and opportunities provisions—will be reviewed. In the next chapter the legal response to the gang problem—or what Spergel and Curry call suppression efforts—will be reviewed.

Spergel and Curry's Typology of Interventions

During the late 1980s, University of Chicago researchers surveyed 254 agencies (criminal justice and community agencies, along with schools) in 45 cities (Spergel and Curry, 1990). In this survey they identified two major types of cities, based on the extent of the gang problem in the area. One type they called chronic gang problem cities, and the other they called emerging gang problem cities. As suggested by these terms, the former are those cities (e.g., Los Angeles, Chicago, and New York) that have had gang problems for many years, while the latter apply to cities (e.g., Milwaukee, Phoenix, and Atlanta) that have experienced such problems only in recent years (although not included in their survey, Las Vegas would be classified as an emerging gang problem city). The distinction between these two types of cities becomes important when considering the effectiveness of the various strategies used to deal with the current gang problem.

In their survey, Spergel and Curry found that the strategies used in these areas to deal with the problem of gangs could be grouped into four broad areas, which they labeled as (1) community organization, (2) social intervention, (3) opportunities provision, and (4) suppression or law-enforcement efforts. These four strategies were found to be the most commonly used in the cities surveyed. In fact, they represent virtually every known type of method that has been tried in the past, is currently being used, and will likely be used in the future. It is within these broad areas that the risk factors noted previously can be reduced and the protective factors enhanced.

Community Organization. This strategy refers to efforts to enhance, modify, or change relationships among various groups and organizations within a city in order to better cope with various problems. The researchers found that respondents in the areas surveyed used such terms as *networking* to refer to this specific strategy. Essentially, such a strategy involves cooperation among various community organizations in order to take advantage of the various skills and knowledge such groups have and to try to avoid duplication of services. It is an attempt to combine all available resources in order to solve what is a community problem involving all citizens, not just those directly affected. Spergel and Curry identified such specific strategies as mobilizing the community, building community trust, educating the community, involving the schools, and involving parent groups in community programs.

Social Intervention. Within this category are some very common methods that have been used for many years to deal with youth and related problems. They include the very popular (and, incidentally, not very successful) strategies of youth outreach and street-work counseling. This general strategy has been defined as follows: "It is the systematic effort of an agency worker, through social work or treatment techniques within the neighborhood context, to help a group of young people who are described as delinquent or potentially delinquent to achieve a conventional adaptation" (ibid.:295).

Social intervention is much broader in scope than the traditional youth-outreach efforts. Among the more common strategies identified by the respondents to the survey by Spergel and Curry included the following: crisis intervention, providing role models for youths, intergang mediation, referrals for services, counseling of gang members, drug-use prevention and treatment, helping members leave the gang, and more general diversion and outreach activities. The general goal of social intervention is "to change the values of youths in such a way as to make gang involvement less likely" (ibid.:296).

Opportunities Provision. This strategy is an attempt to provide jobs, job training, and education, particularly for the most at-risk youths. Within this category, Spergel and Curry found "efforts to stimulate the development of new and improved schools, special training, and job programs, and business and industry involvement in the social and economic advancement of people, including and targeting gang youth" (ibid.:297). More-specific strategies include helping prepare youths to enter the job market (for example, teaching interviewing skills and how to write a resume), job training, placement of youths in jobs (for example, via a youth employment agency), and assisting youths with school problems (for example, special tutors and alternative schooling).

Suppression. The term suppression is used by Spergel and Curry to describe a variety of strictly law-enforcement strategies, including special patrols by police gang units, special prosecution efforts within the district attorney's office, legislation that targets gang activities, and development and implementation of information systems (e.g., the GREAT program, which stands for Gang Reporting, Evaluation, and Tracking). This approach will be covered in Chapter 8.

The Perceived Effectiveness of These Strategies

The respondents in the survey conducted by Spergel and Curry and their colleagues were asked to rank each of these strategies according to which was most often used and which they perceived to be the most effective. It is important to note that the effectiveness of these strategies is based on the opinions or perceptions of those responding to Spergel and Curry's survey rather than empirical evidence. The effectiveness varied according to whether the respondents lived in a chronic gang problem city or an emerging gang problem city:

> In emerging gang problem cities, the perception was that the most effective strategies were the various efforts classified as community organization. Ranked second in effectiveness was that of opportunities provision, with social intervention and suppression ranked third and fourth, respectively. From a statistical standpoint (based on the method used in this survey—analysis of covariance), only community organization was found to be statistically significant.

In chronic gang problem cities, the most effective methods were found within opportunities provision, with community organization ranked second. Ranked third and fourth were suppression and social intervention, respectively. From a statistical standpoint, only opportunities provision was statistically significant.

What is clear from this survey is that if communities rely solely on suppression efforts, the gang problem will not be reduced to any significant degree, regardless of whether the area is a chronic or an emerging gang problem city. Organizing communities and providing opportunities to at-risk youths appear to be the most promising strategies.

What is important to stress is that various components of each of these major strategies should be used in combination. This is because it is erroneous to assume from the data presented by Spergel and Curry that an *entire category* of various strategies will not work. What is needed is to examine each specific type of strategy within each broad category and see which one is most effective. This type of research has not been done as yet. It may be found, for example, that certain specific kinds of law-enforcement procedures are more effective than others (e.g., various forms of community policing may be more effective than traditional police procedures) or that certain specific types of social intervention may be more effective than traditional youth outreach (e.g., providing role models or intergang mediation may be very effective).

What each community needs to do is to study in detail each kind of strategy that it is using to see which is most effective (see the discussion of the risk-focused approach in a later section of this chapter). The effectiveness of a specific strategy may vary according to the type of community where it is used (e.g., providing role models may be more effective than gang mediation in Las Vegas, but the opposite may be true in Phoenix). Such a research effort must necessarily arise from a strong mobilization effort to organize a community and combine both human and nonhuman resources.

Other Intervention Typologies

One of the most comprehensive overviews of delinquency prevention programs is the text by Dryfoos (1990). In this book she addresses four interrelated problems: delinquency, teen pregnancy, drug abuse, and school failure. Although not aimed specifically at gangs, these problems and program typologies can nevertheless be easily adapted to the gang problem. Her review of the research found that the majority of prevention programs fall into one of three broad categories: (1) early childhood and family interventions, (2) school-based interventions, and (3) community-based and/or multicomponent interventions (Dryfoos, 1990:116). Programs that fall within the early childhood and family intervention category include two major types: (1) preschool/Head Start programs and (2) parent training/support programs. Programs found within the school-based intervention category include three main types: (1) curricula, (2) organization of school (teacher training, school team, and alternative schools), and (3) special services (counseling and mentoring programs, health services, and volunteer work). Community-based interventions include three main types: (1) school-community collaboration programs, (2) community education, and (3) multicomponent comprehensive programs.

Dryfoos's review also distinguishes among programs that have been proven to be successful, those that have the potential for success but have not been evaluated systematically, and those for which evaluations have shown negative results. For the prevention of delinquency, some successful models include the following: the Perry Preschool program (a Head Start program in Ypsilanti, Michigan); the Syracuse Family Development Program; parent training programs (e.g., the Oregon Social Learning Center in Eugene); school-based interventions, such as social skills training programs and law-related education; several types of programs that focus on the organization of the school, such as classroom-management programs that attempt to produce greater bonding between the students and the teachers, alternative schools, cooperative learning arrangements (e.g., Positive Action Through Holistic Education, or PATHE, in Charleston, South Carolina; see below for more detail); and, finally, various community-based programs, such as the use of juvenile court volunteers (e.g., Denver Partners) and runaway and homeless youth shelters (e.g., the Neon Street Clinic in Chicago) (ibid.:132–144).

Dryfoos also provides profiles of several successful programs that address the problem of substance abuse (ibid.:155–164). These include such school-based programs, such as Life Skills Training (LST) Programs, Student Assistance Programs, and a program known as Growing Healthy (developed by the American Lung Association), and the use of school-based clinics (e.g., Adolescent Resources Corporation, or ARC, in Kansas City). She cites several community-based interventions, such as The Door (in New York City) and the Midwestern Prevention Project (MPP) in Kansas City.

A major component of any successful program is a focus on the family. Family support is offered in the form of references to social service agencies. These agencies in turn will advocate for the adolescent if it becomes apparent that he or she should be removed from the home. They work to reconnect the family with each other through better communication and education about gangs and gang activity.

Cunningham (1994:98) believes that parents of gang members "need to explore their cultural life, family morals and values, and parental roles and responsibilities." This is often difficult to accomplish. Parents often deny their children's gang affiliations and place the "blame" for illegal, or delinquent, behavior on someone else—usually the child. They are often uncooperative and rarely enter support programs with their children or act on suggestions of those in positions of authority and/or family service agencies. Somehow, they cannot accept the fact that (1) either their child is involved in wrongdoing or that (2) there is no hope for redemption, or positive change, for their child.

Without casting too many aspersions on the parents and families of gang girls and boys, it is important to note that in most cases, the parents are products of the same environment and have little skill in appropriate discipline and/or problem-solving.

Prevention of school failure is another area Dryfoos examines. Schools play a vital role in the success or failure of adolescents. Most gang members are unsuccessful, held back several grades, or socially promoted, frustrated by being in an environment that is difficult to understand and to progress. This is especially true for Latinos and Asians who face language barriers in addition to experiencing all the frustrations that American teens have. Thus it is commonplace for those adolescents to drop out of school. Unable to find employment due to lack of education and marketable skills, they turn to gangs to acquire a different set of skills—the street hustle ("do what is necessary to get by").

Among the most successful programs are the following: (1) early childhood and family interventions, such as the Carolina Abecedarian Program, the Brookline Early Education Project, and Parents as Teachers, and (2) school-based interventions, such as the Comer Process, Success for All (Baltimore), the Transition Project, Twelve-Together (Detroit), Adopt-A-Student (Atlanta), and the I Have a Dream program in East Harlem (Dryfoos, 1990:202–213).

Some school districts are attempting to combat this phenomenon; one example, briefly noted above, is PATHE (Positive Action Through Holistic Education) in Charleston, South Carolina. This program is based on six components (Catalano, 1999:3):

1. Teams of teachers, staff, students, and community members who planned and implemented school improvement programs

2. Curriculum and discipline policies that were reviewed and revised and involved students and ongoing teacher training

3. Academic innovations included study skills and cooperative learning

4. School climate innovations (e.g., peer counseling and expanded extracurricular activities)

5. Career oriented innovations (job skills)

6. Special academic and counseling services for low achievers and disrupters

This program has seen significant decreases in delinquent behavior within the school district. Another Charleston, South Carolina, program is the Multi-modal School-Based Prevention Program. The goals of this program are to improve academic achievement, social competency, and social bonding. Catalano observes that "cooperative learning techniques and career and educational decision skills were employed along with one-on-one tutoring, life skills classes, self-management, modeling behavior, mentoring, self-instruction and violence prevention courses" (ibid:4). The school district reports that the grade-point averages of the youth in the program have improved.

Other notable school-based programs include the School Development Program in New Haven, Connecticut, based on parental involvement and multidisplinary mental health teams to aid staff in managing student behavior problems and a social calendar that integrates arts and athletic programs and parent programs supporting academic and extracurricular activities. The results have been impressive with improved grades, test scores, and an appearance of self-perceived social competence (ibid:3).

Still another program is Project CARE in Baltimore, Maryland. This program takes a team approach to classroom management techniques and cooperative learning. In two years, disruptive behaviors and delinquent acts have decreased (ibid:3–4).

Three other promising programs include (1) Turning Point in Southern California, a cooperative program between the school district and law enforcement to keep the schools safe (Wooden, 1995:216); (2) Ivy Tech (in Indiana), part of a technical school system offering vocational education to youth who are in need of remediation or are functionally illiterate; and (3) Near Peer Tutoring (also in Indiana), a high school program in which honors students tutor junior high probationers (Dronnis and Hess, 1995:503). All of these show potential promise.

Another potentially successful program and one highly praised by former gang members is the Council for Unity (CFU) in Los Angeles. This is a high school organization that mediates violent outbreaks between gangs. The focus in this program is on staying in school, not associating with one's old gang members, and setting life goals and acting on them (Laongo, 1994:121).

Finally, Dryfoos surveys successful teenage pregnancy-prevention programs, which include the following: (1) school-based programs, such as Life Skills Counseling, Fifth Ward Enrichment Program (Houston), the Teen Outreach Project (St. Louis), and school-based clinics (e.g., the St. Paul School Health Program); and (2) community-based programs, such as Mantalk (Winston-Salem, North Carolina), the School/Community Program for Sexual Risk Reduction Among Teens (Charleston, South Carolina), and Impact 88 (Dallas) (Dryfoos, 1990:177–189).

An often overlooked partner in combating gang problems are "social service agencies," which are often the only point of contact with troubled youth. These agencies, including state and local juvenile justice agencies, continue to target males for programmatic services as their numbers demand attention. Again, unfortunately, for many females, social service agencies provide scant aid; the only help they may receive from these agencies is pregnancy counseling. Many of these agencies have recognized that since frequently recipients of their programs are gang members or in a family with gang members, appropriate services for this population are necessary. Mandate services and funding resources help to drive these agencies to address the problem.

There are currently programs such as citywide coordinating groups that aid in gang-control efforts, including the Chicago Intervention Network with field offices in various low-income, high-crime areas of the city, providing services such as neighborhood watches, parent patrols, alternative youth programming, and family support efforts (Siegel and Senna, 1997:151).

In Los Angeles County is found the Gang Alternative Prevention Program (GAPP), designed to provide intensive supervision of at-risk juveniles who are on probation for relatively minor crimes. Juveniles receive prevention services such as individual and group counseling, bicultural and bilingual services to adolescents and their parents, and special programs such as tutoring, parent training, job development, and recreational, educational, and cultural experiences (ibid:152).

Some areas provide economic opportunities as alternatives (e.g., the Chicago Area Project and the Mobilization for Youth in New York City), mixing treatment with economic opportunity.

There are numerous alternative programs that are available to youth through the juvenile justice system. One such program was initiated by the California Youth Authority that includes rigorous outdoor activities and mandatory group counseling. This program "reunites groups of teens from rival gangs in a camplike mountain setting" and has "three primary goals . . . (1) to help teens take responsibility for effective decision making; (2) to clarify facts versus myths among gangs; and (3) to expand each youth's vision of the opportunities available to him or her" (Wooden, 1995:216).

In Indian Head, Maryland, there is the Second Chance Campus–Eckerd Youth Challenge Program, which relies on components such as positive relationships, family involvement, challenging activities, structure and discipline, clinical and educational services, and aftercare. The goal of the program is to improve self-esteem and behavior. Activities include canoeing, biking, ropes course, and community service (Dronnis and Hess, 1995:508).

The Fort Smallwood Marine Institute in Baltimore is for serious and chronic offenders. This is an at-sea experience with a point system that exchanges points for privileges. The recidivism rate is 20 to 30 percent, compared to the recidivism rate for most juvenile programs of 80 percent (ibid:509).

Thistledew Camp in Minnesota offers activities such as fishing, swimming, rock climbing, trapping, and education to nonassaultive youth, while the Youth Environmental Services Camps in Florida has community "clean-up" and vocational training programs for violent youth (ibid:508–509).

Summer youth programs are common to most states. Many offer youth the opportunity to camp and hike as well as to ride horses and go canoeing. In Indiana the Probation Dispositional Alternative Department sponsors such a camp as well as field trips throughout the year for youth in trouble, many of whom are gang members (ibid:503).

Intervention programs must begin with some general assumptions or basic principles to serve as both a practical and a theoretical guide. The Dryfoos overview is one such example of linking interventions with empirical data on the various risk factors associated with delinquency and related problems. Another example is provided by the Office of Juvenile Justice and Delinquency Prevention in their review of efforts to combat serious, violent, and chronic juvenile offenders (Wilson and Howell, 1994). Wilson and Howell note that the research on these types of offenders has concluded that there are several interrelated social and personal factors that serve as basic correlates. These include delinquent peer groups, poor school performance, living in high-crime neighborhoods, weak family attachments, lack of consistent discipline within the home, and physical or sexual abuse. Prevention programs should obviously address these factors. A nationwide comprehensive strategy must follow these five guidelines: (1) strengthen the family, (2) support core institutions (schools, churches, and community organizations), (3) promote delinquency prevention in general (because it is the most cost-effective method of dealing with the problem), (4) intervene immediately and effectively when delinquent behavior occurs, and (5) identify and control the small group of serious, violent, and chronic juvenile offenders.

Borrowing heavily from the social development model devised by Hawkins and Catalano, the Office of Juvenile Justice and Delinquency Prevention suggests that programs should focus on the key risk factors that strongly correlate with serious and chronic delinquency. Five major types of risk factors are identified: (1) individual characteristics, (2) family influences, (3) school experiences, (4) peer-group influences, and (5) neighborhood and community influences. Within each of these five key factors several different types of programs are identified.

One of the major problems with many community-based interventions is the lack of any consistent theoretical rationale behind the programs implemented. Without a stated rationale it is difficult to evaluate such programs. One promising theoretical rationale is the risk-focused approach, based on the social development model introduced in Chapter 7.

A RISK-FOCUSED APPROACH

Risk-focused prevention is based on the assumption that trying to prevent a problem from occurring in the first place is better than trying to deal with it after the fact (similar to the old saying "an ounce of prevention is worth a pound of cure"). More specifically, this approach suggests that the most effective way to prevent a problem is, first, to identify the factors that tend to increase the probability or risk that the problem will emerge in the first place and, second, to find methods to reduce the risks, thereby increasing the protective or resiliency factors (Developmental Research and Programs, 1993:3).

Several researchers at the University of Washington have been working on this approach for the past two decades (Hawkins, Catalano, and Miller, 1992; see also Dryfoos, 1990). They have found that similar factors tend to be associated with a core of serious problem behaviors among youths—delinquency, substance abuse, school problems, teen pregnancy, and gangs. These factors, which they label as risk factors, are grouped into four major categories: (1) community, (2) family, (3) school, and (4) individual/peer.

An important concept in this model is that of protective factors. These are those factors in young people's lives that act as buffers against the risk factors found within their environments. These buffers protect the person by either reducing the impact the risk factor has on the person or altering how a person responds. The goal is to strengthen these protective factors for youths who are at risk. These protective factors are grouped into three major areas: (1) individual characteristics, (2) bonding, and (3) healthy beliefs and clear standards:

Individual Characteristics. These include (1) gender, (2) a resilient temperament, (3) a positive social orientation, and (4) intelligence. The first of these, gender, refers to the fact that girls are less likely than boys to become delinquent or to join gangs. This has a lot to do with gender-role socialization in our culture, where boys are encouraged to be aggressive (or at least they are not sanctioned so much for their aggression). Boys should be socialized to be less aggressive and to learn other methods of measuring their manhood.

The second of these, a resilient temperament, refers to the ability of some young people to adjust to or overcome misfortune. Some young people have the ability to overcome overwhelming odds and numerous barriers to become productive citizens. How one develops such resilience is not completely known; in some cases, this trait may be inherited. Regardless of the source, the existence of such a temperament among high-risk youths should be recognized and capitalized on.

A positive social orientation refers to being friendly and good-natured, having a sense of humor, and enjoying interaction with other people. The development of such traits will reduce the risks of those from disadvantaged backgrounds.

The fourth factor, intelligence, refers to the fact that children who are bright are less likely to become delinquent, although this does not necessarily reduce their risk of becoming substance abusers (ibid.:11).

Bonding. As suggested by the social bond/control theory (see Chapter 7), those with strong bonds to a stable family, teachers, and others are less likely to become delinquent. Children who are from high-risk neighborhoods who do not become delinquent are those with strong bonds with some caregiver (e.g., a family member, a teacher, or another positive adult role model). The elements of the social bond—attachment, involvement, commitment, and belief—all play a significant role in reducing a youth's risks.

Healthy Beliefs and Clear Standards. It is not sufficient to be bonded with just anyone. A child could be bonded with an alcoholic father or with a gang member. In order to reduce risks, those individuals to whom children are bonded must have very clear and positive standards for behavior. For example, this person must take a strong stance against the use of drugs and alcohol. Also, children who have parents with high expectations for their schooling (e.g., the parents support efforts to get good grades and to be successful) are far less likely to drop out of school (and those who do not drop out of school are the least likely to become delinquent). Similarly, clear standards concerning criminal behavior and other forms of deviance would have a positive effect.

THE SOCIAL DEVELOPMENT STRATEGY

Hawkins and his associates at the University of Washington have designed what they call the social development strategy of building strong bonding with the long-term goal of assisting children in developing into healthy adults. It is their contention that to build bonding three main conditions are necessary: opportunities, skills, and recognition.

To begin with, children need to be given opportunities to make a contribution to their schools, their communities, and their families. If these opportunities are beyond their abilities, they will likely experience failure and frustration. On the other hand, if the opportunities are too easy, they will likely become bored. "The challenge is to provide children with meaningful, challenging opportunities that help them feel responsible and significant" (Developmental Research and Programs, 1993:13).

Second, children should develop the skills needed to take advantage of the opportunities provided to them. The most important skills are cognitive ones such as problem-solving and reading, along with communication, the ability to be assertive, and the ability to ask for support. Incidentally, for males, it is much too often the case that they are taught to be aggressive instead of assertive, to believe that it is unmanly to ask for help, and to dominate in conversations with others rather than to develop listening skills.

Finally, children need to be recognized and acknowledged for what they have done, even if they have not done everything perfectly. Such recognition gives them the incentive to contribute more and reinforces their successes. Supportive teachers and recognition from parents are especially important.

The social development strategy recognizes that certain individual characteristics make it easier for children to develop skills, make a contribution, and be recognized. Children with a resilient temperament, for example, are less likely to be frustrated by blocked opportunities and will keep on trying. Those children with high intelligence will tend to develop a variety of skills to help them. Children who are sociable will stand a greater chance to be recognized by adults. Although these traits are often innate, they can be taught and nurtured so that the shy child can become more sociable, the less resilient child can be taught to deal better with blocked opportunities, and the less intelligent child can be helped in improving his or her intelligence.

The social development strategy suggests that increasing opportunities, skills, and recognition leads to greater bonding, which in turn leads to healthier beliefs and clear standards, which in turn lead to healthy behaviors. Thus, prevention programs need to focus especially on providing opportunities, skills, and recognition. Prevention programs also need to develop clear and consistent standards for behavior and to teach skills that will help to develop such standards.

The authors of the social development strategy offer the following specific example of how such a program might work within a family. They suggest that opportunities might include such things as helping to make the rules for the family, helping to make dinner once a week, or helping to find out where the family can get the best buy on a new TV or VCR. Tasks such as making dinner teach skills such as how to measure ingredients, how to use the stove, and how to shop (e.g., helping with coupons). Finally, parents must recognize and praise a child's efforts to help the family (ibid.:14).

A key ingredient of the social development strategy is community mobilization (a strategy proven to be quite successful in solving the gang problem, as noted in the next section). The authors of this strategy borrowed from two very successful models: the Stanford Heart Disease Prevention Program and the Minnesota Heart Health Program. These programs used the mass media very extensively, they used volunteers and educational strategies, and they mobilized the community. The result was a reduction in risks associated with heart disease.

The community approach, as the name suggests, reaches out to include a broad spectrum of individuals, groups, and organizations. The community itself makes it clear that certain unhealthy behaviors are unacceptable and will not be tolerated (e.g., children carrying guns to school, boys harassing girls at school, and drinking and driving). This approach takes advantage of existing community resources in the broadest sense and pools them to develop a communitywide strategy. The mobilization process involves four specific steps: (1) involving key community leaders, (2) forming a community board or task force, (3) conducting a community risk and resource assessment, and (4) planning the program and deciding on evaluation methods. It should be emphasized that this model is based in part on the assumption that problems such as drug abuse, teen pregnancy, and gangs are community problems rather than problems that affect just specific individuals.

Step One: Involving Key Community Leaders Recognized leaders in the community (e.g., the mayor, superintendent of schools, chief of police, business leaders, and youth leaders) are needed in order to begin the process of mobilization. These people have already been recognized as those with whom the responsibility of protecting the best interests of a community has been placed. They are the movers and shakers in the community, the people who get things done. Thus the first step is to get these individuals together. The social development strategy suggests beginning with a one-day orientation meeting, the purpose of which is to (1) "create an understanding of this prevention strategy, its basic premises"; (2) generate a vision of the common goals of the community; (3) decide whether to pursue a risk-focused prevention strategy and, especially, to "commit to a comprehensive, multifaceted, long-term undertaking"; and (4) form a community task force (ibid.:18).

Step Two: Forming a Community Task Force The prevention task force should be the major method of ensuring that the prevention program is completed on a day-to-day basis. The task force should include a diverse group of people, representing existing community coalitions (e.g., the PTA, youths, human service agencies, religious organizations, and the media).

Step Three: Conducting a Community Risk and Resource Assessment This step is crucial, for it involves "taking the pulse" of the community by identifying the risk factors that relate to adolescent problem behaviors in the community. Also involved in this step is the gathering of information on existing prevention programs within the community in order to determine their effectiveness. Here the goal is to focus on outcomes, that is, the impact such programs have on risk factors.

Step Four: Planning the Program and Deciding on Evaluation Methods After the key risk factors within the community have been identified, this final step is to develop specific programs to help reduce these risks and to have a plan for evaluating such programs. The evaluation component cannot be stressed too much, for without it one is doomed to failure. Too often, strategies are put in place without any sort of follow-up evaluation, and programs continue even in the absence of provable beneficial results. The key to evaluating programs is to have access to qualified researchers who are capable of making an objective assessment of what works. Such an investment will save communities a great deal of money over time.

COMPONENTS OF SUCCESSFUL PROGRAMS

Research on the subject of community intervention has covered a wide variety of programs dealing with an equally wide variety of problems, ranging from drug abuse and delinquency to teen pregnancy and school failure. What are the ingredients of programs that have had some success? Do these successful programs have certain features that set them apart from others?

Successful delinquency treatment and prevention programs have several key ingredients, which have been identified by several researchers (Chesney-Lind and Shelden, 1998; Dryfoos, 1990; Falco, 1992; Gendreau, 1991; Hollin, 1993; Schorr, 1989). First, as Falco (1992) and Huff (1990a) suggest with regard to the community's awareness of drug and/or gang problems, there is a need for communities to avoid denial of a problem. Second, programs should target medium- to high-risk youths with intensive, multifaceted approaches that focus especially on the development of social skills (e.g., conflict resolution) and address the attitudes, values, and beliefs that reinforce antisocial behaviors. Third, offer alternatives to gang involvement (recreational programs, school events, jobs, and so on). Gendreau has urged that programs provide explicit reinforcement and modeling of alternatives to pro-criminal styles of thinking, feeling, and acting. Fourth, programs should be conducted within the community with a special focus on families and schools (in an attempt to promote bonding with these two institutions). Fifth, the staff should be well trained and consist of skilled individuals who have developed empathy and an understanding of a youth's own subculture and who do not patronize or discredit his or her beliefs. Sixth, link the program with the world of work by assisting youths in developing job skills. Seventh, the goals of the program should be specific and culminate in some kind of award (e.g., a diploma). Eighth, realize that relapse is normal (whether we are dealing with drug or alcohol abuse or any pattern of negative antisocial behavior) and that treatment is a continual process rather than a single episode; relapse-prevention techniques should always be employed to prepare for community adaptation. Schorr concludes, "In short, the programs that succeed in helping the children and families . . .

are intensive, comprehensive, and flexible . . . Their climate is created by skilled, committed professionals who establish respectful and trusting relationships and respond to the individual needs of those they serve" (Schorr, 1989:259).

SOME SPECIFIC ILLUSTRATIONS OF COMMUNITY-BASED INTERVENTIONS AND PROGRAMS

Much of the public response to the problem of youth gangs has been the creation of programs. Many of these programs are operated by communities themselves or by nonprofit organizations. Against seemingly insurmountable forces (e.g., underfunding, limited power to change economic and social structures), a number of communities have initiated programs that attempted to resolve their local youth gang problems. Ironically, many of the people who live in these communities have themselves been blamed for the youth gang dilemma (e.g., because of having poor parenting skills, failure to produce acceptable role models, being derelict in transferring socially preferred values to their children, and so on). Yet, they continue seeking ways to salvage their communities and their children.

Several public programs designed to abate youth gang activity and violence in their respective communities have been examined (Dryfoos, 1990; Goldstein and Huff, 1993; Martin, 1992). Although many of these programs share common ground in defining their goals (e.g., reduction in drug abuse, violence, and gang membership), they have adopted strategies that range from increased education about violence prevention to community-based centers that provide an array of services (e.g., self-esteem enhancement, job training, drug counseling, crisis intervention, and so on). Some offer recreational alternatives to gang activities (e.g., basketball, football, and so on). The strategies adopted by these programs frequently overlap. Nearly all of these programs suffer from sporadic and insufficient funding, more and more a result of legislative priority shifts from community-based services to law-enforcement intervention. Many of these programs were propagated from community grassroots movements, others have religious foundations, while some have formed alliances with components of the criminal justice system (Martin, 1992).

One of the most popular and long-lasting gang intervention programs has been the so-called detached worker program (Goldstein, 1993:22–32). Such efforts date as far back as the mid-nineteenth century with settlement houses, Boy Scouts, Boys Clubs, and others. The Chicago Area Projects of the 1920s and 1930s utilized various kinds of detached worker programs, as did the New York City Youth Board (with a program called the Street Club Project). By the 1960s such programs could be found in most large urban areas (New York,

Boston, Los Angeles, Chicago, and San Francisco, among others). Unfortunately, the results of these kinds of programs have been disappointing. The theoretical rationale of such programs is that instead of bringing gang youths to programs, the programs should be brought to the gang youths themselves, in their own community or turf. Detached worker programs have typically involved various kinds of social work and counseling interventions, including recreational activities, tutoring, family and individual counseling, casework, and job training. These programs included various kinds of control efforts (e.g., surveillance), treatment (usually based on psychoanalytic perspectives), providing various opportunities (educational, recreational, and/or employment), and changing values. The last (changing values), which over time became one of the main goals of these programs, involved a rechanneling of the beliefs, attitudes, and behaviors of gang youths in more positive directions.

The results of detached worker programs have been mostly negative. For example, the Roxbury Project evaluated by Miller (1974) failed to significantly alter the antisocial behavior of the gang youths who participated. The Los Angeles Group Guidance Project actually made things worse, as delinquency among gang members increased, especially for those who received the most attention from the detached workers (Klein, 1968, 1995). One of the main reasons for the failure of most of these programs is the lack of program integrity. As Goldstein (1993:27–32) notes, many programs suffer from high staff turnover, low or inadequate funding, low staff morale, bureaucratic red tape, and extremely high caseloads (sometimes as high as one caseworker to 92 youths), among other problems. Many programs suffer from the fact that the workers are not as "detached" as the theory suggests they should be, with many spending the bulk of their time in the office or traveling alone from one spot to another. Further, most programs failed to have direct delinquency-reduction techniques and offered no techniques tailored to different kinds of gang youths (e.g., hard-core versus marginal members, aggressive youths versus nonaggressive youths). Finally, detached worker programs have not been comprehensive enough; the workers were not adequately trained and were often overworked.

Another common type of gang intervention program is one that involves opportunities provisions. Such programs have attempted to attack the multiple problems facing gang youths—unemployment, low wages, lack of recreational and educational opportunities, poor health, inadequate housing, and other problems. Among the most popular programs addressing these factors have been Mobilization for Youth (a New York program based on Cloward and Ohlin's [1960] theory), the Ladino Hills Projects (Miller, 1974), the Citywide Mural Project (Albuquerque), the New York City Police Probation Diversion Project, the House of Umoja (Philadelphia), and the Community Access Team, Youth Enterprises, and SEY Yes programs (all in the Southern California area) (Goldstein, 1993:34–35). Opportunities provisions programs have not been systematically evaluated. There is a great deal of anecdotal and impressionistic evidence that such programs are effective, as the survey by Spergel and Curry (1990) found.[1]

Community-based organizations have become increasingly involved in a variety of programs that attempt to address some of the social forces responsible for gang development (noted in Chapters 7 and 8).

The Reverend Eugene Rivers of Boston is but one of a growing number of clergy who appears to be transforming the inner cities and the at-risk youth of those cities. A former gang member and Harvard educated minister, Rivers, in 1992, formed a coalition of churches, law enforcement, and social service agencies in Boston. He believes that it is necessary to "get out of the pulpits and pews and into the hoods." What Rivers does is meet the youth gang members with a radical new approach: "walking the 'hoods, engaging the gangs, pulling the kids out" (*Newsweek,* 1998:22). Rivers and a group of like-minded clergy have formed a coalition to try to reform the "winnable kids." Rather than challenging law enforcement, the group works in conjunction with the police. Police officers identify the youth who are in trouble to the clergy and rely on the clergy to identify and refer back those youth who need to be removed from the street. This has left the clergy to deal with those who may be helped. Since this report an outreach network that includes alternative sentencing programs, job training, and continuing education has been established by Rivers's group. Bostonians credit much of the decrease (71 percent) in gang-related killings and shootings in recent years to this coalition.

Other communities in addressing gang prevention and intervention, while similar in the goal of redirecting gang activities to Rivers's coalition, approach the problem in differing fashion. Chicago has a BUILD (Broader Urban Involvement and Leadership Development) program whose mission is to involve and assist a specific group of young people to become productive individuals. This program has two main components: (1) prevention, which focuses on identifying youth most likely to become involved with street gangs and involving them in alternative activities designed to divert, and (2) remediation, a detached worker project that targets members of street gangs for intervention (Thompson and Jason, 1997:463).

The prevention portion has incorporated several key approaches: classroom sessions (in which the program is introduced, gangs are defined and explained, videos are shown that highlight the risks of membership, substance abuse information is given, and career discussion and values clarification are inducted) and after-school programs (which include athletics and sports clinics and emphasize competition and cooperation with others) (Thompson and Jason, 1997:463).

The Children At Risk Program (CAR) diverts inner-city youth by an intensive program of activities. This includes case management, after-school and summer programs, counseling, tutoring, mentoring, and community expectations. This program is currently offered in Austin, Texas; Bridgeport, Connecticut; Memphis, Tennessee; Newark, New Jersey; Savannah, Georgia; and Seattle, Washington. Qualification for the program is determined by either school-based, family-based, or personal-based factors (Dronnis and Hess, 1995:489).

Programs in Indiana that have met with notable success include Operation Kids CAN (Care About Neighborhoods)–a structured "clean-up"-the-community program that is designed to teach youth about community responsibility. This is coupled with classroom lessons about in the juvenile justice system in the Garden Project, in which youth and their parents plant vegetables in the summer and do crafts in the winter, and Paint It Clean, a program that was designed to decrease gang graffiti in which gang members paint over graffiti in neighborhoods, parks, and buildings. The program also includes youth basketball. The courts and a local Optimist Club have sponsored a basketball league for youth allowing for a structured recreation experience with positive role models (Dronnis and Hess, 1995:503).

Another innovative approach is the prosocial gang. Operating from within the gang and striving to have its members identify themselves, one another, and the community according to prosocial standards, resource workers attempt to tackle gang violence. They begin this prevention process with ART (Aggression Replacement Training). The authors argue that ART "stands alone as a preventive measure because it is one that can be effectively evaluated for quality in integrity, intensity and techniques relevant to delinquency reduction, prescriptiveness and comprehensiveness" (Goldstein and Glick, 1994:102).

The participants redirect overtly aggressive behavior into prosocial activities through the utilization of complementary psychological competencies— "reaching out into their real-world environment in order to bring on board a peer, parent, teacher, sibling, or other to serve as our allies in the generalization effort and such a multichannel-ness is the beginning to a generalization of gain" (Goldstein and Glick, 1994:103).

The Pro-Social Gang Project has two sites in Brooklyn, New York. Managers of the program have noticed improvement in interpersonal skills, reduction in anger, and increase in concern for the feelings of others, including their peers, and some reduction in criminal recidivism (Dronnis and Hess, 1995:515).

The Boys and Girls Clubs of America sponsor a laudable Gang Prevention Through Targeted Outreach Program. Referrals come from social service agencies and courts as well as direct outreach and recruitment. Once in the club, the teens have structured recreation and education activities in which to participate. In a summary of all 157 sites throughout the country, 90 percent of the teens attend once a week or more and 26 percent daily, 48 percent improved in school work, 33 percent had better grades, and 33 percent had better attendance (Thornberry and Burch, 1997:4–5).

Another meritorious program in which teens judge their peers is the Teen Court Program operated by the YMCA in Cleveland, Ohio (Huff and Trump, 1996).

It is important in community programming to include females; as Sikes (1997:68) comments, "There is no equivalent of midnight basketball for girls." Programs to reduce risk behaviors among females "need to either work within the context of the gang structure to alter normative beliefs and behaviors or include components that address the suppression or prevention of gang membership." These authors suggest utilizing the power of the gang's influence to alter its norms in order to "reinforce positive changes in risk behavior" (Harper and Robinson, 1999:402).

There are several other programs of note. The federal government funded (1991–92) the Youth Gang Drug Prevention Program with the primary goal of prevention and intervention of female gang involvement. Several of those sites funded still function (Williams, Cohen and Curry, 1994). Other programs include Boston's FORCE program, designed to build self-esteem and provide girls access to structured social activities and recreation; Seattle's community program for females (40 percent of the girls are former gang members), in which emphasis is placed on individual and group counseling and help with completing school and finding employment; and one in Pueblo, Colorado, that offers a wide range of services to females, half of whom are current or former gang members. The latter program offers mentoring with community adults, self-esteem building, and an emphasis on Mexican-American cultural awareness and conflict resolution (Curry and Decker, 1998:172).

Recently the senior author of this book conducted an evaluation of a unique program in San Francisco, known as the Detention Diversion Advocacy Project (DDAP). The success of this program, plus the fact that it has been replicated in two other parts of the country (Washington, D.C., and Montgomery County, Maryland) and the fact that the evaluation was published by the Office of Juvenile Justice and Delinquency Prevention (Shelden, 1999b), warrants a special section in this chapter. Even though it was not originally established to deal with gangs, it is still worth considering since so many offenders who have participated have been involved in gangs or at least lived in areas where gangs are prevalent.

A Model Program: The Detention Diversion Advocacy Project

The original Detention Diversion Advocacy Project (DDAP) was begun in 1993 by the Center on Juvenile and Criminal Justice in San Francisco, California. The program's major goal is to reduce the number of youth in court-ordered detention and provide them with culturally relevant community-based services and supervision. Youths selected are those that are likely to be detained pending their adjudication. DDAP provides an intensive level of community-based monitoring and advocacy that is not presently available.

Disposition case advocacy is the concept that describes the type of approach being used in this program. This method has been defined as "the efforts of lay persons or nonlegal experts acting on behalf of youthful offenders at disposition hearings" (Macallair, 1994:84). It is based in part on the more general concept of "case management," which has been defined as a "client-level strategy for promoting the coordination of human services, opportunities, or benefits." Case management seeks to achieve two major outcomes: (1) "the integration of services across a cluster of organizations" and (2) continuity of care (Moxley, 1989:11). The main focus of case management is to develop a network of human services that integrates the development of client skills and the involvement of different social networks and multiple service providers (Moxley, 1989:21).

Among the goals the program is designed to accomplish include the following: (1) providing multilevel interventions to divert youth from secure detention facilities, (2) to demonstrate that community-based interventions are an effective alternative to secure custody and that the needs of both the youths and the community can be met at a cost savings to the public, and (3) to reduce disproportionate minority incarceration.[2]

The DDAP program involves two primary components:

1. **Detention Advocacy.** This component involves identifying youth likely to be detained pending their adjudication. Once a potential client is identified, DDAP case managers present a release plan to the judge. The plan includes a list of appropriate community services that will be accessed on the youth's behalf. Additionally, the plan includes specified objectives as a means to evaluate the youth's progress while in the program. Emphasis is placed on maintaining the youth at home, and if the home is not a viable option, the project staff will identify and secure a suitable alternative. If the plan is deemed acceptable by a judge, the youth is released to DDAP's supervision.

2. **Case Management.** The case management model provides frequent and consistent support and supervision to youth and their families. The purpose of case management is to link youths to community-based services and closely monitor their progress. Case management services are "field oriented," requiring the case manager to have *daily contact* with the youth, his or her family, and significant others. Contact includes a minimum of three in-person meetings a week. Additional services are provided to the youth's family members, particularly parents and guardians, in areas such as securing employment, day care, drug treatment services, and income support.

Clients are identified primarily through referrals from the public defender's office, the probation department, community agencies, and parents. Admission to DDAP is restricted to youths currently held, or likely to be held, in secure detention. The youths selected are those deemed to be "high risk" in terms of their chance of engaging in subsequent criminal activity. The selection is based on a risk assessment instrument developed by the National Council on Crime and Delinquency. The target population consists of those whose risk assessment scores indicate that they would ordinarily be detained. This is what Miller has termed the "deep-end" approach (Miller, 1998). This is very important, for by focusing on *detained* youth the project ensures that it remains a true diversion alternative rather than "net widening." Youths are screened by DDAP staff to determine whether they are likely to be detained and whether they present an acceptable risk to the community.

Client screening involves gathering background information from probation reports, psychological evaluations, police reports, school reports, and other pertinent documents. Interviews are conducted with youths, family members, and adult professionals to determine the types of services required. Once a potential client is evaluated, DDAP staff present a comprehensive community service plan at the detention hearing and requests that the judge release the youth to DDAP custody.

Because the project deals only with youths who are awaiting adjudication or final disposition, their appropriateness for the project is based on whether they can reside in the community under supervision without unreasonable risk and their likelihood of attending their court hearings. This is similar in principle of what often occurs in the adult system when someone is released on bail pending their court hearings (e.g., arraignments, trial).

The primary goal of the project is to design and implement individualized community service plans that address a wide range of personal and social needs. Services that address specific linguistic or medical needs are located by case managers. Along with the youth's participation, the quality and level of services are monitored by DDAP staff. It should be noted that the purpose of multiple collaboratives is to ensure that the project is able to represent and address the needs of the various communities within San Francisco in the most culturally appropriate manner. Since youth services in San Francisco have been historically fragmented by ethnicity, race, and community, a more unified approach is being tried with DDAP in that it has become a neutral site within the city and staffed by representatives from CJCJ and several other community-based service agencies (e.g., Horizon's Unlimited, Potrero Hill Neighborhood House, Vietnamese Youth Development Center).

More specific goals include (1) ensuring that a high proportion of the program clients are not rearrested while participating in the program, (2) achieving a high court reappearance rate, (3) reducing the population of the Youth Guidance Center, and (4) reducing the proportion of minority youths in detention. Currently, the Youth Guidance Center is the only place of detention in the city. It has a capacity of 137, but the daily population typically ranges from 140 to 150. The average length of stay is around 11 to 12 days.

The evaluation consisted of comparing a group of youths referred to DDAP with a similarly matched control group that remained within the juvenile justice system (for a complete overview of the evaluation, see Shelden, 1999b). The results showed that after a three-year follow-up, the recidivism rate for the DDAP group was 34 percent, compared to a 60 percent rate for the control group. Detailed comparisons holding several variables constant (e.g., prior record, race, age, gender, and so on) and examining several different measures of recidivism (e.g., subsequent commitments, referrals for violent offenses) showed that the DDAP youths still had a significantly lower recidivism rate.

There may be several reasons for the apparent success of this program. From the data collected here and information from previous research, three reasons seem of paramount importance.

First, the caseloads of the DDAP caseworkers are extremely low in comparison to normal probation officers. The DDAP workers average about 10 cases each. Regular probation officers in major urban areas have caseloads ranging from 50 to 150. Smaller caseloads typically result in more intensive supervision, and more intensive supervision means that the caseworker is constantly "on top of things" with regard to their clients. Indeed, with small case loads they can spend more "quality time" with their clients *in the field* (e.g., in their homes, on the street corners, at school) rather than endless hours in an office doing paperwork, on the phone, and doing other bureaucratic chores.

Second, DDAP is a program that is "out of the mainstream" of the juvenile justice system; that is, it is a true "alternative" rather than one of many bureaucratic extensions of the system. This means that normal bureaucratic restrictions do not generally apply. For example, the qualifications for being a caseworker with DDAP are not as strict as one might find within the juvenile justice system (e.g., age restrictions, educational requirements, arrest records, "street" experience, and so on). From casual observations of some of these caseworkers, this researcher was impressed with their dedication and passion to helping youth. Moreover, the backgrounds of these workers were similar to the backgrounds of some of their clients (e.g., similar race, neighborhood of origins, language, and so on).

Third, the physical location of DDAP seemed to this observer "user friendly" and lacked the usual "macho" appearance of the formal system. There are no bars, no concrete buildings, no devices for screening for weapons as one enters the building, no "cells" for "lockdown," and so on. Further, the DDAP workers are not "officers of the court" with powers of arrest and the usual accoutrements of such occupations (e.g., badges, guns).

There could also be a possible fourth explanation, but one we can only speculate on at this time because we lack the data to draw such a conclusion. It could be that given the low caseloads, DDAP caseworkers are more likely than regular probation officers to be "on top of the case," that is, to be in constant contact with the youth and thus be able to "nip in the bud" potential problems. Also, some police officers, when facing a possible arrest situation and learning that the youth is a DDAP case (presuming the officer knows about DDAP), may be in a position to contact the caseworker, who might be able to persuade the officer that the situation could be handled without a formal arrest. We have no way of knowing whether this occurs with any degree of regularity. Even if it did, such a procedure may be a positive sign since youths from more privileged backgrounds are often treated this way by the police if it is believed that someone in authority can "handle" the youth informally. Many youths have been saved the stigma of formal juvenile processing by such intervention by significant adults in their lives.

Those interested in responding to the gang problem in a more positive way should review this program and attempt to implement it in their own communities.

BROAD-BASED NATIONAL STRATEGIES[3]

Addressing the gang problem will require a national strategy, as the problem is not just local in nature. Several researchers have offered versions of how such strategies should be structured. One example is offered by Elliot Currie (1989).

He suggests five general categories for a national strategy to address the general problem of crime, which by definition also focuses on the gang problem. First, he recommends early educational interventions. These would include programs such as Head Start, based on the assumption that delinquency is related to poor school performance and dropping out, which in turn are related to lack of preparedness for school, especially among lower-class minorities.

Second, the United States should expand health and mental health services, with a special focus on high-risk youths. Such services would include pre- and postnatal care. This is based on evidence that the most violent youths suffer from childhood traumas of the central nervous system, exhibit multiple psychotic symptoms, and have also experienced severe physical and/or sexual abuse (see also Dryfoos, 1990).

Third, he suggests family support programs, especially those dealing with child abuse and other forms of domestic violence. Abused children are far more likely than nonabused children to become abusers themselves. Some recent research indicates that the majority of prison inmates, especially violent ones, experienced severe physical, emotional, or sexual abuse or some combination of all three.

Fourth, he recommends doing something constructive with offenders after they have broken the law. In other words, do not merely warehouse them in a correctional setting. Currie notes that an ingredient found in virtually all successful rehabilitation programs is improving skills—work skills, reading and verbal skills, problem-solving skills, and so on.

Finally, there is a pressing need for drug and alcohol abuse treatment programs. He notes that most recent approaches to the War on Drugs have merely tried to halt the manufacturing and distribution (e.g., the supply side) of drugs rather than the use (e.g., the demand side) of drugs. The effects of this "war" have not only been a failure to reduce the problem but also a tremendous growth in the prison population—most of the increase in the prison population in the last 10 to 15 years has been due to the increase in drug convictions and sentences.

On a more general level, Currie suggests that we as a society need to reduce racial inequality, poverty, and inadequate services and that, perhaps most important, we need to prepare the next generation better for the labor market of the future. With this in mind, Currie outlines four general goals for the decades ahead: (1) reduction of inequality and social impoverishment, (2) an active labor market policy that aims at upgrading job skills, (3) a national family policy (e.g., a family leave bill), and (4) economic and social stability of local communities because we need to prevent the frequent moving of capital and employment opportunities, which has forced so many families to relocate in order to seek better jobs; this relocation has weakened the sense of community and the development of networks that would provide support. Additionally, he suggests the need for a national research agenda to study the effectiveness of these policies in order to find what works.

Mark Colvin (1991) has also written about the need for national strategies. One of his major assumptions revolves around the concept of social reproduction, which refers to the process engaged in by institutions that socialize children and prepare them for productive roles in society—mostly families and schools.

His main thesis is that these institutions have largely failed to give growing numbers of young people social bonds to legitimate avenues to adulthood. The result is that many are becoming marginal to the country's economic institutions. This has been caused by a failure to invest in human development and human capital. This failure has resulted in a growing crime rate and increasing expenditures for welfare and prisons. There is a need for a "national comprehensive program aimed at spurring economic growth, human development, and grass-roots, democratic participation in the major institutions affecting our lives and those of our children" (Colvin, 1991:437).

Colvin argues that neither conservative deterrence approaches nor liberal approaches to rehabilitation have been very effective, mainly because they are reactive policies. Clearly, widespread preventive measures are in order. Some prevention programs do not work because of a lack of funding or a failure to address the larger problems in society or because they often appear to target specific groups (e.g., high-risk poor children) at the expense of middle-class taxpayers.

A comprehensive approach must aim at broader economic and human development programs that affect large segments of the population (e.g., the social security system versus welfare for the poor). The country must do what other industrialized nations do and consider seriously the need to develop human capital for the continued overall well-being of society. In the United States the system is so privatized that public or social needs are often undermined by private investment decisions that result in moving capital all over the world but costing jobs here at home.

We need to redirect our focus away from the question of "what to do about crime" to "what to do about our declining infrastructure and competitiveness in the world economy" (ibid.:439). Further, there is a need to establish an educational-industrial complex to replace the already declining military-industrial complex. Today, our national security threat comes from within, a result of our domestic decline (ibid.:440).

Education is the key here. However, as Colvin notes, education must be more than what the term has traditionally meant, namely, formalized public schooling leading to a diploma. He says that education "must include families, schools, workplaces and communities." The educational-industrial complex must "reduce the marginalization of young people" (ibid.).

Colvin (ibid.:446) offers eight specific proposals. These are as follows:

1. *Short-Term Emergency Measures.* These are needed to reduce immediate problems such as joblessness and human suffering. Programs such as Civilian Employment Training Act (CETA), income subsidies for poor families, and other War on Poverty-type programs are included here. However, he stresses the importance of simultaneously starting more comprehensive programs that affect a broader spectrum of people.

2. *Nationwide Parent-Effectiveness Programs.* These types of programs should be required in the senior year of all high schools and also be offered to adult education classes in high school for new parents. Supplement these with parent-effectiveness counseling programs. The

model used in Oregon by Patterson and his colleagues (1982) could be followed.

3. *Universal Head Start Preschool Programs.* For parents who can afford them, programs for certification and training should be offered. Certified preschool programs should also include free day care programs. These have proven to be very effective in preventing delinquency.

4. *Expanded and Enhanced Public Education.* This includes several interrelated proposals: (1) increase teachers' salaries; (2) change certification to open up the profession to noneducation majors so specialists (especially in math and science) can teach (having to take a year of often-silly education courses, at their own cost, can discourage otherwise qualified people to enter the teaching profession); (3) increase the school year to 230 days (from the 180-day average) to compete with Germany and Japan (which average 240 days per year); (4) focus especially on problem-solving skills; (5) offer nontraditional courses such as "outward bound" and apprenticeships; (6) use peer counseling and student tutoring; (7) eliminate tracking; (8) award stipends for attending school and bonuses for good grades to eliminate the need for students to work (this would also open up many unskilled jobs for unemployed adults); (9) establish nonviolent conflict resolution programs; and (10) get students more active in school policies to help prepare them for participating in democracy as adults.

5. *National Service Program.* On completing high school, a youth should have the opportunity to complete a two-year national service and be given educational and vocational stipends on completion of such service. This service could include a wide variety of services—health care, nursing, environmental cleanup, day care services, care for the elderly, and so on. This could provide much-needed labor for public works projects. It would be good for young people to participate in the improvement of their community, and the community could take advantage of the energy of these youths to help rebuild communities.

6. *Enhancement of Workplace Environments.* Young people must have hope that they are headed for a good-quality job. There need to be labor laws that emphasize workplace democracy to create noncoercive work environments. This helps to attract and reward creative individuals who are needed to compete in a global economy.

7. *Programs for Economic Growth and Expanded Production.* First, investments need to be aimed toward what is good for the general public rather than toward profit for the wealthy few who are interested mainly in short-term profits; second, there should be more investment in research and industrial techniques.

8. *Progressive Income Tax System.* First, the wealthy are now paying proportionately less than they did 30 years ago; second, according to Robert Reich, "Were the personal income taxed as progressive as it was even as late as 1977, in 1989 the top tenth would have paid $93 billion

more in taxes than they did. At that rate, from 1991 to 2000 they would contribute close to a trillion dollars, even if their incomes fail to rise" (Reich, 1991:51).

A variation of the proposals offered by both Currie and Colvin comes from Margaret Phillips (1991) and is a good example of a theory-based intervention. Phillips uses the aphorism from Isaiah Berlin's essay "The Hedgehog and the Fox" (1978) to detail a key factor related to crime—namely, unemployment. Her goal here is to show why there is a connection between these two variables. Her thesis is that the stress associated with poverty and feelings of powerlessness (which are correlated) results in the tendency to be present oriented (i.e., the inability to plan for the future because of a belief that one's life is out of control). This is part of the irresponsibility typically associated with crime and delinquency.

She notes that most theories fall somewhere within the old "nature versus nurture" debate. She gives an interesting account of what was nearly a perfect laboratory test of this debate, which occurred in Austin, Minnesota, in the mid-1980s. A strike at the Hormel Meatpacking Company was broken when the company reopened by hiring workers from outside the town. With many local workers left jobless, the rate of crime—especially domestic violence—and alcohol and drug abuse rose noticeably. These increases were explained by a ripple effect common among plant closures, when crime in general—and domestic violence in particular—increases, along with suicides, stress-related illnesses, and drug and alcohol abuse. What is perhaps most interesting is that there is a corresponding decrease in citizen participation in civic activities, which decreases the amount of informal social control (ibid.:558). She concludes by noting that there is abundant evidence that poverty and economic dislocation play an important role in crime as well as in the lack of self-control.

Phillips's theory tries to combine the role of environmental (especially socioeconomic) factors with individual responsibility and powerlessness. She defines powerlessness and its linkage with irresponsibility in the following manner: "The essence of powerlessness is the feeling that nothing one does matters; taking responsibility for one's acts assumes the understanding that one's acts have consequences. Taking control of one's life implies that understanding that one can have some control over the future. Thus empowerment is a prerequisite for taking responsibility, and the most basic kind of empowerment is economic, the ability to support oneself and a family" (ibid.:558–559).

This would logically lead us to consider full employment as a solution to the crime problem. It even suggests a Works Progress Administration (WPA) project like what occurred in the 1930s. Next, she outlines the link between powerlessness and irresponsibility. She begins by noting that if there is such a thing as a criminal personality type, then such a person would tend to be present oriented and irresponsible. This kind of person sees him- or herself as having little or no control over the future and is therefore extremely tied to the present. This theme can be seen, at least implicitly, in the techniques of neutralization noted by Sykes and Matza (1957). Many delinquents see themselves as effects rather than as active doers. This leads to irresponsibility, which in turn leads to what Matza (1964) called "drift," a condition that places one at risk of becoming a delinquent.

Phillips then turns to an area seemingly unrelated (and usually considered off limits) to sociologists—namely, some medical evidence that links poverty and the lack of security to fatalism and various physiological effects. Quoting studies by an epidemiologist (Sagan, 1989) and a biologist (Sapolsky, 1988), she notes that there is a connection between the symptoms of stress and the lack of control over one's fate. Stress, according to Sagan, stems from such things as a lack of nurturing, not knowing what tomorrow will bring, seeing people suffering and dying on a regular basis, being subjected to criminal victimization, and so on. These stressors are especially pronounced in a society of scarcity (which includes many inner-city ghettos). A person's psychological defenses become limited, and one is unable to develop a sense of autonomy and inner psychological strength to cope. When scarcity exists, a normal psychological defense mechanism is to view one's own situation as uncontrollable and oneself as helpless. This in turn leads to attempts to control others (via various sorts of crime, especially violence).

Thus it is easy to understand why delinquents from these kinds of backgrounds would be so present oriented. Yet it is important to view such characteristics as a result of the stress produced by poverty, discrimination, and oppression, obviously pointing to political and economic solutions.

What is also emphasized is still another characteristic of these individuals and another outcome of the stress associated with poverty—namely, the decrease in the degree of trust. This results in the tendency to view others as potential enemies (a point Jankowski makes). It has also been long recognized that there is a higher incidence of stress-related mental illness in the lower classes.

The longitudinal study by Werner and Smith (1982) reinforces these ideas. Those high-risk children who led fairly stable lives came from families with at least two years between children and had someone in the family with whom they could bond closely. They also had good support networks and developed a belief that they had some control over their fate. In short, they had someone they could trust (ibid.:563).

Phillips next focuses on some common causes of feelings of powerlessness (in addition to poverty itself and the corresponding lack of resources). The main causes are as follows:

1. *Joblessness and Underemployment.* There is a need for jobs with livable wages.

2. *Population Size.* This increases feelings of powerlessness; there is a need to develop small neighborhood units so that people will become more empowered (the "safety in numbers" idea).

3. *Alcohol and Drug Abuse.* Not only is this a way to escape stress, but also such abuse itself results in a lack of control. Addiction, having numerous causes in itself, in turn creates irresponsibility and crime. There is a desperate need for more resources for both treatment and prevention.

4. *Low IQ.* The hard-core offenders, especially those in prison, have lower-than-average IQs. Resources for special education programs early in life would help.

5. *Child Abuse.* As Currie (1985) notes, families most at risk are those with low income and low educational levels and those experiencing stress; such abuse is strongly correlated with crime—a high percentage of inmates experienced severe abuse throughout childhood and adolescence.

Phillips offers several interrelated proposals to address these problems. She begins by noting that programs are needed that empower people—those that help individuals learn to be responsible and able to help themselves independently. Prisons (including the popular boot camp programs) fail to do this. Some alternative sentencing programs may help (e.g., victim-offender reconciliation, probation programs that require substance-abuse treatment, and so on).

On a national level, Phillips suggests that some of the following types of programs might well succeed:

1. *Full Employment.* Examples include WPA-type programs and "reindustrialization from below" (like the old Tennessee Valley Authority of the 1930s).

2. *Welfare Reform.* The inclusion of programs that would provide transitional publicly funded jobs.

3. *Raise the Minimum Wage.* Although Phillips does not mention this, Ron Huff has noted in his discussions with gang members that, when asked what kind of wage would attract them to regular jobs, the answer was usually about $7 per hour.

4. *Health Care Insurance for All.*

5. *Low-Income Housing for the Homeless.*

One way to achieve some of these lofty goals is to have corrections departments and other professional associations endorse proposals like full employment and the channeling of our nation's resources to health care, education, and drug and alcohol treatment. These professionals can explain to policymakers exactly why such programs are needed.

Future research might compare recidivists with successful parolees and probationers in terms of differences in their perception of control to find out what made the difference in staying out of trouble or not. There is some anecdotal evidence from successful parolees/probationers who have given such reasons for success as "finding religion," strong family support, getting a good job, and so on.

In her conclusion Phillips states that the key to solving the problem is empowerment, which begins with having meaningful work at livable wages and developing tools that assist offenders in taking some control over their lives.

SUMMARY

Throughout this chapter the focus has been on intervention strategies for the gang problem at the community and societal levels. These strategies solicit mobilization of community members (e.g., parents and concerned citizens), schools (e.g., teachers), social service agencies (e.g., mental health agencies), and other components germane to the community (e.g., churches) to participate in activities that focus on the family, supervision, and creating opportunities. On a more macro (national) level, policymakers and administrators must make decisions that provide leadership that places prevention before reaction. Policies must be adopted and administered that provide some degree of hope for at-risk youths.

Many of the programs reviewed here have demonstrated some effectiveness in the containment of gang activities and delinquency in general (e.g., DDAP). Such programs, however, have limitations. They cannot do much in regard to the social and economic environments from which most gangs are spawned. Thus a more concerted national program is needed to correct slum injustices that plague our inner cities. Obviously, we must first discover a way in which such a program can be less political and more humanistic.

NOTES

1. Recent reports using the technique of meta-analysis have found evidence that many programs are successful at lowering recidivism rates (see, e.g., Andrews et al., 1990; Garrett, 1985; Lipsey, 1992; Whitehead and Lab, 1989). Hollin (1993:72) defines meta-analysis (quoting from Izzo and Ross, 1990:135) as "a technique that enables a reviewer to objectively and statistically analyze the findings of each study as data points . . . The procedure of meta-analysis involves collecting summary statistics, using the summary statistics from each study as units of analysis, and then analyzing the aggregated data in a quantitative manner using statistical tests."

2. The ability of case advocacy and case management to promote detention alternatives was demonstrated by the National Center on Institutions and Alternatives (NCIA). Under contract with New York City's Spofford Detention Center, NCIA significantly augmented the efforts of that city's Department of Juvenile Justice to reduce the number of youth in detention and expand the range of alternative options (Jefferson and Associates, 1987; this is also documented in Krisberg and Austin, 1993:178–181).

A similar case management system has been in use in Florida through the Associated Marine Institutes (ibid). The Key Program, Inc., also uses the case management approach where in this instance the youth are *closely supervised,* meaning that they are monitored on a 24-hour basis and must conform to some very strict rules concerning work, school, counseling, victim restitution, and so on (ibid.).

Additional evidence in support of the use of case advocacy comes from a study by the Rand Corporation (Greenwood and Turner, 1991). This study compared two groups of randomly selected youths, a control group that was recommended by their probation officers for incarceration, and an experimental group that received disposition reports by case advocates. Of those who received case advocacy disposition reports, 72 percent were diverted from institutional care, compared to 49 percent of the control group. The Rand study also found tremendous resistance from juvenile justice officials, especially probation officers, to alternative dispositions, especially those coming from case advocates. It appeared that the probation staff resented the intrusion into what had heretofore been considered their own "turf" (Greenwood and Turner, 1991:92).

3. The remainder of this chapter is reproduced from the first edition without any changes since we feel that what was said then is even more relevant today. This is not just a local problem, as demonstrated by the proliferation of gangs and ganglike behavior in every major city in the country.

9

✦

Legal Intervention Strategies

A HISTORICAL OVERVIEW

This chapter will be devoted to a detailed examination of the strategy noted by Spergel and Curry in Chapter 8—suppression techniques utilized by the legal system. This will include evaluation of responses to youth gangs by various groups, organizations, and institutions. Responses (e.g., programs, policies, and legislation) to social phenomena do not just happen. There are rationales for these responses; some are based on good intentions, while others are characteristic of reactions of a more dubious nature.

In this recent era of "getting tough," legislatures across the country continue to add stricter codes and harsher sentences for juveniles, especially those with gang affiliations and who commit acts of violence. Often legislative expenditures on incarceration as a result of sentencing statutes reduce the amount of funding for the reduction and prevention of crime. Legislators often allocate scarce resources and make value judgments about the impact or effectiveness of social and criminal justice policies based on their subjective perceptions, ideological preconceptions, political calculus, or wishful hopes rather than on objective data and informed policy analyses. Political slogans, rather than empirical evidence or evaluation research, often guide efforts to formulate youth crime, juvenile court waiver, and sentencing policies (Farrington, Ohlin, and Wilson 1986).

Responses to gang behavior can be grouped into three categories: (1) public—that is, community/neighborhood-based programs (discussed in Chapter 8), (2) official—that is, the criminal justice system, and (3) legislative—that is, local, state, and federal legislative bodies. Combined, these categories form an estranged cooperative, which is often a synthesis of antagonism, competition, mistrust, and self-interest. Mass media can be seen as a dispatcher or messenger for this contentious alliance. By capitalizing on sensational and peculiar events, the mass media have actually been able to shape public perceptions of youth gangs (Vago, 1994) while simultaneously, and with shocking accuracy, predicting the responses of the cooperative (Quinney, 1970; Reiman, 1995;

Schlesinger and Tumber, 1993; Williams and Dickinson, 1993). The mass media are able to produce and reproduce our perceptions of and responses to youth gang activities and behavior (Goldstein, 1991; Hagedorn, 1998; Huff, 1990; Jankowski, 1991; Klein, 1995; Moore, 1993; Padilla, 1993; Vigil, 1988). In other words, the mass media may, on command (internal or external), create or re-create public interest in youth gangs while simultaneously orchestrating responses to this phenomenon by manipulating the extent and intensity of youth gang behavior.

Suppose for a moment that the public develops a perception that youth gangs are becoming increasingly troublesome, and let us assume that this perception is largely the result of the mass media—a phenomenon that is becoming more and more frequent. Following the cultivation of public interest/unrest (public response), policymakers scurry to introduce legislation (legislative response) they anticipate will appease the appetites of their disgruntled constituents (particularly those constituents who are most likely to vent their feelings in the voting booth). This legislation nearly always ignores the etiology and epidemiology of the youth gang phenomenon and falls far short of offering meaningful solutions to the alleged problem. It is difficult to discern whether this failure to consider the causes or extent of the youth gang phenomenon is intentional or unintentional. Nevertheless, the criminal justice apparatus responds (official response) by formulating and adopting policies and procedures in a frantic attempt to comply with legislative requirements. Often these policies and procedures (e.g., general sweeps of targeted areas by police, filing by prosecutors of more conspiracy and enhancement charges, and judges handing down longer prison sentences mandated by legislated sentencing guidelines) are counterproductive. In many instances, these reflexive responses do little more than intensify existing tensions within the target communities, congest the courts, and fill the prisons. The heightening of tensions within communities is compounded when the extent of gang activity is grossly exaggerated or fabricated (Padilla, 1992). If the alleged problem persists, the mass media can instigate further pressure on both the criminal justice apparatus and legislators; if the problem diminishes, the mass media can either change their focus (look for another potentially commercial phenomenon) or reproduce the initial production. Society's willingness to consume and ingest as much violence as is produced by the media renders it susceptible to this form of media manipulation.

The mass media capitalize on the public's appetite for violence by sensationalizing exciting stories related to youth gangs (e.g., drive-by shootings, alleged gang members caught with large amounts of cash and/or drugs, assaults that involve alleged gang members, robberies committed by alleged gang members, and so on). Regarding youth gangs, the mass media have the best of both worlds: (1) they have an addicted/interested audience (the public) for whom they "perform," and (2) they are not bothered with the cumbersome responsibility of examining hard data, nor are they required to demonstrate the validity of their "performance." Jankowski points out that

> the violence and crime associated with gangs are perfect topics of this
> because they accommodate the public's interest in violent acts, while

avoiding many of the technical problems that reporters encounter with other stories related to violent crime. . . . In most cases involving gangs, the suggestion that the events reported are verified facts is somewhat deceptive. . . . The news industry is able to report an interest-generating crime (event) without having to identify specific persons or group of persons who committed it. . . . It creates reader–listener interest with few journalistic responsibilities (Jankowski, 1991:286).

A gang member in Detroit asked, "Where do they [newspaper and television reporters] get their information? I live on these fucking streets and don't see half the shit they say happens regular. How the fuck can it be regular if it hardly ever happens?" During an interview with one reporter at a major newspaper in Detroit, it was divulged that "gang news is good news. It is reliable. Readers enjoy the story, and the circulation department is happy. It's good business. That's what counts."[1]

We are not suggesting that destruction and violence cannot be associated with youth gangs—there are casualties resulting from gang violence (e.g., drive-by shootings, assault, murder, rape, and so on) as well as victims of other forms of socially irresponsible behavior acted out by many of these youths (e.g., drug dealing, theft, vandalism, and so on). We do, however, support the notion that the two concepts—violence and youth gang—are not necessarily synonymous. We further contend that by using these concepts interchangeably the problem can be, and perhaps is, overstated and self-serving for commercial and political value.

THE LEGAL RESPONSE TO YOUTH GANGS

Four components of the criminal justice system are included in the "legal" category. These components include (1) law enforcement, (2) prosecution, (3) the courts, and (4) legislatures. Each component has a particular role in dealing with youth gangs, although they all share common ground—they are all subject to political and legislative pressures and mandates.

Law Enforcement

It has been argued that law enforcement represents society's first line of defense against crime. Consequently, law enforcement is the first segment of the criminal justice system that responds to the youth gang dilemma. Obliged to cater to the whims of lawmakers who frequently underestimate the dynamics associated with youth gangs, law enforcement is faced with the question "What can we do?" Law enforcement has responded to youth gangs with a conglomeration of maneuvers.

California's State Task Force (1986:37) offered a number of policy (and legislative) suggestions to combat youth gangs: (1) design and develop statewide gang information systems, (2) launch school-based gang and narcotics prevention programs, (3) provide technical assistance in gang analysis to local law-enforcement agencies, (4) identify gang members under the supervision of the California Youth

Authority and intensify parole supervision, (5) establish and expand special units in probation to supervise gang members, (6) create a Southeast Asian youth gang prevention and intervention program, (7) establish standards throughout the correctional system that discourage gang membership, and (8) using ex–gang members and community street workers, establish a model gang intervention program. Although many of these suggestions do not affect law enforcement directly, they all have an impact on law enforcement's role in policing youth gangs.

In a desperate attempt to find solutions to the problem of youth gangs, violence, and drugs, law enforcement has embarked on a voyage from the proactive/policing approach of creating and sponsoring new programs with catchy acronyms such as DARE (Drug Awareness Resistance Education) and SANE (Substance Abuse Narcotics Education) to paying gang members to fight crime (*New York Times,* 1994). Some promote the notion that foot patrols should be a major tactic used against gangs (Wilson and Kelling, 1989); others, such as Boyle and Gonzales (1989), embrace police programs that target schools and neighborhoods and provide instruction on developing self-esteem, dealing with peer-group pressure, and decision-making, among others. Still others, however, such as Morrison (1992:31), suggest that "police can only do so much, even if they can identify the problems."

The main underlying rationale of the law enforcement approach is that of *deterrence.* In fact, all efforts that come under the more general banner of "suppression" are based on deterrence theory. Klein observes that the essence of suppression is that (1) there is little emphasis on prevention and treatment; (2) the highest priority is on "street crimes," which typically means the most visible (e.g., drug crimes); and (3) there is a strong emphasis on surveillance and "selective enforcement" (meaning harassment) with (4) a corresponding assumption that gang members and potential gang members will respond in a "rational" manner and choose to refrain from continued involvement in gang activities (Klein, 1995:160).

An example of suppression tactics can be seen in the case of "Operation Hammer" and similar police suppression tactics in Los Angeles during the late 1980s. This was a major police response to gangs in south-central Los Angeles under the administration of Police Chief Daryl Gates. The crackdown began in April 1988 and focused on 10 square miles in the south-central area. It was like a "search and destroy" mission in Vietnam (Miller, 1996). A total of 1,453 arrests were made, mostly for minor offenses like curfew, disturbing the peace, and so on. Hundreds more had their names and addresses inserted into an "electronic gang roster" for "future intelligence" (Davis, 1992:268). To aid in this repressive activity the police used a special "mobile booking" operation next to the Los Angeles Coliseum. The overall purpose was merely social control (of African-American youth) rather than a serious attempt at reducing crime. Proof of this is the fact that out of the 1,453 arrests, 1,350 (93 percent) were released without any charges filed. More interesting is that half of them turned out *not* to be gang members. Only 60 felony arrests were made and charges were filed on only 32 of these. Around 200 police officers were used, while during the same period there were two gang-related homicides (Klein, 1995:162).

Similar suppression efforts in the "war on gangs" and "war on drugs" in Los Angeles have met with similar results. For example, Chief Gates launched the Gang Related Active Trafficker Suppression (GRATS) program in February and March 1988, just before Operation Hammer took place. This program targeted so-called drug neighborhoods for raids by 200 to 300 police officers. They stopped and interrogated anyone suspected of being a gang member based on how they dressed or the use of "gang hand signals." Nine of these sweeps took place, resulting in 500 cars being impounded and around 1,500 arrests. Gates wanted to "get the message out to the cowards out there . . . that we're going to come and get them." Apparently the message did not get through, for after the chief gave a speech praising his sweeps, a few Crips fired on a crowd on a street corner in south-central, killing a 19-year-old woman (Davis, 1992:268–274).

Such a crackdown was supported by many conservative leaders, including County Supervisor Kenneth Hahn, who asked for the use of the National Guard, suggesting that Los Angeles was "fighting the war on gang violence . . . that's worse than Beirut," while a state senator's press secretary argued that "when you have a state of war, civil rights are suspended for the duration of the conflict." Meanwhile, the NAACP reported that during these events there were hundreds of complaints about unlawful police conduct and that the police were in effect contributing to gang violence by leaving suspects stranded on enemy turf and even going so far as to write over Crip graffiti with Blood graffiti and vice versa (Davis, 1992:274).

Moore notes a similar crackdown on gangs in Los Angeles that took place on four consecutive weekends in the late 1980s that netted a grand total of 563 arrests (mostly on outstanding warrants), three ounces of cocaine, and a total of $9,000 in cash related to the drug trade (Moore, 1991: 3–4). In San Diego a similar sweep resulted in 146 arrests during a one-week period (mostly minor offenses, as usual), and only 17 were still in custody at the end of the week. Similar suppression efforts have been tried, with the same results, in such cities as Chicago, Milwaukee, Baltimore, and Boston (Klein, 1995:162, 166).

In still another crackdown, Chief Gates ordered a raid that turned into what some called an "orgy of violence" as police punched and kicked residents, threw washing machines into bathtubs, smashed walls and furniture with sledgehammers and axes, and even spray painted slogans on walls, including "LAPD Rules." The result: two minor drug arrests. The police took disciplinary action against 38 officers, including a captain who ordered his officers to "level" and "make uninhabitable" the apartments that were targeted (Davis, 1992:276)—another example of a "search and destroy" type of activity, similar to that used in Vietnam.

Another Gates program was called CRASH (Community Resources Against Street Hoodlums), which was originally called TRASH, with the "T" standing for "Total," but the name was changed for obvious reasons. Under this program the police engaged in "surveillance and harassment" with the explicit purpose being, to use one officer's words, to "jam" suspected gang members (i.e., harass and then move on, with no arrest being made in most cases). The officers were rotated out after two or three years and thus never had a real opportunity to develop detailed knowledge about the communities (Klein, 1995:164–165).

Operation Hammer and other "suppression" efforts resulted in the arrests of an estimated 50,000 African-American youth, with as many as 90 percent never being formally charged. Yet Chief Gates continued such sweeps as a sort of "semipermanent community occupation" or "narcotic enforcement zones," one known as "Operation Cul-de-Sac." These "zones," sort of like the Berlin Wall, were extended all the way from south-central to the San Fernando Valley, just to the north (Davis, 1992:277).

Behind such crackdowns—and the "war on gangs" in general—is a widespread racist belief system. Typical of such racist beliefs was one expressed by Chief Daryl Gates, chief architect of gang suppression efforts in Los Angeles. Concerning the scandal involving the deaths of African-American men because of the police use of the "chokehold," he remarked as follows: "We may be finding that in some Blacks when [the carotid chokehold] is applied the veins or arteries do not open up as fast as they do on normal [*sic*] people" (ibid).

What about the deterrent effect of such efforts? Concerning the effects of such "sweeps" as Operation Hammer, Klein offers the following humorous scenario that may take place. It begins when a gang member, on being released from the mobile booking area near the Coliseum, returns to his neighborhood and meets up with some of his homies. Klein continues (1995:163):

> Does he say to them, "Oh, gracious, I've been arrested and subjected to deterrence; I'm going to give up my gang affiliation." Or does he say, "Shit man, they're just jivin' us—can't hold us on any charges, and gotta let us go." Without hesitation, the gangbanger will turn the experience to his and the gang's advantage. Far from being deterred from membership or crime, his ties to the group will be strengthened when the members group together to make light of the whole affair and heap ridicule on the police.

Despite repeated failures such as Operation Hammer many police officials continue with similar suppression tactics, often based on the assumption that they are "sending a message." Obviously the message is not getting through very clearly, as the number of gangs and gang members continues to grow.

Some individual police officers are more realistic than their superiors. One officer, who has worked with gang members for nearly eight years, in the course of his regular patrol duties stated, "Many of these kids have zero options. They live in a shit hole. I can arrest them. They may, in rare instances, actually do some time. When they get out, they are dumped back into the same shit hole."[2] Another officer pointed out that "these kids have no place to play. They find some structure (e.g., a street-light pole) to nail a backboard and hoop, and play basketball in the middle of the street. They disrupt traffic and make drivers mad. Pretty soon the kids just say fuck it and go find something else to do—they go banging." Most interesting is the reference to "kids," suggesting an acknowledgment by these officers that these youths are not necessarily gangsters or criminals; rather, many are children. This language is qualitatively different from the rhetoric used by those who have transposed the term *kids* (a term frequently associated with a stage of the human development process) to other less flattering abstractions, such as *scavengers,* which is used by Taylor (1990b:105). Of course, in a broader sense, these officers are drawing attention to structural issues germane to many neighborhoods in the inner city.

The interdiction dimension of law enforcement's response to youth gangs is a reflex of the tremendous pressure placed on police to produce results. Many law-enforcement agencies have come to rely on special units. Some scholars have pointed out advantages in the creation of these units (Skolnick, 1994; Skolnick and Bayley, 1986). Others are less than enthusiastic about the special-unit approach (Goldstein, 1990; Walker, 1994). With a nearly impossible mandate (to eradicate, or at least control, youth gangs), many law-enforcement administrators and local governments often find themselves financially driven to replenish insufficient resources.

During the past few years, the federal government has provided assistance in funding through block grants designated for youth gang interdiction. Most often, these grants are used to create and support social-control strategies rather than solution-oriented approaches. We found one law-enforcement agency that formed a special gang unit in order to compete for a piece of the block-grant pie. Surprisingly, we discovered that this particular jurisdiction did not have a youth gang problem at the time of application, nor does this jurisdiction have a gang problem now. During an interview with the detective in charge of the newly formed gang unit, it was revealed that "the mayor wanted a gang unit because he had heard that federal grant money was available for police departments that had adopted this sort of special unit." When asked what his gang unit did, he responded, "Nothing. We don't have any gangs in this community. We have some kids who play with spray paint. At best, we have a few gang wannabes."[3]

In Las Vegas, despite the lack of firm evidence that gangs are responsible for many serious crimes, the police department's gang "unit" was recently re-named a "Gang Bureau." With this categorization comes, not surprisingly, more money for more officers and equipment. Naturally, in recent years the number of "gangs" and "gang members" has increased.

These "gang units" have spread throughout the nation. In a national assessment, 53 of the 72 police departments surveyed maintained separate gang units, whose efforts include processing information, prevention (mediation programs), suppression efforts, and follow-up. Eighty-five percent of these units provide personnel with special training in gang control; 73 percent have specific policies directed at dealing with gang boys, and 62 percent enforce special laws designed to control gang activity (Siegel and Senna, 1997:145).

The Chicago Police Department has more than 400 officers in its gang crime section. Some police departments offer school-based lectures, police-school liaisons, information dissemination, recreation programs, and street worker programs that offer counseling assistance to parents and community organizations, among other services. Some have "gang-breaking" activities, for example, Los Angeles police who conduct intensive anti-gang "sweeps" in which more than 1,000 officers are sent to the identified gang neighborhoods to arrest and/or intimidate gang members (Siegel and Senna, 1997:146).

In another instance, one major midwestern urban police department has a gang unit consisting of more than 60 officers. This unit is composed of five components: administrative, enforcement, investigative, intelligence, and surveillance.[4] The general responsibilities of this gang unit include the following:

1. Identify and patrol intense youth group activity and "shooting scenes" that do not result in death and are not dealt with by other special units.
2. Identify active criminal youths and their leaders.
3. Collect, analyze, and disseminate all information related to youth group problems.
4. Investigate, enforce, and gather intelligence related to all youth group criminal activities.
5. Deploy both uniformed and plainclothes officers as required to respond to scenes of youth group criminal problems. This includes planned youth events that have the potential for youth criminal problems and violence (e.g., rock concerts, rap concerts, high-school sporting events, ethnic festival events, and so on).
6. Restrict surveillance responsibilities to youth-oriented activities.
7. Be responsible for handling, investigating, and securing warrants in probate and recorder's court for all arrests and detentions stemming from firearms offenses occurring in and around public and private schools in the city.

Specific "enforcement unit" duties include the following:

1. Aggressive enforcement action within established target areas which have a *potential* for youth crime activity (e.g., schools, gatherings of youth for social functions, and neighborhoods experiencing high incidents of street shootings and gang activity).
2. Advocation of aggressive enforcement techniques, including traffic stops, stop and frisk, reasonable suspicion, and probable cause, are used in legally obtained evidence of serious crimes.
3. Respond to radio runs, which involve youth crime activity and all shooting incidents for which this unit has primary responsibility.

The duties of the "investigative unit" include the following:

1. Investigation and prosecution of all youth crime activity.
2. Determine whether the criminal activity is germane to the purpose of the gang squad.
3. Conduct live "show-ups" and prepare warrant requests for the prosecution of gang members and their associates.

Among the "surveillance unit" duties are the following:

1. Surveillance of targeted individuals, vehicles, groups, or locations based on information provided by the investigation and intelligence units.
2. Provide *factual* information based on their observations to the intelligence investigation and enforcement units.
3. Provide eyewitness accounts of criminal activity.

The "intelligence unit" is responsible for the following:

1. Evaluation, maintenance, and statistical analysis of intelligence data collected. In addition, disseminate the information to the investigative and enforcement units for action in particular target areas.
2. Prepare profiles on perpetrators of criminal acts who are involved with various gangs.
3. Maintain files with information relevant to gangs (e.g., nickname file, vehicle file, gang membership, affiliation with other gangs, and so on).
4. Develop informants both in the community and within gangs.
5. Maintain liaison with the board of education.
6. Be familiar with upcoming gangs, change in names, membership numbers, leadership changes, and so on.

Gang members are identified by this special gang unit using the following criteria (these criteria are similar to those of many other jurisdictions):

1. When an individual admits membership in a gang.
2. When a reliable informant identifies an individual as a gang member.
3. When a reliable informant identifies an individual as a gang member and this information is corroborated by independent information.
4. When an individual resides in or frequents a particular gang area; adopts the gang's styles of dress and use of hand-signs, symbols, and tattoos; and associates with known gang members.
5. When an individual has been arrested several times in the company of identified gang members for offenses that are consistent with usual gang activity.
6. When there are strong indications that an individual has a close relationship with a gang but does not fit the above criteria. He shall be identified as a "gang associate."

An obvious paradox exists for this gang squad when one considers the specific duties of each element within the context of what the unit calls its underlying philosophy: "The gang unit is a proactive unit that curtails the activity of youthful offenders through proactive enforcement in areas that are heavily concentrated with gang members."

On any given day, rarely are there more than four or five officers actually working on gang-specific cases within their jurisdictions. Typically, dealing with gangs for this unit is limited to conducting investigations when alleged gang members are possible suspects in a crime. Moreover, it is common knowledge among police officers throughout this department that assignment to the gang unit provides strong credentials for promotion—thus the gang unit in this jurisdiction is little more than a political position. Several officers agreed with one officer's perception: "Members of the gang unit profile around and play cowboy. When they do make contact with gang members they do little more than harass them." Another officer stated, "We [patrol officers] are the ones who work the gangs. We deal with them on a daily basis. The gang squad is too busy dealing with the media, and kissing the Chief's ass." Suggesting that this perception may extend beyond this midwestern jurisdiction, a San Jose, California, police veteran of 22 years told Brown, "Gang units are like every other special unit in policing—full of bullshit and totally political."[5]

One of the best-known and widely duplicated law enforcement programs is G.R.E.A.T. (Gang Resistance Education and Training). Developed by practitioners, the components of the program have been linked to control theory and social learning theory (Winfree, Esbensen, and Osgood, 1995).

This is a curriculum taught by uniformed police officers to sixth and seventh graders in hourly sessions over an eight-week period. This program emphasizes skill training and information that may help youths resist peer pressure, improve self-esteem, shun violence, and ignore gang influences. The assessment of this program is mixed. G.R.E.A.T. has been found to modestly improve attitudes but may fall short of persuading adolescents not to join gangs, and participants have lower levels of gang affiliation and self-reported delinquency, including drug use, minor offending, property crimes, and crimes against persons (Howell, 1998:13).

Gang suppression and reduction programs within police departments are numerous. Several of the most active are highlighted in the following discussion. Boston's Youth Violence Strike Force employs a gun user reduction strategy in collaboration with police and probation officers. This strategy relies on the premise that guns are vital tools to gang members, especially in resolving gang conflicts. By removing guns from the street and from the possession of gang members, that vitality is effectively reduced (Lasley, 1998:4).

Atlanta's police department has a model program, recognized by the Department of Justice's PACT (Pulling America's Communities Together). GANGIS, the Gang Intelligence System, is locally developed and supported by the federal government. Its goals are to improve and share intelligence and to support family ties and community values (Jackson and Gordon, 1995)— lofty in theory, but there is an indication (perhaps only perceived by citizens) that this unit has been effective in reducing the number of gang incidents in the community.

The Comprehensive Community-Wide Approach to Gang Prevention, Intervention and Suppression Program, developed by Spergel and his colleagues (Spergel, 1995), contains 12 program components for the design and mobilization of community efforts by police, prosecutors, judges, probation and parole officers, corrections officers, school officials, employers, community-based agency staff such as street outreach workers, and a range of grassroots organizations' staff (Howell, 1998:13–14). A pilot of this model is the Chicago Police Department's Gang Violence Reduction Project, which has been touted by city officials. The target of this project is Latino youth involved in serious gang crime and violence. "A core team of workers delivers relevant services, provides opportunities and carries out suppression strategies in highly coordinated and integrated matters. The level of serious gang violence is decreasing; there are fewer arrests; gang members are referred to, or provided with a variety of counseling, crisis intervention, job placement, family, school and special education programs and services" (Thornberry and Burch, 1997:3).

Another law-enforcement strategy is the implementation of the OJJDP's Comprehensive Strategy for Serious, Violent and Chronic Juvenile Offenders, which targets gang members for graduated sanctions, including priority arrest, adjudication, vertical prosecution (the prosecutor filing the case and remaining responsible for it throughout the prosecution process), intensive probation supervision, incarceration, and transfer to the criminal justice system (Howell, 1998:14).

TARGET (Tri-Agency Resource Gang Enforcement Team) in the Los Angeles area (the Westminster Police Department, the Orange County district attorney's office, and the Orange County Probation Department) utilizes this strategy. It focuses on three actions: interdiction, apprehension, and prosecution. "The Gang Incident Tracking System identifies and tracks gang members, providing the information base . . . uses intelligence gathering and information sharing to identify and select appropriate gang members and gangs for intervention" (ibid:14).

A tactic used by the Los Angeles Police Department was Operation Cul de Sac, in which traffic barriers were placed in neighborhoods where gangs and gang violence had become a dominant force. The year before the project was implemented, these neighborhoods had seen the highest number of drive-by shootings, gang homicides, and street assaults in the city. Drugs were being sold in open disregard for the law. As automobile access to the area was reduced, crime was reduced; homicide and aggravated assault rates fell and were not displaced to other areas. This action, while measurably successful, was initiated and evaluated in this singular area (Lasley, 1998:4). Lasley suggests that the lack of the displacement of gang-related crime "lies in the nature of gang ties to specific neighborhoods or turf. . . [they] may have refrained from committing crimes in surrounding neighborhoods because these neighborhoods are the turf of rival gangs . . . rival gangs traveling . . . in the general vicinity of the site may have been given word to stay clear . . . avoiding [the site] and contiguous neighborhoods altogether" (ibid:4).

This project makes the assumption that gang violence is partly the result of criminal opportunity. This program "directly challenged the popular notion that gang rivalries are so deep-seated, emotionally charged, and irrational that they cannot be mitigated or stopped by specific deterrence measures" (ibid:4). Operation Cul de Sac did provide deterrence as opportunities were blocked by limited street access (see also Klein, 1995:166).

Clark (1992) has further developed this notion of criminal opportunity by defining what he terms "situational crime prevention." This idea assumes that crime can be reduced by pinpointing and blocking the forces that facilitate would-be offenders' criminal acts. These individuals make rational choices in planning their acts, as Lasley (1998:2) offers: "For example, gangs may choose a particular street to commit a crime because they rationally determine that the way the street is situated provides them with ready access and exit, thereby creating an opportunity to move easily elude arrest."

Others would argue that these law enforcement tactics are not effective. Recent (1999) action by the U.S. Supreme Court in striking down antiloitering methods employed by law enforcement against gangs has curtailed this tactic. A Chicago loitering ordinance that had been enforced (45,000 arrests in three years) was ruled unconstitutional by the Court, which said, "If the loitering is in fact harmless and innocent, the dispersal order itself is an unjustified impairment of liberty" (Carellic, 1999:4A). The ordinance required police to order any group of people standing around with no apparent purpose to move along if an officer believed any one of the members of the group belonged to a gang. Chicago's city attorney, Lawrence Rosenthal, said that gang crime is "different from every other form of criminal activity" because street gangs "rely on their ability to terrorize the community" with their mere presence. Gang members just "hang around" innocently by the time police arrive on the scene (ibid.).

Conducting sweeps, or rousts, of targeted areas is another strategy employed by police. Sweeps are tactics whereby many police officers converge on a target area for the purpose of eradicating (or relocating) specific forms of criminal or undesirable behavior. Similar methods were employed by the SS to relocate the Jewish population in Nazi Germany; however, we suspect that the American public, including political officials, are not willing to go quite that far to provide a solution to the youth gang problem. Following public outcries to local officials about prostitution, police have had some success in relocating prostitutes using these maneuvers. In the case of youth gang interdiction, this tactic is analogous to an attempt to put out a forest fire with a water bucket. While it is possible to remove prostitutes from a particular neighborhood (at least for a period of time), it is more difficult, and legally and morally questionable, to remove youth gang members from their neighborhoods, homes, and/or families. Often this tactic can do more harm than good; this is particularly true when local citizens view this approach as an example of racism (e.g., in Watts, Newark, and Detroit during the 1960s and instrumental in events leading to the riots in south-central Los Angeles in 1992).

Ironically, one of America's gross social injustices (also believed to be a contributing factor in the proliferation of youth gangs)—racial segregation—may actually assist law enforcement in their quest for victory over youth gangs. There are social-control advantages reached through segregation. Jackson (1992:90) writes, "Segregation may reduce the pressure on authorities to police minority populations, since segregation reduces interracial crime, the phenomenon most likely to result in pressure on crime control authorities." Moreover, she adds, "fear of crime, coupled with fear of loss of dominance, provides fertile ground for a mobilization of policing resources" (ibid.).

A recent development is the use of specialized information systems, consistent with the proliferation of high-tech computers in recent years. There has been an increase of computer-based intelligence information and the sharing of such information across jurisdictional lines. One example was GRATS (Gang Related Active Trafficking System), begun in Los Angeles in 1988. This proved to be of little use and was soon abandoned. The GREAT (Gang Reporting Evaluation and Tracking) program soon took its place (Spergel, 1995:196–211). The latter consists of information on more than 100,000 gang members. GREAT has been accessed by more than 150 law-enforcement agencies nationwide (including the Bureau of Alcohol, Tobacco and Firearms), based on the assumption (unproven) that gang members from Los Angeles are constantly spreading out all over the country. The chance of misinformation is, not surprisingly, quite high, especially since membership turnover is a constant within gangs and usually leads to an inflation of the actual number of gang members (but with the seemingly unstoppable flow of federal and state dollars, law-enforcement agencies probably do not care)—not to mention the civil liberties problems when gang members move to other areas and are immediately under surveillance (Klein, 1995:191–192).

The overall effectiveness of police anti-gang efforts has not been demonstrated, despite law-enforcement claims to the contrary, usually based on dubious and typically anecdotal evidence (Spergel, 1995:199).

Prosecution

There are three principle types of disputes (conflicts of claims or rights) brought before the court: (1) private dispute, which addresses civil matters; (2) public defendant dispute, which holds government officials and agencies accountable; and (3) public-initiated dispute, whereby the state holds norm violators accountable for their infractions (Goldman and Sarat, 1989). It is to the instance of public-initiated disputes that we turn our attention. The public-initiated dispute is a response by the state (also referred to as "the people") seeking to enforce social norms or to punish violators of those norms (Vago, 1994). It is the prosecutor, acting on behalf of the state (or people), who brings these disputes to the attention of the courts.

The prosecutor may be considered the regulator within the criminal justice system. Whereas law enforcement may be the first line of defense against crime in society, it is the prosecutor who actually establishes the parameters for that defense. The prosecutor has no direct regulatory authority over law enforcement; however, as Katzman (1991:124) points out, "For an investigator, a primary goal is to develop cases which will be accepted by the prosecutor for prosecution." Thus, without support from the prosecutor, law enforcement has no means to process its "product" through the courts. Like law enforcement, the prosecution enjoys a substantial amount of discretion in processing criminal cases through the criminal justice system; in most instances, however, the law looks less favorably on the use of discretion employed by the police (LaFave and Israel, 1992). From an idealistic standpoint, the decision to prosecute a case is grounded in the concept of justice. In *Burger v. United States,* it was argued, "The United States Attorney is the representative not of an ordinary party to a controversy, but of a sovereignty whose obligation to govern impartially is as compelling as its obligation to govern at all; and whose interest, therefore, in a criminal prosecution is not that it shall win a case, but that justice shall be done."[6]

Realistically, the decision to prosecute a particular case is based on several factors: (1) the severity of the offense (more serious offenses are likely to be prosecuted), (2) public sentiment (political consideration), and (3) the strength of the evidence (if the case can result in a conviction). Decisions to prosecute cases are rarely the subject of legal review (Chambliss and Seidman, 1971). The prosecution of defendants is usually carried out by the prosecutor with little animus; however, there have been instances of prosecutor vindictiveness brought before the higher courts (Zalman and Siegel, 1991).[7]

There is also the issue of the prosecutor exercising discretion not to prosecute. LaFave and Israel (1992) identified five general situations that may influence the prosecutor's decision not to prosecute a case: (1) when the victim expresses a desire that the offender not be prosecuted, (2) when the cost of prosecuting a case is too exorbitant, (3) when prosecution would result in undue harm to an offender, (4) when the offender is capable of assisting other enforcement goals, and (5) when the injury committed by the offender can be resolved without prosecution. Donald Black (1976) suggests that social stratification is a factor associated with the decision either to prosecute or decline prosecution. Others, such as Chambliss and Seidman (1971), Gordon (1990), Quinney (1970, 1974, 1977), and Reiman (1998), suggest that social class and race are catalysts in the decision either to prosecute or decline prosecution.

Similar to law-enforcement agencies who have adopted special units to respond to the youth gang dilemma, prosecutors' offices have also designed and launched their own special prosecuting units to address this problem. Typically, the duties of these special units include designing and maintaining data banks that track gangs and their members, coordinating their efforts with law enforcement, and, most frequently, practicing vertical prosecution (the prosecutor initially assigned to a gang case remains with that case until final disposition). In a study of gang prosecution in America conducted by the Institute for Law and Justice (1994:2–13), it was reported that 32 percent of the large jurisdictions studied have gang units, whereas only 5 percent of the smaller jurisdictions have special units to deal with gangs.[8]

Characteristics of the strategies employed by prosecutors against youth gangs may be viewed in the context of either utilizing existing laws or employing a new set of gang statutes. Examples of the old legislation include certification (transferring jurisdiction of the juvenile to adult court), taking advantage of forfeiture laws (confiscation of vehicles used in drive-by shootings), and filing enhancement charges when the opportunity exists (e.g., crimes committed in or near a school, use of a weapon, elderly victim). New gang-directed legislation has provided prosecutors with additional tools. Prosecutors in many jurisdictions now confiscate weapons used by gang members, impose parental liability for damages caused by gang members, enhance penalties for vandalism (graffiti), and prosecute gang members who threaten or use coercive methods of intimidation on members who want to leave the gang or youths who do not join a gang. But new does not necessarily mean better or more efficient. It was found that prosecutors in many jurisdictions with statutory provisions for gangs have a broader range of problems. For example, "Prosecutors in gang-statute states complained in greater proportions about the lack of resources for various gang prosecution than did their colleagues in non-gang-statute states. The sharpest disparity is in lack of early intervention programs for youth at risk of gang involvement" (ibid:2–20).

One of the prototypical prosecutorial efforts was that of "Operation Hardcore" started in Los Angeles in the 1980s. Central to this is what is known as "vertical prosecution," where one deputy district attorney is involved with the case from the start to the end. This operation also included special training given to both the police and members of the district attorney's investigation staff, use of witness protection programs, elimination of plea bargaining, use of high bail, and others. As usual, they used rather narrow and conspiratorial definitions of "gangs." Although the operation in Los Angeles achieved a high rate of convictions (95 percent) and was copied all over the country, it narrowed the targets to mostly homicide cases. Also, the focus was clearly on "special" rather than "general" deterrence (Klein, 1995:173). The "special deterrence" emphasis quite naturally resulted in a policy of "incapacitation." However, while trying to "send a message" to gang members and wannabes (e.g., they created posters which read "Gangs—Prison! Think Twice"), there is no evidence that the intended recipients actually received it, let alone paid any attention.

Unlike law enforcement, which is policy driven (i.e., creating policies that conform to legislative activity, local government mandates, and prosecutor-established standards), the prosecutor is often guided by political realities or ambitions. The prosecutor is usually an elected public official and is frequently provided with access to an assortment of resources capable of promoting a desired public image that is politically marketable. The numbers of cases prosecuted, with particular attention to conviction rates, are the staples of reelection campaigns for prosecutors. Conversely, low numbers become targets for prosecutor wannabes. Youth gangs provide another commodity in which bargains can be made (plea bargains) and reputations constructed. This commodity is a component of the lower class, which is unable to purchase the "expensive spread" (private attorneys) of legal representation. In a way, prosecutors are analogous to journalists who cover youth gang stories. Neither are account- able for their decisions. Both can be viewed as being in the business (which, incidentally, justifies many types of behaviors) of marketing; one is marketing a tangible product (news), and the other is often marketing a political career.

The Courts

The third segment of the legal response to youth gangs is the judiciary, of which there are three components. Of immediate interest to our work are (1) the juvenile court, (2) the adult court, and, at the apex of the judiciary, (3) the Supreme Court. Each component has played a role in the adjudication process of accused members of youth gangs. The juvenile courts have provided elevated statuses for convicted youths (Thrasher, 1927), adult courts have at- tempted to satisfy the public's voracious appetite for revenge by sending youths to prison, and the Supreme Court has oscillated in its decisions regarding youths—mirroring changes in the political and public atmospheres. The courts are presumed to consist of the following:

> (1) an independent judge applying (2) preexisting legal norms after
> (3) adversary proceedings in order to achieve (4) a dichotomous decision
> in which one of the parties was assigned the legal right and the other
> found wrong (Shapiro, 1986:1).

Beyond this quite idealistic perception is another collection of court functions.
    The courts legitimize government and its social-control apparatus—the criminal justice system (Heydebrand and Seron, 1990). In addition, the court has other functions, such as serving as trial referee (Frankel, 1975) and provid- ing for the routinization of administrative legal procedures such as uncon- tested adoption cases and previously negotiated plea bargains (Spitzer, 1982) and lawmaking (Holmes, 1881; Shapiro, 1986; Vago, 1994). Many of these functions are relative to historical epochs (Hurst, 1950). In fact, the courts may be viewed as a forum that engages in the reification of the utility of criminal law. Reiman suggests,

> The criminal law enshrines institutions as equivalent to the minimum
> requirements for any decent social existence—and it brands the individual
> who attacks those institutions as one who has declared war on all
> organized society and who must therefore be met with the weapons of
> war (Reiman, 1993:141).

Judges, as a whole, attempt to present an image of objectivity and maintain a posture that is somewhat distanced from the youth gang issue. However, on an individual basis, some judges have begun to take a broader view of youth gangs.
    The juvenile court, sometimes called family court, was founded on the principle that children must be treated differently from adults when their be- havior is antithetical to standards adopted by society. In a quixotic sense, this court would provide the best of both worlds: (1) due process protection and

(2) care and treatment during the dispositional phase. Of course, this has not always been the case (Faust and Brantingham, 1979). It was established that, through the juvenile court, every effort would be exhausted to return the delinquent child to a socially accepted status (ibid.). Of course, middle–class philanthropists were designated to establish the criteria for social acceptability (Platt, 1969). Through *parens patriae,*[9] the state assumed the role of parent, acting on behalf of the delinquent child, and the juvenile court judge represented the state. Julian W. Mack notes,

> The problem for determination by the judge is not, has this boy or girl committed a specific wrong, but what is he, how has he become what he is, and what had best be done in his interest and in the interest of the state to save him from a downward career (Mack, 1989).

Mack also notes that

> the child who must be brought into court should, of course, be made to know that he is faced with the power of the state, but he should at the same time, and more emphatically, be made to feel that he is the object of its care and solicitude (ibid.).

In a similar vein, Walter H. Beckham suggests,

> It should be understood that a juvenile court proceeding is not a trial of anyone on criminal charges but, according to the laws of most states, is an "investigation" into the conduct of a young citizen to determine not whether punishment should be inflicted, but what action or program should be adopted for the welfare of the child (Beckham, 1949).

Times have obviously changed.

Today, there is a tendency, particularly in the case of alleged youth gang members, to change the adjudication jurisdiction. In some states, a juvenile judge makes the determination whether the accused (1) committed a serious offense, in which case she or he is certified as an adult and referred to adult court for prosecution, or (2) can benefit from available rehabilitation facilities and programs established for juveniles. In other states, legislatures have removed this function from the juvenile courts. The difference between juvenile and adult jurisdiction over the individual is significant, particularly with the current application of capital punishment in most states. In the juvenile court the child is subject to a relatively short period of incarceration, whereas in the adult court the same child faces long-term incarceration or death. Based on public opinion polls, it is clear that society wants children who commit violent offenses treated as adults. For example, when asked the question, "In your view, should juveniles who commit violent crimes be treated the same as adults, or should they be given more lenient treatment in juvenile court?" 68 percent indicated, "Treated the same as adults" (Maguire and Pastore, 1994:196). Thirty-five states allow for transferring juveniles to adult court, for various violent offenses, at 14 years of age or younger (Maguire, Pastore, and Flanagan, 1993:145–147). Moreover, race appears to be a major factor in the certification process. For example, in 1991 white youths accounted for 65.1 percent of all offenses (person, property, drug, and public-order offenses), compared with 31.6 percent for blacks (Maguire and Pastore, 1994:548). Yet, 1.1 percent of the petitioned cases involving white youths were waived to adult court, compared with 2.0 percent of the petitioned black youth cases (ibid.:549). Another obvious fact surfaces in the analysis of these data—despite public sentiment to treat youthful offenders as adults in cases involving violence, the courts have been reluctant to transfer many of these to adult jurisdiction. Of course, this does not take into account legislative mandates that remove decisionmaking from the courts.

During a recent discussion with a midwestern district court judge about the certification process of youth gang members, the following information was revealed:

> I was trained in the logic and rationale of the law. Those are the two principle abstractions that accompanied me to the bench. Now, I see these youngsters [gang members] standing before me, and I realize the ineffectiveness of the system I have supported all my life. Although I am bound by statute to sentence many of these defendants to prison, I understand that it is to no avail. They simply return to the environment that manufactured the behavior which brought them to me in the first place. Society has elected to accept this cycle; this defies all logic and rationale.[10]

When asked why society continues embracing its current retributive position, the judge replied,

> I want to believe that most of society is ignorant of the conditions in these environments; in which case they may be excused, in this instance, for their ignorance. In this instance, the solution lies with educating society. On the other hand, it may be that people who have the capacity to act in a positive manner do not feel obliged to act, and that means people will not be apprised of the situation. Of course, there is also the possibility that people just don't care anymore.[11]

As previously stated, the Supreme Court stands at the apex of America's judicial system. This judicial body is entrusted with the responsibility to ascertain the factual, procedural, and legal basis of criminal charges while simultaneously ensuring that stipulations set forth in the U.S. Constitution are observed by the entire court system. In other words, the lower courts are operationally confined by the latitude allowed and established by the Supreme Court. As Scheb and Scheb point out, "The Supreme Court has jurisdiction to review, either on appeal or by writ of *certiorari,* all the decisions of the lower federal courts and many of the decisions of the highest state courts" (Scheb and Scheb, 1994:26).

There is another aspect of the Supreme Court—a more politicized element that is generally masked from public consideration. This component is obscured behind an illusion of preoccupation with deference to evidence and fact-finding; both dimensions are subject to pressure from the legislative branch of government as well as from within the Supreme Court itself. The Supreme Court may reverse lower-court decisions on the facts in criminal cases, but *only* when the lower court's record contains *no evidence* to support the conviction. The reason for this reluctance to overturn convictions is that the principal job of an appellate court is lawmaking.

The Supreme Court continually seeks to reiterate its connection with the basis of all judicial legitimacy: dispute settlement. As Shapiro notes,

> So long as the appellate courts do their lawmaking under the guise of doing substantial justice between man and man in particular cases—and they must do this if they are to be perceived as and supported as courts— they will keep clawing their way back towards the facts (Shapiro, 1986:42–43).

Although the Supreme Court is frequently involved in political issues, it is not necessarily considered a factor in politics because of its low-key posture as an institution that enjoys much public support, even though the majority of the cases brought before the Supreme Court are not widely publicized in the general media (Zalman and Siegel, 1991). Moreover, the Supreme Court is most likely to cater to cases submitted for review by the government. O'Brien points out that

> the government has a distinct advantage in getting cases accepted, but its higher rate is not surprising. Since the creation of the office in 1870, the solicitor general of the United States assumed responsibility for representing the federal government. From the Court's perspective, the solicitor general performs an invaluable service. He screens all prospective federal appeals and petitions and decides which should be taken to the Court. . . . Since he typically argues all government cases before the Court, the solicitor general has intimate knowledge of the justices and has been characterized as the Court's "ninth-and-a-half" member. . . . By contrast, indigents like Gideon are unlikely to have their cases given full consideration (O'Brien, 1990:249–250).

The Supreme Court, responding largely to the demands of the criminal justice apparatus and perhaps under political pressure because of public outcry, has heard cases pertaining to gangs. Supreme Court rulings date back at least to 1939. In the *Lanzetta et al. v. New Jersey* case, the Supreme Court overturned the conviction on the basis of ambiguity of the concept of *gang,* and its dependent term *gangster,* in the New Jersey law.[12] This definitional problem with the concept of gang would cause legislatures in the 1980s and 1990s to reconsider their statutory definitions of similar concepts. In another case, *Abel v. U.S.,* the question was raised whether belonging to a gang or organization that was involved in illegal activity could stand alone to justify criminal conviction.[13] The Supreme Court ruled that one may not be convicted merely for belonging to an organization that advocates illegal activity. In order to get a conviction, the government must provide evidence that the individual knows of, and personally accepts, the tenets of the organization or gang. To a large degree, the Supreme Court has allowed legislative bodies to redefine the law—tailoring it to meet society's demand for vengeance against criminal youths.

Legislatures

From a most naive perspective, legislative bodies act on the sentiment of society. Of course, most people (1) recognize that they are completely ignorant of legislation passed at the state and federal levels or (2) find that their representative voted contrary to what the constituents wanted. This is probably best referred to as politics—supporting a candidate who supports legislation contrary to what he or she claimed to support during an election campaign. What is most interesting about this phenomenon is that the same people return to the polls and reelect their "nonrepresentative."

Political actors often wrap themselves around platforms that draw attention to episodes of youth gang activities.[14] The validity and extent of these indictments make little difference. Rarely do these actors address economic, social, and political factors that have a contributing causal link to delinquent behavior among many of society's youths (e.g., poverty, unemployment, discrimination in school funding, absence of constructive activities for youths, and so on). In fact, laws that govern political campaigns do little to discourage or restrict false information (this holds true for arguments between opposing candidates and for their distortions of social issues). An excellent example is the Republican Party's 1994 Contract with America, which is characterized by denial, ignorance, and misrepresentation. (Chomsky, 1996:113–117).

In their attempt to resolve the youth gang dilemma and appease disgruntled constituents, legislators across America have enacted new laws and revisions to existing ones. Frequently, their legislation begins with a consideration of the feasibility of existing laws. Legislators struggle with the troublesome question "What constitutes a gang?" Armed with arrogance, ignorance, and indifference, legislative bodies (federal, state, and local) spend much of their time reacting to the gang dilemma, preferring creative sanctions rather than a subscription to social justice. In the process, many legislators believe it is necessary to fracture the U.S. Constitution; they begin by undoing many of the tenets set forth by the Founding Fathers and reaffirming earlier dogmas by the Warren Court—particularly in the area of due process. There seems to be significant support for reducing the protection afforded through due process, such as justification to implement the "no-knock warrant" (Allegro, 1989). The concept of toughness stands in the way of more tolerant concepts such as individual rights, human rights, dignity, and compassion, which could be used to direct legislation. Clearly, the intended social-control–oriented ends of the Republican Congress are believed to justify their cruel and haphazard means (e.g., program cuts and eliminations and reduction in vital community services). The vigor with which these ideologues apply their pragmatism to the development of strategies in their youth gang war is reminiscent of two earlier statesmen (Nixon and Kissinger) in a previous war (Vietnam). As one compares the two events, there is a striking parallel in the outcomes (increases in body counts, and no end in sight). Moreover, both incidents were avoidable and preventable—assuming, of course, that ignorance is not replaced by rational thought complemented with humanistic consideration.

Two types of legislation have typically resulted. The first involves passing new laws that would cover gang activity (e.g., covering drive-by shootings, graffiti, preventing gang members from frequently certain areas, targeting "crack houses"). The second involves using existing laws but providing "enhancements" on the penalties when gangs are involved (McCorkle and Miethe, 2001:211).

A perfect example of the latter was California's Street Terrorism Enforcement and Prevention Act (STEP). This was a classic example of legislatures accepting uncritically law enforcement and media stereotypes and exaggerations about gangs. The word "terrorism" conjured up highly professional and highly organized groups analogous to the popular terrorists of the Middle East. Furthermore, the definition of "gang" and "gang member" was dubious at best. The statute read in part as follows:

> Any person who actively participates in a criminal street gang with knowledge that its members engage in or have engaged in a pattern of criminal activity, and who willfully promotes, furthers, or assists in any felonious criminal conduct by members of that gang, shall be punished in the county jail for a period not to exceed one year, or by imprisonment in the state prison for one, two or three years (California Penal Code, Section 186.22; quoted in McCorkle and Miethe, 2001: 212).

The definition of a "street gang" was similar to other law enforcement definitions (part of this was quoted in Chapter 1). The key part of the definition was where it was stated that a "criminal street gang," which was, of course, quite vague and could theoretically be applied to many groups, especially if they happen to be young and members of a racial minority. As Klein notes, the framers of this law supported a rather conspiratorial view of gangs and "saw only the worst cases" while never seeing the "normal, humdrum existence of most gang members on most days." Rather, they "saw violence as the core of gangs" (Klein, 1995:179).

Other examples of anti-gang legislation has included civil abatement laws, which, among other things, seek to punish landlords for allowing gangs to flourish on their property (e.g., apartment complexes), as if these landlords can control the activities of youth vaguely defined as "gangs." Another example would be closing off certain cul-de-sacs to gang members or even prohibiting "known gang members" from associating with one another in a certain part of town, such as parks. Also common has been the use of RICO statutes (federal racketeering laws) applied to gangs, as if they were like the Mafia. The Wisconsin Street Gang Crime Act, known as Wisconsin State Senator Chuck

Chvala's "Gangbuster bill," added additional penalties for certain acts (e.g., "drive-bys") or doubled the penalties for "gang-related" crimes. Many new bills have specifically targeted juveniles (Klein, 1995:184–186).

The Omnibus Crime Bill of 1994 is an excellent example of legislative creativity. In response to well-orchestrated public paranoia about crime, this bill reaches into all facets of crime in America. First, it provides seed funding for 100,000 new police officers. Then, in anticipation of increases in arrests, almost $10 billion is set aside for new prison construction. There is an additional $2.6 billion reserved for additional funding for the DEA, FBI, INS, U.S. attorneys, the Treasury Department, and other Justice Department components. Federal courts are also beneficiaries. Of course, there is $6.1 billion for prevention programs, but many of these programs are contingent on law-enforcement cooperation and/or participation—which suggests a social-control version of prevention programs (more DARE programs that touch out-of-risk youngsters). There is also a gang component—new and stiffer penalties for violent and drug-trafficking crimes committed by gang members.

Dissatisfied with this antiquated crime bill, which was viewed as being soft on criminals, the House of Representatives passed yet another panacea-for-crime bill in early 1995. This bill transfers much of the crime-fighting funding to the states based on the argument that crime control is a local issue (just as we were getting used to the presentation that crime was a national dilemma) and that local authorities are more knowledgeable about local needs.[15] Interestingly, the new House bill removes the "pork" in program spending while also limiting the number of appeals for death-row inmates. Moreover, a principal target of this bill reduces and in some cases eliminates the cumbersome search warrant.

In 1994, Governor John Engler of Michigan signed into law P.A. 328 of 1994, which mandates the permanent expulsion of public-school students (few African-American students, compared with white students, attend private schools) who are in possession of dangerous weapons as defined by the school code. These dangerous weapons include firearms, daggers, stilettos, knives with a blade over three inches long, pocket knives that are opened by a mechanical device, iron bars, and brass knuckles. When asked about the permanent expulsion law, several gang members in Detroit stated, "We can't believe it. Engler is actually recruiting for us."[16]

A case study of the legislative response to gangs in the state of Nevada provides a fascinating glimpse of the effect of a "panic" over gangs and how elected officials succumb to horror stories and scare tactics used by criminal justice officials and the media. McCorkle and Miethe (2001) note that between 1989 and 1991 a total of 10 different pieces of gang legislation were passed. The new laws were put together based solely on popular images of gangs provided by the police and the media. McCorkle and Miethe provide us with an apt description of the legislative process in Nevada and elsewhere when they remark that

> without firsthand knowledge of gangs, Nevada law makers were forced to rely on media accounts that distorted and exaggerated the threat.
> Moreover, during numerous committee hearings on street gangs, the

testimony provided by law enforcement officials would only heighten their fears. Armed with charts, figures, and frightful anecdotes, in public hearings police portrayed gangs as a clear, present, and extreme danger to the community. . . . Warned that only heroic action would curb the escalating threat, law makers moved swiftly to pass new laws (McCorkle and Miethe, 2001:209).

It seems as though much of the legislation being passed, particularly that which attempts to target gang activity, is done so without any real understanding of youth gangs. For example, more prisons will simply mean that there will be more people in prison. When a gang member is imprisoned, similar to the incarceration of drug dealers, another takes his place on the street. During a two-year study of 79 gang members in Detroit, it was found that nearly 86 percent were not worried about legal sanctions or prison. More than 90 percent indicated that they were not particularly concerned about their own safety related to gang violence or encounters with authorities. These data are not surprising, given that almost one-third of the subjects defined having fun as making money (which should be alarming when one considers that these youngsters ranged in age from 13 to 17).[17]

What seems clear at the start of a new century is that the crackdown on gangs has not resulted in an abatement of gangs or their activities. As so many gang researchers have noted, the gang is a sort of "oppositional subculture," and attempts to break them up by the authorities merely solidifies them even more. Far from acting as a deterrent, such threats of punishment may function to perpetuate gangs and criminal activity (Klein, 1995:186). Years of deterrence research has confirmed this simple fact (Zimring and Hawkins, 1973).

SUMMARY

The notion that violence and youth gangs are not necessarily synonymous serves as a catalyst for this chapter in the exploration of the legal response to gangs. Three components of the criminal justice system (law enforcement, prosecution, and the courts) are addressed in the discussion and analysis. Beginning with law enforcement, it becomes obvious that current practices of law enforcement are not only ineffective in their attempt to suppress gangs but may indeed perpetuate youth gangs. Although many police administrators ignore the futility of relying solely on social-control policies directed toward youth gangs (demonstrated by their adoption of certain policies and tactics), many police officers recognize the necessity of providing viable options for many youths who find themselves involved in gangs.

Second, this chapter also points out that prosecutors—key agents of the state—have a tremendous amount of discretionary power and that they can be quite political in dealing with gang members. As elected officials, prosecutors have a political agenda driven by a combination of public perceptions and fears (which can be and have been manipulated by a zealous media) and self-interest (getting reelected or running for higher office).

Third, this chapter presents a discussion of the judiciary and its response to gangs. The judiciary is largely a passive institution in that it relies on others (police and prosecutors) to generate clients. Although judges do have a degree of discretion, their options continue to be reduced as more and more jurisdictions establish guidelines that limit the options available to these jurists. At the higher-court level (i.e., the Supreme Court and other appellate courts) there has been a tendency to allow legislative bodies to redefine the law. This tendency has contributed to the increased number of youths who are certified as adults in the adjudication process.

Finally, we have looked at legislative bodies and their impact on youth gangs. Political actors often wrap themselves around platforms that promote "get tough on crime" policies. Gangs are frequently incorporated into these policies. Sometimes, fact has little room in their political rhetoric. Variables such as economic deprivation, racism, and segregation are sometimes neutralized by references to family values and individualism in political orations. One fact is quite clear, however: The legal response demonstrates that practitioners, with few exceptions, do not *listen to gang members.*

These policies have all been based on the deterrence model of the legal system. The intention has always been to "send a message" (via threats) to those who are already in a gang and to those who might want to be in a gang that "crime does not pay." The messages have not been well received, judged by the continuous presence of gangs and gang members in every major city in the country.

NOTES

1. These quotes are taken from an interview by Brown during a study of youth gangs in Detroit, Michigan (Brown, 1998).

2. This and subsequent quotes from police officers are from interviews by Brown during a study in Detroit (Brown, 1998).

3. Interview by Brown, at a suburban police station in Detroit (Brown, 1998).

4. Data provided to co-author Brown.

5. Interview by Brown.

6. 295 U.S. 78, 55 S.Ct. 629, 79 L.Ed. 1314, 1935.

7. See *Blackledge v. Perry* (417 U.S. 21, 94 S.Ct. 2098, 40 L.Ed. 628, 1974).

8. The Los Angeles prosecutor's office was found to have the largest gang unit (48 lawyers).

9. *Parens patriae* is the philosophy that the state can assume the role of parent when parents are deemed unfit. For a detailed discussion of this philosophy within the context of the emergence of the juvenile justice system see Shelden, (2001).

10. Interview by Brown with a midwestern district court judge.

11. Ibid.

12. 306 U.S. 451, 59 S.Ct. 618, 1939.

13. *Abel v. U.S.,* 362 U.S. 217, 80 S.Ct. 683, 1960.

14. In a campaign for county sheriff in Las Vegas, Nevada, in the early 1990s, the two major candidates focused on the local gang problem, almost to the total exclusion of any other major problem related to crime. The impression was given that gangs were responsible for almost all the crime problems in this county, which is patently untrue. Nevertheless, these candidates kept trying to

outdo each other with their own versions of a gang policy.

15. *Time* magazine released an article (America Online, February 20, 1995) that directs attention to the states' abilities to determine their crime problems and develop their own resolutions through block grant funding. For example, North Carolina commissioned a $27,000 study that focused on why inmates want to escape. In 1972, Florida law-enforcement agencies shared a $350,000 grant that urged people to notify the police if they see or hear anything suspicious. Indiana used $84,000 for a twin-engine Beechcraft plane for the purpose of crime fighting. Flight logs, however, revealed that the aircraft was used by the governor, his family, and friends to travel around the country—one trip was to fly to Washington to pick up a "moon rock." Heflin, Alabama, used federal crime money to buy an unmarked police car, which was used exclusively for private use by the mayor. Louisiana used $79,000 of federal crime money to purchase riot-control equipment. The bulk of the equipment included machine guns and an armored personnel carrier. In fact, the article cites a House subcommittee's finding that millions of dollars in grant money had been "parked by local governments in bank accounts or had been used to invest in U.S. Treasury bills . . . .The Federal Government ended up paying interest on its own largesse."

16. Interview by Brown of *Cash Flow Posse* members (Brown, 1998).

17. Study by Brown of Detroit gang members (Brown, 1998).

10

♦

Conclusions

> We begin with a fundamental realization: No amount of thinking and no
> amount of public policy have brought us any closer to understanding and
> solving the problem of crime. The more we have reacted to crime, the
> farther we have removed ourselves from any understanding and any
> reduction of the problem. In recent years, we have reformulated the law,
> punished the offender, and quantified our knowledge. Yet the United
> States remains one of the most crime-ridden nations. In spite of all its
> wealth, economic development, and scientific advances, this country has
> one of the worst crime records in the world (Quinney and Wildeman,
> 1991:vii).

This quote should send us an important message, and we should all remember
it and seriously reflect on it. It must be said at the outset that the prospects for
the future are not very good, as long as we stay in the past. As a philosopher
once stated, "Those who fail to study history are doomed to repeat it." We in
American society do not study history; thus we do repeat it. Such is the case
in our response to the problem of crime and delinquency in general and of
gangs in particular.

This book has offered a comprehensive review of youth gangs in America.
We may be no closer to an answer as to what we as a society can do to stem
the criminal actions and violence of these groups, but our intent at the outset
was to provide an *understanding* of the phenomenon of gangs. We are convinced
that we have added to the knowledge base regarding this phenomenon. We are
somewhat less frustrated over the inability of gangs and their communities to
communicate with one another. But it is not because people are not trying. A
flurry of activity takes place throughout the country every day of the week—
board meetings, seminars, lectures, discussions, projects, and programs. These
are actions that are driven by youth gangs. They capture the time and energy
of many individuals and groups who focus mostly on getting rid of youth
gangs. The focus is on what to do and how to do it *now;* most often this takes
the form of a new policy for law-enforcement agencies to implement. Politi-

cians and administrators are continually participating in a search for methods of eradicating gangs and restoring safe and secure streets for the remainder of the population.

Despite the recent influx of research on gangs, there is still much to be learned. This is especially true when considering the wide variations in gang structures from one city to another. Hagedorn has made the following persuasive observation:

> A major conclusion of this study is the uniqueness and variability of modern gangs and the importance of local factors in understanding and fashioning a flexible response. But on another level, this book is a challenge for both sociologists and practitioners to go beyond the law enforcement paradigm in both theory and policy. The development of an urban minority underclass in the last decades, first in large cities and more recently in middle and small sized cities, has altered the nature of gangs and demands new investigation and new policies (Hagedorn, 1998:33).

In a similar vein, Horowitz concludes that

> gang research has progressed substantially in the last several years, though the results are difficult to compare in part because of the small number of cases included in most of the studies. It may not be possible yet to develop a general theory of gangs. We do not know the parameters of what makes up a "gang" and enough about the nature of the gangs as social/business organizations or the relationships among gang organizations and ethnicity, the local community and its institutions, the wider society, and the legal and illegal activities of members (Horowitz, 1990:52–53).

But do we really need more data from scientific research on the problem of gangs? Is there something missing from our usual analyses of social problems? Richard Quinney has written that "we of the West live in an age of lost meaning. The ethos of the Enlightenment has come to an end. We can no longer believe fully in scientific rationalism as the source of all knowledge and human progress. The Enlightenment liberated us from the tradition of one era only to be captured by the materialistic ethic of another" (Quinney, 1991:108–109). Perhaps it is time to seek new levels of understanding.

Indeed, in this era of materialism and selfishness, there is an emptiness to so many lives. Little wonder that so many of our youths, desperate for some recognition and a place in the world, seek out similarly situated young people for protection and a sense of belonging and empowerment. Seeing the greed and search for power and control among the adults of the world, is it any wonder that so many youths have been caught up in a similar search for power and control? And should we be surprised that so many young people (especially urban minorities) have little hope for the future or at least have some serious doubts about it? Two personal stories told by one of the authors (Brown) highlight what we are talking about here. The stories are from his own personal experiences and are taken from two seemingly different social contexts—Vietnam and Detroit, Michigan. But a closer examination of these two stories will reveal that the two contexts are more similar than different.

The first story is about an experience Brown had several years ago while giving a lecture to a group of social science students at a university in Ho Chi Minh City, Vietnam.[1] We will let Brown tell the story in his own words:

> During the lecture several students raised questions about homelessness in America. They were unable to understand how, in a country with so much prosperity, there could actually be people without a place to live. To be certain, there were many without homes in Ho Chi Minh City during the early 1990s. And for Vietnam, it was relatively simple to explain this phenomenon. Vietnam was one of the poorest countries in the world. Western businesses, with their advanced technology, were beginning to displace a form of labor which had dominated Vietnam for centuries. People were migrating from the countryside to the city in search of work.
>
> I spent several hours walking those streets late at night and observing people huddled in corners, some lying beside cooking fires trying to keep warm. Yet, in this classroom, I found it difficult to explain why there were so many homeless people in America. I attempted to explain changes in the American economy, and the displacement of workers in recent years. "But America is rich with resources," replied several knowledgeable students. "How can it be that these people have nowhere to live?" Clearly, this was one of the most difficult discussions I had ever encountered. My lecture turned to the topics of fear, complacency, insensitivity, competition, greed, power, and hate, and eventually discussing issues related to human rights.

The second story is about a 15-year-old African-American youth named Jimmy.[2] Brown met Jimmy as a result of his observations of gang life in Detroit. Brown relates his story as follows:

> My wife and I had previously discussed the prospects of taking Jimmy somewhere for his birthday. The difficulty, however, was where does a white, middle-class couple take a black, soon-to-be-15 gang member for his birthday? Drawing from our limited middle-class options, and recalling the interests of our two daughters who have since grown up, we decided that the Detroit Zoo, followed by a movie, and perhaps dinner, would be both appropriate and appreciated. Having made our decision, I had obtained permission from Jimmy's sister (Jimmy's mother was in prison, and he had never met his father) to take him on an outing for his birthday. The irony, of course, was that several months earlier Jimmy had introduced me to a contact who arranged my first visit to a crack house (in and of itself, a zoolike environment). Unknowingly, I was now going to introduce Jimmy, who had been born and raised in this city, to the Detroit Zoo. It had never occurred to me, nor to my wife, that an inner-city child, soon to be 15, had never visited a city zoo.

The day was absolutely perfect, given the unpredictability of late spring in southeastern Michigan. The sky was clear, and a slight breeze carried the pleasant scent of Lake St. Clair across the city. Jimmy was "hanging" outside his apartment, located in a complex that many would be inclined to label "the projects." Although attempting to maintain the normal attitude of a streetwise kid, there was a hint of excitement in Jimmy's voice as we exchanged greetings. His sister had already left for work (she also received food stamps due to the low wages she received), so we got into the car and drove to Woodward, turned left, and traveled north to Ten Mile Road.

The Detroit Zoo is located off of Woodward at Ten Mile Road. Those who are familiar with Detroit are aware that, as one drives north out of the inner city, Eight Mile Road represents the Mason-Dixon line of this city. North of Eight Mile Road is white country, and south of this "line of ignorance" is black country. Although some suburban and state policymakers attempt to deny this fact, one need only to look at the occupants of vehicles and at people on the streets. The social reality of racial segregation is self-evident at the Eight Mile Road boundary.

Although I knew that Jimmy had been involved in illegal drug sales, and I suspected he was still involved in this enterprise to some extent, he was, as usual, broke. Many people believe that these kids make large amounts of money running drugs, but I had found that most of the youngsters I have studied have little or no money. This observation has also been noted by others who have conducted ethnographic studies of youth gangs (Padilla, 1992). I gave Jimmy $20 so that he could have some sense of independence. As we paid for our tickets (Jimmy paid for his own from the $20 I had given him) and walked into the zoo, my wife reached out to hold Jimmy's hand in a protective sort of way. For a moment he did not resist, then politely withdrew his hand. My wife was concerned about Jimmy's safety in this very secure setting, yet Jimmy had been taking care of himself on the streets of Detroit for several years now! We walked around the zoo for nearly six hours. It was interesting, to say the least, to watch Jimmy eat cotton candy, ice cream bars, popcorn, and so on like a normal kid on an outing. I had seen him navigate around a crack house and stand up for himself, on many occasions, in less than calm situations.

Following the zoo experience, we went to a movie. I welcomed the rest. Jimmy ate two more boxes of popcorn and one ice cream sandwich and drank an extra-large drink. I attempted to calculate the transition of calories into pounds had I attempted this quest to devour these treats. After the movie we went to a preselected restaurant. At the restaurant we encountered many stares and subtle examples of disapproval from many of the occupants. There were instances during our visit to this restaurant when I wanted to respond to some of the rude onlookers, but this was Jimmy's day. I am certain that Jimmy was aware of the ugliness associated with those demonstrations of white ignorance, but it didn't have much impact on his appetite—after ordering, and eating, a prime rib dinner, he ate an obscene slice of chocolate cream pie. Before leaving the restaurant, I telephoned Jimmy's sister and told her we were on our way home. Obviously concerned, and now relieved, she asked how Jimmy had behaved (in direct contradiction of those who think parental interest and family values are lacking in the inner city), specifically drawing attention to his manners. I told her that he had been absolutely wonderful, and I really meant it. Returning to our table, I found Jimmy and my wife engaged in deep conversation about basketball—an activity about which she has neither knowledge, nor interest to acquire knowledge. Later, when I asked her about their discussion, she replied, "I just wanted him to be able to talk about whatever he wanted to talk about. I felt very sad because I realized that we had to take him home soon."

We left the restaurant about 10 o'clock and began our journey back to Jimmy's home. Jimmy had also realized that the day had come to a close. In retrospect, my wife and I developed an analogy about this event. Imagine a delicate flower kept in a refrigerator. The petals are drawn closely together in defense against the cold—trying desperately to survive. This represents Jimmy on the morning that we drove toward the zoo. At some point during our tour of the zoo, Jimmy, responding very much like that delicate flower when warmth entered that cold environment, began to open his petals. Throughout the day that flower remained in full bloom. Looking across the seat on the way home, it became obvious that the closer we got to Eight Mile Road, the more the flower began to close. By the time we arrived at Jimmy's apartment, the petals had closed—realizing that survival was foremost.

My wife and I will never forget Jimmy's 15th birthday. It was a day filled with good intentions. We both wanted that day to be special for Jimmy—and it was. That day was also filled with cruelty. We removed Jimmy, for a day, from "the projects." We showed him what life would be like if he were white or middle class. We gave him a glimpse of life outside his natural environment. But Jimmy is not white, nor is he middle class. He is black. He lives, like so many other black kids, in poverty. The future is very uncertain for him. The probability of escape for Jimmy, and the thousands of "Jimmys" like him, is very low—despite all the political rhetoric of "American opportunity."

I have seen Jimmy many times since his 15th birthday. Each time he talks about our outing. In his own way, he always expresses his gratitude for that day. But, like any delicate flower, he has come to accept his lot in life. While it may be very cold in his environment of poverty, he feels that it is better than the pain of experiencing brief encounters in an environment that he believes is beyond his reach. Thus, he has never asked to repeat the experience.

Since the first edition of this book, Jimmy's life has changed for the worse. We have learned that he is now in prison (one of several in the northern peninsula of Michigan) following a conviction for burglary and drugs. Jimmy's story is not unusual for African-American youth growing up in today's inner cities. According to one estimate, more than one-fourth (28.5 percent) of all African-American children will end up in prison some time in their lifetime (Proband, 1997:22).

It seems that there is either a lack of interest or an absence in effort in truly understanding what is going on in our inner cities—beyond the reflexive responses of repressed people. Understandably, the "haves" desire to retain that which they perceive to be legally theirs. There are vested interests that continue to repress the "have nots." This, it has been suggested, is human nature. Adoption of this perspective is understandable, albeit inexcusable, for policymakers who desire only to be reelected and to continue their careers as power brokers. But it is unconscionable for social scientists, in constant pursuit of government grants, to ignore social facts (the plight of inner-city youth) and continue focusing on, and perpetuating, social control. Many social scientists may argue that their work is objective research conducted in the name of science (part of the "publish or perish" doctrine within academia).[3] Many social scientists may argue that they are not necessarily responsible for the actions of policymakers and social-control agents who respond to the findings of their research. Richard Quinney points out that

> as social scientists (as we are called in this age), we give witness to the possibility of social existence. The tragic character of our project is the continuing disparity between our interpretive constructions and the knowledge of the symbols that are necessary in the struggle for social existence. That there are moments when our efforts are appropriate is the hope and objective of critical reflection. We are in the long tradition of the world coming to know itself. The meaning of social existence is being revealed to us (Quinney, 1982:15).

Jimmy is a human being—not a social statistic. Jimmy, although he has definitely engaged in criminal activity during the few years of his existence, is a victim—he is neither a variable nor a numerical digit keyed into a database. Jimmy does not need a program;[4] like thousands of kids in similar situations, he needs hope. This is an ideal that every human should expect to possess. It is not a new concept, not a fad, not wishful thinking; it can be found in a Christian religious promise given nearly 2,000 years ago: "Love . . . hopeth all things. . . . But now abideth faith, hope, love, these three" (I Corinthians 13:7–13). Yet the concept is something that is hard to grasp and to hold on to when the reality of the neighborhood in which one lives speaks to something other than hope; it speaks to despair and dismay, to frustration and failure. This is the environment for the youths who comprise most of the gangs in our society today; still, we—the middle class, the professionals, the politicians—too often believe that the responses of these youths should nevertheless be positive, conforming, and "decent." We need to return hope to these youths in the form of education, job skills, decent housing, and adequate health care. David Dawley spoke powerfully as he issued the following challenge to all of us who are sincere about ending the suffering:

> In foreign affairs, Desert Storm demonstrated the power of defined goals, massive force and political resolve. Now the question is: can we mobilize similar political commitment and economic investment in a coordinated campaign to bring opportunity, hope and justice to the Third World within our own borders? (Dawley, 1992:198)

The story of Jimmy begs an answer to the question, What would these kids be like if meaningful environmental changes were introduced to the inner cities of America? Yet we seem preoccupied with asking questions that support more social control on the streets, efficiency in the courtrooms, easier methods to certify juveniles as adults, and how long we can "lock 'em up." We (social scientists, policymakers, social-control agents, and all others who make up humanity) *must* begin to open our eyes and recognize the social existence of the youths who are members of gangs, those who are contemplating membership, and those who will inevitably join existing and future gangs. It is irrational to declare war on a symptom while the causes are ignored.

Classifying all gang members as garbage, scum, or other such epithets denies their humanity. It is clear that most of the youths who join gangs are "the people society gave up on—the bottom of the barrel." Yet they are "also people who want love, respect, responsibility and friendship. They are like most young people, growing up with many of the same personal needs. For most, the gang is the only real family they know; the gang is survival, protection, recognition, education" (Dawley, 1992:189).

What we also need is a truly progressive criminology for the new millennium, a criminology that must be a combination of enlightenment, empowerment, and reinforcement.[5] It is a criminology that strives for peace and social justice (Quinney and Wildeman, 1991:110–119). A progressive criminology must have, at its core, an appreciation for human rights. Human rights must be viewed as nonnegotiable. *People* must replace statistics. It is not likely, looking at much of the conservative and liberal publications that fill our professional journals, that assistance will be forthcoming from conventional criminologists or sociologists. Many criminology and criminal justice programs situated in major universities appear to be breeding grounds for conservative social and criminological thought. Many have grown accustomed to the Bureau of Justice funding trough. A progressive criminology must, as Richard Quinney suggests, come from *within* concerned parties, regardless of their discipline. Members of a progressive criminology must not become involved for the purpose of radicalism or self-promotion; rather, they must be devoted to social change that empowers the disenfranchised and strives to improve the quality of life for all people.

As these words are being written, we have entered into not only a new century but a new millennium. Looking back 1,000 years, to the dawn of the modern age, we have certainly improved not only social conditions in general but also our system of justice. Yet it is ironic that at the beginning of this new age what passes for a system of "justice" still tends to concentrate mostly on punishing the "dangerous classes" (Shelden, 2001). Despite the vast amount of knowledge about crime and the enormous sums of money available, sometimes our methods of social control seem like what occurred at the start of the old millennium. We are, as Elliott Currie has remarked, "at one of those critical watersheds in our history when it comes to crime and justice." On the one hand, writes Currie, "there are tremendous opportunities for serious reform." On the other hand, "there is also the very real danger that things could get much worse—especially if the recent era of economic prosperity comes to a halt." We could easily find ourselves in "a country where, even more than today, endemic tendencies toward social disintegration are held in check by an increasingly pervasive penal system and an increasingly militarized and uncontrolled police." Currie suggests that criminologists must be willing to "stick their necks out" and "do a better job of public education and public advocacy than we've been able to muster in the last quarter-century" (Currie, 1999:18).

Put somewhat differently, criminologists, especially those of us affiliated with universities, where we have at our disposal such vast amounts of information and the leisure time to pursue the truth, must take serious Noam Chomsky's "call to action" more than 30 years ago when he wrote of the "responsibilities of intellectuals." In this classic statement, Chomsky said that this responsibility is quite simple: "It is the responsibility of intellectuals to speak the truth and to expose lies"(Chomsky, 1987:60). Thus it is our responsibility to expose the lies about gangs, about who they are and who they are not, about what kinds of social conditions create and perpetuate gangs and gang activities, and about what should and should not be done about the problem. We hope that in this book we have contributed, in some small way, to a more enlightened view of this problem and that we have been responsible.

NOTES

1. For a more detailed discussion of Brown's experiences in Vietnam, see Brown (1994).

2. Jimmy is a pseudonym for a Detroit gang member who is included in Brown's study of youth gangs.

3. Historian Howard Zinn put it well when he wrote, "We publish while others perish" (Zinn, 1990:5).

4. During a discussion with one gang member, focusing on possible programs to get kids out of the gang, Brown was told, "The only thing programs do is try to make 'good niggas' out of us. There's no difference between a 'good nigga' and a 'bad nigga.' You're still just a 'nigga.' I'm a person. Society don't give a shit, my brothers do."

5. For a fuller exposition of these ideas, see Shelden, Macallair, Schiraldi, and Brown (1995).

Bibliography

Abadinsky, H. 1993. *Drug Abuse: An Introduction.* 2d ed. Chicago: Nelson-Hall.

Abel, R., ed. 1982. *The Politics of Informal Justice.* New York: Academic Press.

Adler, F. 1975. *Sisters in Crime.* New York: McGraw-Hill.

Albeda, R., N. Folbre, and the Center for Popular Economics. 1996. *The War on the Poor.* New York: The New Press.

Allegro, D. B. 1989. "Police Tactics, Drug Trafficking, and Gang Violence: Why the No-Knock Warrant Is an Idea Whose Time Has Come." *Notre Dame Law Review.* 64(4):552–570.

Anderson, E. 1978. *A Place on the Corner.* Chicago: University of Chicago Press.

———. 1990. *Streetwise: Race, Class and Change in an Urban Community.* Chicago: University of Chicago Press.

———. 1994. "The Code of the Streets." *The Atlantic Monthly.* May:81–94.

Andrews, D. A., I. Zinger, R. D. Hoge, J. Bonta, P. Gendreau, and F. T. Cullen. 1990. "Does Correctional Treatment Work? A Clinically Relevant and Psychologically Informed Meta-analysis." *Criminology.* 28:369–404.

Asbury, H. 1927. *The Gangs of New York.* New York: Alfred Knopf.

Associated Press. 1999. "Whites Leaving Welfare Faster than Minorities, Survey Reveals." March 30.

Atlanta Gang Conference. 1992. "Gangs Prevention Training." Sponsored by Carondelet Management Institute. Atlanta, GA. October 9 and 10.

Auletta, K. 1983. *The Underclass.* New York: Vintage Books.

Bagidikian, B. 1987. *The Media Monopoly.* Boston: Beacon Press.

Baker, B. 1988a. "Tough Boss Shows Gang Members New Way of Life." *Los Angeles Times.* April 15.

———. 1988b. "Gang Murder Rates Get Worse." *Los Angeles Times.* April 10.

———. 1988c. "Homeboys: Players in a Deadly Drama." *Los Angeles Times.* June 26.

Bartlett, D. L. and J. B. Steele. 1992. *America: What Went Wrong?* Kansas City, MO: Andrews and McMeel.

Bartollas, C. 2000. *Juvenile Delinquency.* 5th ed. New York: Macmillan.

Beccaria, C. 1963. *On Crimes and Punishment.* New York: Bobbs-Merrill.

Becker, H. S. 1963. *Outsiders: Studies in the Sociology of Deviance.* New York: Free Press.

Beckham, W. H. 1989. "Helpful Practices in Juvenile Court Hearings." In McCarthy and Carr, eds. *Juvenile Law and Its Processes.*

Bell, D. 1987. *And We Are Not Saved.* New York: Basic Books.

Bensinger, G. 1984. "Chicago Youth Gangs: A New Old Problem." *Crime and Justice.* 7:1–16.

Berlin, I. 1978. "The Hedgehog and the Fox." In H. Hardy and A. Kelly, eds. 1978. *Russian Thinkers.* New York: Viking.

Berrick, J. D. 1995. *Faces of Poverty: Portraits of Women and Children on Welfare.* New York: Oxford University Press.

Bing, L. 1991. *Do or Die.* New York: HarperCollins.

Bjerregard, B. and C. Smith. 1993. "Gender Differences in Gang Participation, Delinquency, and Substance Abuse." *Journal of Quantitative Criminology.* 4: 329–355.

Black, D. 1976. *The Behavior of the Law.* New York: Academic Press.

Block, C. R., and R. Block. 1993. *Street Gang Crime in Chicago.* Washington, DC: U.S. Department of Justice, National Institute of Justice, Research in Brief.

Block, C. R., A. Christakos, A. Jacob, and R. Przybylski. 1996. *Street Gangs and Crime: Patterns and Trends in Chicago.* Research Bulletin. Chicago: Illinois Criminal Justice Information Authority.

Bluestone, B., and B. Harrison. 1982. *The Deindustrialization of America.* New York: Basic Books.

Blumberg, A., ed. 1974. *Current Perspectives on Criminal Behavior.* New York: Knopf.

Bobrowski, L. J. 1988. *Collecting, Organizing and Reporting Street Gang Crime.* Chicago: Chicago Police Department, Special Functions Group.

Bogardus, E. 1943. "Gangs of Mexican-American Youth." *Sociology and Social Research.* 28:55–56.

Bonfante, J. 1995. "Entrepreneurs of Crack." *Time.* February 27:22–23.

Bookin-Weiner, H., and R. Horowitz. 1983. "The End of the Youth Gang: Fad or Fact?" *Criminology.* 21:585–602.

Bordua, D. J., ed. 1967. *The Police: Six Sociological Essays.* New York: Wiley.

———. 1961. "Delinquent Subcultures: Sociological Interpretations of Gang Delinquency." *Annals of the American Academy of Social Science.* 338:119–136.

Bowker, L., ed. 1978. *Women, Crime and the Criminal Justice System.* Lexington, MA: Lexington Books.

——— and M. Klein. 1983. "The Etiology of Female Juvenile Delinquency and Gang Membership: A Test of Psychological and Social Structural Explanations." *Adolescence* 13: 739–751.

Boyle, J., and A. Gonzales. 1989. "Using Proactive Programs to Impact Gangs and Drugs." *Law and Order.* 37(8):62–64.

Brace, C. L. 1872. *The Dangerous Classes of New York.* New York: Wynkoop and Hallenbeck.

Brown, W. B. 1994. "Reconciliation in a Back-Alley Cafe of Saigon." *Humanity and Society.* 18:75–84.

———. 1998. "The Fight for Survival: African-American Gang Members and Their Families in a Segregated Society." *Juvenile and Family Court Journal.* 49: 1–14.

———. 1999. "Surviving Against Insurmountable Odds: African American Mothers and Their Gang Affiliated Daughters," in *Humanity and Society,* 23: 102–124.

Brown, W. B., and R. Shelden. 1994. "Gangs and Gang Members as Victims and Victimizers." February. Berkeley, CA: Western Society of Criminology.

Brown, W. B., R. Shelden, and A. Kiesz-Mrozewska. 1994. "Social, Economic, Political, and Legal Quandaries Following Solidarity: Changes in Crime and Delinquent Behavior in Poland." March. Chicago: Academy of Criminal Justice Sciences.

Brown, W. K. 1977. "Black Female Gangs in Philadelphia." *International Journal of Offender Therapy and Comparative Criminology*. 21:221–228.

———. 1978. "Black Gangs as Family Extensions" and "Graffiti, Identity, and the Delinquent Gang." *International Journal of Offender Therapy and Comparative Criminology*. 22:39–48.

Burgess, E. W. 1925. "The Growth of the City." In R. E. Park, E. W. Burgess and R. D. McKenzie, eds. *The City*. Chicago: University of Chicago Press.

Camp, G. M., and C. G. Camp. 1985. *Prison Gangs: Their Extent, Nature and Impact*. Washington, DC: U.S. Department of Justice.

Campbell, A. 1984a. *The Girls in the Gang*. Cambridge, MA: Basil Blackwell.

———. 1984b. "Girls' Talk: The Social Representation of Aggression by Female Gang Members." *Criminal Justice and Behavior*. 11:139–156.

———. 1990. "Female Participation in Gangs." In Huff, *Gangs in America*.

———. 1993. *Men, Women, and Aggression*. New York: Basic Books.

Carey, A. 1995. *Taking the Risk Out of Democracy*. Chicago: University of Illinois Press.

Carellic, R. 1999. "Supreme Court Strikes Down Anti-loitering Law Aimed at Gangs." *Savannah Morning News*. Savannah, GA. June 11: 4A.

Catalano, R., R. Loeber, and K. McKinney. 1999. "School and Community Intervention to Prevent Serious and Violent Offending." Office of Juvenile Justice and Delinquency Prevention. Washington, DC: U.S. Department of Justice.

CBS. 1992. "Girls in the Hood." *Street Stories*. August 6.

Cernkovich, S., and P. Giordano. 1987. "Family Relationships and Delinquency." *Criminology*. 16:295–321.

Clark, R., ed. 1992. *Situational Crime Prevention: Successful Case Studies*. New York: Harrow and Heston.

Chambliss, W. J. 1975. "The Saints and the Roughnecks." In Chambliss, W. J., ed. *Criminal Law in Action*. New York: John Wiley.

———. 1993. "State Organized Crime." In W. Chambliss and M. Zatz, ed. *Making Law: The State, the Law and Structural Contradictions*. Bloomington: Indiana University Press.

———, and R. B. Seidman. 1971. *Law, Order, and Power*. Reading, MA: Addison-Wesley.

Champion, D. J. 1998. *The Juvenile Justice System*. 2d ed. Upper Saddle River, NJ: Prentice-Hall.

Chesney-Lind, M. 1993. "Girls, Gangs and Violence: Reinventing the Liberated Female Crook." *Humanity and Society*. 17:321–344.

———. 1986. "Women and Crime: The Female Offender." *Signs*. 12: 78–96.

———, and R. G. Shelden. 1998. *Girls, Delinquency and Juvenile Justice*. 2d ed. Belmont, CA: Wadsworth.

———, R. Shelden, and K. Joe. 1996. "Girls, Delinquency and Gang Membership" in Huff, *Gangs in America*. 2d ed.

———, A. Rockhill, N. Marker, and H. Reyes. 1994. "Gangs and Delinquency:

Exploring Police Estimates of Gang Membership." *Crime, Law and Social Change*. 21: 210–228.

Chicago Crime Commission. 1995. *Gangs: Public Enemy Number One, 75 Years of Fighting Crime in Chicagoland*. Chicago: Report of the Chicago Crime Commission.

Chin, L. 1990. "Chinese Gangs and Extortion." In Huff, *Gangs in America*.

———. 1996. "Gang Violence in Chinatown." In Huff, *Gangs in America*. 2d ed.

Chin, K. 1990. *Chinese Subculture and Criminality.* Westport, CT: Greenwood Press.

Chomsky, N. 1989. *Necessary Illusions: Thought Control in Democratic Societies.* Boston: South End Press.

———. 1993. *Year 501: The Conquest Continues.* Boston: South End Press.

———. 1996. *Class Warfare.* Monroe, ME: Common Courage Press.

———. 1998. *The Common Good.* Monroe, ME: Odonian Press.

Cleeland, N. 1999. "Temps Become Full-Time Factor in Industry." *Los Angeles Times.* May 29: A1, A12.

Clemmer, D. 1958. *The Prison Community.* New York: Holt, Rinehart and Winston.

Cloward, R., and L. Ohlin. 1960. *Delinquency and Opportunity.* New York: Free Press.

Cloyd, J. W. 1982. *Drugs and Information Control: The Role of Men and Manipulation in the Control of Drug Trafficking.* Westport, CT: Greenwood Press.

Cohen, A. 1955. *Delinquent Boys: The Culture of the Gang.* New York: Free Press.

———. 1990. "Foreword and Overview." In Huff, *Gangs in America.*

Cohen, L., and M. Felson. 1979. "Social Change and Crime Rate Trends: A 'Routine Activities' Approach." *American Sociological Review.* 44: 588–608.

Cohen, S. 1980. *Folk Devils and Moral Panics: The Creation of the Mods and Rockers.* 2d ed. New York: St. Martin's Press.

Cole, D. 1999. *No Equal Justice: Race and Class in the American Criminal Justice System.* New York: The New Press.

Colvin, M. 1991. "Crime and Social Reproduction: A Response to the Call for 'Outrageous' Proposals." *Crime and Delinquency.* 37:436–448.

Commission on Behavioral and Social Sciences and Education. 1993. *Losing Generations: Adolescents in High-Risk Settings.* Washington, DC: National Academy Press.

Connell, R. W. 1987. *Gender and Power.* Palo Alto, CA: Stanford University Press.

Conot, R. 1967. *Rivers of Blood, Years of Darkness.* New York: Bantam.

Cook, T. D., H. Cooper, D. S. Cordray, H. Hartmann, L. V. Hedges, R. I. Light, T. A. Lewis, and S. M. Mosteller, eds. 1992. *Meta-analysis for Explanation: A Casebook.* New York: Russell Sage Foundation.

Cook, P. J. 1986. "The Demand and Supply of Criminal Opportunities." In *Crime and Justice,* Vol. 7, edited by M. Tonry and N. Morris. Chicago: University of Chicago Press.

Coontz, S. 1992. *The Way We Never Were: American Families and the Nostalgia Trap.* New York: HarperCollins

———. 1997. *The Way We Really Are: Coming to Terms with America's Changing Families.* New York: Basic Books.

Cottingham, C., ed. 1982. *Race, Poverty, and the Urban Underclass.* Lexington, MA: Lexington Books.

Covey, C., S. Menard, and R. Franzese. 1992. *Juvenile Gangs.* Springfield, IL: Charles S. Thomas.

Covington, J., and R. B. Taylor. 1991. "Fear of Crime in Urban Residential Neighborhoods: Implications of Between- and Within-Neighborhood Sources for Current Models." *Sociological Quarterly.* 32:231–249.

Crittenden, D. 1990. "You've Come a Long Way, Moll." *Wall Street Journal.* Jan. 25: A14.

Cunningham, R. M. 1994. "Implications for Treating the Female Gang Member." *Progress: Family Systems Research and Therapy.* 3: 91–102.

Cummings, S., and D. J. Monti, eds. 1993. *Gangs: The Origins and Impact of Contemporary Youth Gangs in the United States.* Albany, NY: SUNY Press.

Curran, D., and S. Cook. 1993. "Growing Fears, Rising Crime: Juveniles and China's Justice System." *Crime and Delinquency.* 39:296–315.

Currie, E. 1985. *Confronting Crime.* New York: Pantheon.

———. 1989. "Confronting Crime: Looking Toward the Twenty-First Century." *Justice Quarterly.* 6:5–25.

———. 1998. *Crime and Punishment in America.* New York: Metropolitan Books.

———. 1999. "Radical Criminology—or Just Criminology—Then and Now." *Social Justice.* 26: 16–18.

Curry, G. D. 1998. "Female Gang Involvement." *Journal of Research in Crime and Delinquency.* 35: 100–118.

Curry, G. D., and S. H. Decker. 1998. *Confronting Gangs: Crime and Community.* Los Angeles: Roxbury Press.

———, and I. A. Spergel. 1988. "Gang Homicide, Delinquency, and Community." *Criminology.* 26:381–405.

———, R. A. Ball, and R. J. Fox. 1994. "Gang Crime and Law Enforcement Recordkeeping." *National Institute of Justice, Research in Brief.* August:1–11.

———, and S. Decker. 1996. "Estimating the National Scope of Gang Crime From Law Enforcement Data." In Huff, *Gangs in America.* 2d ed.

Curtis, L. A. 1985. *American Violence and Public Policy.* New Haven, CT: Yale University Press.

Datesman, S. K., and F. R. Scarpitti, eds. 1980. *Women, Crime, and Justice.* New York: Oxford University Press.

Davis, J. R. 1982. *Street Gangs: Youth, Biker, and Prison Groups.* Dubuque, IA: Kendall/Hunt.

Davis, M. 1992. *City of Quartz.* New York: Vintage Books.

Davis, N. 1999. *Youth Crisis.* Westport, CT: Praeger.

Dawley, D. 1992. *A Nation of Lords: The Autobiography of the Vice Lords.* 2d ed. Prospect Heights, IL: Waveland Press.

Decker, S. H., and J. L. Lauritsen. 1996. "Breaking the Bonds of Membership: Leaving the Gang." In Huff, *Gangs in America.*

Derber, C. 1998. *Corporation Nation.* New York: St. Martin's Press.

Developmental Research and Programs. 1993. *Communities That Care: Risk-Focused Prevention Using the Social Development Strategy.* Seattle, WA: Developmental Research and Programs, Inc.

Dolan, E. F., and S. Finney. 1984. *Youth Gangs.* New York: Simon and Schuster.

Domhoff, G. W. 1998. *Who Rules America? Power and Politics in the Year 2000.* 3d ed. Mountain View, CA: Mayfield.

Dronnis, R., and K. Hess. 1995. *Juvenile Justice.* Belmont, CA: Wadsworth.

Dryfoos, J. 1990. *Adolescents at Risk.* New York: Oxford University Press.

Durkheim, E. 1950. *Rule of the Sociological Method.* Glencoe, IL: Free Press (originally published in 1895).

Duster, T. 1987. "Crime, Youth Employment and the Underclass." *Crime and Delinquency.* 33:300–316.

Dyer, J. 2000. *The Perpetual Prisoner Machine: How America Profits from Crime.* Boulder, CO: Westview Press.

Easton, A. 1991. *Adolescent Culture.* New York: New York University Press.

Eastman, M., trans. and ed. 1959. *Capital, The Communist Manifesto and Other Writings.* New York: The Modern Library.

Esbensen, F. A., and D. W. Osgood. 1997. "National Evaluation of G.R.E.A.T.: Research in Brief." Department of Justice. Washington, D.C.

———, E. P. Deschenes and L. T. Winfree. 1999. "Differences Between Gang Girls and Gang Boys." *Youth and Society.* 31: 27–53.

———, and D. Huizinga. 1993. "Gangs, Drugs, and Delinquency in a Survey of Urban Youth." *Criminology.* 31: 565–589.

Edwards, R. C., M. Reich, and T. E. Weisskopf, eds. 1986. *The Capitalist System.* 3d ed. Englewood Cliffs, NJ: Prentice-Hall.

Eitzen, D. S., and M. B. Zinn. 1998. *In Conflict and Order.* 8th ed. Boston: Allyn and Bacon.

Elikann, P. 1999. Superpredators: *The Demonization of Our Children.* Reading, MA: Perseus Books.

Elliott, D. S., D. Huiziinga, and S. S. Ageton. 1985. *Explaining Delinquency and Drug Use.* Beverly Hills, CA: Sage.

Engels, F. 1993 [1845]. *The Condition of the Working Class in England.* New York: Oxford University Press.

Erlanger, H. S. 1979. "Estrangement, Machismo and Gang Violence." *Social Science Quarterly.* 60:235–249.

Fagan, J. A. 1989. "The Social Organization of Drug Use and Drug Dealing Among Urban Gangs." *Criminology.* 27:633–667.

———. 1990. "Social Processes of Delinquency and Drug Use Among Urban Gangs." In Huff, *Gangs in America.*

———. 1996. "Gangs, Drugs, and Neighborhood Change." In Huff, *Gangs in America.* 2d.

———, E. S. Piper, and M. Moore. 1986. "Violent Delinquents and Urban Youth." *Criminology.* 23:439–466.

Falco, M. 1992. *The Making of a Drug-Free America.* New York: Times Books.

Farrington, D., L. Ohlin, and J. Q. Wilson. 1986. *Understanding and Controlling Crime: Toward a New Research Strategy.* New York: Springer-Verlag.

Faust, F. L., and P. J. Brantingham. 1979. *Juvenile Justice Philosophy.* St. Paul, MN: West.

Federal Bureau of Investigation. 1995. *Crime in America: Uniform Crime Reports.* Washington, DC: U.S. Department of Justice.

Fishman, L. T. 1988. "The Vice Queens: An Ethnographic Study of Black Female Gang Behavior." Paper presented at annual meeting of American Society of Criminology.

Fleisher, M. S. 1995. *Beggars and Thieves: Lives of Urban Street Criminals.* Madison, University of Wisconsin Press.

Flowers, R. B. 1987. *Women and Criminality.* New York: Greenwood Press.

Folbre, N., and the Center for Popular Economics. 1995. *The New Field Guide to the U.S. Economy.* New York: The New Press

Fones-Wolf, E. 1994. *Selling Free Enterprise.* Indianapolis: University of Indiana Press.

Ford, R. 1998. "Razor's Edge." *Boston Globe Magazine.* May 24.

"Fort Worth Pays Gangs to Fight Crime." 1994. *New York Times.* May 13:A13.

Fox, J. 1996. Trends in Juvenile Violence: A Report for the U.S. Attorney General on Current and Future Rates of Juvenile Offending. Washington, DC: U.S. Department of Justice.

Fradette, R. 1992. "Gang Graffiti and Tattoos." Unpublished seminar paper, Department of Criminal Justice, University of Nevada, Las Vegas.

Frankel, M. 1975. "The Search for Truth: An Empirical View." *University of Pennsylvania Law Review.* 123:1031.

Frias, G. 1982. *Barrio Warriors: Homeboys of Peace.* Los Angeles: Diaz Publications.

Gans, H. 1995. *The War Against the Poor: The Underclass and Antipoverty Policy.* New York: Basic Books.

Garabedian, P. G., and D. C. Gibbons, eds. 1967. *Becoming Delinquent.* Chicago: Aldine.

Garrett, C. J. 1985. "Effects of Residential Treatment on Adjudicated Adolescents: A Meta-analysis." *Journal of Research in Crime and Delinquency.* 25:463–489.

Gendreau, P. 1991. "General Principles of Effective Programming." Paper delivered at National Coalition of State Juvenile Justice Advisory Groups. April.

Gibbs, J. T., ed. 1988. *Young, Black, and Male in America: An Endangered Species.* Dover, MA: Andover House.

Giddens, A. 1971. *Capitalism and Modern Social Theory.* New York: Cambridge University Press.

———. 1990. *Introduction to Sociology.* New York: Norton.

Gilbert, D. 1998. *The American Class Structure.* 5th ed. Belmont, CA: Wadsworth.

Gillespie, E., and B. Schellhas, eds. 1994. *Contract with America.* New York: Random House.

Gilligan, C. 1991. *Women's Psychological Development: Implications for Psychotherapy.* New York: The Haworth Press.

Giordano, P. 1978. "Girls, Guys and Gangs: The Changing Social Context of Female Delinquency." *Journal of Criminal Law and Criminology.* 69:126–132.

Glascow, D. C. 1981. *The Black Underclass.* New York: Vintage Books.

Glueck, S., and E. Glueck. 1950. *Unraveling Juvenile Delinquency.* Cambridge, MA: Harvard University Press.

Golden, R. 1997. *Disposable Children: America's Welfare System.* Belmont, CA.: Wadsworth.

Goldman, S., and A. Sarat, eds. 1989. *American Court Systems: Readings in Judicial Process and Behavior.* New York: Longman.

Goldstein, A. P. 1991. *Delinquent Gangs: A Psychological Perspective.* Champaign, IL: Research Press.

———. 1993. "Gang Intervention: A Historical Review." In Goldstein and Huff, *The Gang Intervention Handbook.*

———, and B. Glick. 1994. *The Prosocial Gang: Implementing Aggression Replacement Training.* Newbury Park, CA: Sage.

———, and C. R. Huff, eds. 1993. *The Gang Intervention Handbook.* Champaign, IL: Research Press.

Goldstein, H. 1990. *Problem Oriented Policing.* New York: McGraw-Hill.

Goode, E., and N. Ben-Yahuda. 1994. *Moral Panics: The Social Construction of Deviance.* Cambridge, MA: Blackwell.

Gora, J. 1982. *The New Female Criminal: Empirical Reality or Social Myth.* New York: Praeger.

Gordon, D. R. 1990. *The Justice Juggernaut: Fighting Street Crime, Controlling Citizens.* New Brunswick, NJ: Rutgers University Press.

———. 1994. *The Return of the Dangerous Classes: Drug Prohibition and Policy Politics.* New York: W. W. Norton.

Granovetter, M. 1992. "The Sociological and Economic Approaches to Labour Market Analysis: A Social Structural View." In M. Granovetter and R. Swedberg, eds. 1992. *The Sociology of Economic Life.* Boulder, CO: Westview Press.

Greenburg, D., ed. 1991. *Crime and Capitalism.* 2d ed. Palo Alto, CA: Mayfield.

Greenwood, P. W., and S. Turner. 1991. *Implementing and Managing Innovative Correctional Programs: Lessons from OJJDP's Private Sector Initiative.* Santa Monica, CA: Rand Corporation.

Hagan, J. 1993. "The Social Embeddedness of Crime and Unemployment." *Criminology.* 31:465–491.

———, and B. McCarthy. 1992. "Streetlife and Delinquency." *British Journal of Criminology.* 43:533–561.

Hagedorn, J. M. 1998. *People and Folks: Gangs, Crime and the Underclass in a Rustbelt City.* 2d ed. Chicago: Lakeview Press.

———. 1994. "Neighborhoods, Markets and Gang Drug Organization." *Journal of Research in Crime and Delinquency.* 31: 264–294.

———. 1990. "Back in the Field Again: Gang Research in the Nineties." In Huff, *Gangs in America.*

———. 1991. "Gangs, Neighborhoods, and Public Policy." *Social Problems.* 38:529–542.

Hanson, K. 1964. *Rebels in the Streets: The Story of New York's Girl Gangs.* Englewood Cliffs, NJ: Prentice-Hall.

Harper, G., and L. Robinson. "Pathways to Risk Among Inner-City African American Adolescent Females: The influence of Gang Membership." *American Journal of Community Psychology.* 27: 383–404.

Harrington, M. 1962. *The Other America: Poverty in the United States.* Baltimore, MD: Penguin Books.

———. 1984. *The New American Poverty.* New York: Penguin Books.

Harris, M. G. 1988. *Cholas: Latino Girls and Gangs.* New York: AMS Press.

———. 1997. "Cholas, Mexican-American Girls, and Gangs." In Mays, ed., *Gangs and Gang Behavior.*

Harper, Gary, and W. LaVonne Robinson. 1999. "Pathways to Risk Among Inner-city African-American Adolescent Females: The Influence of Gang Membership." *American Journal of Community Psychology.* 27(3): 383–404. June.

Hawkins, J. D., and J. G. Weis. 1985. "The Social Development Model: An Integrated Approach to Delinquency Prevention." *Journal of Primary Prevention.* 6:73–79.

Hawkins, J. D., R. F. Catalano, and J. Y. Miller. 1992. "Risk and Protective Factors for Alcohol and Other Drug Problems in Adolescence and Early Adulthood: Implications for Substance Abuse Prevention." *Psychological Bulletin.* 112:64–105.

———, R. F. Catalano, D. M. Morrison, J. O'Donnell, R. D. Abbott, and L. E. Day. 1992. "The Seattle Social Development Project: Effects on the First Four Years on Protective Factors and Problem Behaviors." In McCord and Tremblay, *The Prevention of Antisocial Behavior in Children.*

Hay, D., P. Linebaugh, J. Rule, E. P. Thompson, and C. Winslow, eds. 1975. *Albion's Fatal Tree: Crime and Society in Eighteenth-Century England.* New York: Pantheon.

Heilbroner, R. L. 1985. *The Nature and Logical of Capitalism.* New York: W. W. Norton.

Heinz, A., H. Jacob, and R. L. Lineberry. 1983. *Crime in City Politics.* New York: Longman.

Helmer, J. 1975. *Drugs and Minority Oppression.* New York: Seabury Press.

Herman, E., and N. Chomsky. 1988. *Manufacturing Consent: The Political Economy of the Mass Media.* New York: Pantheon.

Heydebrand, W., and C. Seron. 1990. *Rationalizing Justice: The Political Economy of Federal District Courts.* Albany: State University Press of New York.

Hindelang, M. J., M. R. Gottfredson, and T. J. Flanigan, eds. 1981. *Sourcebook of Criminal Justice Statistics, 1980.* Washington, DC: U.S. Department of Justice, Bureau of Justice Statistics.

Hirschi, T. 1969. *Causes of Delinquency.* Berkeley: University of California Press.

———. 1983. "Crime and the Family." In J. Q. Wilson, ed., *Crime and Public Policy.* San Francisco: Institute for Contemporary Studies.

Hochhaus, C., and F. Sousa. 1988. "Why Children Belong to Gangs: A Comparison of Expectations and Reality." *The High School Journal.* December–January:74–77.

Hollin, C. 1993. "Cognitive-Behavioral Interventions." In Goldstein and Huff, *The Gang Intervention Handbook.*

Holmes, O. W., Jr. 1881. *The Common Law.* 58th printing. Boston: Little, Brown.

Hooks, B. 1995. *Killing Rage: Ending Racism.* New York: Henry Holt and Company.

Horowitz, J. 1960. *The Inhabitants.* New York: World.

Horowitz, R. 1982. "Masked Intimacy and Marginality: Adult Delinquent Gangs in a Chicano Community." *Urban Life.* 11:3–26.

———. 1983a. "The End of the Youth Gang." *Criminology.* 21:585–600.

———. 1983b. *Honor and the American Dream.* New Brunswick, NJ: Rutgers University Press.

———. 1987. "Community Tolerance of Gang Violence." *Social Problems.* 34:437–450.

———. 1990. "Sociological Perspectives on Gangs: Conflicting Definitions and Concepts." In Huff, *Gangs in America.*

Howell, J. C. 1997. "Youth Gangs, Drug Trafficking and Homicide: Policy and

Program Implications." *Juvenile Justice.* 4:9–20.

———. 1998. "Youth Gangs: An Overview." Office of Juvenile Justice and Delinquency Prevention. Washington, D.C.: U.S. Department of Justice.

Horowitz, R., and G. Schwartz. 1974. "Honor, Normative Ambiguity and Gang Violence." *American Sociological Review.* 39:238–251.

Huff, C. R. 1989. "Youth Gangs and Public Policy." *Crime and Delinquency.* 35:524–537.

———. 1990b. "Denial, Overreaction, and Misidentification: A Postscript on Public Policy." In Huff, *Gangs in America.*

———. 1993. "Gangs in the United States." In Goldstein and Huff, *The Gang Intervention Handbook.*

———, ed. 1990a. *Gangs in America.* Newbury Park, CA: Sage.

———, ed. 1996. *Gangs in America,* 2d ed. Thousand Oaks, CA: Sage.

———. 1998. "Criminal Behavior of Gang Members and At-Risk Youth." National Institute of Justice, Research in Brief. Washington, D.C.: U.S. Department of Justice.

———, and K. S. Trump. 1996. "Youth Violence and Gangs." *Education and Urban Society.* 28: 492–503.

Hurst, J. W. 1950. *The Growth of American Law: The Lawmakers.* Boston, MA: Little, Brown.

Hutchinson, R. 1993. "Blazon Nouveau: Gang Graffiti in the Barrios of Los Angeles and Chicago." In Cummings and Monti, *Gangs: The Origins and Impact of Contemporary Youth Gangs in the United States.*

Ignatieff, M. 1978. *A Just Measure of Pain.* New York: Columbia University Press.

Inciardi, J. A., R. Horowitz, and A. E. Pottieger. 1993. *Street Kids, Street Drugs, Street Crime.* Belmont, CA: Wadsworth.

Institute for Law and Justice. 1994. *Gang Prosecution in the United States.* Washington, DC: U.S. Department of Justice, National Institute of Justice.

Irwin, J. and J. Austin. 1997. *It's About Time: America's Imprisonment Binge,* 2d ed. Belmont, CA: Wadsworth.

Izzo, R. L., and R. R. Ross. 1990. "Meta-analysis of Rehabilitation Programs for Juvenile Delinquents: A Brief Report." *Criminal Justice and Behavior.* 17: 134–142.

Jablon, R. 2000. "L. A. Prepares for Worst as Police Scandal Grows." *Associate Press,* Feb. 19.

Jackson, C. B., and J. Gordon. 1995. "Atlanta's GANGIS Advances Fight Against Crime." *The Police Chief.* May 11.

Jackson, P. G. 1989. "Theories and Findings About Youth Gangs." *Criminal Justice Abstracts.* June:313–329.

———. 1991. "Crime, Youth Gangs, and Urban Transition: The Social Dislocations of Postindustrial Economic Development." *Justice Quarterly.* 8:379–398.

———. 1992. "Minority Group Threat, Social Context, and Policing" In Liska, *Social Threat and Social Control.*

Jackson, R., and W. D. McBride. 1992. *Understanding Street Gangs.* Placerville, CA: Copperhouse.

Jankowski, M. S. 1990. *Islands in the Street: Gangs and American Urban Society.* Berkeley: University of California Press.

Joe, D., and N. Robinson. 1980. "Chinatown's Immigrant Gangs." *Criminology.* 18:337–345.

Joe, K., and M. Chesney-Lind. 1995. " 'Just Every Mother's Angel': An analysis of Gender and Ethnic Variations in Youth Gang Membership." *Gender and Society.* 9: 408–431.

Johnson, B. D., P. J. Goldstein, E. Preble, J. Schmeidler, D. Lipton, B. Spunt, and T. Miller. 1985. *Taking Care of Business: The Economics of Crime by Heroin Abusers.* Lexington, MA: Lexington Books.

Johnstone, J. C. 1983. "Youth Gangs and Black Suburbs." *Pacific Sociological Review.* 24:355–373.

Judd, D. R. 1999. "Symbolic Politics and Urban Policies." In A. Reed Jr., ed.,

Without Justice For All. Boulder, CO: Westview Press.

Katzman, G. S. 1991. *Inside the Criminal Process.* New York: W. W. Norton.

Keiser, R. L. 1969. *The Vice Lords: Warriors of the Streets.* New York: Holt, Rinehart and Winston.

Kelly, D. H., ed. 1993. *Deviant Behavior.* New York: St. Martin's Press.

"Kids Who Kill." 1991. *U.S. News and World Report.* April 8:26–34.

Kitchen, D. B. 1995. *Sisters in the Hood.* Ph.D. Dissertation, Western Michigan University.

Klein, M. 1968. *The Ladino Hills Project. Final Report.* Washington, DC: Office of Juvenile Delinquency and Youth Development.

———. 1971. *Street Gangs and Street Workers.* Englewood Cliffs, NJ: Prentice-Hall.

———. 1995. *The American Street Gang.* New York: Oxford University Press.

Klein, M., and C. Maxson. 1985. " 'Rock Sales' in South Los Angeles." *Sociology and Social Research.* 69:561–565.

———. 1989. "Street Gang Violence." In Wolfgang and Weiner, *Violent Crime, Violent Criminals.*

———. 1990. *Street Gangs and Drug Sales.* Los Angeles: University of Southern California, Center for Research on Crime and Social Control.

Klein, M., C. Maxson, and L. C. Cunningham. 1988. *"Crack," Street Gangs, and Violence.* Los Angeles: University of Southern California, Social Science Research Institute.

Klein, M., C. Maxson, and M. A. Gordon. 1984. *Evaluation of an Imported Gang Violence Deterrence Program: Final Report.* Los Angeles: University of Southern California, Social Science Research Institute.

———. 1985. "Differences Between Gang and Non-Gang Homicides." *Criminology.* 23:209–220.

Kluegel, J. R., ed. 1983. *Evaluating Contemporary Juvenile Justice.* Beverly Hills, CA: Sage.

Kobrin, S., J. Puntil, and E. Peluso. 1987. "Criteria of Status Among Street Groups." *Journal of Research in Crime and Delinquency.* 4:98–118.

Kornblum, W. 1987. "Ganging Together: Helping Gangs Go Straight." *Social Issues and Health Review.* 2:99–104.

Kotlowitz, A. 1991. *There Are No Children Here.* New York: Doubleday.

Kozol, J. 1992. *Savage Inequalities: Children in America's Schools.* New York: Harper Perennial.

Krisberg, B., and J. Austin, 1993. *Reinventing Juvenile Justice.* Newbury Park, CA: Sage.

LaFave, W. R., and J. H. Israel. 1992. *Criminal Procedure.* 2d ed. St. Paul, MN: West.

Laidler, K. A., and G. Hunt. 1997. "Violence and Social Organization in Female Gangs. *Social Justice.* 24: 148–169.

Lanier, M. M., and S. Henry. 1998. *Essential Criminology.* Boulder, CO: Westview Press.

Laongo, T. 1994. "I Was a Gang Girl." *Mademoiselle.* July.

Lasley, J. 1998. *Designing Out: Gang Homicides and Street Assaults.* Washington, DC: National Institute of Justice.

Latimer, D., and J. Goldberg. 1981. *Flowers in the Blood: The Story of Opium.* New York: Franklin Watts.

Lauderback, D., J. Hansen, and D. Waldorf. 1992. " 'Sisters Are Doin' It for Themselves': A Black Female Gang in San Francisco." *The Gang Journal.* 1:57–72.

Lavigne, Y. 1993. *Good Guy, Bad Guy.* Toronto, Canada: Random House.

"Life and Death with the Gangs." 1987. *Time.* August 24:21–22.

Lee, F. R. 1991. "For Gold Earrings and Protection, More girls Take the Road to Violence." *New York Times.* Nov. 25: A1.

Lemert, E. 1951. *Social Pathology.* New York: McGraw-Hill.

Lewis, N. 1992. "Delinquent Girls Achieving a Violent Equality in D.C." *Washington Post.* Dec. 23: A1, A14.

Lipsey, M. 1992. "Juvenile Delinquency Treatment: A Meta-Analysis Inquiry into the Variability of Effects." In Cook, et al., *Meta-analysis for Explanation: A Casebook.*

Liska, A. E., ed. 1992. *Social Threat and Social Control.* Albany: State University of New York Press.

Loeber, R., and M. Stouthamer-Loeber. 1986 "Family Factors as Correlates and Predictors of Juvenile Conduct Problems and Delinquency." In M. Tonry and N. Morris, eds., *Crime and Justice: An Annual Review.* Chicago: University of Chicago Press.

Loper, A. B., D. G. Cornell. 1995. "Homicide by Girls." Paper presented at the Annual Meeting of the National Girls Caucus, Orlando, Florida.

Los Angeles County. 1992. *L.A. Style: A Street Gang Manual of the Los Angeles County Sheriff's Department.* Los Angeles: Los Angeles County Sheriff's Department.

Lour, G. C. 1987. "The Family as Context for Delinquency Prevention: Domographic Trends and Political Realities." In J. Q. Wilson and G. C. Loury, eds., *From Children to Citizens, Volume III: Families, Schools, and Delinquency Prevention.* New York: Springer-Verlag.

Loury, G. C. 1985. "The Moral Quandary of the Black Community," *Public Interest.* 79: 11.

Macallair, D. 1994. "Disposition Case Advocacy in San Francisco's Juvenile Justice System: A New Approach to Deinstitutionalization." *Crime and Delinquency.* 40: 84–95.

Machiavelli, N. 1950. *The Prince and the Discourses.* New York: Modern Library.

Mack, J. W. 1989. "The Juvenile Court." In McCarthy and Carr, *Juvenile Law and its Processes.*

MacLeod, J. 1987. *Ain't No Makin' It: Leveled Aspirations in a Low-income Neighborhood.* Boulder, CO: Westview.

Maguire, K., and A. L. Pastore, eds. 1998. *Sourcebook on Criminal Justice Statistics—1997.* Washington, D.C.: Department of Justice, Bureau of Justice Statistics.

Maguire, K., A. L. Pastore, and T. J. Flanagan. 1993. *Sourcebook of Criminal Justice Statistics, 1992.* Washington, DC: U.S. Department of Justice, Bureau of Justice Statistics.

Males, M. 1999. *Framing Youth: Ten Myths About the Next Generation.* Monroe, ME: Common Courage Press.

Mann, C. R. 1984. *Female Crime and Delinquency.* University: University of Alabama Press.

Marinucci, C., S. Winokur, and G. Lewis. 1994. "Ruthless Girlz." *San Francisco Examiner.* Dec. 12: A1.

Martin, D. E. 1992. *Promising Programs Addressing Youth Violence.* Detroit, MI: Wayne State University, Center for Urban Studies, Urban Safety Program.

Marx, K. 1964. *The Economic and Philosophic Manuscripts of 1844.* New York: International.

Marx, K., and F. Engels. 1947. *The German Ideology.* New York: International.

Maslow, A. H. 1951. *Motivation and Personality.* New York: Harper & Row.

Massey, D. S., and N. A. Denton. 1993. *American Apartheid: Segregation and the Making of the Underclass.* Cambridge, MA: Harvard University Press.

Matza, D. 1964. *Delinquency and Drift.* New York: Wiley.

Mauer, M. 1999. *Race to Incarcerate.* New York: The New Press.

Mays, G. L. 1997. *Gangs and Gang Behavior.* Chicago: Nelson-Hall.

Maxfield, M. 1987. "Household Composition, Routine Activities, and Victimization: A Comparative Analysis." *Journal of Quantitative Criminology.* 3: 301–320.

Maxson, C. L. 1998. *Gang Members on the Move.* Bulletin. Washington, DC: U.S. Department of Justice, Office of Justice Programs, Office of Juvenile Justice and Delinquency Prevention.

———. 1999. Personal communication with Shelden via fax.

———, Woods, K. J., and M. W. Klein. 1996. "Street Gang Migration: How Big a Threat?" *National Institute of Justice Journal*. 230: 26–31.

———, and M. W. Klein. 1983a. "Agency Versus Agency: Disputes in the Gang Deterrence Model." In Kluegel, *Evaluating Contemporary Juvenile Justice*.

———. 1983b. "Gangs: Why We Couldn't Stay Away." In Kluegel, *Evaluating Contemporary Juvenile Justice*.

———. 1990. "Street Gang Violence: Twice as Great or Half as Great?" In Huff, *Gangs in America*.

Mays, L. 1997. *Gangs and Gang Behavior*. Nelson-Hall. Chicago.

McCarthy, F. B., and J. Carr, eds. 1989. *Juvenile Law and Its Processes*. 2d ed. Charlottesville, VA: Michie Company Law Publishers.

McCord, J., and R. Tremblay, eds. 1992. *The Prevention of Antisocial Behavior in Children*. New York: Guilford.

McCorkle, R. and T. Miethe. 1998. "The Political and Organizational Response to Gangs: An Examination of a Moral Panic." *Justice Quarterly*. 15: 41–64.

———. 2001. *Panic: Rhetoric and Reality in the War On Street Gangs*. Saddle River, NJ: Prentice-Hall.

McNaught, S. 1999. "Gansta Girls." *The Boston Phoenix*. May 20–27.

Mendez, D. 1996. "More and More Girls Joining Violent Male Gangs." *The Seattle Times*. Oct. 27: A7.

Messerschmidt, J. 1993. *Masculinities and Crime*. Baltimore, MD: Rowman and Littlefield.

Merton, R. K. 1968. *Social Theory and Social Structure*. New York: Free Press.

Messner, S., and K. Tardiff. 1985. "The Social Ecology of Urban Homicide: An Application of the Routine Activities Approach." *Criminology*. 23: 241–267.

———, and R. Rosenfeld. 1997. Crime and the American Dream. 2d ed. Belmont, CA: Wadsworth.

Mieczkowski, T. 1986. "Geeking Up and Throwing Down: Heroin Street Life in Detroit." *Criminology*. 24: 645–666.

Miller, J. 1996. *Search and Destroy: African-American Males in the Criminal Justice System*. New York: Cambridge University Press.

———. 1998. *Last One Over the Wall: The Massachusetts Experiment in Closing Reform Schools*. 2d ed. Columbus, OH: Ohio State University Press.

Miller, J. M., and A. Cohen. 1995. "A Brief History of Gang Theories and Their Policy Implications." In Miller and Rush, *A Criminal Justice Approach to Gangs: From Explanation to Response*.

Miller, J. M., and J. P. Rush, eds. 1995. *A Criminal Justice Approach to Gangs: From Explanation to Response*. Cincinnati, OH: ACJS/Anderson Monograph Series.

Miller, W. B. 1958. "Lower Class Culture as a Generating Milieu of Gang Delinquency." *Journal of Social Issues*. 14: 5–19.

———. 1974. "American Youth Gangs: Past and Present." In Blumberg, *Current Perspectives on Criminal Behavior*.

———. 1975. *Violence by Youth Gangs and Youth Groups as a Crime Problem in Major American Cities*. Washington, DC: U.S. Department of Justice.

———. 1980a. "The Molls." In Datesman and Scarpitti, *Women, Crime, and Justice*.

———. 1980b. "Gangs, Groups, and Serious Youth Crime." In Schichor and Kelly, *Critical Issues in Juvenile Delinquency*.

———. 1982. *Crime by Youth Gangs and Groups in the United States*. Washington, DC: U.S. Department of Justice.

———. 1990. "Why the United States Has Failed to Solve Its Youth Gang Problem." In Huff, *Gangs in America*.

Mills, N. 1997. *The Triumph of Meanness: America's War Against Its Better Self*. New York: Houghton Mifflin Company.

Miringoff, M., and M. Miringoff. 1999. *The Social Health of the Nation.* New York: Oxford University Press.

Molidor, C. 1996. "Female Gang Members: A Profile of Aggression and Victimization." *Social Work.* 41: 251–257.

Moore, J. W. 1978. *Homeboys: Gangs, Drugs, and Prisons in the Barrio of Los Angeles.* Philadelphia: Temple University Press.

———. 1985. "Isolation and Stigmatization in the Development of an Underclass: The Case of Chicano Gangs in East Los Angeles." *Social Problems.* 33:1–10.

———. 1988. "Gangs and the Underclass: A Comparative Perspective." Introductory chapter in Hagedorn, *People and Folks: Gangs, Crime and the Underclass in a Rustbelt City.*

———. 1991. *Going Down to the Barrio: Homeboys and Homegirls in Change.* Philadelphia: Temple University Press.

———. 1993. "Gangs, Drugs, and Violence." In Cummings and Monti, *Gangs: The Origins and Impact of Contemporary Youth Gangs in the United States.*

Moore, J. W., D. Vigil, and J. Levy. 1995. "Huisas of the Street: Chicana Gang Members." *Latino Studies Journal.* 6: 27–48.

Moore, J. W., D. Vigil, and R. Garcia. 1983. "Residence and Territoriality in Chicano Gangs." *Social Problems.* 31:182–194.

Morris, N., and M. Tonry, eds. 1989. *Crime and Justice: An Annual Review of Research.* Vol. 12. Chicago: University of Chicago Press.

Morrison, R. D. 1992. "Gangs: Police Strategies for the Nineties." *The Police Marksman.* 17:30–31.

Moxley, R. 1989. *Case Management.* Beverly Hills, CA: Sage Publications.

Murray, C. 1993. "Tomorrow's Underclass." *The Wall Street Journal.* October 29.

Musto, D. 1973. *The American Disease: Origins of Narcotics Control.* New Haven, CT: Yale University Press.

National Drug Intelligence Center. 1996. *National Street Gang Survey Report.* Johnstown, PA: National Drug Intelligence Center.

National Law Enforcement Institute. 1992. *Gang Manual.* Santa Rosa, CA: National Law Enforcement Institute.

NBC. 1993. "Diana Koricke in East Los Angeles." *World News Tonight.* Mar. 29.

Needle, J. A., and W. V. Stapleton. 1983. *Police Handling of Youth Gangs.* Washington, DC: American Justice Institute.

New York Times. 1999. "Bold Effort Leaves Much Unchanged For The Poor." December 30.

Newsweek. 1998. "God and Gangs." June 1: 21–24.

O'Brien, D. M. 1990. *Storm Center: The Supreme Court in American Politics.* 2d ed. New York: W. W. Norton.

O'Connor, A. 2000. "Police Scandal Clouds List of Gang Members." *Los Angeles Times,* March 25.

Padilla, F. 1992. *The Gang as an American Enterprise.* New Brunswick, NJ: Rutgers University Press.

Patterson, G. R., P. Chamberlain, and J. B. Reid. 1982. "A Comparative Evaluation of a Parent-Training Program." *Behavior Therapy.* 13:636–650.

Pearson, G. 1991. "Goths and the Vandals: Crime in History." In Greenburg, *Crime and Capitalism.*

———. 1983. *Hooligan: A History of Reportable Fears.* New York: Schoeken Books.

Pelz, M. E., J. W. Marquart, and C. T. Pelz. 1991. "Right-Wing Extremism in the Texas Prisons: The Rise and Fall of the Aryan Brotherhood of Texas." *Prison Journal.* LXXI:23–37.

Pennell, S., and C. Curtis. 1982. *Juvenile Violence and Gang Related Crime.* San Diego, CA: San Diego Association of Governments.

Perkins, U. E. 1987. *Explosion of Chicago's Black Street Gangs: 1900 to the Present.* Chicago: Third World Press.

Phillips, K. 1990. *The Politics of the Rich and the Poor.* New York: Random House.

Phillips, M. B. 1991. "A Hedgehog Proposal." *Crime and Delinquency.* 37:555–574.

Piven, F. F., and R. A. Cloward. 1971. *Regulating the Poor: The Functions of Public Welfare.* New York: Vintage Books.

Platt, A. M. 1977. *The Child Savers.* 2d ed. Chicago: University of Chicago Press.

Polakow, V. 1993. *Lives on the Edge: Single Mothers and their Children in the Other America.* Chicago: University of Chicago Press.

Polk, K. 1984. "The New Marginal Youth." *Crime and Delinquency.* 30:462–479.

Portillos, L., and M. Zatz. 1995. "Not to Die For: Positive and Negative Aspects of Chicano Youth Gangs." Paper presented at the American Society of Criminology, annual meeting, Boston.

Proband, S. C. 1997. "Black Men Face 29 Percent Lifetime Chance of Prison." *Overcrowded Times.* 8:1.

Project TEAM. 1991. *Report to the Community.* Sierra Vista, AZ: Sierra Vista New Turf Project.

Prothrow-Stith, D. 1991. *Deadly Consequences.* New York: HarperCollins.

Quadegno, J. 1994. *The Color of Welfare: How Racism Undermined the War on Poverty.* New York: Oxford University Press.

Quicker, J. C. 1983. *Homegirls: Characterizing Chicana Gangs.* San Pedro, CA: International University Press.

Quinn, J. and B. Downs. 1995. "Predictors of Gang Violence: The Impact of Drugs and Guns on Police Perceptions in Nine States." *Journal of Gang Research.* 23: 15–27.

Quinney, R. 1970. *The Social Reality of Crime.* Boston: Little, Brown.

———. 1974. *Critique of Legal Order: Crime Control in Capitalist Society.* Boston: Little, Brown.

———. 1977. *Class, State, and Crime: On the Theory and Practice of Criminal Justice.* New York: David McKay.

———. 1982. *Social Existence: Metaphysics, Marxism, and the Social Sciences.* Beverly Hills, CA: Sage.

———. 1991. *Journey to a Far Place: Autobiographical Reflections.* Philadelphia: Temple University Press.

Quinney, R., and J. Wildeman. 1991. *The Problem of Crime: A Peace and Social Justice Perspective.* 3d ed. Mountain View, CA: Mayfield.

Reckless, W. 1961. *The Crime Problem.* 3d ed. New York: Appleton-Century-Crofts.

Regoli, R. M. and J. D. Hewitt. 2000. *Delinquency in Society.* 4th ed. New York: McGraw-Hill.

Reich, R. B. 1991. "The Real Economy." *The Atlantic.* 267:35–52.

Reiman, J. 1993. "A Radical Perspective on Crime." In Kelly, *Deviant Behavior.*

———. 1998. *The Rich Get Richer and the Poor Get Prison: Ideology, Crime, and Criminal Justice.* 5th ed. Boston: Allyn and Bacon.

Reiner, I. 1992. *Gangs, Crime and Violence in Los Angeles: Findings and Proposals from the District Attorney's Office.* Arlington, VA: National Youth Gang Information Center.

Rice, R. 1963. "A Reporter at Large: The Persian Queens." *The New Yorker.* 39 (October 19).

Rifkin, J. 1995. *The End of Work.* New York: G.P. Putnam.

Ritzer, G. 1996. *The McDonaldization of Society* (revised ed.). Thousand Oaks, CA: Pine Forge Press.

Roberts, S. 1972. "Crime Rate of Women Up Sharply Over Men's." *New York Times.* June 13.

Robins, L. 1966. *Deviant Children Grown Up.* Baltimore: Williams and Wilkins.

Rothman, R. A. 1999. *Inequality and Stratification: Race, Class, and Gender.* 3d ed. Upper Saddle River, NJ: Prentice-Hall.

Rubin, L. B. 1994. *Families on the Fault Line.* New York: HarperCollins Publishers.

Ruigrok, W., and R. van Tulder. 1995. *The Logic of International Restructuring.* London: Rutledge.

Rusche, G., and O. Kirchheimer. 1968. Originally published 1938. *Punishment and Social Structure.* New York: Russell and Russell.

Sachs, S. L. 1997. *Street Gang Awareness.* Minneapolis, MN: Fairview Press.

Sagan, L. A. 1989. *The Health of Nations.* New York: Basic Books.

Sampson, R. J. 1986. "Effects of Socioeconomic Context on Official Reaction to Juvenile Delinquency." *American Sociological Review.* 5:876–885.

———, and B. W. Groves. 1989. "Community Structure and Crime: Testing Social-Disorganization Theory." *American Journal of Sociology.* 94: 774–802.

Sanders, W. 1994. *Gangbangs and Drivebys.* New York: Aldine DeGruyter.

Sanders, W. B. 1970. *Juvenile Offenders for a Thousand Years.* Chapel Hill: University of North Carolina Press.

Santiago, D. 1992. "Random Victims of Vengeance Show Teen Crime." *The Philadelphia Inquirer,* Feb. 23: A1.

Santrock, J. W. 1981. *Adolescence: An Introduction.* Dubuque, IA: William C. Brown.

Sapolsky, R. M. 1988. "Lessons of the Serengeti: Why Some of Us Are More Susceptible to Stress." *The Sciences.* May/June:38–42.

Savitz, L. D., L. Rosen, and M. Lalli. 1980. "Delinquency and Gang Membership as Related to Victimization." *Victimology.* 5:152–160.

Scheb, J. M., and J. M. Scheb II. 1994. *Criminal Law and Procedure.* 2d ed. Minneapolis/St. Paul, MN: West.

Scheinfeld, D. H. 1983. "Family Relationships and School Achievement Among Boys of Lower-Income Black Families." *American Journal of Orthopsychiatry.* 53.

Schichor, D., and D. Kelly, eds. 1980. *Critical Issues in Juvenile Delinquency.* Lexington, MA: D.C. Heath.

Schlesinger, P., and H. Tumber. 1993. "Fighting The War Against Crime: Television, Police, and Audience." *British Journal of Criminology.* 33:19–32.

Schorr, L. 1989. *Within Our Reach: Breaking the Cycle of Disadvantage.* New York: Anchor.

Schur, E. 1971. *Labeling Deviant Behavior.* New York: Harper & Row.

Schwendinger, H. and J. 1985. *Adolescent Subcultures and Delinquency.* New York: Praeger.

Seagal, D. 1993 "Tales from the Cutting-Room Floor: The Reality of 'Reality-Based' Television." *Harper's Magazine.* November.

Shapiro, I., and R. Greenstein. 1997. "Trends in the Distribution of After-Tax Income: An Analysis of Congressional Budget Office Data." Center on Budget and Policy Priorities, Washington, D.C., August 14.

Shapiro, M. 1986. *Courts: A Comparative Political Analysis.* Chicago: University of Chicago Press.

Shaw, C., and H. D. McKay. 1942. *Juvenile Delinquency in Urban Areas.* Chicago: University of Chicago Press.

Shelden, R. G. 1995. "A Comparison of Gang and Non-Gang Juvenile Offenders." Paper presented at the Pacific Sociological Association annual meeting, April.

———. 1999a. "The Prison Industrial Complex." *The Progressive Populist.* 5(11) November 1.

———. 1999b. *Detention Diversion Advocacy: An Evaluation.* Washington, DC: U.S. Department of Justice, Office of Juvenile Justice and Delinquency Prevention. Juvenile Justice Bulletin.

———. 2001. *Controlling the Dangerous Classes: A Critical Introduction to the History of Criminal Justice.* Boston: Allyn and Bacon.

———, and W. B. Brown. 1997. "The Crime Control Industry and the Management of the Surplus

Population." Paper presented at the annual meeting of the Western Society of Criminology, February.

———, D. Maccalair, V. Schiraldi, and W. B. Brown. 1995. "Toward a Progressive Criminology." Paper presented at the annual meeting of the Western Society of Criminology, February.

———, T. Snodgrass, and P. Snodgrass. 1992. "Comparing Gang and Non-Gang Offenders: Some Tentative Findings." *Gang Journal*. 1:73–85.

Shellety, J. E. 1993. "Residents Speak Out on Growing Gang Presence." *Salt Lake Tribune*. October 3.

Shoemaker, D. J. 1996. *Theories of Delinquency*. 3d ed. New York: Oxford University Press.

Short, J. F., ed. 1968. *Gang Delinquency and Delinquent Subcultures*. New York: Harper & Row.

———. 1990. "Gangs, Neighborhoods, and Youth Crime." *Criminal Justice Research Bulletin*. 5.

———. 1990a. "New Wine in Old Bottles? Change and Continuity in American Gangs." In Huff, *Gangs in America*.

———. 1996. "Gangs and Adolescent Violence." Unpublished report. Boulder, CO: Center for the Study and Prevention of Violence.

Short, J. F., and F. Strodbeck. 1965. *Group Process and Gang Delinquency*. Chicago: University of Chicago Press.

Siegel, L., and J. Senna. 1997. *Juvenile Delinquency*. Belmont, CA: Wadsworth.

Sikes, G. 1997. *Eight Ball Chicks*. New York: Anchor Books.

Simon, R. 1975. *Women and Crime*. Lexington, Mass.: Lexington Books.

Sipchen, B. 1993. *Baby Insane and the Buddha*. New York: Bantam Books.

Sklar, H. 1998. "Let Them Eat Cake." *Z Magazine*. (November).

———. 1999. "For CEO's, a Minimum Wage in the Millions." *Z Magazine*. (July/August).

Skogan, W. G. 1990. *Disorder and Decline: Crime and the Spiral of Decay in American Neighborhoods*. Berkeley, CA: University of California Press.

Skolnick, J. H. 1990. Draft paper. *Gang Organization and Migration*. Berkeley, CA: Center for the Study of Law and Society.

———. 1994. *Justice Without Trial: Law Enforcement in Democratic Society*. 3d ed. New York: Macmillan College.

———, and D. H. Bayley. 1986. *The New Blue Line: Police Innovation in Six American Cities*. New York: Free Press.

———, T. Correl, E. Navarro, and R. Rabb. 1990. "The Social Structure of Street Drug Dealing." *American Journal of Police*. 9:1–41.

Smith, A. 1976. *The Wealth of Nations*. Oxford: Clarendon Press.

Speir, H. 1994. "Folks Nation, Inc., Apply Within." *Gwinnett Loaf*. 2 (September 10):7–9.

Spergel, I. A. 1964. *Racketville, Slumtown and Haulberg*. Chicago: University of Chicago Press.

———. 1984. "Violent Gangs in Chicago: In Search of Social Policy." *Social Service Review*. 58:199–225.

———. 1989. "Youth Gangs: Continuity and Change." In Morris and Tonry, *Crime and Justice: An Annual Review of Research*.

———. 1990. *Youth Gangs: Problem and Response*. Chicago: University of Chicago, School of Social Service Administration.

———. 1995. *The Youth Gang Problem: A Community Approach*. New York: Oxford University Press.

———, and G. D. Curry. 1990. "Strategies and Perceived Agency Effectiveness in Dealing with the Youth Gang Problem." In Huff, *Gangs in America*.

———, and S. F. Grossman. 1997. "The Little Village Project: A Community Approach to the Gang Problem." *Social Work*. 42: 456–470.

Spitzer, S. 1982. "The Dialectics of Formal and Informal Control." In Abel, *The Politics of Informal Justice*.

———. 1975. "Toward a Marxian Theory of Deviance." *Social Problems.* 22: 638–651.

Stabile, C. A. 1995. "Feminism Without Guarantees: The Misalliances and Missed Alliances of Postmodernist Social Theory." In A. Callari, S. Cullenberg, and C. Biewener, eds., *Marxism in the Postmodern Age.* New York: Gulliford Press.

Stark, R. 1987. "Deviant Places: A Theory of the Ecology of Crime." *Criminology.* 25: 893– 909.

State Task Force on Youth Gang Violence. 1986. *Final Report.* Sacramento, CA: California Council on Criminal Justice.

Steffensmeier, D. J., and Steffensmeier, R. H. 1980. "Trends in Female Delinquency: An Examination of Arrest, Juvenile Court, Self-Report, and Field Data." *Criminology.* 18:62–85.

Stover, D. 1986. "A New Breed of Youth Gangs Is on the Prowl and a Bigger Threat Than Ever." *American School Board Journal.* 173:19–24, 35.

Stryker, S. 1980. *Symbolic Interactionism.* Menlo Park, CA: Benjamin/Cummings.

Sullivan, M. L. 1989. *Getting Paid: Youth Crime and Work in the Inner City.* Ithaca, NY: Cornell University Press.

Sutherland, E. H., and D. R. Cressey. 1970. *Criminology.* 8th ed. Philadelphia: Lippincott.

Suttles, G. 1968. *The Social Order of the Slum.* Chicago: University of Chicago Press.

Sykes, G., and Matza, D. 1957. "Techniques of Neutralization." *American Journal of Sociology.* 22:664–670.

Taylor, C. S. 1990a. *Dangerous Society.* East Lansing, MI: Michigan State University Press.

———. 1990b. "Gang Imperialism." In Huff, *Gangs in America.*

———. 1993. *Girls, Gangs, Women, and Drugs.* East Lansing: Michigan State University Press.

Thompson, D. W., and L. A. Jason. 1997. "Street Gangs and Preventive Interventions." In Mays, ed., *Gangs and Gang Behavior.*

Thornberry, T. P., and J. H. Burch. 1997. "Gang Members and Delinquent Behavior." Office of Juvenile Justice and Delinquency Programs. Washington, D.C.: Office of Justice Programs. U.S. Department of Justice.

———, M. Krohn, A. Lizotte, and D. Chard-Wierschem. 1993. "The Role of Juvenile Gangs in Facilitating Delinquent Behavior." *Journal of Research in Crime and Delinquency.* 30: 55–87.

Thrasher, F. 1927. *The Gang.* Chicago: University of Chicago Press.

Toy, C. 1992. "A Short History of Asian Gangs in San Francisco." *Justice Quarterly.* 9: 647–665.

U.S. Department of Commerce, Bureau of the Census. 1989. *Statistical Abstract of the United States: 1994.* Washington, DC: U.S. Government Printing Office.

———. 1990. *1990 Census, Summary Tape, File 3C.* Washington, DC: U.S. Government Printing Office.

———. 1994. *Statistical Abstract of the United States: 1994.* Washington, DC: U.S. Government Printing Office.

———. 1995. *Statistical Abstract of the United States, 1995.* Washington, D.C.: U.S. Government Printing Office.

U.S. Department of Justice, Office of Justice Programs. 1999. *1996 National Youth Gang Survey.* Washington, DC: Office of Juvenile Justice and Delinquency Prevention.

U.S. Department of Justice. 1998. *Addressing Community Gang Problems: A Practical Guide.* Washington, DC: Office of Juvenile Justice and Delinquency Prevention.

Vago, S. 1994. *Law and Society.* 4th ed. Englewood Cliffs, NJ: Prentice Hall.

Valentine, B. 1978. *Hustling and Other Hard Work: Life Styles in the Ghetto.* New York: Free Press.

Vigil, J. D. 1983. "Chicano Gangs: One Response to Mexican Urban Adaption," *Urban Anthropology.* 12:45–68.

———. 1988. *Barrio Gangs.* Austin, TX: University of Texas Press.

———. 1990. "Cholos and Gangs: Culture Change and Street Youths in Los Angeles." In Huff, *Gangs in America.*

———, and S. C. Yun. 1996. "Southern California Gangs: Comparative Ethnicity and Social Control." In Huff, C. R. (eds.), *Gangs in America.* 2d ed.: Thousand Oaks, CA: Sage.

Vigil, J. D., and J. M. Long. 1990. "Emic and Etic Perspectives on Gang Culture: The Chicano Case." In Huff, *Gangs in America.*

Vigil, J. D., and S. C. Yun. 1996. "Vietnamese Youth Gangs in Southern California." In Huff, *Gangs in America.*

Waldorf, D. 1993. "When the Crips Invaded San Francisco: Gang Migration." *Gang Journal.* 1(4):11–16.

Walker, S. 1994. *Sense and Nonsense About Crime and Drugs.* Belmont, CA: Wadsworth.

Wang, Z. 1995. "Gang Affiliation Among Asian-American High School Students: A Path Analysis of Social Developmental Model." *Journal of Gang Research.* 2: 1–13.

Warr, M. 1996. "Organization and Instigation in Delinquent Groups." *Criminology.* 34: 11–37.

Weber, M. 1946. *From Max Weber: Essays in Sociology.* Trans. H. Gerth and C. W. Mills. New York: Oxford University Press.

———. 1958. *The Protestant Ethic and the Spirit of Capitalism.* New York: Charles Scribner.

Werner, E. E., and R. S. Smith. 1982. *Vulnerable, but Invincible: A Longitudinal Study of Resilient Children and Youth.* New York: McGraw-Hill.

Werthman, C. 1967. "The Function of Social Definitions in the Development of Delinquent Careers." In Garabedian and Gibbons, *Becoming Delinquent.*

Werthman, C., and I. Piliavin. 1967. "Gang Members and the Police." In Bordua, *The Police: Six Sociological Essays.*

West, D. J., and D. P. Farrington. 1977. *The Delinquent Way of Life.* London: Heinemann.

———. 1973. *Who Becomes Delinquent.* London: Heinemann.

Whitehead, J. T., and S. P. Lab. 1989. "A Meta-Analysis of Juvenile Correctional Treatment." *Journal of Research in Crime and Delinquency.* 26:276–295.

Whyte, W. F. 1943. *Street Corner Society.* Chicago: University of Chicago Press.

Wilkinson, K. 1974. "The Broken Home and Juvenile Delinquency: Scientific Explanation or Ideology? *Social Problems.* 21: 726–739.

Williams, P., and J. Dickinson. 1993. "Fear of Crime: Read All About It? The Relationship Between Newspaper Crime Reporting and Fear of Crime." *British Journal of Criminology.* 33:33–56.

Williams, T. 1989. *The Cocaine Kids: The Inside Story of a Teenage Drug Ring.* Menlo Park, CA: Addison-Wesley.

Williams, K., M. Cohen, and G. D. Curry. 1994. "Evaluation of Female Gang Prevention Programs." Paper presented at the American Society of Criminology, annual Meetings, Miami, FL.

Wilson, H. 1980. "Parental Supervision: A Neglected Aspect of Delinquency," *British Journal of Criminology.* 20.

Wilson, J. J., and J. C. Howell. 1994. *Comprehensive Strategy for Serious, Violent, and Chronic Juvenile Offenders.* Washington, DC: Office of Juvenile Justice and Delinquency Prevention.

Wilson, J. Q., and G. L. Kelling. 1989. "Making Neighborhoods Safe." *Atlantic Monthly.* February:46–52.

Wilson, J. Q. and R. Herrnstein, 1985. *Crime and Human Nature.* NY: Simon and Schuster.

Wilson, W. J. 1987. *The Truly Disadvantaged.* Chicago: University of Chicago Press.

———. 1996. *When Work Disappears: The World of the New Urban Poor.* New York: Vintage Books.

Wilson-Brewer, R., S. Cohen, L. O'Donnell, and I. F. Goodman. 1991. *Violence Prevention for Young Adolescents: A Survey of the State of the Art.* Washington, DC: Carnegie Corporation of New York.

Winfree, L. T., Jr., F. Esbensen, and D. W. Osgood. 1995. "On Becoming a Youth Gang Member: Low Self-Control or Learned Behavior?" Paper presented at the Academy of Criminal Justice Sciences, annual meeting, Boston.

Wolff, E. 1995. *Top Heavy: A Study of Increasing Inequality of Wealth in America.* New York: The Twentieth Century Fund Press.

Wolfgang, M., R. Figlio, and T. Sellin. 1972. *Delinquency in a Birth Cohort.* Chicago: University of Chicago Press.

Wolfgang, M. E., and N. A. Weiner, eds. 1989. *Violent Crime, Violent Criminals.* Newbury Park, CA: Sage.

Wooden, W. S. 1995. *Renegade Kids, Suburban Outlaws.* Belmont, CA: Wadsworth.

Woodson, R. L. 1985. "Self-Help, Not Big Daddy, Must Rescue the Black Underclass," *Washington Post.* May 12.

Wright, E. O. 1997. *Class Counts.* London: New Left Books.

Zalman, M., and L. Siegel. 1991. *Criminal Procedure: Constitution and Society.* New York: West.

Zatz, M. S. 1987. "Chicano Youth Gangs and Crime: The Creation of a Moral Panic." *Contemporary Crises.* 11:129–158.

———. 1985. "Los Cholos: Legal Processing of Chicano Gang Members." *Social Problems.* 33:13–30.

Zepezauer, M. and A. Naiman. 1996. *Take the Rich Off Welfare.* Emeryville, CA: Odonian Press.

Zimring, F. 1998. *American Youth Violence.* New York: Oxford University Press.

———, and G. J. Hawkins. 1973. *Deterrence: The Legal Threat in Crime Control.* Chicago: University of Chicago Press.

Zinn, H. 1990. *The Politics of History.* 2d ed. Urbana: University of Illinois Press.

———. 1994. *You Can't Be Neutral on a Moving Train.* Boston: Beacon Press.

Zopf, P. E., Jr. 1989. *American Women in Poverty.* New York: Greenwood Press.

Name Index

Subject Index